THE TRIBAL WORLD OF VERRIER ELWIN

THE TRIBAL WORLD OF VERRIER ELWIN

VERRIER ELWIN

GYAN

Published by

Gyan Publishing House
5, Ansari Road
Daryaganj, New Delhi-110002
Phone: 011-47034999, 9811692060
E-mail: books@gyanbooks.com

Distribution Network
gyanbooks.com
India, USA, Canada, UK, Australia

ISBN: 978-93-7447-437-2 (HB)

First Published, 1964

2nd Impression 2025

Printed at: Gyan Press, Delhi.

THE TRIBAL WORLD OF VERRIER ELWIN
Author: VERRIER ELWIN

Photo, Sunil Janah

The author in 1953

The Tribal World of Verrier Elwin

AN AUTOBIOGRAPHY

1964

OXFORD UNIVERSITY PRESS

NEW YORK AND BOMBAY

To Eldyth & Basil
my oldest friends

Preface

THIS is the story of one who for many years has lived between the two worlds of Britain and India and who has in his own experience, if it is not too pompous to say so, found that 'East and West are but alternate beats of the same heart'. My journey from a deeply religious evangelical home to modernist and catholic Oxford and then through Gandhi's settlement at Sabarmati to the tribal hills of India involved many changes in my outlook and way of life. I was ordained an Anglican priest at Oxford and had almost settled down to the life of a don there, when India caught my imagination and transported me to another hemisphere. After some years of struggle I left the Church, though I have never turned from the life of scholarship. My contact with Gandhi wedded me to India and I am today an Indian citizen. Although I loved, and still love, great and ancient cities, I have lived, by choice, in remote and primitive villages. I have married into tribal society and found felicity there. In India I have found sorrow and joy, disappointment and fulfilment but above all reality, an answer to the prayer: 'From the unreal, lead me to the real.'

In spite of these changes I find a consistent thread running through my life, a perennial philosophy which has survived the loss of a conventional faith. My childhood had impressed on me that here we have no abiding city and that there is an elusive treasure far above the prizes of the world. At school I learnt to love Wordsworth with his stress on the essential quality to be found in the countryside and among poor people. At Oxford I developed the habit of thinking in neo-Platonic terms by which one can build up a store of inner strength that will be independent of external circumstances. Without this I do not think I could have endured the isolation and the tragedies of village life. My early years in India, and specially those in

Gandhi's settlements, were a training for an experience that was hard and difficult, though very well worth while. Even now, when my home is no longer in a village, I spend much of my time and most of my thought among the tribal people.

I am enormously proud of India, and that I have become an Indian, but I am also proud of Britain in whose culture I have my roots and origins. 'The transfer of power in India,' Dr Radhakrishnan has said, 'was one of the greatest acts of reconciliation in human history.' And nothing could be happier than the way the old quarrels, some of which are reflected in the early chapters of this book, have been resolved. In mentioning these I had no desire to revive unhappy memories, but the incidents of the British period are important for the story of my life and I had to include some of them. But I agree with Arthur Koestler when he says of the British Empire: 'The fall of each of the great Empires of the past was an ugly and catastrophic event. For the first time in history we see an Empire gradually dissolving with dignity and grace. The rise of this Empire was not an edifying story; its decline is.'

Europe is deep in my bones, but India has gone even more deeply now, as I came to realize when I set out to write this book, for much of it is written from the Indian point of view and most of its characters are Indians. It could hardly be otherwise with an Indian wife and home, Indian interests, a majority of Indian friends, and above all my absorbed and concerned attachment to India's tribes.

In this book I have tried to tell both Western and Oriental readers a little of how I, having had a certain kind of experience and having become what I am, look on things and react to them.

I have tried to show my life as a whole and to describe those things in it that have been important to me. I have not put in everything. In a recent discussion in the *Times Literary Supplement*, it is suggested that while, inevitably, every autobiography is an essay in omission, readers in the modern world are no longer content with a self-idealized *persona*, 'something not too wide of the mark—but, please Heaven, not too close either': they want the full man. The realistic Confession, the unexpurgated Diary is what appeals today and 'the blacker the picture of a lifetime the louder the applause with which it is likely to be acclaimed'. The difficulty is that the writer and his readers may have very different ideas about what is important, even about what is black.

My path has sometimes been shadowed by clouds and I have hinted at them in the following pages, but I have not enlarged on them, for I don't think they are very interesting. Other matters, which some readers may envy or even admire, and others will condemn, are my own business and, whatever the modern trend may be, I do not think that in an autobiography a man is required to lower the barriers of the discreet reticence which would govern his everyday conversation. On the whole, though I would not call my life successful (for I have not thought in terms of success), it has been very rewarding, and a portrait of inner happiness is not a mere *persona* but, realistically, the whole man.

Admittedly then, I have not put in everything. Nor have I put in everybody. I am, I think, a friendly and affectionate person and I have made a great many friends. But an autobiography is not a catalogue and I have not been able to mention many people who have meant much to me at different times. I hope they will forgive me and not assume that this is because I have forgotten them, but will realize that it is simply because an author, if he wants his book to be read, must not make it too fat.

V. E.

Shillong, July 1963

Note

I am indebted to Shamrao Hivale for a number of passages reproduced from his book *Scholar Gypsy* ; and to All India Radio for quotations from my Patel Memorial Lectures. There are some paragraphs from various journals and newspapers—the *Geographical Magazine,* the *Statesman* and the *Illustrated Weekly of India* —as well as from some of my earlier books.

I am specially grateful to a number of friends who read this book in manuscript and criticized it—N. K. Rustomji, B. Das Shastri, P. H. Trivedi, Margot Gilkey, Juliana Kadleczovics and my sister Eldyth—and above all to my friends in the Oxford University Press. The title of the book was suggested by the Wasant of chapter 11.

Contents

Illustrations

The Tribal World of Verrier Elwin

1

Angel Infancy

I WAS born at Dover in Kent, England, in 1902, on the early morning of 29th August, a day which is traditionally associated by the Church with the beheading of John the Baptist. This was, of course, on the birthday of King Herod, which was celebrated by a performance of what would probably today be called tribal dances. It is perhaps significant that I should have arrived in the world on an anniversary marked by dramatic action against a well-known Puritan reformer.

I was the eldest of three children, my sister Eldyth being two years, and my brother Basil some five years, younger.

I was baptised with the names Harry Verrier Holman Elwin by no fewer than three Bishops; long afterwards one of them told me, 'Three of us tried to cast the devil out of you, with remarkably little success.'

My father, Edmund Henry Elwin, was himself an Anglican bishop holding the see of Sierra Leone, but he had been appointed Bishop of Bristol when he suddenly died of yellow fever at the age of 38, when I was seven, only a few weeks before returning to England to take up his new assignment. He had been at Merton, which was to be my own college later on, and after serving as a curate in Oxford he went to West Africa as a missionary. He was at first principal of Fourah Bay College but soon became the youngest bishop in the Church of England.

West Africa, at the beginning of the century, must have been of unusual interest to anthropologists and our house was full of what the family called curios—my mother had the amiable habit of going into heathen temples and removing the idols which she ultimately brought home. I wish I had some of them now. West Africa was an exciting place at that time and the family tradition was that my mother, having wandered by accident into a cannibal village, was on the point of being eaten when my father arrived with a rescue party and delivered her from the cooking-pot.

I hardly ever saw my father, for he was constantly on tour in Africa, and my own memories hardly go beyond two occasions when he gave me a beating for being naughty. One of these, which I still remember vividly, was for running off at the age of six to the railway station, against his orders, to say good-bye to my mother who was going away somewhere.

My mother was a beautiful, intelligent and imaginative woman. Witty and well-read, she liked all the right things, poetry, music and art, but unfortunately her fundamental interest was in a form of religion that was the negation of all of them. Had my father lived and we had gone to Bristol to the beautiful Cathedral Close to live in dignity and with financial security, her life would have been very different. As it was, my father's death left a gap which could only be filled by a passionate devotion to her children and an equally passionate devotion to religion. There was hardly any money. All her life my mother was afraid of boredom. Apart from us children there was nothing for her to do. She could not settle down and so we lived in 'rooms'—furnished apartments, generally one bedroom and one sitting-room with a bathroom which we shared with the other lodgers. My mother was continually moving from one place to another, for she could not get on with landladies and we grew up in an atmosphere of catastrophic rows with these formidable women. This meant that as children we had few friends, there was never a garden to play in, very little privacy, and we were generally on 'tour' or 'transfer'.

Always religious by temperament, mother turned to Jesus to fill the emptiness of her heart and give an interest to life. Evangelical Anglicanism, or 'low Church', which was that aspect of religion which claimed my father's allegiance, is one of the dullest types of religion in the world and it certainly did not satisfy my mother. While remaining loyal to her Church, therefore, she sought consolation in the revivalism which characterizes some of the evangelical groups. This was much more exciting: one might fall into trance, speak with

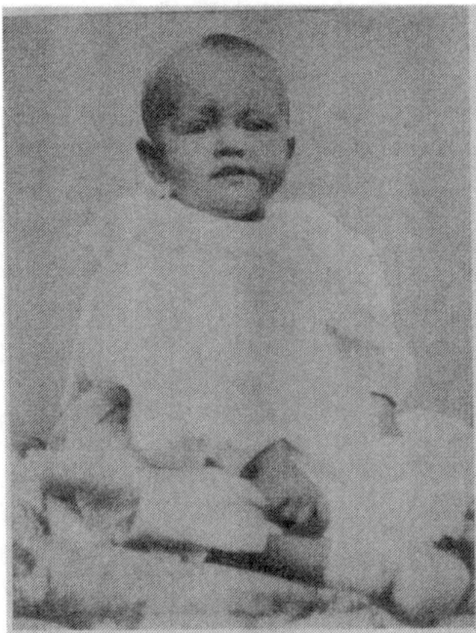
As a baby

With his sister Eldyth
and brother Basil

At the age of 2 with his parents

At a school prize-giving, 1919

As a young don at Oxford, 1927

In his library at Shillong, 1961

tongues, dance in ecstasy before the Holy Table. Dear mother tried very hard, but she never succeeded in reaching these heights. Nor did I, little boy with wondering, expectant eyes, hoping for the best.

But there were three big things. There was an unswerving belief in the Bible as the literally inspired word of God, almost a book of magic ; we sometimes opened it at random to get a 'message'. Then there was a conviction that at any moment Jesus would come again in clouds of glory, that those who believed in Him would be caught up to meet Him in the air, that He would destroy the bad old world and create a better one.

Thirdly, there was a strong faith in the possibility of immediate communion with God and possession by the Holy Ghost.

These beliefs had very practical results. We could never go to a theatre, cinema, circus or other place of entertainment, for it would have been rather embarrassing if Jesus had arrived in the middle of the programme. I remember, in a house where my bedroom was above my mother's, creeping downstairs almost every night to listen outside her door for her breathing in case she had been caught up into the air after going to bed. I never could really believe that I was sufficiently good to earn this distinction and the possible sudden disappearance of my mother was a constant cloud on my happiness.

This was the atmosphere in which I grew up. It was well calculated to impress on a child the importance of the treasures of the spirit, for here there were certainly no treasures of the flesh ; it was easy to believe that here we had no abiding city, for we were always moving on.

All this meant that as a small boy I had to entertain myself in all sorts of ingenious ways. When I was going through a purgatory with the dentist, I spent a lot of time stopping holes in the garden wall, devising horrid probing instruments and drills. I invented a universal language, the first—and fundamental—sentence of which was '*Oo lovessisia eiya*', 'I love you'. I used to paint my own stamps on large sheets of paper and later made what today would probably be a fairly valuable collection, for I found many of the rarest Indian issues in packets of old letters stored away in dilapidated boxes: like a fool I sold it for £5 to the Army and Navy Stores (our ticket number was 37176) when I went to India.

One great deprivation of those years was lack of reading matter. We could not afford to buy books (this was before the days of cheap paperbacks): we did not discover lending libraries till much later. But I did buy, out of my little pocket money, the *Boy's Own Paper* every week. How excitedly I looked forward to it, but when it came I had to ration it, one story a day, to make it last as long as possible.

How mother did it I have no idea, but every year she took us for a holiday. It must have meant her doing without new dresses, new hats, going by bus instead of taxi, cutting out the cakes when she had tea at Lyons—all the things that children do not realize at the time. So one year we went to Cromer, another to Corfe Castle and later to Eastbourne, Swanage and North Wales. These were the bright moments of our young days.

At this time our Relations were very important to us. There were a great many of them and I will describe first my mother's family, for we saw more of them and liked them better. Mother's maiden name was Holman, and the Holmans as a clan were generous and lovable. Their ancestry, however, is not very well documented. My great-great-grandmother was Augusta Anderson who was born in Queenstown: her mother was in turn a Melville who had married a Dr Anderson of Dublin. In April 1826 at the age of seventeen, Augusta married a soldier called James Campbell (whose people were connected with a Paisley-shawl factory) and he went with the Army to India where the couple had three sons and three daughters, one of them being Flora Campbell, our immediate grandmother.

One of her sisters was Great-aunt Jane who married a man called Slane, who seems to have been an engineer, at the age of eighteen. She died a year later and her husband was thrown down the well at Cawnpore during the Mutiny.

William Laban Holman, our grandfather, ran away from home and joined the East India Company. He helped to build the road to Murree in unpartitioned India: he was one of the founders of this attractive hill station, and my mother was born there.

There is no doubt that there was a lot of Scottish blood in my mother's family and, since there was also some link with Ireland, I hope that there was some injection of Irish blood as well.

The Scottish and, desirably, Irish element in their ancestry gave the Holmans, and my mother herself, their human, witty and enthusiastic attitude to life. Some of them were not very interested in religion and Grannie Holman, for example, objected vociferously to her daughter Minnie's marriage to a mere clergyman, though she thawed a little when he became a bishop. She never went to church, did not read her Bible, but from us children's point of view the most exciting thing about her was a guilty secret. She drank. I don't suppose the poor old thing ever got very much, but there was usually a bottle of brandy tucked away behind voluminous black dresses in the wardrobe, and Granny seems to have taken little nips of this when she felt so disposed.

One of the absorbing topics of conversation between Eldyth, Basil and myself was: 'Will Granny go to hell?' Technically, we admitted, this was inevitable, for Granny was not saved. But how could this happen to one who was such a dear, so liberal —out of her small income we received a steady flow of half-crowns, and sometimes even a golden sovereign or half-sovereign —such a character and still so good-looking (long ago, in India, she had been known as the Beauty of the Punjab and people used to come out of their houses as she rode by just to have a glimpse of her)? We shuddered at the thought of those eager flames devouring her kindly face for ever and ever, and mother too hedged a bit when we asked her the dreadful question, even hinting that some special arrangement might be made for the old lady after she passed over.

This applied also to the two worldly uncles, my mother's brothers, to whom we were all devoted. One was Uncle Fred, a physician, who had some sort of job as house-doctor to a titled family living in a castle in Scotland. This was one of the few things that brought colour into our lives. Uncle Fred was a very generous person and baskets of pheasant, grouse, salmon, tutti-frutti and other delicacies used to arrive once or twice a year at our lodgings and mother, who was an excellent cook, would prepare them with all the trimmings.

Uncle Fred was a sportsman, fishing, shooting, yachting, and he always seemed to be in funds. He would bring us boxes of lead soldiers and little cannon and we had wonderful games.

Uncle Herbert, a soldier, was even more exciting. He had an adventurous life, for he qualified as a first-class interpreter in Russian, French and German and this led to his being sent about the world on special missions. At the end of the last century he went with the Chinese Expeditionary Force to assist in the suppression of the Boxers. Some years later, he went to Manchuria where he saw something of the Russo-Japanese War, being attached to the Russian Forces. After distinguished service in the First World War, he was selected in 1919 as Chief of the British Mission to South Russia, where the Bolsheviks declared that, if they caught him, they would crucify him upside down.

In the year that I went up to Oxford he returned to India, where many years before he had been posted to the 16th Bengal Lancers, and held commands, first in Sindh-Rajputana and then in Mhow. He had a hatred of red tape and was known as 'Burn-the-Files Holman' after making a bonfire of documents (including, unfortunately, some irreplaceable land records) in Simla. He finally attained the rank of Lieutenant-General and retired from the Army in 1928 with a row of letters after his name—K.C.B., C.M.G., D.S.O. For over twenty years he was Colonel of the 6th Duke of Connaught's Own Lancers (Watson's Horse). In his company we felt that we were in touch with Distinction, part of a wider world.

Among the aunts our favourite was Aunt Polly. She was one of those unfortunate women who have to sacrifice everything to possessive mothers. She never married, she wasn't allowed to, for she had to look after Grannie Holman. She was very good to us, and perhaps mother's greatest friend, a cathartic, sensible, delightful person. She was her father's favourite and he left her a little money which she invested in a small house in Worthing. Since she lived alone, we often went to stay with her and as a boy I used to see Lord Alfred Douglas about the town, though I was never invited to one of his famous small-boy tea-parties. Perhaps it was just as well. Aunt Polly was more indianized than the others; we were always hearing about 'dak', the 'dhobi' and there was an occasional bad word—'*Suar ka batcha*' (son of a pig) I can still remember. She made a delicious curry (so did mother) and was an expert at jelabies.

Then there was Aunt Loo, a stout homely person, married to a desiccated architect, with a lot of sons, our cousins; one was commander of a submarine and went down in it in the First World War; another died in Japanese hands after the loss of Singapore in the Second.

Finally there were the relations we hushed up. One of these was poor Cousin Louie, who had committed the desperate crime of joining the Church of Rome. I have vague recollections of a kindly gentle faded little lady wearing a crucifix, but we were naturally not allowed to have much to do with her.

Then there was Cousin Hugh, who was at once an embarrassment and a source of deep satisfaction to the whole family. He was embarrassing because we managed to get him into the Army in the early days of World War I, when the recruiting officers were not very particular, and within a few months of his taking the oath, he went off his head. As he was a full-fledged soldier, Government had to look after him for the rest of his life, thus saving everyone a great deal of money. Cousin Hugh was really, I think, just 'simple'. He was allowed out from time to time and we enjoyed his visits. He used to sing to us, pathetic little ballads like 'Wrap me up in a tarpaulin blanket'; he was convinced that my mother was the Virgin Mary and revered her accordingly, though I did not get the position that this flattering belief should have awarded me.

In contrast, my father's family, the Elwins, were a little dull.

The Elwins are an Anglo-Saxon, not a Welsh, family—Elwin is a Christian name in Wales, a surname in Kent—and *Burke's Landed Gentry* (oddly enough my name occurs in this snob volume, though the only land I am ever likely to possess is a six-foot grave) traces their pedigree to 1531. None of these ancestors were very notable; in 1600 Henry Elwyn, as the name was then spelt, was 'one of the ancients or senior barristers of New Inn'; two hundred years later we find a Michael Elwin as one of the officials of the Naval Victualling Department at Dover; for the most part the Elwins were solicitors, officials and, in recent years, clergymen. Two of my uncles were in the ICS, which they left at the time of the Morley-Minto Reforms, and the two sons of the younger of them, D. H. Elwin in the Madras and R. B. Elwin in the Punjab cadres, were also in the ICS from which they very properly resigned at Independence. I think that, with the exception of Margaret Elwin, not listed in Burke, who was burnt as a witch in 1615 for plotting to burn a town in Norfolk and raise a wind to fan the flames, I was the first of the Elwins to depart from the strict and narrow path of orthodoxy in religion and politics since the family began four hundred years ago.

The Elwins, so far as I know, were strictly religious in a conventional way, very definitely Low Church.

Much later my ex-ICS Uncle Edgar Elwin forbade the female members of the family to read any of my books.

Not exactly a relation, but my god-father, Bishop Taylor-Smith, was Chaplain-General to the Armed Forces in the First World War and became notorious for his refusal to allow Anglican chaplains to use crucifixes. His other special aversion was masturbation. He was always talking to me about it, how semen was forty times as valuable as blood, how if one lost it one got dark rings under the eyes and deteriorated mentally, how it stunted one's growth even more than smoking.

I remember later, at a 'squash' at Oxford, how he stood up and, beating his Tarzan-like chest, declared: 'I've never touched a woman and look at me.'

As most of his audience were passing through a (doubtless temporary) homosexual phase, this went down very well. Another friend of my father's, a type called Tyndale-Biscoe, was always telling me to be a MAN, and to this day I can't hear the expression without feeling a little queer.

We grew up. Eldyth became an exquisitely pretty little girl, I a chunky small boy with a prognathous jaw (it had to be pulled back by a dreadful machine attached to it every evening), and Basil was the pet of the house. Eldyth and I naturally joined together to intrigue against him. When I was six, there was a governess who made me learn the first chapter of St John's Gospel by heart. Despite this elevating experience, a year or two later I had a spell of naughtiness and was sent, in the hope of it doing me good, as a boarder to a small private school in London. My classmates were all girls and they gave me hell. They used to tie me up, put me under a table and prick my bottom with pins. I also didn't like the food, and after half a term mother came up to London (we were then living in a small town called Wallington) and took me home. We then moved to Reigate, where we hired a whole house, which was fun. There was a garden, and mother did most of the cooking, lovely food. We employed a servant, but after a few weeks she ran away in one of mother's dresses with a hundred pounds worth of silver cutlery. This was my first experience of the police and a flattering one. I found one of the defaulter's shoes with finger-prints on it, and I still remember the best notice I've ever had, my mother's 'Verrier, you're a brick.' Fortunately the stuff was insured and the money came in very useful, and the incident probably gave me my lifelong attachment to crime fiction.

I went to school in Reigate, a good sound evangelical school, and remember nothing except that I once got six of the best on the old spot for organizing the boys into a sort of union, which demanded shorter hours and better food for lunch. Mother summoned the headmaster to the house and of the two of us I think he suffered the most.

I then went on to another Prep. school at Eastbourne. The headmaster was an enormous red-faced man called Mr P., who taught me one lesson of lifelong value.

One of the assistant masters used to enjoy hanging round the bathrooms and making improper proposals to the little boys as they came out. This dubious pleasure was, in due course, brought to the attention of Mr P., and he held an inquiry, to which I was summoned as a witness. This was my very first introduction to the harsh realities of sex, if that is the right name for it, and I was embarrassed and confused.

As a result I blushed and stammered through my interrogation and Mr P., towering above me like Jehovah, boomed, 'Call a spade a spade, boy, call a spade a spade.' Ever since, and specially in my book *The Baiga,* I have tried to do this.

When I was thirteen there was the problem of a Public School. In choosing this the family and their advisers were dominated by the desire to keep me untainted by the Church of Rome and the infidelity which they believed to come from the application of modern scholarship to the Bible.

My father had hoped that I would go to Westminster, but to the family's sheltering eyes there was some danger of Popery there. They tried Rugby, but on cross-examination Dr David, the headmaster, admitted that he accepted the first chapters of the book of Genesis as true only in a symbolic sense, so that was no good.

Finally, on the advice of a missionary friend, I was sent to a west-country school, Dean Close, Cheltenham, which had been founded to uphold the basic principles of evangelical religion, and where certainly there was never any nonsense about applying the ordinary standards of intelligence to the Word of God.

Religion, which played such a strong part in my childhood, therefore, continued to be important at school. There were not only the regular prayers and chapel services but there were such institutions as the Sunday prayer-meeting, where a few of the more pious boys (I among them) met in a dreary classroom and gave little sermons in turn. At the end of the talk we were each expected to offer up an extempore prayer, which personally I found a considerable ordeal. Then there was what was called the Crusaders, which was rather similar but not considered quite so spiritual—even though it was held in the early morning before breakfast. Finally there was the Scripture Union, whose members had to promise to read a scheduled passage of the Bible every day of their lives. As this involved reading through the entire Bible every few years, the passages were often highly unsuitable for young people. But since we had no other form of sex-instruction it probably served a useful purpose.

The headmaster of Dean Close school was Dr W. H. Flecker, the father of James Elroy Flecker, whom I still consider a good poet. When I was at school he was at the height of his fame for, with Rupert Brooke, he was the most popular of the earlier poets of the First World War. We used to sing some of his poems, set to music, in the chapel; one of them was the beautiful *Masque of the Magi* which we performed every December in anticipation of Christmas.

We had a rather heavy dose of the Fleckers. There was a younger son who for some time taught us classics; there was a daughter Joyce who taught science; and old Mrs Flecker once tried to teach me Hebrew. She, however, impinged on our lives more obviously by a nightly inquisition. She would stand at the end of the dining-room and all of us below a certain age used to file past saying, 'Yes (or 'no'), Mrs Flecker; four (or whatever it might be) for tea.' The 'yes' or 'no' was a report on the movement of one's bowels and the 'four for tea' referred to the number of slices of dry and tasteless bread that one had managed to consume during the high tea which was the main meal of the day.

Dr Flecker himself was, I have little doubt, something of a great man. He built up the school almost from scratch and gave it some sort of position, at least in the west country. He was a brilliant preacher, to whose sermons we actually used to look forward, and he had a sensitive understanding of literature. I remember him once giving an exceptionally fine lecture on Milton. He had a certain amount of German blood, and in the bitter days of the War this went against him. On one or two occasions the good people of Cheltenham walked out of local churches when he was invited to preach.

Dean Close was perhaps not a very good school but there was always something going on. I describe later the thrilling incidents of the Green Bicycle Murder. Another day, equally exciting, Dr Flecker stood up in Hall and declared that he had been arrested in the Army and Navy Stores for stealing a Bible, a tin of sardines and a packet of toilet paper. This was obviously due to either a minor breakdown or a sheer fit of absent-mindedness, but anti-German feeling at that time was so strong that the police actually pressed the case to the courts, though it was naturally at once dismissed.

At this time I was a shy, not very attractive little boy, terribly priggish, filled by my uncles with conventional Imperialist ideas and by my mother with the belief that there was nothing, nothing in the world, to compare with the joy of leading souls to Jesus.

On one occasion, I made a list of the boys in my class with columns in which I gave each so many marks for morals, intelligence, religion and attractiveness and a note on whether they were saved or not. The instincts of the anthropologist, in however bizarre a form, were already at work. Unfortunately I left the incriminating document one day in the school lavatory and later had the mortification of seeing parts of it copied out on a blackboard, with dire consequences to myself from the boys whom I had marked low for 'attractiveness'.

From the age of about seven and continuing until my third year at Oxford, a very important part of our life was concerned with the Children's Special Service Mission (CSSM). This was an enterprising organization which arranged missions at seaside resorts throughout the country during the pleasant holiday month of August. A team of workers would descend on some place like Eastbourne or Llanfairfechan and embark on an ambitious programme of meetings, sports and entertainments.

These missions were generally very well done. A sand pulpit was built on the beach and decorated with shells and seaweed. There was a red banner and a lot of jolly singing. There were competitions, all sorts of games, and such things as processions with Chinese lanterns. One of the hymns we sang was 'I am H.A.P.P.Y.'. Another was 'Joy, joy, joy—with joy my heart is ringing' and this accurately expressed my feelings at the time.

But there were two things which were not so good. The first was that the CSSM created a forced and unnatural religious precosity. I remember sitting on the beach at the age of seven and, under the inspiration of a hearty evangelical clergyman, declaring that I had given my heart to Jesus two years before. I added with a touch of condescension that I had never regretted it. Later this led to a clash with Eldyth, for she too claimed that she had given her heart to Jesus and I was furious at this invasion of my monopoly.

'I am the only member of the family,' I declared, 'who has done it,' and I knocked her on the head with a celluloid doll.

Her physical injury was not serious but the blow to her feelings was severe and I was punished by being locked up in a bedroom all day and having the school crest removed from my blazer. It is curious to reflect that today Eldyth is the only member of our family likely to get to heaven; it will be a thoroughly well-deserved award.

The CSSM, like the Buchmanism of a later period, fostered an upper-class religion. Its meetings and entertainments were confined to 'visitors', and town-people were not admitted. Visitors, that is to say the children of parents who could afford to pay for a holiday at a seaside resort, were considered to be of higher caste than the children of residents, who had to be content for their spiritual pabulum with the local Sunday Schools. The result was that, while the CSSM enabled us to make attractive, well-dressed friends of the right class, it introduced a caste barrier based on economic standards which was obviously shocking, and looking back I am astonished that it never occurred to any of us all through those years that there was anything wrong about it. Since then the social revolution in Britain may have changed the CSSM, if it still exists. I hope so, for this was one of the things that I am really ashamed of in my youth. Yet at this time it brought thrills and variety into what was otherwise a rather unexciting life.

Just after I went to Dean Close school the First World War broke out. We were far away in the west country and at first it had little effect on us. I was only twelve years old. But gradually, as some of the best masters were called up, the names of old boys began to appear in the casualty lists and the food steadily got worse, some idea of the realities of war began to come home to us. As the days went by we finally found ourselves eating horseflesh and jealously watching our rations of sugar, butter and bread. We used to swop pats of butter for white mice and postage stamps, and food became a sort of currency.

Later the great influenza epidemic struck the school with great force. It seemed to break out simultaneously in every dormitory and, even more disastrously, in the servants' quarters so that for the first two days there was no one to look after us and no proper food. I remember crawling on hands and knees from my dormitory down to the kitchen in the hope of getting some milk to drink. One of my most admired friends, a really lovely little boy, died. Finally, army nurses came in and took charge.

The war naturally gave a great stimulus to the Officers' Training Corps. I was never very keen on games and used the OTC as an outlet for my surplus energies. Ultimately I rose to be Sergeant-Major and I greatly enjoyed swaggering about in my Sam Brown. I was an expert on bombs and in the written exam. for Certificate A I got 98 per cent marks for my paper on the theory of bombing. I could draw a plan of the inside of a Mills Bomb and various other sinister weapons. Unfortunately, I was not quite so good on the practical side and, on the one occasion when we were permitted to use live bombs, I threw mine straight up into the air and nearly killed the C.O.

When victory came we were as excited at school as anywhere in the country and as Sergeant-Major I let off a barrage of crackers from the top of the school tower in the early morning of Victory Day. Later, I led a procession that escorted a captured German tank through the streets of Cheltenham.

It never occurred to anyone that there was the least inconsistency between the Scripture classes, where we were taught to love our enemies, and the Bombing classes, where we were taught to kill them.

One of the strongest influences in my life was a young woman—whom I never saw. I was seventeen years old when she was murdered and she was twenty-one. Her name was Bella Wright, pretty and forthcoming, engaged to be married to a stoker. One day her dead body was found on an old Roman road near Leicester.

Six months later one of our masters at Dean Close, a Mr Ronald Light, was arrested and charged with her murder. Mr Light had been teaching me, and I shall never forget the thrill when Dr Flecker rose solemnly in the Great Hall and told us about it. We had sardines and sausages for high tea that evening, just as we had when Dr Flecker himself was arrested, to create an optimistic atmosphere.

Mr Light was ultimately acquitted, and we were all happy about it, for he was a pleasant little man, but he did not come back to the school. It was hard to get masters in those war days and we therefore remained one short.

I had managed to establish myself by that time as a special case, for I had decided to take English literature, and the cut fell on me. There was no one to teach me and so Dr Flecker turned me loose in the library and told me to teach myself. Bella Wright's murder thus had the unexpected result that for a whole year I had the opportunity of rummaging about in an excellent collection of books and exploring the main roads and by-ways of poetry. I had to. There was no one to make me work but myself. For someone of a less studious temperament this might have been fatal, but since I was already approaching books in the spirit of a lover, the opportunity to work in freedom gave me those habits of research which I still have.

An Anglo-Catholic clergyman, to whom a friend of mine confessed that he had got into trouble by going after girls, suggested to him that 'he might try boys: for they were "cleaner" and safer'.

For many years I thought this was rather shocking, until one day quite recently I read the first volume of Victor Gollancz's autobiography. Gollancz had one great love, for a boy, during his schooldays, but it was a passing phase and he goes on to say: 'Though devoid of homosexual leanings myself (since that one experience) and strongly sexed in the normal manner, I wonder whether homosexual love may not sometimes be purer (purer in heart) than the average heterosexual love; and whether to give everything and demand nothing, after the fashion of chivalry, may not commonly be the mark of it.' He wonders whether the 'strong sweetness, the unfeverish intensity, the quality of acceptance rather than of seeking' does not suggest that schoolboy and schoolgirl 'pashes' and 'crushes' may not be 'among the best things in life'.

I have never before found anyone who had the courage to say this but I think there is something in it. Dean Close school was riddled, as the headmaster put it, with 'impurity' and though I left school without ever knowing exactly what he meant, I think masturbation and certainly 'little boys' must have been in his mind. Official opposition naturally developed interest in our pretty juniors into what was almost a cult; so far as I know, and certainly in my own case, nothing ever 'occurred', but there was a sweetness and charm, all the attraction of forbidden fruit. There was one boy especially whom I loved, a gifted and beautiful child. We read Rossetti's Italian poems in the original as a romantic way of learning the language; he went to Cambridge and I once stayed with him in King's College after I had gone to Oxford: the luminous beauty of the surroundings and the joy of simply being with him kept me mentally intoxicated for months.

Until I was twenty-one I knew nothing about women and certainly never could have anticipated that one day I would be mentioned half-a-dozen times as an authority on the sexual behaviour of the human female in the Kinsey Report. Tribal children know all about a woman's anatomy, the rules of menstruation and—whatever Malinowski may have said—how babies come, before they are five years old. I knew nothing when I was four times that age. Most tribal children have had exciting and ecstatic experiences by twelve or thirteen. All I had were timid glances. The first I exchanged, when I was about seven, was with my cousin Joan, a gloriously pretty child of six ; the second, when I was twelve, with a girl of my own age called Robina whom I still remember as the most sexually exciting creature I have ever encountered. Except, however, for carrying her pick-a-back in the CSSM sports at Eastbourne, I made no advances and so never arrived.

My boyhood was thus a rather curious affair. During the holidays, we had a life with very few comforts, and virtually no amusements (except religious ones): in those days there were few cinemas and few cars. We met very few people and my father's friends, such as Willie Holland, Alec Fraser, Tom Alvarez, Walter Miller (names famous in missionary history), who used to come to see that we were all right, were all of a certain highly religious type. We had to work very hard and only once did we have a servant for a short time. My mother did the cooking, cleaning, most of the washing and we children used to help as much as we could. This, so far as I remember, we did not mind at all. It was all rather fun and we did not, in fact, realize at that time how greatly restricted our horizons were nor how much more life had to offer.

But there was one thing, completely inconsistent with the rest, that made all the difference. When I was about sixteen I discovered poetry and fell in love with the beauty of words. At first, perhaps naturally, I was attracted by Tennyson and similar poets ; a little later I was intoxicated by Swinburne ; I bought a volume of Yeats' poems out of my meagre pocket-money. But my great joy was Wordsworth.

In the early mornings at school I used to wander out into the woods and fields with a little blue-bound selection of his poems, and I would sit in the peace of that gentle countryside absorbing the gentle message of the poet. This stimulated my love of natural beauty and later I knew no greater happiness than to make walking-tours in the Lake District ; once I traced the poet's steps up the River Duddon to its source, reading the Duddon sonnets along the way.

In fact, for the last two years at school I lived in a sort of trance of delight. I was in two worlds which could not be reconciled. Orthodox evangelicalism stood strangely beside the mystical pantheism of Wordsworth, and at that time, and for several years afterwards, I did not know which was the real thing for me. I think I was rather a puzzle to the school staff and I remember one day walking through the headmaster's garden, which had a superb display of roses, with Mrs Flecker and quoting Richard Jefferies to her about 'that pure colour which is rest of heart'. I have rarely seen a woman look so astonished.

I would not like to say that my schooldays were unhappy. As I look back I feel mostly a certain regret, not about happiness but that I could have had so much better an education if I had been put in a different kind of school, taught in a different way and had made other friends. Yet even so I did learn much about the beauty and joy of life.

My home was a place of intense affection. Mother was a darling and looked after us wonderfully. But we were poor and had to grow up the hard way. I am not sorry about that, any more than I regret the later troubles with the Church and the police. The result has been that later, since I had learnt not to expect anything, I was often agreeably surprised, and even now, when anything nice happens to me, I feel grateful to life for being so pleasant after all.

2

Youth of Delight

Youth of delight, come hither,
And see the opening morn,
Image of truth new-born.
—*William Blake*

I

I WENT up to Oxford in the autumn of 1921. My knowledge of life was almost entirely literary, based on books in the school library. I had very little money, it was the first time I had ever been on my own, and I felt rather lost. Moreover, it was a disturbing period for, as Roger Fulford says, in *Right Honourable Gentleman,* of the Oxford of 1921-2:

> Never has undergraduate life been more terrifyingly, more scorchingly brilliant than in the years when England settled down to enjoy the peace. The young men of Oxford drank their wines and spirits, spent their fathers' modest fortunes, and put the world to rights with all the poise and sophistication of Victorian clubmen; they gossiped about one another with such backbiting gusto that the University at times recalled the cackling malice of a tea-party at a bridge club for ladies. The fashion for disguising intelligence by behaving like an enthusiastic wasp had spread rapidly to Oxford from Bloomsbury. Discussion of subjects, which is generally profoundly boring, had given place to discussion of people, which is always fascinating; tartness and wit were the essential ingredients of conversation. It is not only the passage of years, not only the tricks of memory, not only the blandishments of social historians which conjure up this sparkling vision; it was in sober fact a brilliant epoch. Oxford in 1922 whispered the last enchantments of the Edwardian Age.

According to my calculations, it was in the third year of my undergraduate tutelage that Claude and Eustace (in *Right Ho, Jeeves*) were sent down, their amiable lunacy being characteristic of my own day. I myself led a procession along the High and ended up with a passionate speech from the steps of the Police Station protesting against the admission of women to the University.

My college was Merton, as it had been my father's, and the Warden, Tommy Bowman, always wrote my father's initials instead of mine. I had very small rooms under the roof in Mob Quad, immediately below the Chapel and facing the famous Library which dates back to 1377.

My scout was called Hobbes. A sign of his approval was to give a cup of early morning tea, free of charge, to his special young men. I took some time to win this accolade, though when I did it was enthusiastic, but for the first year I had the mortification of seeing my neighbours get their tea while I didn't.

In my second year I moved to the ground floor and henceforth all was well. The two years I spent in this large room with its dark red hangings, its enormous mirror with a bullet hole made by a drunken undergraduate trying to commit suicide by shooting at his reflection, its ghosts (two witches were supposed to have been burnt on the site), and a host of friends were probably the happiest in my life.

We had a distinguished set of dons. The greatest, I suppose, was A. C. Bradley, who had a profound influence on T. S. Eliot who had spent a year at Merton reading the Posterior Analytics with Professor Joachim. There was also Sir Walter Raleigh, who tutored me for all too short a time ; and W. W. How, the Senior Tutor, who took me through some books of Livy in my first term.

The most remarkable of the dons was, however, H. W. Garrod, the authority on Keats and Wordsworth, a rather devastating person whom I adored.

After suffering the indignity of Pass Mods., which at that time you had to do as a preliminary for a number of Honours Schools, in my third term I started on English Literature. Everyone advised against it, as it was a new School and was said to be one in which it was very hard to get a First. My tutor was David Nichol Smith, a great specialist on eighteenth-century poetry, unbelievably handsome, charming and quiet. Merton also had H. C. Wyld, the terror of generations of women students, my terror too until I came to know him, and I was also taught by Sir George Gordon for a short time.

Since in 1921 English literature had not yet established itself as a respectable subject in the University, there was no scholarship in the subject offered at Merton to which, as my father's college, my family was anxious I should go. Accordingly, I went up as a Commoner and was condemned for three years to wear the little jacket which was not altogether unlike, except in its dull sub-fusc colour, an Adi or Mishmi coat of a kind which I often wear today.

In my second term I was awarded the Fowler Exhibition but this did not give me the privilege of wearing a scholar's gown. A year later I sat for a coveted University scholarship, the Charles Oldham, which was awarded for Shakespeare studies. The preparation for this took me out of the ordinary rut of Schools, for I had to go into problems of textual emendation and bibliography and I was very excited and pleased when I won it. The remuneration, in terms of the purchasing power of the rupee today, was something like three thousand rupees, and in addition the College gave a handsome prize of books.

After I got my degree I won another University prize, the Matthew Arnold, for an essay, 'The Poetry of Revolution', which rather interestingly anticipated later events.

My chief failure was the Newdigate. The subject for the poem was Michelangelo and I came fifth out of a large field. 'It was too much of a sermon,' said Garrod.

The teaching at Oxford is, of course, quite different from anything in the world and almost the opposite of the kind of instruction inflicted on students in India. I myself never sat through a single course of lectures in my five years (for I have always believed that the need for lectures disappeared in the fifteenth century, when the printing-press came into use) though I attended a few which promised unusual entertainment. Since most of the dons read out their lectures I did not see why I could not obtain the same result in comfort by reading the stuff in a book. In fact, I was only actually taught for one hour a week but it was extraordinary how effective that teaching could be.

My official studies in English stopped at the year 1800. It was possible to take a further paper covering the whole of the nineteenth century but my tutor advised against it. There was too much 'literature' in it; it was too readable and the examiners accordingly tried to make it as difficult as possible. You were not asked straight questions, for example, about Matthew Arnold's philosophy but were told to compare it with that of some obscure clergyman, nor would you get a simple question on Carlyle's style. There would always be a catch in it. The result was that my approach to modern poetry was entirely non-professional and I was able to read the Victorians for pleasure and not as a duty.

On the other hand, I never suffered from the undue professionalism of which Eng. Lit. has frequently been accused. It was a new School then and everyone was exploring. In fact, it was a great thing to be forced to study Shakespeare properly, which I would probably never have done otherwise. A great range of seventeenth-century poetry (John Donne especially) would have been lost to me if I had not had to read it for Schools. The chief thing, however, was that I came to know and love the eighteenth century. My tutor Nichol Smith's house was full of its books and I suspect that he never read an eighteenth-century poem except in its first edition. After I had taken my degree he asked me to give him a little help in editing *The Oxford Book of Eighteenth Century Verse* and I read through vast quantities of good and bad poetry in the eighteen volumes of Chalmers's *English Poets*. Once a week I used to go to Nichol Smith in the evening and we would sit together for a couple of hours separating the gold from the dross. In these sessions I probably learnt more about good taste and the essential nature of poetry than in all the rest of my studies put together.

The eighteenth century included, of course, a good deal of Blake, and Wordsworth and Coleridge up to the publication of the *Lyrical Ballads*. Nichol Smith would never agree that the eighteenth-century poets were indifferent to Nature and put me on to discovering Nature-poetry among writers who were popularly supposed to be entirely urban in outlook. It was worth while doing the School if only to learn to appreciate Pope and Dryden, and fall under the spell of Boswell and Johnson. Nichol Smith, as a true eighteenth-century man, believed in plain straightforward prose and discouraged the purple patch.

I went through a D. H. Lawrence period which was bad both for my style and my thinking, but I soon left it behind. My discovery of the great moderns, T. S. Eliot and Ezra Pound, was delayed until I went to the Indian forest and it was not until I was in Shillong that I developed my enthusiastic admiration for W. H. Auden.

From time to time I was given some very good advice. Sir Walter Raleigh warned me never to claim, as I had claimed, to enjoy *The Faerie Queene.* 'It immediately', he said, 'stamps you as a humbug.' Once in an essay I brought in a quotation in Italian, a language which I knew very slightly. Garrod criticized this saying, 'It looks as though you have brought it in simply to show you can.'

I had a certain gift of making epigrams at that time, and Garrod encouraged me in this but he jumped on me when I made a reference in an essay to the 'essential gutlessness' of somebody. I had been inspired to it by something, I think, in Kipling but Garrod would have none of it.

'Mr Elwin, Mr Elwin,' he moaned, 'never, never do a thing like this again.'

I think the very first time I appeared in print was when Garrod, who had been asked to write an article for some University journal on the seventeenth-century dramatist Middleton, wrote half of it and asked me to complete it for him. This was a rather alarming honour, since Garrod was undoubtedly the greatest authority on the subject in the University. However, I produced a draft of a complete article and he accepted it without making any alterations. I expressed the fear that people might notice the decline in style in the part which I had written, whereupon he said, 'There are no two human beings, Mr Elwin, who will read this article with the same attention which you and I have given it.'

In these days I am often asked to prepare drafts for other people, who are not always as kind to me as Garrod was when

I was just a beginner. A thing which frequently amused me in Shillong when K. L. Mehta was Adviser was his habit, when I put up a draft, of altering almost every word and then writing in the margin, 'An excellent draft. I have ventured to make one or two verbal alterations.' On the whole, however, I enjoy both preparing drafts and correcting those prepared by other people. In the first case one writes with a certain sense of irresponsibility and freedom, in the second with a schoolmasterish pleasure in putting others right.

Another valuable piece of advice was from a visitor to Oxford, the great evangelist, Dr J. J. Meyer, who came to give a number of sermons, and whom I persuaded to have tea in my rooms. I had naturally tidied up everything and carefully emptied my waste-paper-basket. After we had talked a little while I saw his eyes stray to my desk and he presently said, 'If you want to make progress in the world of literature or scholarship, you must constantly tear up what you have written and write it again. I always judge a scholar by the amount of discarded paper in his waste-paper-basket.' This has always remained with me and I am afraid I have got through an enormous quantity of waste paper in the past thirty years of writing, quite apart, of course, from what I have actually published.

In 1924 I took my English Finals and was awarded a First. Professor Wyld, rather grumpily, told me that it was a good one and that I had got Alpha Plus for three papers and Alphas for the rest, including, to my great surprise, the three Old English and Language papers. It is significant of the uselessness of much education that within a few years I had forgotten every single thing about Anglo-Saxon and Middle English, at which I had presumably done reasonably well.

II

After finishing my English course I decided to stay on for another two years and do the Theology Finals, which means you take your B.A. degree all over again, and Merton gave me a generous grant of money to enable me to do so. In my fourth year I had to go out of college and I found digs, near what is now St Peter's College, which I shared with a very close friend of mine, George Bosworth. I can remember little about the year I spent in lodgings except that they were almost next door to the Church of St Peter-le-Bailey, where my father had his first curacy, and that George had a favourite quotation, from *Ecce Homo* I think, that he never tired of using: 'No love is pure that is not passionate, no virtue safe that is not enthusiastic.'

My theological tutor, F. W. Green, was a High Churchman with modernist leanings, that is to say, he was a deeply religious man who believed in Truth. There was a story in my day attributed to Cardinal Newman that when he was asked what kinds of protection there were against the modern German 'higher criticism', he replied, 'One is the shield of the Holy Spirit and the other—an ignorance of the German language.' However, I started to learn German but did not get very far with it. But Green knew it well and gave me vast piles of notes which he had taken from the most advanced German theologians. My outlook, therefore, became more or less that of a book famous in my time through doubtless forgotten now—*Essays, Catholic and Critical.*

In those days the old controversy about the verbal inspiration of the Bible was still very much alive. Green's contribution to it was characteristic. The one thing he said that he really believed in about the Bible was its verbal inspiration, at least that of the King James's men who did the Authorized Version. In fact, all the great Elizabethans were verbally inspired. It was not the language of the Bible but its opinions that he considered sometimes dubious.

In my fourth year the annual Church Congress was held in Oxford, and the authorities thought they might brighten it up by having a session on the subject: 'What Youth asks of the Church'. I was chosen to represent Oxford and an old classmate (as he would be called in India), S. C. Neill, represented Cambridge. Neill was not exactly a 'fellow-student', for at school he had always been in quite a different class to me, earning scholarships and prizes with rather intimidating brilliance. He is now a bishop but still, I believe, a very learned man. Shortly before the Congress he wrote to me asking for a copy of my speech and in all innocence I sent it to him. He did not return the compliment, with the result that when the day came he was in a very favourable position to make some carefully prepared cracks at my expense. I still remember his referring to 'the warm streams of oratory that had descended on the audience from Oxford' (loud laughter) and his going on to say that he spoke for 'the sheep that had no shepherd', which was exactly what I thought I had been doing myself.

This speech of mine got me into the headlines and for the first time in my life I saw myself in big type. I had made some remark that older people seemed to think that all youth was interested in was 'Food, Felix and Football'—Felix was a feline forerunner of Mickey Mouse. Feeble as this was, it stood out in the dull deliberations of the churchmen and the newspapers splashed it in large capitals. The intoxicating effect of this, for the first drink is always the best, was increased by an enthusiastic letter from no less a person than Margot Asquith agreeing with everything which I was reported to have said.

My mother took a furnished house on Headington Hill, a very old and charming house where I used to spend my Sundays. I was fond of cycling in those days and the joy of free-wheeling down into Oxford more than atoned for the labour of pushing my bike up the hill.

Another place in the lovely neighbouring countryside which I often visited was a farm at Elsfield, the home of a great friend of mine at Univ., Mervyn Hatt. There was a mother, almost paralysed by arthritis but a most heroic and witty person. There was the father, a typical English farmer of the old school, and two very pretty sisters, and a number of us used to go up there and enjoy the warmth and hospitality of English village life.

Mervyn qualified as a doctor, a very good one, and later went to India to work in the CMS hospital at Ranaghat near Calcutta, where he was well known as both physician and surgeon. He was, to some extent, influenced by Gandhi's ideas and inspired the staff of the hospital to do away with sweepers: everybody agreed to do the sweeping themselves. This valiant attempt to banish untouchability unfortunately did not have the desired effect, for the sweepers were furious at losing their jobs and their discontent was fanned by a number of Communist agitators. One evening in November 1949 someone appeared with a gun at the window of the room where the hospital staff were having supper and killed Mervyn himself and two of his nurses. Even at Oxford Mervyn had some of the marks of a true saint and his early death was a tragic loss both to medicine and the cause of genuine religion.

After a year in digs, as George Bosworth went to take up his work in a parish, I moved into Wycliffe Hall. This was a theological college in North Oxford which was devoted to teaching theology of a protestant and evangelical character. I did not, however, at this time, have any tuition from the Hall itself as I was still studying through Merton under Green. My mother bought a house for about a thousand pounds in North Oxford—1 Warnborough Road—so I was able to live quite near the family, whom I visited frequently. This year too passed without any very striking outer events and at the end of it I sat for my second final school, which I did with much greater nervousness than before, but again was fortunate enough to get a First.

In 1925 Magdalen College required a Fellow to teach English literature and I applied for the post. Nichol Smith did not think I had very much chance, for among the other candidates was a formidable opponent, the C. S. Lewis who was to become famous as a writer on very varied subjects—literary criticism, religious propaganda and science fiction. He had originally come up in 1917, had some war experience, gained a First in Greats and was considerably more mature than I was at the age of twenty-three. Nichol Smith was right, for Lewis was elected but I was runner-up and got so far as having an interview with the President, Sir Herbert Warren, and being invited to High Table so that the dons could see what my manners were like.

During that dinner at which, so far as I remember, I was surprisingly free from nerves, somebody told the story of the candidates for a Fellowship who were offered stewed cherries as a test. The first spat the stones on to his plate; he was rejected. The second put the stones into his spoon and arranged them neatly on the side of his plate; he too was rejected.

The third swallowed the stones and was unanimously elected, but died of appendicitis before he could take up the appointment.

Another story was going round Oxford at this time about Sir Herbert, who was well known to be one of the greatest snobs living.

Mrs Besant came to Oxford to put her ward, Krishnamurti, into one of the colleges. She naturally went straight to Magdalen and interviewed the President. When Sir Herbert showed some reluctance to accept her candidate, Mrs Besant exclaimed, 'But my ward is a very special person. I don't want to stress it, but he does happen to be the Son of God.'

Sir Herbert replied, 'Madam, we have the sons of many distinguished people in this college.'

Many years later I told this story to Sardar Panikkar, distinguished writer and former Indian Ambassador to France, when he visited Assam as a member of the States Reorganization Commission.

'Where did you hear that?' he said.

I told him that it was an old chestnut from my Oxford days. 'Do you know,' he replied, 'I invented that story myself as a young man when I was hard up in Paris and wanted to earn a little money by writing for the American papers? The story appeared first in America; it was repeated in the London *Times* and so found its way to Oxford.'

I have never been much of a one for taking exercise. Like Sherlock Holmes I have always looked upon aimless bodily exertion as a waste of energy but, unless one was to be thought pansy, one had to put in an appearance on some playing-field. At school I won a copy of *Through the Looking-Glass* as a prize for boxing. Later, however, I came round to Bertie Wooster's opinion that this extravagant exercise was better left to muscular females like Honoria Glossop. My father had been in the Merton boat, but had had the intelligence to obtain the post of cox as I did of goal-keeper in another discipline, thus keeping actual physical exertion to a minimum. By following this sensible policy, I rose ultimately to be Captain of the Merton Second Eleven in soccer. That season was a disastrous one for the College, for my team lost every single match, usually by about fifteen goals to nil, and I then gave up any pretence of being an athlete.

I liked swimming, however, and was often to be found at Parson's Pleasure, where everyone bathed nude, after which I would float down the river lying comfortably in a punt.

One summer afternoon Bernard Aluwihare and I took Dr Radhakrishnan, now President of India, who was then a Fellow of All Souls, out with us in such a punt. I still remember with shame asking him if he knew anything about comparative religion.

I never smoked at Oxford and drank very little. It was only in my third year that I began to take an occasional beer or shandy, though I used to enjoy wine at College or Club dinners. This, of course, is the proper way to drink—in public and with one's food—and for those of us who come to live in the East, perhaps the change-over from wine to spirits is the most uncivilized of the new habits we adopt.

After going to India and until I was about forty I suffered continually from malaria. I attribute this to the fact that in those days I was a non-smoker. Since I took to cigars (I have never smoked cigarettes) I have not had a single attack of malaria and my general health has greatly improved.

In England and on the Continent the cigar is a mark of the plutocrat—Communist cartoons often picture the capitalist with a large corona in his mouth. But in India, the home-made cigar is really a cheroot and works out a little cheaper than the cigarette.

III

What a lot of time I wasted during my undergraduate days on religion! The narrow ideas that I had then disappeared from my life long ago and I am doubtful whether at any time they did me very much good. But religion was very exciting then and it did, I suppose, provide an alternative interest, taking the place of bridge or racing.

We held prayer-meetings and gave 'squashes'. One would get hold of some distinguished evangelist or orthodox don and invite twenty to thirty friends, and particularly friends whose souls one desired to cure, to one's rooms. After feeding them with a large tea, which generally included anchovy toast, crumpets and cakes, when they were nicely mellow, the evangelist would give his talk.

A much more ascetic kind of spiritual exercise was held at the Martyrs' Memorial at 8 o'clock on Sunday evenings. Here a little crowd of what were surely rather heroic undergraduates would assemble. Someone would produce a harmonium (and I think this is one of the reasons for my lifelong antagonism to this abominable instrument), hymn-sheets would be handed round and we would embark on an hour's performance of prayer, hymn-singing and sermons. Standing on a rickety chair and shouting at the top of my voice a speech that was supposed to change the lives and outlook of my audience, which often consisted of rather derisive undergraduates, was as brave a thing as I have ever done—and, I fancy, as useless. Through this, however, I found some very true friends, Lindesay Godfrey, Noel Wardle-Harpur and F. W. Dillistone.

Another type of religious enterprise which occupied a lot of my time was concerned with what was known as the OUBU—the Oxford University Bible Union—of which I ultimately became President. This was the successor of the old OICCU (which corresponded to a Cambridge Society with a similar name) which some years earlier had gone off the rails and amalgamated with the Student Christian Movement which we considered 'unsound'. The OUBU, therefore, was the most orthodox and reactionary of all the religious societies in Oxford and, as its name implied, took a four-square stand on the verbal inspiration of the Bible. Meetings used to be held in St Peter's Hall every Friday evening and distinguished visitors as well as members were invited to give addresses. There was hymn-singing and prayers and, though the membership was limited to seventy or eighty undergraduates, it certainly held them together and was the source of inspiration of a certain kind.

Although my actual activities in the religious field for my first three years at Oxford were confined to this sort of thing, I had a great deal to do with the Anglo-Catholics. In Mob Quad my neighbour was Alston Dix, one of the most brilliant young men I have ever met, who later became a monk—Dom Gregory —and a well-known theologian. Another neighbour was Max Petitpierre, a gangling youth with a heart of gold, immensely pious. There was also a great character who during my first year lived in the rooms which I was to inherit from him—Reggie Smith, who was a leading personality in the OUDS; he did a quite wonderful Falstaff.

All these three were Anglo-Catholics and from the very first week they started a campaign to convert me. They used flattery (I was far too good to waste my time on these unintelligent evangelicals), arguments of a kind for which nothing I had learnt at school had prepared me, and much affection. When one of them was arguing with me, another would be on his knees in the bedroom, praying that my heart would be touched. The Anglo-Catholics did one very well and, as I will show, they ultimately succeeded.

Later, towards the end of my time at Oxford, yet another religious influence arrived in the University. This was Frank Buchman and I had the privilege of being present at the very first meeting in Oxford of what was later to be called the Oxford Group and later still Moral Rearmament.

Directly I was introduced to Buchman he pointed his finger at me and exclaimed, 'There is a secret sin in your life.'

There was, of course, but even at that date, simple as I was, I felt it was a little phoney, for it would be a fairly safe bet to say this to anyone in Oxford and hit the mark. I attended two or three of Buchman's meetings for, while I strongly disapproved of the whole thing, they were certainly interesting.

I particularly liked the public confessions which I believe have now disappeared from the programme (a great pity). I remember one little first-year student, innocent as a baby, who, when his turn came to confess, could not think of anything to say and was reduced to admitting that he had once blown his nose on a public towel in the Union bathroom. On another occasion a woman student confessed that she had sinned against morality, whereon a loud trans-Atlantic voice exclaimed: 'Be more explicit, sister.'

Although Buchmanism took some hold in colleges like Worcester and among the Rhodes Scholars, it did not, at least in my day, have very much real success. It was obviously no use to the Anglo-Catholics and the great authority of Bishop Chavasse condemned it for the evangelicals.

Immediately after I finished my Theology Finals I was appointed Vice-Principal of Wycliffe Hall and a friend of mine, Julian Thornton-Duesbury, who also got a First in the same examination, became Chaplain. A few months later I was ordained in Christ Church Cathedral by Tommy Strong, the Bishop of Oxford, to whom I was greatly devoted and who was, I think, a little fond of me. We used to have fantastically learned talks about the pseudo-Dionysius the Areopagite and Caesarius of Heisterbach, though he rarely used words of more than two syllables and gave me a lasting inclination towards simplicity in speech and writing.

Strong was a wonderful friend and guide to young men, but it was generally accepted that, while he was an ideal Dean of Christ Church and Vice-Chancellor of the University, he was less suitable as Bishop of Oxford, for he was bored by public occasions, particularly objecting to those people who specialized in ecclesiastical small talk. He disliked sermons, thought hymns were quite unnecessary and tended to measure the success of a church service by the speed with which it could be brought to a conclusion.

'I think,' writes his biographer, 'that he probably could not really understand why anyone wanted to listen to sermons. They seemed to him to have very little to do with religion.' And he tells how on one occasion, when instituting an incumbent in a small village parish, Strong insisted in robing in the car (which involved something like a wrestle with his chaplain), in order that he might not have to meet the assembled clergy. On arrival at the church, when asked what hymns he would like, he answered: 'No hymns.' He got through the service at breakneck speed, escaped from the procession into his car, shook hands with the new incumbent, said, 'I hope you will be happy,' and rapidly drove away.

Although the habit did not affect me when I was in the Church, it did have considerable delayed-action influence in my later life, revealing itself in a very similar attitude to receptions, committees, and all ceremonial occasions. If I can't get away, I do what Tommy Strong presumably did not: I sit patiently, reciting to myself the matchless words of the *Dhammapada*—'All created things are grief and pain: all created things perish; all forms are unreal.' The unreal things pass away in time.

As Vice-Principal I got a good set of rooms in a wing of the Hall where I was entirely by myself and I had the task of giving regular lectures and holding tutorials, as well as performing the routine duties of an Anglican clergyman.

At Merton I gave a series of lectures on the Epistle of St James. This little-regarded work can be described as an attempt by its author to put the Christian message in a form likely to appeal to Jewish readers—the Jews were to develop along the lines of their own genius; their faith was the ally rather than the rival of Christianity. Thus I was already thinking in terms of a policy which I have followed all my life. In Poona I tried to express Western mysticism in Hindu categories and later among the tribes I have always tried to express the new ideas that the modern world is bringing them in a way that will be familiar and will result in an evolution from their past and not be a break with it. I started, therefore, very early on this sort of thing.

I only stayed for a year as Vice-Principal and outwardly the life was conventional and a little dull. Inwardly, however, it was a time of intense excitement. In the first place, I developed my studies in mysticism and my practice of religion to a greater degree than I had ever attempted before.

I had taken a special paper in the Theology Schools on mysticism with special reference to William Law, and this naturally involved a close study of the works of Jacob Boehme. I was fascinated by Plotinus and once had a talk with Dean Inge about him. I collected an unusual library of mystical books, spending every penny that I could save on them, and I read them voraciously. I was very much in earnest in the search for God. I used to fast every Wednesday and Friday, taking nothing to eat until 7 o'clock in the evening. Sometimes I stayed up all night at prayer and vigil. I was in love with the Beauty ever-ancient, ever-new that centuries ago had stirred the passionate heart of Augustine. 'The love that moves the sun and the other stars' possessed me. In God's will was my peace, and I cried in the solitude of my room: 'Thou hast made me for Thyself, and my heart is restless until it can rest in Thee.'

At the same time my old affection for the bad boys of my college grew greater and I had quite a number of them in my confidence. I was also made Chaplain of Merton and used to conduct matins and evensong regularly there in addition to what I did at Wycliffe.

It was thus not unnatural that I should find myself definitely turning to Catholicism, not the real thing, but its substitute in Anglo-Catholicism. I had no objection to Rome, but it was unfamiliar and would have been altogether too much for my dear mother. Anglo-Catholicism had poetry and beauty as well as mysticism of a kind which the evangelical party in the Church of England could not provide.

I made my first confession to Green in Merton Chapel and was so nervous that I went beforehand into the vestry and drank about half a bottle of the communion wine to stimulate me for what seemed to me an appalling review of a sinful life. When I think of it now I am astonished how little there was really to tell—then.

This, of course, put me in a rather difficult position. I was an important official of an institution which represented the spearhead of opposition to the Anglo-Catholic movement. I was expected to teach theology from a particular angle and to give the arguments against the Mass, confession, Mariolatry and other exercises of religion connected with the Church of Rome. Towards the end of my year it became evident that the position was impossible.

In the vacation term of the summer of 1927 the Principal had arranged an expedition to Palestine. The staff and students of the Hall would go and spend a couple of months studying the Bible and its history in the very place where its great events had occurred. For a whole year I had looked forward to this but I felt that it would be wrong for me to take advantage of it and that the path of sincerity demanded that I should resign my post before and not after this adventure. This was certainly a very idealistic way of doing things, but I thought it was right.

I went to see the Principal, Graham-Brown, and had a most

unpleasant interview. 'I have long suspected,' he said, 'that you have been going to confession,' in the tone of voice that he might have used had he suspected me of visiting brothels. In fact, the attempt of my relations and former colleagues to create a guilt-complex in me over what was after all a struggle for the truth taught me at least one thing—never to interfere with the journey of a soul towards what it believes to be the light. I felt that I was giving a lot of pain to my family and friends and this, for I have always been very sensitive, undoubtedly cast a cloud on what should have been a felicitous progress of the mind and spirit towards reality.

At the end of that summer term, therefore, I found myself without a job and went to live at home with my mother. I was faced with a number of possibilities. I was already Chaplain at Merton and it would not have been difficult to establish my position there. There was a possibility of my going to the House and the offer of a Fellowship at Keble. I was certain of getting something, and something attractive, by the autumn term.

IV

But during the summer vacation I had to face something more than a change of religious allegiance. I had to consider the entire shape of my future life. Until then my path had seemed fairly straightforward. I had done well in Schools ; I had been appointed to two Examining Chaplainships ; there was talk of Fellowships in three different colleges. We had even bought the house in North Oxford.

But my resignation from Wycliffe Hall set me thinking again. My former tutor, Green, a very wise man who always had a great influence on me, felt strongly that I should not stay in Oxford and insisted that I should go to a parish in the slums of London or one of the industrial cities and live among poor and ordinary people. I did actually try to arrange this but it fell through. Other influences then began to turn my thoughts to India.

I do not think I have loved anything in the world all my life so much as I loved Oxford in those days. It had everything

I wanted and the things I wanted then were not just the temptations of the flesh, a life of comfort and ease. *John Inglesant* was one of the books that influenced me. Oxford offered the search for truth, the dignity and interest of a life of scholarship, friendships of the most stimulating kind, surroundings of great beauty. Yet it did not satisfy me ; 'some life of men unblest' troubled me as it had troubled the Scholar Gipsy and driven him into the wilds.

At that time, and, in fact, for many years afterwards, I was completely indifferent to finance. My mother had brought us up to believe that there was something a little undignified about wanting money. The family was not particularly distinguished but I don't think that any of its members had ever gone in for trade. The children of merchants, however wealthy, or of shopkeepers, however charming, were not considered our suitable companions. Although poor mother was continually struggling to make both ends meet, there was a persistent atmosphere that it was not money that brought happiness and that gentlefolk did not really bother about it.

The result was that, although I got some fairly handsome rewards in the way of prizes and scholarships, they didn't affect me very much and I gave whatever I could save to the family. When I was invited to accept the post of Vice-Principal at Wycliffe Hall I never even asked what the emoluments were. Actually they were £200 a year plus board and lodging for about thirty weeks. This looks very little, yet in purchasing power £200 a year in 1927 was probably equal to a thousand rupees a month now. But the point was not whether it was a lot or a little but that I was not in the least concerned about it.

I was also curiously indifferent to ambition, as I have always been. My family never even suggested to me that one should make one's plans with a view to future preferment. The thing to do was quite simply, as we put it at that time, to discover the Will of God and follow it.

My choice, therefore, was simplified to some extent and it was obvious that there was a great deal to be said for India. My family had a very long connexion with the country. Even more impelling was an impulse which was very real indeed at the time and had a strong influence on my thinking.

The Catholic religion lays stress on a spiritual ideal which is known as reparation. Christ made reparation for the sins of the world. The saints through their prayers and sufferings make reparation for their own sins and those of others. During my later years in Oxford this became translated into the desire to make reparation to the poor for the way more privileged people had behaved to them. Now in relation to India I remembered how my family had made its money, such as it was, out of India, and my countrymen had gone to India to exploit it and to rule.

I thought, therefore, that I might go to India as an act of reparation, that from my family somebody should go to give instead of to get, to serve with the poorest people instead of ruling them, to become one with the country that we had helped to dominate and subdue. This idea became sufficiently important to break up my Oxford career and was the driving force that carried me through many difficult years in India.

When I made this decision I felt that I was leaving for ever the life of scholarship and plunging into an unknown world. Had I realized it I was, in fact, stepping on to a path that would offer me infinitely greater opportunities of research than anything I could have found among the books of Oxford. My self-imposed exile enabled me to study endlessly varied human beings along untrodden ways. Fourteen years later Oxford give me the D.Sc. for these researches.

When I first went up to Oxford I knew nothing about India except what my more conventional relations had taught me. Indians were wogs or natives. They were incapable of self-government and had to be kept in their proper place. In my third year, however, I met Bernard Aluwihare who, although he came from Ceylon and not from India, was an ardent supporter of the Indian national movement and in his own charming person was the best possible antidote to the ideas about Asia in which I had been brought up. He introduced me to the writings of Tagore and the opinions of Gandhi. He lent me books on Indian philosophy and gradually changed my entire outlook.

I became fired by the ideals of Indian nationalism: in particular, the personality of Gandhi absorbed my attention. Hindu mysticism greatly attracted me. I did not know many Indian students but among them was a boy from St John's, who was later to play an important part in the life of India, Jaipal Singh, already famous as a distinguished athlete.

In my fifth year and during the year I was teaching in North Oxford other influences strengthened my interest in India. A gentle and spiritual Christian ascetic, the Sadhu Sunder Singh, visited Oxford and made a deep impression on many of us. Professor Heiler visited the University a little later and gave some lectures: he was, I think, the first German theologian to come to Oxford after the War and, as he had written a book on the Sadhu, we had interesting discussions about the mysticism of East and West. Then came Jack Winslow.

V

Father Jack Winslow was the founder of an ashram-settlement called the Christa Seva Sangh. He had been a missionary in western India for many years, but after a time had decided to break away from conventional ecclesiastical activity in order to identify himself more closely with the poor and with Indian nationalism and culture. There was a great deal to Winslow. He had studied certain aspects of Indian mysticism and made them his own. He knew a lot about yoga in theory and practice. He might have been a great Christian leader. He certainly was a powerful Christian stimulant—but subsequent history proved that you cannot live on cocktails. At all events he captivated me and others with a vision of what Christianity might be once it became truly oriental in character.

I took to this new idea with enthusiasm and before I had left England I had made some study of Hindu philosophy and religion and had worked out various ways in which Christian architecture, art, philosophy, mysticism and worship could be approximated to the oriental model. Even today, when these things, I am afraid, are not so important to me as they once were, I believe that the suggestions I made then were valid.

The Christa Seva Sangh was founded to explore the possibilities of the reorientalization of the Christian religion. This was no new thing. Father Stevens, the Jesuit, one of the first Englishmen to come to India, wrote a version of the Bible in the form of a Purana. The Abbé Dubois lived and dressed in Indian style and is said to have composed a supplement to the Vedas proving the truth of Christian doctrine. In more modern times, the well-known Bombay historian, Father Heras, had worked at the indianization of Church architecture.

The Christa Seva Sangh set out ambitiously enough to develop this, though it did not carry on long enough to have much effect.

Two of my best friends—one from Oxford, Oliver (Bernard) Fielding-Clarke, and the other from Cambridge, Algy Robertson—were attracted by Winslow's plan, and in the summer of 1927 resolved that they would join him and help to build up the small Order which he had founded in Poona. After a long struggle I finally decided to go with them.

This meant more than merely leaving Oxford for an unknown India. It also implied that there was a serious possibility that we would become monks, ultimately taking vows of poverty, celibacy and obedience. For about three years we were all very serious about this and Algy continued as a monk or rather as a sort of friar to the end of his life, though Bernard and I both for various reasons gave up the idea.

Fortunately my mother, though she disliked the 'monkish' side, did not object to my going abroad, and Eldyth was keen on it. Gandhi's ideas, while irritating enough to the British politicians and the orthodox bishops, were proving rather stimulating to the more unconventional. My mother, for example, whom one would not have thought likely to be attracted by one who was in some ways a rival and critic of Christianity, became interested in Gandhi, and five years later when he visited England for the Round Table Conference and he went to visit her in her house at Oxford, she became enthusiastic. She carried on a lengthy correspondence with his secretary, a remarkable man called Mahadev Desai, and was perhaps typical of many who were attracted by the new Indian political philosophy.

The deep impression that Gandhi made on my mother is revealed in a letter which she wrote to me many years later after receiving the news of his assassination. 'What a great soul has left this poor, sad, struggling world and what a picture of sacrifice and endurance—great and wonderful courage—and what love. I shall ever remember his look and smile of love, not a "put on" one. The misery of his people, whose hope he was, breaks my heart. The despair of those masses on their terrible march! It is like a fantastic nightmare to think of them and a wicked cruel thing.'

My mother described how she had just gone into lunch when someone, who had heard the news on the radio, announced the tragedy and she came away weeping, for it was impossible for her to eat. 'I have rarely', she said, 'felt such a shock and grief. Bapu is now called the greatest man in the world. What a mockery from those who so often nailed him to the cross!'

After deciding to join the erratic, but devoted, company of the CSS I busily got ready to go to India. I received no money from the Society. Indeed, the idea was that we would get no money for we should not need it, and if we had any we should in any case have to hand it over, since we would not be allowed to have private possessions. In actual fact, I was, by the end of my time at Oxford, almost penniless and in considerable difficulty until we left. The Society bought us third-class tickets by rail across Europe and then on a French passenger boat leaving Genoa for Colombo. Third-class passengers who, before being allowed on board, were examined for venereal disease, were herded into cabins of six or eight at a time. We were incredibly uncomfortable but each of us saw himself as a young apostle braving all discomforts and we were carried along on a wave of excitement.

3

Saints and Satyagrahis

Look East, where whole new thousands are!
In Vishnu-land what Avatar?

—Browning

I

WE arrived at Colombo on November 30th 1927 and after a few days in Ceylon, during which we visited Kandy, we went up to Malabar. How thrilling it was to stand at last on Indian soil which to my youthful and romantic imagination was sacred, hallowed by the feet of countless saints, mystics and seekers after truth. How beautiful it was—Malabar in early December, fresh and green. I had read of the dirt, the squalor, poverty and ignorance of India, and I remember how astonished I was at the cleanliness, the people well-fed and well-dressed, and the thousands of boys and girls pouring into the schools. I was to see poverty in plenty later on, but not at first.

The reason we broke our journey here was to go on pilgrimage to a small monastery among the hills which had been established by a bishop of one of the Eastern Churches, Mar Ivanios, a man of singular devotion. It was run on primitive Franciscan lines and we were all deeply impressed by the simplicity, discipline and joy of the monks there. This was the kind of life I wanted and expected: I certainly had no idea of the strange experiences that were waiting for me. At this time in fact I shrank from politics, unaware that soon they would become, and would remain, a major interest. It never occurred to me that I could actually meet and talk to Gandhi: I had not realized how accessible India's leaders were. I had no idea of India's tribes, though they were all round me in Malabar. This was probably the one time in my life when Goodness had priority over Truth, Love or Beauty as my central aim.

Then we travelled by train across India to Poona, where we found a disconcertingly conventional group of buildings in the middle of a large field on the outskirts of the town, very near the Agricultural College, with Father Winslow and some Indian brothers of the Christa Seva Sangh to greet us. We immediately settled down to a rather odd life, certainly very odd by the standards of 1927 when Englishmen, especially the clergy, were expected to behave properly. We slept on the floor and, in fact, since there was practically no furniture, we did everything on the floor, which was very much in line with the practice of Hindu homes in western India at that time. We ate Indian food (with dispensation for invalids) and were rather particular about the way this was served, in the proper dishes—big brass plates, with a number of little pots—and the ceremonial washing of the hands before and after meals. We naturally removed our sandals whenever we entered a building. The regular dress of members of the Sangh was white khadi made into a 'habit' and those who had taken preliminary vows were entitled to wear saffron girdles.

Winslow was an excellent linguist and he insisted that we should give first priority to learning the Marathi which was spoken all round us. For this purpose the Sangh employed a number of pandits who came over from the city to teach us. I was fortunate in having a wonderful old Brahmin, H. V. Harshe, who was the embodiment of the best kind of traditional Hinduism. We spent most of my language-lessons discussing Hindu mysticism and philosophy with the result that after six months I knew the Marathi or Sanskrit words for most of the higher spiritual states, yogic postures and exercises but I was quite incapable of ordering lunch at a railway station.

Our inner lives were in a state of constant turmoil and excitement, but the first external event of note was a visit to Sabarmati in January 1928. Bombay has always been a cosmopolitan and liberal city and a number of intellectuals there had recently started a branch of the Inter-Religious Fellowship—the President was the veteran Professor P. A. Wadia. This body met regularly in Bombay for what were called non-denominational prayers and once a year had a conference which was attended by adherents of all religions. In 1928 the venue of the conference was in Mahatma Gandhi's ashram at Sabarmati near Ahmedabad.

From the moment of my arrival there I was doomed. For long a sympathetic fellow-traveller, I now became an ardent disciple. At this time, the national movement of India had risen to a pitch of sincerity and devotion that has rarely been equalled in the political upheavals of the world. The ashram itself, standing on the tall banks of the Sabarmati river, was the home of some hundreds of people marked by that quiet and disciplined devotion to hard work and to the poor which was then characteristic of the best type of Congressman. Among them Gandhi walked in almost unearthly dignity and beauty. That was the first thing that struck me about him—his beauty, and the inner spiritual power that transformed his frail body and filled the entire place with kindliness and love.

The impact of those few days at Sabarmati was extraordinary. It was as if I had suddenly been reborn as an Indian on Indian soil. Everything fell into place so naturally that I did not, I think, realize at first how very serious was the new attitude I adopted or what the consequences would be.

At first I did not see the conflict as between India and Britain but rather as between two different kinds of people. My theme was freedom and this was not confined to India. The prize-essay on the poetry of revolution which I wrote at Oxford had shown me how many Europeans, and particularly how many of the English poets, had treasured liberty. Many of the ideas inspiring India's national movement came originally from the West. Tolstoy and Ruskin had a profound influence on Gandhi. The first result of my contact with him, therefore, was to put me among those Europeans, those Englishmen, to whom colonialism or imperialism was intolerable, to whom the freedom of subject peoples everywhere was a passion, a consuming ideal.

I do not remember that this set up any conflict or caused me anguish of spirit. After I had met Gandhi it seemed to be the only possible attitude. This may seem surprising but it was, I suppose, easier for me because at that time I hardly knew any

Europeans in India. I belonged to no club which might have boycotted me for my opinions. I had never met a British official (except one or two Anglican bishops) and many of my friends in England, with whom I corresponded, were themselves inclined to a liberal attitude towards India's cause.

Later, as the struggle developed, I became more aware of the implications of my new devotion to Gandhi and his movement. As I gradually met more English people and some officials it was impressed on me, not always very kindly, how badly, from their point of view, I had gone off the rails. This was sometimes embarrassing, occasionally distressing, but the idea of freedom is so intoxicating, to work for it is so rewarding that I cannot say that I minded very much.

Perhaps I only fully realized the implications of my association with the national movement much later, when at a lunch party of British officials in Jubbulpore at the height of the Second World War my host asked me what I would do if India became an independent country and war broke out between her and Britain. 'That is the real test,' he said, 'of anyone who takes the Indian side.' I replied that in any case I did not believe in war, but in such a situation I would certainly be for India. I can still remember the hush of shocked incredulity that fell on the table, and I realized that these good people were obviously thinking that here was a potential traitor whom it would be rather embarrassing to shoot. Yet I could never think of myself really as a traitor but rather as someone who was loyal to the highest principles which Britain herself had taught the world.

I have, I am afraid, gone too far ahead in my chronology: I must come back to the early years. After Sabarmati and its stirring consequences, the next dramatic event in my life was that I very nearly died. All through 1928 I was undoubtedly playing with my health. I not only sat and slept on the floor. I went a little further and sat and slept on a cement floor with nothing to protect me but a thin piece of sacking. I gave up my mattress and even my pillows in an ardour for self-discipline. I went barefoot, ate anything I was given. This was all right during the earlier part of the year but, when the hot weather, which at least kept the cement warm, yielded to the rains, it should have been obvious to anybody but a young idiot that what he was doing was very silly. Someone remarked that I was only kept going by Wodehouse, whisky and the Holy Ghost.

The result was that, despite these prophylactics, I developed dysentery in an acute form, was rushed to hospital and for six weeks hovered, as they say, between life and death. I was unconscious for part of the time and only those who have had a severe attack of dysentery in the days before the new antibiotics were invented, will know the intense pain and appalling exhaustion it caused. Telegrams were sent to my family in England preparing them for the worst and I was told (afterwards) that suitable arrangements had been made with the local undertaker. The Bishop of Bombay came to give me the last rites—Extreme Unction, which prepares the soul for death.

At the same time the bishop, Palmer of Balliol who possessed to the full the Oxford blend of idealism and commonsense, brought three bottles of champagne under his cassock and persuaded the doctors that this was really the best thing they could give me. Even if it failed to keep me alive, he pointed out, it would dispatch me on my long journey in the right mood. In actual fact, I suspect that the bishop's champagne saved my life. From the very first glass I began to mend and within a month I was tottering about, extremely weak but fit to go on living.

But the Poona doctors were emphatic that I would need a full year of convalescence and it was decided that the best thing for me to do would be to return to Oxford and do a little research there in the hope that I would be able to come back again to India at the end of that period.

II

This year in England was a profitable one. I spent almost all the time in Oxford in my mother's house and this gave me the opportunity to read widely in the Bodleian and other libraries. In fact, I hardly did anything else except read and write and I actually produced three small books. One was a study of mysticism in a book which I called *Christian Dhyana*. This is an account of an anonymous fourteenth-century mystical classic, *The Cloud of Unknowing*, a book which, as I wrote, 'might have been written by some Christian Sadhu, so entirely does it express that rhythmic philosophy, that deep, slow breath of thought characteristic of the East. How to be free from petty mundane distractions, how to be purified from the sin that separates, how to unify and concentrate the mind, how to discipline the self and bring it to perfection and to God—such urgent and practical questions are asked by all lovers of the Infinite. In *The Cloud of Unknowing* the answer will be found.'

A second was a little book called *Studies in the Gospels* which I had been asked to write by the Inter-Religious Fellowship; similar studies of the *Koran* and the *Bhagavad-Gita*, the latter by C. Rajagopalachari, appeared at about the same time. My book was exceptional in that I illustrated many of the gospel-passages by quotations from such liberal Hindu writers as Keshab Chandra Sen, Ram Mohan Roy and others.

The third book, which I did not complete immediately, though I collected all the materials, was a study of the English mystic, Richard Rolle, whose message I tried to express in terms of Hindu *bhakti*. Later, in Karanjia, I wrote a companion book on St Francis of Assisi, whose life and message I also tried to interpret in Indian terms.

In the autumn of 1929 I was considered well enough to return to India and I travelled, first to Assisi and then, in the agreeable company of Leonard Schiff, to Palestine.

After going to Assisi I visited a group of Italian Sisters in a beautiful little convent among the olive-trees high up in the hills not far away. For some time past these Sisters, who formed an unconventional community of women who lived according to the primitive Franciscan rule in complete poverty and had an intense sympathy for Gandhi and India, had corresponded with me. They sent me a special blessing, which I have quoted in *Leaves from the Jungle*, but which I will give again here, for at one time it brought us a great deal of comfort, especially the bit about *funzionari noiosi*.

State sani e allegri,
senza troppo caldo,
senza patire la pioggia,

senza zanzare,
senza colera e malaria
e altre malattie,
senza funzionari noiosi
e altre persone moleste,
senza scrupoli e malinconie,
in pace, lìbertà e fortezza.

May you be fit and cheerful,
free from excessive heat,
free from the pouring rain,
free from gnats,
free from cholera and malaria
and other diseases,
free from troublesome officials
and other tiresome persons,
without doubts or sadness,
in peace, freedom and strength.

Here was the Catholic ideal at its purest and best and I count myself very fortunate that at this time of my life I had the opportunity of seeing this in Europe and Hindu life at its purest and best in Gandhi's Sabarmati.

The visit to Palestine was most enjoyable. We were well escorted by an eccentric but knowledgeable Anglican clergyman who had spent many years in the country. In Jerusalem and Bethlehem I lived in a rapture of spiritual excitement and spent many hours in the holy places, and specially in the great Church of the Holy Sepulchre. Later we went out into the wilderness of Judea and visited a number of monasteries and churches of the Orthodox Church, one of which was built on the very face of a precipice: we could look down through a crack in the floor to the rocks hundreds of feet below. The régime of these monasteries was severe and their great religious celebrations began about two o'clock in the morning and lasted till dawn. But the singing was so beautiful and the whole setting so romantic that one forgot to be tired, and at five in the morning we were taken into a little vestry and revived with fried eggs and vodka.

From Palestine we went on to India and reached Poona at

the end of November. We found that the Christa Seva Sangh had now become, both in appearance and organization, much more of a real monastery or ashram. It was a pretty place and was running in a more ordered fashion.

Almost immediately, however, Winslow decided to go on leave and, rather to my dismay (for I was far too young), left me in charge. This had an unexpected result. Winslow was very sympathetic to India's desire for freedom, but he belonged to the ranks of those liberal-minded Englishmen who talked about fulfilling India's legitimate aspirations, which could mean almost anything according to the interpretation you put on the word 'legitimate'. He had always managed to keep in with both parties to this great dispute.

When he left we rather let ourselves go: with the mouse away the cats had a great time. I hoisted the revolutionary tricolour over the ashram on the plea that since the Anglican cathedral in Bombay flew the Union Jack from its spire there was no reason why we should not fly the flag of India. The real crisis, however, came not through anything I did myself but from a lecture which I arranged to be given in the ashram hall.

At this time the press was excited by the appearance in India of a young Englishman who was chosen by Gandhi to be the bearer of one of his famous letters to the Viceroy. Gandhi's emissary, with his flaxen hair and khaki shorts, breaking into the world of immaculately dressed ADC's, excited public imagination almost as much as the half-naked fakir striding up the steps of Viceregal Lodge to parley with the King's Representative on equal terms. He was Reginald Reynolds, who later married Ethel Mannin, wrote a history of water-closets and became my very dear friend. At that time Reginald, like myself, suffered from the unpardonable crime of youth. Nothing he said could be correct; nothing he did could be proper, because he was young. In his untimely death a few years ago he finally paid his debt to the enthusiasms of his younger days.

At that time I hardly knew who Reginald Reynolds was. But when he wrote to me asking for the hospitality of the ashram for a few days on his way to England, I naturally sent him, as I sent everybody, a warm invitation to stay with us. He came and charmed us all by his simplicity and wit. I asked him to give a lecture in the ashram on the Gandhian philosophy, and he gave an unusually fine address to a great crowd of people, in which he stressed those aspects of Gandhi's teaching which make for international peace and national progress. There was not a word in the speech that could not have been delivered in any cathedral in England.

But this was too much for Government, and they at last got busy. I was expecting the police, which shows how little I knew about the Church of England. What I got, of course, was the Archdeacon. He wrote to me saying that Government was seriously upset at our entertaining a person like Reginald Reynolds, and asking for an explanation of my conduct. There was not much that *could* be explained, but I remember saying how astonishing I found it that this question should be raised by a representative of the Church instead of the CID.

After this I was chased by the police and shadowed by chaplains of the Establishment.

It says much, however, for the Christa Seva Sangh that it did not allow the constant pressure from the Church leaders and increasing vexations from the CID to turn it aside from what it felt to be right. With the full approval of the other members, for example, I entertained Subhas Chandra Bose and at the end of 1930 I was allowed to accept an invitation from Sardar Vallabhbhai Patel, later Home Minister in the Government of independent India to visit Gujarat and make an inquiry into police repression of the No-Tax Campaign that had been started there.

This campaign was on a very wide scale, and the Government had taken strong measures to counter it, so strong indeed that in many places almost the whole population had migrated into the neighbouring Baroda State. I visited over sixty villages in five talukas—Anand, Nadiad, Borsad, Bardoli and Jalalpur—and wrote a report which appeared first in the *Bombay Chronicle* and later as a small booklet, *In the Deserted Villages of Gujarat*. I was then, of course, still a Christian clergyman, and I wrote very strongly, appealing to the 'Christian' Government to observe the principles of its own professed religion.

'Surely,' I said, 'it is possible to meet even such an emergency as this by methods which are true to the principles of Law and

Justice, Righteousness and Humanity, and not by those which betray them.

'I would urge on all my fellow-Christians who read these pages, not least on any English Government servants, if they have the good fortune to meet their eye, that the principles of Christ apply equally to public and private life . . . If they would put all they know of the principles of Christ into the conduct of public affairs in Gujarat, then whatever the issue of the present struggle may be, they will have preserved intact the authority of Law, the sanctity of Justice and left behind no heritage of bitter memories.'

In Poona we used to conclude the morning and evening worship with the ancient Indian prayer: 'From the unreal lead me to the real: from darkness lead me to light; from death lead me to deathlessness.' Bernard Fielding-Clarke, a strong socialist in outlook, once remarked on the very different meanings this had for him and for me: for me, he said, it was obviously the desire to penetrate beyond or through the unreal transitory world to the eternal reality; for him it was the struggle away from the unreality of a life of social, political or even religious interests to the harsh realities of misery and pain. This was probably true when I first came to India, but very soon I was interpreting the verse just as Bernard did and I still do so, though I take both meanings now and look for the treasure of the true reality behind all appearance, as well as the reality of poverty and suffering.

III

While I was in Poona the ashram attracted to its membership a number of remarkable Indians, among whom was one who was to be my lifelong friend and ally. This was Shamrao Hivale, whose name appears frequently in these pages.

Shamrao was about six months younger than me, yet directly he came to the ashram he took me under his wing, initiated me into Indian ways, looked after me and probably saved my life by rushing me to hospital when I fell ill. He is a person of unusual attractiveness with a smile that charms everybody. He has 'a tamelessness of soul' that draws people to him. Like his brother, the late Dr B. P. Hivale who became famous in western India as the founder of a flourishing college in Ahmednagar, he has great determination and usually gets his way. He had long dreamt of going to England and finally persuaded the CSS to send him to Mirfield, a theological seminary of the Anglo-Catholic persuasion, where he remained for about a year. Before going there he had accompanied me on the Gujarat inquiry and when he returned from England, at the time I left the CSS, he went with me to the North-West Frontier. After this we planned everything together and worked together for many years until I went to NEFA. It was not easy in those days for an Englishman (as I still was) to find his way about outside the narrow circle of the sahibs and I could have done little had I not had Shamrao with me. He was (and is) a wonderful companion and his simplicity of heart and unfailing cheerfulness carried us through many difficulties.

IV

The years 1928 to 1932, during which I was closely in contact with Gandhi and his followers, were critical for India's future. It was now that the old national demand for dominion status was abandoned in favour of a demand for complete independence. It was now that Nehru clarified and proclaimed his views on republicanism and socialism and the Congress gradually found itself committed to a socialist pattern of society.

From 1928 onwards there was a great change in the people of India. There was a stir among the peasants; industrial workers began to organize themselves. Vallabhbhai Patel came into prominence and started the first of his anti-Government campaigns in Gujarat. The provocation of the Simon Commission, which had come to India at the end of the previous year, roused the intellectuals and the younger generation. Shortly after my first visit to Sabarmati Lala Lajpat Rai was beaten up by the police in Lahore and died. A few weeks later Nehru too was beaten in Lucknow. Terrorist activities began in the Punjab and Bengal.

On a walk with Gandhi

Talking to Mirabehn in the Sabarmati ashram

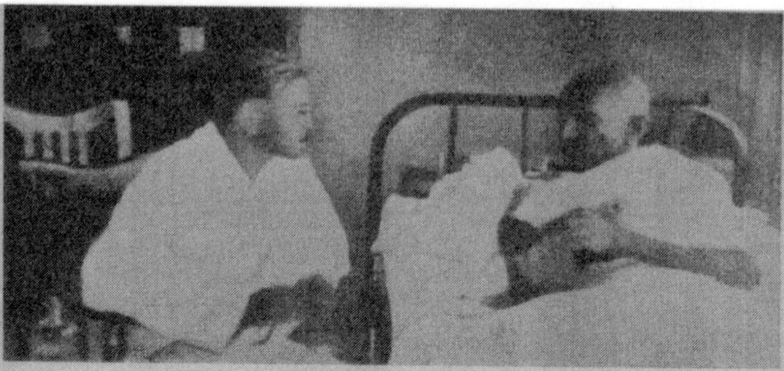

Talking to Gandhi after one of his fasts

On a visit to Dhulia jail, talking with Jamnalal Bajaj and Gandhi's secretary, Pyarelal

Government's reaction was severe and as Civil Disobedience spread throughout the country thousands went to jail. In December 1929 the annual meeting of the National Congress was held at Lahore with Nehru as President. Impatient with the dilatory and unfulfilled promises of the British Government, on January 26, 1930 millions of people throughout India recited the first Independence pledge:

We believe that it is the inalienable right of the Indian people, as of any other people, to have freedom and to enjoy the fruits of their toil and have the necessities of life, so that they may have full opportunities of growth. We believe also that if any Government deprives a people of these rights and oppresses them, the people have a further right to alter it or to abolish it.

The following year public imagination was captured by Gandhi's march to Dandi to break the salt laws. He was arrested on May the 5th, Nehru having been jailed three weeks earlier, and now Civil Disobedience became very widespread. Nearly a hundred thousand people went to jail and the Government became seriously alarmed. I remember Emerson, then Home Secretary to the Government of India, telling me a little later that nothing had disturbed him more than the great awakening among Indian women and the part that they had begun to play in politics. The whole of India was in a ferment and the movement spread even to the North-West Frontier.

Motilal Nehru died in February 1931 and later in the same month Gandhi, who was always seeking for peace, began talks with Lord Irwin. The British people, however, were still under the influence of the old imperialist ideas and, although the kindly Lord Irwin did everything possible to find a settlement, not very much progress was made. It was, however, decided that everything should be discussed at a Round Table Conference in London and on August 29th Gandhi left India to take part in it. At the end of December he returned and on January 4th, 1932, he was, as I shall describe later, arrested and remained in jail for many long months.

During these years my association with the Christa Seva Sangh was gradually waning, and I paid a number of visits to the Sabarmati ashram.

For my first long stay there I was lucky to get a room in

Gandhi's own house. From the cottage I looked out across the great expanse of sand and water of the Sabarmati river. On the further bank I could see in panorama many of the forces against which Gandhi was in revolt. There were the tall chimneys of the factories which were helping to destroy the hand-spinning industry. There was the palace of the Collector, symbol of a foreign domination which had sapped the manliness of India. There was the railway which, in Gandhi's view, had done so much to ruin the quiet peasant life of the villages. Opposite were the low roofs of the simple dwellings of the ashram. The forces of the world and the forces of the spirit were here in vivid symbol arrayed against one another—machine-force against soul-force, force of arms against love-force. At the time of my first visit, the river was slowly rising: soon the dry and barren sand-hills would disappear, and what all through the hot weather had been a tiny stream would soon be a great and irresistible torrent. 'Is this too a symbol?' I wrote, for I was young then. 'Is a new civilization based on love and justice and sacrifice, about to flow down from the hills of God into the arid desert of our modern world?'

The programme of the ashram was a strenuous one. The rising bell went at 4 o'clock in the morning and was followed, twenty minutes later, by prayers, in the open air whenever possible, which lasted for about an hour. At 6.0 there was a light breakfast—a cup of milk and a piece of bread—and then during the morning there was a succession of engagements, including classes in spinning, carding and Hindi. At 10.0, everyone went for their baths and washed their clothes, for there was no one to perform this duty for you. At 10.45 there was the midday meal of chapatis, boiled vegetables and curds.

Then again from 12.30 to 5 there was a programme of weaving and spinning. There were sometimes lectures on technique but at least two hours were spent hard at work in the weaving shed and another hour in spinning. At 5.30 there was the evening meal of chapattis, boiled vegetables, a little rice and milk, some fruit. This was followed at 6.15 by the evening walk, which for me was always a time of excitement as we used to go in a group round Gandhi and he would single us out one by one for conversation. At 7.30 there were the evening prayers, followed by a period of recreation, and at 9 o'clock the bell called us to bed.

It was exactly like being back at school again. I went in terror of being late: Gandhi (whom we usually called Bapu) compared the events of the day to a railway-train—if you arrive late at the station, you miss the train ; if you arrive late for a meal, you miss the meal. The discipline was very strict. There was a roll-call at the morning and evening prayers, and in the evening we had to say how much yarn we had spun during the day. My name was called along with the students'. There were about 150 people, boys and girls, men and women, both married and unmarried, when I was there. The strictest chastity both outside (naturally) but even within the marriage tie, was enjoined. The ashram was, in fact, an interesting experiment in co-monasticism: how far it worked I would not like to say.

The chief features of the life were given as Body-labour (everyone was expected to do eight hours' work a day), Economy (expenses were reduced to Rs. 12 a month, and no private property was permitted), Discipline, Cleanliness, Punctuality. Full members took six vows—Truth, Ahimsa (Love), Celibacy, Control of the Palate, Non-stealing (in the sense that it is theft if we have articles which we do not really need) and Non-possession.

Bapu once told me that he found Control of the Palate the most difficult of these vows for, he confessed, in a rather shy whisper, he loved good food. And in Gujarat the best Indian vegetarian food is quite wonderful.

Bapu himself set the pace. He adopted manual labour and filled his life with ceaseless toil. He reduced his food to the smallest quantity possible. His clothing was that of the poorest peasant. I once had the honour of washing his famous loin-cloth and I was able to see how the very minimum of cloth was used, even the ends being cut away to provide handkerchiefs. He always travelled third-class. He exercised no copyright over his many books. His cottage at Sabarmati, his hut at Keradi where he was arrested, were plain, sparely-furnished dwellings where his humblest followers could feel at home. He wrote his countless letters on tiny scraps of paper, used with rigid economy. For him simplicity of living was a religious adventure, an act of worship.

Bapu's asceticism did not express itself in sitting on a bed of spikes, but in the careful keeping of accounts.

Soon afterwards I wrote, rather poetically: 'Bapu's asceticism is of the open air. See him asleep beneath the stars, restful and calm. I associate him with growing flowers, fresh fruit, the wide and open river, the prayer before the morning star has risen, the walk in the unsullied air of dawn.'

I enjoyed my experiences in the spinning and carding classes and in the weaving shed. It was all very new to me, this body-labour, but it was enthralling, the triumph of drawing a perfect thread of even count, the excitement of seeing the white fleecy cloud of cotton rise up under the twanging carding-bow, the struggle with the complex processes of weaving, and the pleasure of watching the cloth grow beneath one's hand. I wish now that I had kept it up. It would have been as soothing as cigars.

Here I saw Bapu from yet another angle—as the monastic founder and spiritual director. On the way to see the Viceroy, he would be writing endless notes of spiritual advice to members of the ashram. He knew them all, heard their confessions, gave them counsel, was always at their service. 'I went to him', a boy of seventeen told me, 'and told him all the bad things in my life, and what a relief I felt when the burden of my sin was removed.' To one who asked advice about his life-work, he said, 'Seek first Truth, and everything else will come to you.' He was very stern, made tremendous demands, yet was sure to understand. He had the power of giving himself completely even to the apparently unimportant.

A few years earlier, Miss Slade, who soon became famous in India under her new name, Mirabehn, had joined the ashram at the inspiration of Romain Rolland.

She was a talented and attractive girl of colossal determination and came of a distinguished naval family, but by the time I reached the ashram she had cut off all her beautiful hair.

Bapu regarded her as his daughter and I was greatly excited one day in 1930 when he said to me, 'As Mirabehn is my daughter, so you shall be my son.' From that day I regarded myself as a citizen of India.

It was Mirabehn who looked after me. I told Bapu that I really could not say prayers at 4.20 in the morning unless I had a cup of tea. I believe I was one of the very few people who ever got the necessary dispensation and Mirabehn used to provide me with the healing brew.

My great trial in the ashram was the visitors. My room had windows with bars to them instead of glass, giving the impression that one was in a sort of cage. Crowds of visitors came daily to the ashram, and they all came to look at me, peering through the bars. I might be sleeping, or dressing, or eating, it didn't matter. And they often mistook me for Mirabehn who, with her shaven head, looked a little masculine, while I, in my flowing robes, might have been anything. You heard them gather at the window, they lifted up the children to see better. There was a pause while they drank me in. And then a whisper: 'To think that is the daughter of an English Admiral!'

We all had to do our turn as sweepers, and one of the attractive things about the ashram was that there were no futile lavatory inhibitions. Bapu had no sense of smell and when he did his inspections, Mirabehn, and sometimes I too, went with him so that our more sensitive noses might report on the sanitary conditions.

Looking back I feel, though I did not feel so at the time, that there was far too much stress on celibacy. Husbands and wives had to live together as brothers and sisters and this put a great strain on their nerves. Sexual irregularities were treated with a severity out of all proportion. On one occasion I was present when Bapu held an inquisition on an unhappy young couple who had fallen into sin. I remember he began, 'In my own experience in South Africa . . .' but Mrs Gandhi, who was there, said, 'No, no, no, you can leave that alone.'

The way things went to excess is illustrated by a curious incident in Bombay. One day I went to lunch with Mirabehn who was staying in a flat overlooking the sea. We were having a pleasant talk when the food was brought in and spread on the floor, whereupon Mirabehn got up and shut the windows.

I protested, for it was very hot, but she said sternly, 'No, Verrier, the sea-breeze carries particles of salt. These will fall on our food and it will make it more difficult for you to control your passions.'

Bapu himself, however, thought of everything in terms of Truth. At the beginning of 1933 I nearly got married and I wrote to Bapu, who was then in the Yeravda jail, to tell him so. He sent me this affectionate and characteristic reply:

My dearest son,

Son you have become of your own choice. I have accepted the responsible position. And son you shall remain to the end of time. The tie between you and me is much thicker and tougher than blood. It is the burning love of Truth at any cost. Therefore, whatever you will do will not disappoint me. But I was sad.

I am not thinking of superiority of celibacy over marriage. I am thinking of what you had intended, almost pledged yourself to be. But I know that you had to be true to yourself and appear as you were.

He went on, however, to give his blessings to the marriage, which never actually came off, but ended by saying that if I did decide not to marry, 'Your love of Truth will transmute your desire for exclusive marriage into the universal marriage with Truth. In this divine marriage we men and women are all women and Truth is the only lord, master and husband.'

V

I did not keep very many personal recollections of those days, but here is an account of a journey in 1931.

Three small third-class carriages were reserved on the night-train for Bombay. I arrived first on the platform: then Mirabehn turned up with a sick boy and a sick woman whom Bapu was taking for treatment to Bombay. Then Pyarelal arrived with a bus-load of luggage, piles and piles of it, boxes of files, rolls of bedding and baskets of food, spinning-wheels, water-pots—it was all cascaded into the tiny carriage. Finally at the last moment, Bapu and Mrs Gandhi with Jamnalal Bajaj and the secretaries arrived. No one knew that Babu was going, so there was no demonstration, though about a hundred people gathered round the carriage. There was no shouting as the train left the station. Directly we were on the move, Bapu got up and told us that his day of silence had begun and would continue till the following evening. Mirabehn had just made his bed, and he went straight to it. Within five minutes he was fast asleep. The rest of us tossed about on the hard narrow seats till midnight. At every station someone had to get up and guard the windows to prevent people waking Bapu up. Old women want to touch his head ; others want to give him presents, or they thrust lanterns into the carriage and just look at him. It was a beautiful thing to see his peaceful childlike sleep, undisturbed by the jolting train, or by the memory of the endless files that were piled up around him.

At four we all got up for prayers, and in the darkness as the train rushed onward, the familiar songs were sung, and the verses from the *Bhagavad-Gita*—about control of mind and body, and the peace that comes from it, were recited.

I stayed a few days in Bombay. On the last morning about six-thirty as I was preparing to catch the eight o'clock train to Poona, a phone message come to say that I was to go round to Laburnum Road at once to see Bapu. This sounded very important, so I went round immediately and went upstairs.

It was the day of critically important All-India Congress Committee meetings. Bapu was sitting in a tiny room talking to some man who was involved in trouble with the police. He had an air of repose and calm such as you or I might possibly obtain on a good holiday.

I waited a little, and then he said that he had sent for me because he knew I was in perplexity about my future, and he had thought that he might perhaps be of use to me. It was just then that I was thinking so hard about my relations with c s s of which Mirabehn had told him something. He had it all in his mind—and on such a day. Then for twenty minutes he talked to me about the whole business with the most perfect tact and understanding, giving several examples from his own career. He told me of his own relations with the Servants of India Society, and why he did not join them.

'If you are doubtful of your position in a Society,' he said 'tell them the worst about yourself. Even exaggerate the difficulties. Then if they will swallow that, you will be all right.' 'It is normally a good rule not to go till you are turned out.' 'But you musn't have a constant burden on your mind, the thought that you are embarrassing your Society. Even if the thought is imaginary, it is very real in its effects. If I imagine a ghost in my room—even if there is not a ghost in the whole world—I shall be unable to sleep. And this ghost you must lay. Smite it, kill it—no room for Ahimsa here.' Finally he urged me to go to Almora in the Himalayas, and recover my health fully, at his own expense.

My experiences during these months were decisive for my whole life. I came to the conclusion that I must leave the Christa Seva Sangh and go to live in some very poor village where I would be in closest contact with the people. The prayer 'Lead me from the unreal to the real' had taken its new meaning. At that time I thought of going to the untouchables, and to Gujarat.

But Sardar Vallabhbhai Patel persuaded me against this. 'The untouchables', he said, 'are not your problem. They are the sin of the Hindus, and it is the Hindus who must make reparation to them.' He also pointed out that Gujarat was already full of social workers and missionaries, and I should find it very difficult to establish myself in a clear field. This I should find among the tribal people.

One day as I was driving through the streets of Ahmedabad with Sardar Vallabhbhai and Seth Jamnalal Bajaj, I heard for the first time in my life—from the lips of Jamnalal—the magic word 'Gond'.

'Why don't you come to the Central Provinces,' he said, 'and do something for a tribe which is almost entirely neglected both by national workers and by missionaries?'

I liked what Jamnalal had to tell me about the Gonds, and decided to visit their country before the end of the year.

In the meantime I had written to Shamrao in England, telling him of my plans and asking him if he would join me. We were still, it must be remembered, thinking of ourselves as members of the Church, and Shamrao still hoped to be ordained. To join me at that moment meant cutting short his training in England. Our idea was that we would live together in a small ashram in a Gond village. We would identify ourselves with the positive aspects of the national movement. We would continue to be members of the Church, and would draw up a Rule of Franciscan living. We would not, however, do any missionary work or preaching, and we would not aim at any kind of conversion. Our ashram would be open to people of any faith or of none.

Such a plan might not have been possible in England, for I do not think any bishop there would have been able to accept it. But it seemed to me that in India there was no reason whatever why groups of national-minded Christians should not associate themselves with members of other faiths in the most intimate manner for the service of poor people without in any way losing the distinctiveness of their own religion.

After long discussions, and much good advice from Gandhi himself, Shamrao finally sent me a cable saying that he would join me at the end of the year. This brought my plans within the realm of practical politics, and I resigned from the Christa Seva Sangh. We arranged that Shamrao should come back to India in Gandhi's party.

This was a tremendous plunge in the dark. We had no idea what our new country would be like. We knew nothing about the tribes. We had practically no money and were not at all sure how we were to get any. For our immediate needs our new friend Jamnalal Bajaj was ready to provide, and we can never forget how he helped us through those difficult days.

Yet the actual break with the Christa Seva Sangh, which I had recognized as inevitable a year or two earlier, was easy when it came at last. It did not involve any very serious change of outlook: it was an amicable retirement from an institution, not a drastic reversal of ideas. For Shamrao and I proposed to do much the same things as before, only with greater freedom and without the specifically missionary element which we had come to recognize in the Sangh's policy. We hoped at that time to continue in the Church, if only on the fringe of it. We were still interested in the mystical aspect of Christianity blending with the mysticism of the Hindus.

In its ultimate result, of course, my resignation had far-reaching and drastic results, but it took time. In 1931 the chief practical result was that I no longer had a Society to pay my bills.

I stayed on in Poona for a few weeks, and then set out on my wanderings. I went first to stay at the Satyagraha Ashram at Sevagram near Wardha, Gandhi's favourite home, where he used to go whenever he wanted rest and retreat, and where later he established his headquarters. There was none of the romantic river-scenery of Sabarmati here. Sevagram was in the dusty plains of central India ; it could get oppressively hot ; and Gandhi used to take his morning and evening walks along the railway-line. It was as though he wanted a place where there would be nothing beautiful or sensuous to distract the soul, and his followers could devote themselves entirely to the needs of the poor, the challenge of the search for Truth.

I used to stay sometimes in Sevagram, more often with Jamnalal Bajaj who lived not far away. Jamnalal was a man of great property ; a merchant prince who ten years previously had left his palatial home for a small overcrowded bungalow, where he lived a life of great simplicity. He still owned a good deal of property, but he regarded himself as a trustee, and the whole of his fortune was at the public service. He was a typical product of the Indian national movement: he had given his life to the winning of freedom through national reconstruction. Long ago he threw open the doors of his family temple to the 'untouchables'. He was a leader of the khadi movement which brought some help to the homes of the very poor. While I was with him, we went to open a number of wells to the 'untouchables' and some temples too were freed from the burden of caste restrictions. Only a very few Englishmen visited Wardha in those days and Jamnalal was never so well known to them as some other Congress leaders, largely because of his unwillingness to talk much in English. I think that was a pity, for there was a great deal in him—his simplicity, his straightforwardness and plainness of speech (I remember him rebuking me for saying 'thank you' so often, which he said I could not possibly mean), his Quaker-like attitude to existence would have made a strong appeal to them.

Jamnalal went, of course, to jail and one day I travelled to Dhulia to see him. I was so shocked at the way he, as a class

C prisoner, was being treated that I took a vow (everyone was doing this sort of thing then) that I would go barefoot until India won her independence. The only exception to this was that I should not make myself conspicuous and so I put on sandals when I visited a town. I kept this vow for about fifteen years and got so used to it and saved such a lot of money on socks, shoes and polish that I felt rather sorry when I no longer had an excuse to continue.

About this time I went with A. V. Thakkar (Thakkar Bapa), perhaps the most prominent of the social workers of his day, on a ten-day tour to see what was being done for the 'untouchables' and this made a great impression on me. We first went to Bombay, and put up at the Servants of India Society, where we were most kindly received by the labour leader, N. M. Joshi. In Bombay, we spent some crowded days visiting the tenements of the Bhangis (the sweepers who, in the absence of the flush-system, remove the refuse from the lavatories). These 'untouchables' were in the employment of the Municipality, and lived in municipal dwellings.

I quote an extract from a letter I wrote immediately afterwards.

The worst slums in London are nothing to these tenements laden with humanity, mostly tall buildings with hundreds of little rooms. In these some of the rooms are clean and airy, but overcrowded. A very few are single-storied dwellings, well built, clean and open. The majority, four-storied or single-storied, are dark, overcrowded, intolerably filthy. One settlement, typical of several others, was no more than a collection of tiny kennels, the house built of scraps of kerosene tins nailed together, without windows, on ground which—when the rain pours down—becomes a swamp exhaling poisonous vapours. Here live our own people, condemned by social custom to a life of degrading toil. The theatre of their joys and sorrows are these dark hutches. I went into one of them: the family was sitting and lying in the pitch darkness: the hut was heavy with the damp-laden heat of Bombay. Scarcely able to breathe, I backed out into the familiar sunlight. Here children come to birth, the first joys of love awaken, fevers and choleras must be endured, until death comes to free them—these brothers and sisters of our own whom society has made into parasites on human excrement.

We went to the central sewage station. It was fairly clean —but the smells! Smells, astonishing, shocking, bewildering smells! a whole new world of possibilities in horror! smells mixed and blended to produce new smells ; every second they came ; in their infinite variety, they swarmed about you, now stimulating, now depressing you, unforgettable, amazing. And past many of the sweeper-settlements, where live little children whose affinities are with blue skies and 'all enchanting innocencies', the open sewer carries its slow-moving, hideous cargo.

From Bombay Thakkar Bapa and I went on to a place called Jalhod, where we stayed with a landowner, and a deputation of sweepers waited on Thakkar Bapa, but they were not admitted to the house or even to the courtyard, and we had to talk to them sitting in the street under a steady downpour of rain.

We went then to Dohad, the centre of Thakkar Bapa's work among the Bhils. Here I had the (to me) novel experience of opening and naming a street—Thakkar Street.

On Jamnalalji's advice I went up to Betul, a charming country town on the Satpura plateau, to see whether I could find a suitable place for our headquarters in that tribal area. I had an introduction to a leading merchant and landlord, Seth Dipchand Gothi, who entertained me royally in the bosom of his family, and took me about the countryside to see as many places as possible. Although a man of considerable wealth, he had no motor car.

'If I get one,' he said, 'it will always be commandeered by officials, and I should feel so annoyed that I prefer to go on foot.'

So we went down by train to the Tapti river, and tramped on foot through the jungle, visiting a number of Gond villages. Afterwards we made a long journey by bullock-cart in the Korku country. I liked Betul very much and was fascinated by the Gonds and Korkus, even though I had a foretaste of what village life would mean in the way I was pursued by the police wherever I went. At that time I used to wear a dhoti tied Madrasi-fashion and a long shirt which hung down outside. Both, of course, were of khadi. For a few days I even put on a Gandhi cap. But this gave me so criminal an appearance in the eyes even of my dearest friends that I abandoned it. It was not remarkable, therefore, that an Englishman so unorthodoxly dressed should have attracted the notice of the police, especially as Betul had been the scene of some violent struggles between Government and the tribesmen.

From Betul I went to Chhindwara, where I was fortunate to have a car put at my disposal, and I was taken up to the beautiful village of Tamia on the Pachmarhi road. Unhappily, I was not the first person to think Tamia a suitable place to live in. There were missionaries in the neighbourhood, a Government dispensary and even a dak bungalow. Beautiful as it was, therefore, I had to abandon the idea of settling in Chhindwara.

When I got back to Wardha I found myself at a loose end, for it was not possible for me to go and settle in a village until Shamrao returned, even if I could have got land and made arrangements in time, and he was not due back from England until Christmas. I went, therefore, to stay with Acharya Kripalani, later a celebrated and controversial politician, at Meerut.

After a few days studying the khadi industry there, I went with Kripalani on a tour in the United Provinces. I could not have had a better companion and we visited all the bigger places and many of the smaller and more interesting ones—Muttra, Brindaban, Hardwar, Hrishikesh, Ayodhya. We were chiefly concerned on this occasion in promoting the cause of khadi, and we used to give a number of reasons why people should wear it—because it was the symbol of freedom, equalized people by dressing rich and poor alike in the same cloth, put money in the hands of the peasants instead of the capitalists and was a constant reminder of Gandhi's philosophy. We then usually gave a brief outline of that philosophy, stressing particularly the note of universal love, non-violence and the new peaceful method of political agitation which Gandhi had introduced.

During my tour in the United Provinces, I came for the first time into real contact with Indian poverty, for the villages of the C P and the U P were much poorer than those of Gujarat or Maharashtra. As Kripalani said to me, 'No one with any imagination should visit these places. It is almost more than I can bear.' He was right. I wrote:

It is utterly heart-breaking to see these wretched tumbledown villages, with their pools of filth, their cheerlessness, the thin scarcely-clad bodies of their inhabitants, with hunger and despair in their eyes. Near Meerut, a villager was crippled in an accident. All day he had to lie on his rough bed. No one could be spared to nurse him. As the time for paying the rent drew near, the family began to wonder how he was to be fed. They carried him tenderly to the doctor. I saw the poor man with his body covered with ghastly bed-sores. And his friends who loved him said to the doctor, 'We cannot feed him. There is no one to care for him. Can't you give him something to take him to another world ?'

The tour was surprisingly uneventful. But we were investigated by the police on various occasions, and once, in Cawnpore, an order was passed forbidding us to hold any public meeting.

Our last visit on the way down to Bombay to meet Gandhi on his return from the Round Table Conference—Shamrao too was travelling with him—was to Jubbulpore. Here I gave precisely the same lecture which I had delivered in every large town in the United Provinces, urging the people to remain non-violent, to love their enemies and, while fighting bravely for freedom, to keep the spirit of peace in their hearts. The local CID, whose agent was not apparently very familiar with the English language, sent in a report that I had advocated violent revolution, and had praised the terrorist Bhagat Singh, who had recently been executed. I had made some reference to the *Bhagavad-Gita,* and no doubt the reporter had confused the two names.

What followed was typical of what was continually happening all over India. The report went up to the Commissioner. On reading it he at once recommended my deportation from India.

From Jubbulpore, Kripalani and I travelled down to Bombay. For Kripalani, of course, the great event was the arrival of Mahatma Gandhi. For me Shamrao's return to India seemed even more important. I managed to get a special pass to go on board the boat. It was a very impressive sight that morning, for the whole of the great city seemed to have turned out to welcome Gandhi, and the immediate approaches to the docks were lined with saffron-robed Desh Sevikas.

I found Shamrao looking very well but I contented myself with greeting him and my old friend Bernard Aluwihare ; I had never felt it was proper for people of no importance in the political world, just because they were Europeans, to push themselves forward into the presence of Gandhi. However, we were invited to go to his house, where we shared a room with the Privats, an enthusiastic Swiss couple who had travelled to India with the party.

The following day Shamrao and I went up to Matheran in order to make our plans for the future in some degree of quiet. But after only three days a telegram arrived from Mahadev Desai asking us to come at once. We left in less than ten minutes, got a couple of horses, and rode down the hill to a station from which we could get a quick train to Bombay.

VI

Gandhi was staying in a house called Mani Bhuvan and he invited us to stay with him there. There was great excitement in the city ; the Viceroy had finally rejected the Congress offer of peace ; Nehru was already in jail, and the arrest of other national leaders was expected at any moment.

But when we reached Mani Bhuvan and climbed to the roof, we found a great serenity in astonishing contrast to the crowds and turmoil outside. The roof was a very pleasant place. Low tents had been erected, and there were palms and plants: at least 300 people could gather there. It was cool and you could see the stars. Bapu was sitting at the wheel quietly spinning. He had already begun his weekly silence. I carried on a one-sided conversation with him, and he wrote down his questions and replies on a scrap of paper which I still have. I must have begun by asking if there was anything I could do.

He wrote:

I have sent for you for that very purpose. I have told Mahadev all I have been revolving in my mind. When he comes he will tell you or I shall briefly write what is wanted.

How are you keeping in health?

He [Mahadev] should be coming shortly. If he does not

during the time I finish this I shall write out what I want to say.

You are sleeping here? If so is your bedding etc. arranged?

Then Shamrao and I retired to the smaller tent and Bapu lay down about three yards from us, while some thirty others lay on the roof under the canvas shelter. Mrs Gandhi and Mirabehn gave us a surprisingly satisfying supper of dates, nuts and fruit. But I could not sleep. As I wrote at the time, 'I felt I had to keep vigil, and for hours I was under those splendid stars that rose, tier upon tier above me, while beside me Bapu slept like a child committed to his Father's hands. I thought of Christ going up to Jerusalem, his eyes filled with determination and courage: and I seemed to see the Spirit of Christ travelling the centuries like a bright sword turned against all wrong and injustice. Among these sleeping friends so dear to us, brave, pure-hearted, sincere, the spirit of Love was manifest and unconquerable'.

At last I lay down between Shamrao and Bernard on my hastily improvised bed on the floor, just beside Bapu, and fell into a deep sleep, when suddenly like the coming of a dream there was a stir and a whisper: 'The police have come.'

We started up and I saw what I shall never forget—a fully uniformed Commissioner of Police at the foot of Bapu's bed, and Bapu just waking, a little bewildered, looking old, fragile and rather pathetic with the mists of sleep still on his face.

'Mr Gandhi, it is my duty to arrest you.'

A beautiful smile of welcome broke out on Bapu's face and now he looked young, strong and confident. He made signs to show that he was keeping silence.

The Commissioner smiled and with great courtesy said, 'I should like you to be ready in half an hour's time.'

It was five minutes past three. Bapu looked at his watch and the Commissioner said, 'Ah, the famous watch!' And they both laughed heartily. Bapu took a pencil and wrote, 'I will be ready to come with you in half an hour.'

The Commissioner laid his hand on Bapu's shoulder with a gesture so full of affection that I thought it was an embrace, until I realized that it was the formal token of arrest. Bapu then cleaned his teeth and retired for a moment. The door was guarded, and all of us who were on the roof sat round in a circle. I looked out on to the road where some had been keeping all-night vigil and where a little crowd, very quiet and orderly, had collected, but there were no special police precautions.

When he was ready, Bapu sat in the midst of us for the prayers and we sang together the Song of the True Vaishnava. Then Bapu took pencil and paper and wrote a few messages, some last instructions to his followers and a letter to Sardar Vallabhbhai, which was as follows:

'Infinite is God's mercy' (these were the first words to be written after his arrest). 'Please tell the people never to swerve from truth and non-violence. Never to flinch, but to give their lives and all to win Swaraj.' He then wrote a short note and gave it to me:

My dear Elwyn,

I am so glad you have come. I would like you yourself to tell your countrymen that I love them even as I love my own countrymen. I have never done anything towards them in hatred or malice and God willing I shall never do anything in that manner in future. I am acting no differently towards them now from what I have done under similar circumstances towards my own kith and kin.

with love
yours
M. K. Gandhi

Then Bapu stood up to take farewell. It was a strange sight: the police at the door, Mirabehn and Devadas bustling to and fro with the baggage which was already packed, Bapu surrounded by his friends, many of them weeping. Mrs Gandhi with tears running down her cheeks said, 'Can't you take me with you?' Everyone in turn touched his feet, and when I said goodbye he pulled my ear with a smile. He was in very good spirits: he might have been going to a festival rather than a jail.

Then, followed by the whole company, he went downstairs. Shamrao and I watched from the roof. The tiny figure got into the car and the crowd surged round it. It was a wonderful tribute to India's non-violence that there were only a few policemen and they were able to be in the midst of the crowd without fear of danger. Just at that moment a message came to say that

Sardar Vallabhbhai, the Congress President, had also been arrested. And then the crowd scattered as the car bearing the very soul of India drove away through the dark and deserted streets.

VII

Among the instructions scribbled for Mahadev Desai after the arrest was one asking me to go to the North-West Frontier Province to discover what was really happening there. Disquieting reports had filtered down to Bombay about the severe repression of the 'Red-Shirt' movement; no journalists were admitted, all press reports were strictly censored, and as a result there was a great deal of concern about the fate of the Pathans who had so unexpectedly adopted Gandhi's non-violent technique. I was the first 'reporter' to get in, and this, I later heard with some complacency, rather annoyed the India Office.

This all happened long ago and I must put the reader briefly in the picture. Nationalist activities in the NWF Province were largely associated with the name of Khan Abdul Ghaffar Khan. This splendid and heroic figure captured the imagination of the Pathans. His name was constantly linked with that of Gandhi, though his speeches were more fiery, and he had not the latter's power of winning the hearts of his enemies. He was a competent organizer, an autocrat, essentially a leader, yet very gentle, with a sincere love for his villagers. The very spirit of non-violence shone in his face. When I saw him some years later, I thought of Wordsworth's lines on another great Highlander:

> In him the savage virtue of the Race,
> Revenge, and all ferocious thoughts were dead;
> Nor did he change; but kept in lofty place
> The wisdom which adversity had bred.

At the beginning of 1930, Abdul Ghaffar Khan started an organization which aimed at developing into an army of non-violent warriors. They were called 'Khudai Khidmatgars'

(Servants of God). At first they had no uniform, but one day a volunteer turned up on parade with a shirt which had been dipped in brick-dust mixed in water. It looked well and was convenient, so it was adopted as a uniform—an unfortunate accident which gave rise to the alarming name of 'Red-Shirts'. But there was nothing 'Red' about the Red-Shirts; they had nothing whatever to do with Moscow and nothing to do with violence. In happier times, they might have developed into a Frontier Scout Movement. The movement was highly organized: it had its Generals, Colonels, Captains, and its rank and file: it even had its own C.I.D. The whole country was divided into 'Districts': there was a 'civil' as well as a 'military' administration; each District had its Jirga or Local Board with President and committee, as well as its 'garrison' in charge of a Colonel or Major.

Abdul Ghaffar Khan made a point of taking no important step without consulting Gandhi, and his supreme achievement during this period was to drive home the message of non-violence, which was a very great thing. The Pathan was naturally violent and revengeful; he possessed arms; and for hundreds of years he had lived by the law of retaliation. There was no greater insult than to be beaten, and in front of women. To bear such insult without retaliation, to fight with the strange, clean weapon of Satyagraha, was the new ideal set before the Frontier by Abdul Ghaffar Khan. He used to say, 'You are to be an army of sufferers, not of avengers. Only by patience will you be victorious.' And the Afridis who carried their merchandise to the bazaars of Peshawar and saw the picketers there suffering without retaliation, returned to their mountain fortresses with rage and wonder in their hearts.

Government soon began to be seriously worried. The numbers of the Red-Shirts swelled to over a hundred thousand; their organization was excellent: they were in a position to paralyse the administration; a parallel Government had practically been established: the prestige and influence of Abdul Ghaffar Khan was paramount. Towards the end of the year, therefore, an ordinance was promulgated and the entire General Staff of the Red-Shirts was arrested. Abdul Ghaffar Khan himself went to jail on Christmas Day. Within a week, every Red-

Shirt officer, from Colonel to Subedar, and every President and Secretary of the district Jirgas was in jail.

Mahadev Desai wanted us (for I insisted on taking Shamrao with me) to start for Peshawar at once but I had no money for the fare, nor had anyone else. Devadas Gandhi, therefore, took us round to visit two or three wealthy merchants in Bombay and very quickly collected the small sum—I think it was only 300 rupees—which we felt (as usual thinking that money didn't matter) would be required.

I have always looked back on this incident with great satisfaction, for it was the one time in my life when I have been a man of action and gone into a certain amount of danger. Always a devotee of thriller fiction, I now found myself plunged into the most exciting cloak-and-dagger adventures. It was obvious that if I went as I was, in the Gandhi uniform, I would be arrested immediately, so I borrowed a suit made in London which belonged to Bernard Aluwihare and which, though far too small for me, at least made me look respectable. We travelled Inter Class, which personally I thought would attract attention but, as it turned out, enabled us to get through the police cordon that was drawn round the Province. Government got information that I was on the way and expected me to be travelling First Class and, in consequence, arrested a perfectly innocent English businessman to his great indignation. Under the cover of the flap caused by this gentleman we managed to get through.

We had to spend some hours in Delhi and there was an exciting interview at night with some contacts under the walls of the Red Fort. I forget exactly what it was about except that it had something to do with gold. Later, on the Lahore platform, I met dear Bul (Korshed Naoroji) who told us something of what we might expect.

When we reached Peshawar we found ourselves in a strange confusing world. Everything had been arranged in a great hurry and I had no idea where to go or how to begin. Devadas, however, had given us the name of a merchant in the city and we drove by tonga to his house, only to be kept waiting for an hour while he deliberated whether or not it was safe to see us. Shamrao has described our arrival and its immediate sequel.

The merchant was dressed very smartly and looked quite brave. We thought we should get a lot of help from him. But as soon as he read our letter of introduction he trembled all all over his body. 'The man you want is very old and blind, and is unable to see anyone,' he said. However, we did not give up hope, but sat there talking to him. Verrier is very good at getting information out of people, and we were able to learn a good deal of the situation even from this panic-stricken friend, who was in himself a vivid illustration of the reign of terror on the Frontier. He thought that I looked suspicious in my Maharashtrian clothes, and lent me some of his baggy Pathan trousers and Russian shoes. After about an hour, the merchant whom his brother had described as old and blind came in. He was about thirty-five and was perfect in feature. He helped us a good deal, though very cautious that no official should discover that he had anything to do with us.

Our first plan was to stay with him as if we were merchants come to deal with his firm, but we soon found that this would not do, since no Englishman ever stayed in an Indian home in the City. So we drove off, through several police guards, to the biggest hotel in the Cantonment where many Englishmen and officers were living.

The hotel, however, although extremely comfortable, was too expensive for our small budget and the next day we moved into the Dak Bungalow, where I actually filled in a form under my own name for the police who, I believe, got a rocket for not having spotted me. The awkward thing was that I had to pretend to treat poor Shamrao as if he was a servant. There was only one room available and Shamrao had to sleep outside on the veranda where it was very cold. But Englishmen and Indians were not supposed to be familiar in those days on the Frontier and had we shared a room it would have created immediate suspicion. When we got our bill there were two items—'Food for the Sahib' and then, 'Food for the Fellow' at half-price. Happily we knew each other far too well for any of this to matter.

In spite of all difficulties, however, we managed to get a certain amount of information in Peshawar, though it was very difficult to persuade people to say anything and most of them would only come to see me at night, creeping furtively to the back door of a house or meeting me in some obscure room.

On the third day we visited a number of villages round Peshawar and on the fourth day had a wonderful drive through the wild and rugged hills to Kohat in a car we managed to hire. We were frequently stopped on the way and at one place the police came and asked me if I had a pistol. When I said 'No', they were astonished and even offered me one, but I nonchalantly lit a cigarette (I never smoked ordinarily in those days and put it out directly we got through). This seems to have convinced them that I was a sahib.

Shamrao did most of the work in Kohat, for it would have been impossible for me to go round the town getting information.

On the fifth day we went up the Khyber Pass, walking down from Landi Kotal to Zintara. There was cccasional rifle fire round us—'Just a family feud,' said our guide casually. We visited some of the tribal villages and discussed the situation with the Afridis. I remember telling Shamrao, as we approached Peshawar again, that as we now had finished our work, all we had to do was to become heroes by being arrested. Before going up the Pass I had sent a letter to the Deputy Commissioner telling him why we had come and asking him if I could have an interview so that I could hear the official view of things and so make my report more balanced. When we got out of the station at Peshawar I received the answer to my letter in two English police officers and some constables with the following order of deportation:

ORDER

In exercise of the powers delegated to me under Section 4(1) (c) Emergency Powers Ordinance, it is hereby directed that the Reverend Verrier Elwin shall forthwith remove himself from and shall not return to the North-West Frontier Province.

The penalty to which he becomes liable for breach of this Order should be explained to Mr Elwin.

O. K. Caroe,
District Magistrate,
Peshawar

15.1.32

The policeman who actually arrested me was an amusing person and kept on saying he was 'damned sorry'. They took us back to the Dak Bungalow and searched our baggage but were unable to find anything. We were allowed to stay on in our rooms under open arrest, but Caroe ordered that I should leave Peshawar by the most inconvenient train in the day. My friend, the Inspector of Police, sent over a note to this gentleman saying that I was ready to give my parole if I could leave the following morning by the Frontier Mail but Caroe insisted that I should have an uncomfortable night in the train and go at once. 'That', said my friend, 'is what is called imperialism.'

After a drink or two with my policeman we went down to the station where a dozen seedy-looking CID men paraded before me looking at me with sinister attention. This was so that they would recognize me if I ever tried to be naughty again. Mr Pickwick had the same experience 'sitting for his portrait' at the Fleet.

The one thing the police were after was documentary evidence but I managed to hide all my notes, as well as certain papers which would have got some of the Peshawar people into trouble had they been found, in a packet of 'Force'. This stood, like Poe's Purloined Letter, in full view on a table in our room, and though the police searchers went through everything else like a dose of salts, they ignored the innocent-looking packet of breakfast cereal. I carried it down in triumph to Bombay and was able to write and publish a report in consequence. This was immediately declared forfeit to His Majesty and, though it was reissued in London later, for many years even I myself was unable to get a copy. But it was nice to think of King George having it.

VIII

Back in Bombay we had to face another problem. Shamrao had returned from England and sacrificed his higher education to work for the tribal people. My own inclination was in the same direction. But now, and specially since Gandhi's arrest and my own deportation, a good deal of pressure was put on me to enter politics. For example, at this time the Congress was planning to appoint a series of Presidents which would include members of every community, and Jamnalal Bajaj asked me if I would be willing to become Congress President when it was the turn of an Englishman to occupy that high office. It would not, he pointed out, mean a great deal of work, for I would certainly be arrested and imprisoned within a week. I told him that I was willing and I have sometimes wondered what would have happened if I had gone through with it.

But when Shamrao and I talked it over, we came to the conclusion that this was not really our line. I have always been a little doubtful of the value of the intervention of European political amateurs in matters at which they are not expert. And, though I have always regretted that I did not go to jail, it was obvious that Government would not have given me that privilege, but would have deported me from the country, and that would merely have been a humiliation. And so we decided to keep to our original plan of going into the Gond country in the Central Provinces.

As I had been unable to get land in Betul and most of my friends were now in jail, I asked the Bishop of Nagpur (for it must be remembered I was still a loyal, if somewhat unorthodox, member of the Church of England) for his advice. This was Bishop Wood, a brave, strong man, with a sincere affection for the tribes and an equal devotion to the British Empire. His biographer says of him: 'He was always on the most friendly terms with Forest officials.' 'How fully he won the confidence of Government is evident from the fact that in his third year in India he was awarded the Kaiser-i-Hind Medal.' In his dealings with us he fully justified that confidence.

The bishop recommended Karanjia, a Gond village in the Mandla District, as particularly suitable for me. Of the last five Europeans to stay in this part of the world, he pointed out with relish, four had died within a year. This sounded very much what we wanted and so, on the 28th of January, 1932, a day which marks the central turning-point in my life, Shamrao and I started out in a bullock-cart, with only a couple of hundred rupees between us, through the jungle into the Maikal

Hills. Two days later we reached Karanjia, ahead of our baggage and supplies, tired and hungry. No one would come near us: we could not get so much as a pot of water. Shamrao went to try and make arrangements and I sat waiting by the roadside. I can still remember the appalling sense of desolation that swept over me then, the sudden fear that I had staked everything on the wrong horse. My mind went back to Oxford: there were friends there, friends of my own kind. Would there be any here? There was comfort in Oxford: there was certainly no comfort here. In Bombay, Poona, Sabarmati, Wardha there were allies, people you could work with. In this unfamiliar Central Provinces, in Mandla District and its cold welcome, this strange remote frightened village, I felt very much alone. Above all, I felt that I should be wasted, useless: it would have been better to have faced deportation or, if I had been lucky, imprisonment. And why, O why, did I leave the lovely books and libraries of Oxford and London?

We spent that night in a small, cold, dirty Forest Bungalow and the next morning went to visit the village. Karanjia consists of ten hamlets and the nearest had the attractive name of Tikera Tola (a *tikera* is a small hill standing by itself: ever since, even in Shillong, I have lived on *tikeras*). Here we found an impoverished but friendly Mussalman who had married a Gond girl and adopted the tribal way of life. He agreed to rent us, for three rupees a month, a small shed in which he kept his goats, and gave us the use of a veranda near by for a kitchen. The bargain struck, he turned out the goats, had the hut washed with cowdung, warm piles of straw were heaped on the floor, a small hearth was built on the veranda, someone brought wood and water, and that evening we were in our new home.

As I lay down to sleep on that mud floor the doubts and fears of the previous day vanished. never to return. In that little goat-shed I realized that I was caught, that never would I be able to escape the call of the primitive world; for better or worse I was committed. Yet at that moment, there was little that was beautiful, or exciting, or romantic: the Gonds of Tikera Tola seemed a little dull (no dances to welcome us), very poor, dirty, timid and shockingly diseased. But I had had the first glimpse of the 'elusive treasure' and I knew I must search till I found it, even if it took all my life.

At first, however, it looked as if we should not be able to search for very long. I wrote, as a matter of courtesy, to the Deputy Commissioner at Mandla, and soon afterwards received this remarkable letter in reply:

In reply to your letter of the 29th January, the Commissioner has asked me to inform you that in view of your political record, we do not want you in this district.

Yours sincerely
D. V. Rege

We took no notice of this letter and expected to be arrested at any moment; in fact, we posted a boy on the top of a neighbouring hill to keep a look-out for the police so that we would have time to destroy any incriminating papers before they arrived. Nothing much, however, happened except that one day we were raided and searched by the police and a little later Rege himself came and, sitting on the floor of our hut, had a very pleasant chat. In actual fact, Rege was a good person and privately very sympathetic with the Congress movement: he explained that he had had to write as he did under the orders of the Commissioner. We were raided on one or two other occasions and the police went off with some of my books, fortunately not ones that I was very fond of.

From the point of view of our work this was, of course, exactly what was wanted. It meant that we got off on the right foot with the local villagers. We must be decent people, they thought, very like themselves; the police bothered them and they bothered us. We were clearly on the same side.

During those first months in Karanjia I wrote a small book which I called *Truth about India,* though the publishers changed this, rather cynically I thought, to *Truth about India —Can we get it?* I had my typewriter with me but no furniture and I typed the entire book sitting on the mud floor of our little hut.

I will go back a little here and mention other things of the kind which I had done earlier. The most important of them was a joint book by Winslow and myself called *The Dawn of Indian Freedom* which had a foreword by Archbishop Temple;

it seems to have done some good, especially in religious circles, in Britain. My contribution consisted of two long chapters, one a study of Gandhi, the other a 70-page sketch of the history and principles of Satyagraha. My chapters were violently attacked in the *Times of India*, which also told the archbishop that 'he would have done better not to meddle in a matter of which he knew so very little'. But elsewhere the book was sympathetically received, even by those who disagreed with it.

While I was in Sabarmati I had come to know the gifted artist Kanu Desai and he asked me to write a prefatory essay to an album of his paintings and sketches of Gandhi. I took a lot of trouble over this and it was published in London by the Golden Vista Press, and was later reprinted in India by a publisher who misspelt my name throughout.

My booklet *Christ and Satyagraha* was a sort of guide-book for the Christian revolutionary; it united the Fathers of the Church and the religious teachers of modern times to prove the right and duty of Christians to overthrow a foreign or despotic Government. I gave a number of circumstances when a Government should, on principles generally accepted by the Church, be resisted. The first was when its authority was not just but usurped. 'It is the universal belief in India that the foreign and unnatural Government now in existence, began in usurpation, continued in usurpation and must end as soon as possible.' Then a Government may be resisted when it commands that which is unjust, when it is not the expression of the general will, when it impoverishes the common life, when its laws violate some higher law of ethics or religion.

Above all things [I wrote] the Christian's task is one of reconciliation. 'Blessed are the peace-makers, for they shall be called sons of God.' To be a peace-maker does not mean that a man must be politically neutral, but that, while believing whole-heartedly in the justice of his own cause, he tries to see and to make known all that is good on the other side, and never shuts any possible doorway into peace. 'I have dedicated my whole life,' says Romain Rolland, 'to the reconciliation of mankind.' This ideal is one that is not out of reach even of the combatant in the present bloodless war. For us in India today, reconciliation does not mean giving in before the goal is won;

it does not mean a cry of Peace, Peace, when there is no peace. What it does mean is that we should carry on our war always with a view to peace; that we should so act that no bitter memories, no poignant regrets, shall arise to haunt our future; that we should always behave to our enemies as if they were one day to be our friends.

In one sense, every war is a civil war; all strife between men is a domestic strife: there is only one nation, one race, one family; we all belong to the nation, the race, the family of God.

I also published a small booklet, *Religious and Cultural Aspects of Khadi,* with a foreword by Acharya Kripalani, and many articles on religious subjects—the Nivritti-Marga, the religion of Bhakti, the mysticism associated with the idea of Light—in the *Ashram Review.* I also did a study of *Mahatma Gandhi's Philosophy of Truth,* which appeared in the *Modern Review.* I first surveyed historically those Western mystics who had thought of religion primarily in terms of Truth, from Plato and Plotinus to the present day, and then made a detailed study of Gandhi's own philosophy, which I summarized as follows:

The identification of the Ultimate Reality with Truth is very old, and Mahatma Gandhi is original not so much in speaking of Truth as in speaking of practically nothing else. His conception of Truth is metaphysical, mystical and moral; there is no aspect of it which is not real to him. It has been his special task to bring this lofty philosophical idea down to earth, to introduce it as a working principle into the lives of ordinary people, to direct its austere moral challenge upon world-politics, to exalt it as a practical basis of business and personal relations and to work out with great exactness what is implied in the quest for its realization.

What a fuss people made about me in those days! Years afterwards a high official of the Government of India told me that the Central Provinces Government had been very worried about me and what I might be up to. I was also rather worried about them for, although I realized that it was all part of the game and I have always enjoyed the company of senior police officials, it is rather distracting to have your letters read, your house searched and to be followed about everywhere by policemen of the lower grades who are often lacking in manners and in our case did their best to obstruct our work.

IX

In 1932, I decided, rather unwisely as it turned out, that I should go to England during the rains, partly to try to arouse people there to the seriousness of the Indian situation, and partly to see my mother who had been very ill. Shamrao and I went down to Bombay, and there I nearly abandoned the trip. My passport had expired and the Bombay Government refused to renew it except for a period of three weeks, which would just allow me to reach England, but not to return. So I gave up the idea of going, and announced the fact in the press.

There was an immediate outcry; the *Bombay Chronicle* devoted its morning leader to the subject, and was good enough to point out that it was men like me 'who enable Indians to believe that the British nation does not consist entirely of Imperialists, commercial exploiters, swashbuckling special correspondents. They are the one link that holds the attenuated chain of Indo-British relations together'.

Soon afterwards, I received a friendly letter from the Chief Passport Officer, asking me to go and see him, which I did. This official explained that even if he renewed my passport for five years, Government could always cancel it at any moment, but that actually his own refusal to extend it for a longer period was due to purely technical reasons, and he saw no reason why I should have any difficulty in getting it renewed for the full period after I had reached England.

I was much simpler then than I am now. I should, of course, have seen very clearly, especially in view of the Commissioner's attempt to get me deported, that Government was only anxious to get me out of India without a press agitation. But I was really keen to visit England, and after arranging that Shamrao should go for medical training at the Tirupattur Ashram, I said goodbye to him and left Bombay.

I had an interesting journey across Europe, making contact with the pro-Indian groups in Italy, Switzerland and France.

In Siena and Florence I went about with a grand old English lady, Miss Turton, splendid and energetic for all her seventy-five years, one of India's unofficial publicists. At Siena, I stayed in the lovely palace of Ravizza, where the family was equally enthusiastic for the Indian cause. In Florence I spent a day in a finely decorated house, the Villa Star, whose private chapel was being painted by the artists Giovanni and Mai Costetti. Giovanni was writing a little book in Italian about Gandhi and asked me to contribute a foreword, though in the end nothing came of it.

I went on to visit Villeneuve and M. and Mme Privat: I stayed with Romain Rolland and his sister on the way back. In Paris I visited the little flat of Mme Guiyesse in the Latin quarter. She had founded a society called the Friends of India and published a paper, *Nouvelles de l'Inde.*

When I reached London I had a regular reception at Victoria Station, and a full programme was arranged for me. My first meeting was at Kingsley Hall in Bow, where Gandhi had stayed in London, with George Lansbury (then Leader of the Opposition in the House of Commons) in the chair. 'The only solution of the present situation', I declared, 'is to give India what she wants, that is self-government. But if Britain will not do this, she at least ought to fight with clean hands.' I concluded: 'I long to see my countrymen achieve a sufficient degree of greatness to rise to the chivalrous appeal of Mahatma Gandhi. If we do so we shall show that brute force is not the only power, and that the principles of Jesus Christ are still being applied in the conduct of great peoples towards one another.'

At a later meeting, presided over by C. F. Andrews, I described the condition of India, the oppression by the police, the sufferings of the imprisoned. I again pleaded for justice. 'Surely to do justice to a country that wants to be free is no betrayal, but the highest loyalty to our own traditions . . . While the statesmen of Europe are endeavouring to abandon brute force, Britain is employing that force in India.' I described Gandhi's arrest earlier in the year and said that as I saw the Mahatma and the Police Commissioner face each other I 'had no doubt that Mahatma Gandhi's empty hands were the stronger hands and that if they took away from England her

Empire they might restore to her a feeling of chivalry in dealing with a subject race'.

I addressed many other meetings and had a number of interviews with members of Government, among them Lord Irwin, as he then was. I got to know the Lord Chancellor, Lord Sankey, quite well, and among my trophies is a copy of *The Spirit of Man,* in which he marked his favourite passages. But Sir Samuel Hoare (later Lord Templewood), who was then Secretary of State for India, refused to see me on the ground that I had behaved 'in an indiscreet way' and that 'it would not be appropriate that he should receive me' at the India Office. In fact, when I went to see Lord Irwin he began by saying, 'In loyalty to my colleagues, I must tell you that the Secretary of State for India has the lowest possible opinion of you. But having said this, let us talk as friends.'

Sir Samuel showed his displeasure in a very practical way. I applied for a renewal of my passport immediately, getting George Lansbury to sign my application, but a week later I received the following letter:

> The Chief Passport Officer presents his compliments to the Reverend H. V. H. Elwin and, with reference to his application for the renewal of his passport, begs to inform him in accordance with a request made by the Secretary of State for India that he cannot be granted passport facilities for entry into India.
>
> If Mr Elwin desires his passport to be renewed this will be done but the passport will have to be endorsed as not valid for India.

'This document', I wrote shortly afterwards, 'was one of the most shattering I have ever received, and yet I am glad I had it, for it revealed to me, as nothing else could have done, something of the helplessness of being a political outcaste, a condition into which so many thousands of people have been thrown both by British imperialism and by the dictatorships of the last decade. It was impossible to get an interview with anyone. Nobody would answer your letters. I was not important enough for the British press to take up my cause. I felt as though I was standing in front of a great precipice up which there was no hope of climbing. I approached everyone I could, and they told me of the great difficulty they too found in persuading the authorities even to discuss anything to do with me.' My sufferings were very small compared to those of others, but they did at least give me some idea of what it must be like to lose one's passport.

But I had a few friends, and some of them, working behind the scenes, were able ultimately to put enough pressure on the India Office officials to get them to consent to allow me to return to India, provided that I signed an undertaking:

That I would confine myself entirely to work among the Gonds;
take no part in civil disobedience or any other political movement;
refrain, as far as possible, from associating with any persons engaged in political agitation;
refrain from writing articles against the Government;
and would observe the undertaking in the spirit as well as the letter.

Here was another crisis. C. F. Andrews thought I should not sign; others thought I should. Krishna Menon, later Defence Minister of India, was very helpful. I myself had no doubt of my duty. I had started my tribal work and I must go on with it. I signed, and caught the first available boat for India. When they heard about it later, both Gandhi and Jamnalal Bajaj approved of my decision and, looking back, I have no doubt it was right.

But it meant, of course, the end of my active political interests; it meant some misunderstanding, much isolation—for I was cut off from everyone. But it actually worked out very well. Sir Francis Younghusband remarked, 'I will always be grateful to Sam Hoare for one thing at least, that he forced Elwin from politics to poetry.'

I was not, however, isolated entirely from Bapu and continued to correspond with him, even when he was in jail. I have a packet of precious letters in his own hand—the quaint little home-made envelopes, the letters on tiny scraps of paper.

One of Gandhi's greatest concerns was the abolition of untouchability and in 1933 he was greatly disturbed by the arrangements made by Ramsay MacDonald's Government which provided separate electorates for the untouchables.

Though well-intentioned, Gandhi felt that this would still further divide the caste Hindus from their brethren and he wrote to the British Prime Minister declaring that if this plan went through he would fast unto death in protest against it. This dramatic gesture was scheduled for the 20th of September and on the 16th Bapu wrote to me from the Yeravda Central Prison.

My dear Verrier,

You had, I hope, no difficulty in understanding the step I am about to take. This is therefore just to tell you that all my English friends were before my mind's eye when I penned my letters to the Prime Minister. May God bring good out of this.

My love to you all in which Sardar and Mahadev join.

We sing the hymn this evening (Friday).

Bapu

Happily the untouchable leaders and the Indian moderates modified the original scheme sufficiently to enable Gandhi to break his fast after six days. He does not seem, however, to have been altogether happy about it and he decided in May of the following year to undertake a 'self-purificatory fast' for twenty-one days, in spite of Nehru's determined opposition. This fast began on the 8th of May and the previous day Gandhi wrote to me again from prison.

My dear Verrier,

I cannot enter upon the ordeal without talking to you. It is a matter of great joy to me that I have the prayers of many many true friends to speed me on—Truth is God and he will give me all the food I shall need during the fast. I wish I had time to talk more to you.

I hope you are all well.

Love to you all,

Bapu

The following day Government released him and he went to continue the fast in the house of a friend in Poona. A week after his ordeal had concluded he wrote to me from there, speaking of the 'very wonderful twenty-one days' which he had passed.

My dear Verrier,

Of course I have been having news about you and now I have your letter before me of the 31st ultimo.

Yes, God has been good to me. He has been a friend in need. He never forsook me during all those very wonderful 21 days. But I must not dictate a long letter, after having dictated one long letter to Mira who stood in need of one. I do not want you to come here merely for the purpose of meeting me. The temptation to say 'come' is there but I know that I must resist it. You have your work cut out for you and you must not be disturbed.

I am glad you all seem to be keeping well. Do send my love to mother, Eldyth and the Italian sisters when you write to them. I am flourishing.

Love
Bapu

Shortly after Gandhi's arrest in 1932, I wrote to a number of friends in India and Europe, as well as to Gandhi himself, to suggest that we should all sing the hymn 'Lead, kindly Light' on Friday evenings as an act of unity and friendship between those in jail and the rest of us. This is the hymn to which Gandhi refers in the first of his letters. The idea caught on and was continued for several years.

I have many other letters from Bapu, nearly all in his own hand. In July 1939, he wrote to me about spinning, whose utility for the Gonds I had questioned. He replied that he did not want us to spin unless we had a living faith in it. The cause of spinning, he said, 'is passing thro' a severe trial. To me it is on the same level with the war against untouchability. Even if Indian humanity did not rise to them, I should be spinning and warring against untouchability. Without them non-violence cannot be established nor truth vindicated.'

Bapu had described me to someone as *naram* and I wrote to ask what he had in mind.

I forget the connexion in which I used the adjective *naram* about you. *Naram* means soft, gentle, yielding, unsteady. All these adjectives can be applied to you in certain circumstances. I cannot recall the circumstance which prompted the use of that adjective and in what sense. If you cannot recall the connexion, do not trouble. It is enough for me to know, as I do know, that you regard no sacrifice too great for the pursuit of truth.

Later in the same year, I wrote Bapu a rather depressed letter, for which he rebuked me.

> God has saved you for greater service. You must not give way to dejection. Dejection is the measure of one's want of faith. . . I understand the persecution to which you have been subjected. But that is the moment of your trial. Your faith must be immovable like the Himalayas. But they will suffer decay, not so your faith if it is worth anything. No, no, it won't do. You must cheer up. No more of idle sorrow.

He ended by sending 'a cartload of love' to Shamrao.

During the forties my links with Gandhi weakened. My closest friends among his followers, Jamnalal Bajaj and Mahadev Desai, died. With some of the others (except for his secretary Pyarelal) I found myself a little out of sympathy. For Gandhi my affection never wavered, but I allowed the differences between us to keep me away from him. I suffered a great disillusion when I discovered that the khadi programme was not suitable for our tribes. I have always been a strong supporter of handloom weaving, but spinning, for very poor people and in places where cotton did not grow, seemed to me artificial and uneconomic.

Gandhi's emphatic views on Prohibition (which I considered damaging to the tribes), his philosophy of sex-relations, especially as exaggerated by some of his followers (which I considered damaging to everybody), and what seemed to me a certain distortion of values—the excessive emphasis on diet, for example, further separated me from him. Today I feel very sorry about this, for it was in his last years that Gandhi reached his highest stature and I deprived myself of the warmth of his affection and the strength he would have given me during a difficult period. But it was a feeling about Truth that kept me from going to see him and from this point of view my instinct was right.

4

Bishops and Bayonets

Does the Bishop think that every sturdy bullock whom he tries to sacrifice to the Genius of Orthodoxy will not kick, and push, and toss ; that he will not if he can, shake the axe from his neck, and hurl his mitred butcher into the air ?

—Sydney Smith

DURING the next few years I moved slowly, but inevitably, away from the Church into a life of religious and intellectual freedom. The process was difficult and painful, for in the beginning I was intensely devoted to the Christian religion and to its expression in Anglo-Catholicism. I always dislike hurting people and unfortunately the controversies in which I was involved gave pain to my family and to many of my older friends.

There were two main points on which I came into conflict with the ecclesiastical authorities. The first was concerned with the Christian's part in politics, the second with his attitude to the non-Christian. My view was that it was quite untrue, as so many of the clergy and officials used to say at this time, that 'Christianity had nothing to do with politics'. I insisted, as Gandhi insisted, that 'religion' had an important place in political life and that the Christian community not only had a right but a duty to bring its message and spirit into public affairs. On this subject generally I set out my views in *Christ and Satyagraha,* in which I called a great deal of evidence from the Fathers of the Church and advanced religious thinkers of modern times to maintain the right and even the duty of the Christian to overthrow a foreign or despotic Government by non-violent means.

I will discuss the question of conversion later, for my

immediate difficulties arose from political rather than theological problems. So long as I was living in the diocese of Bombay there was no actual breach with the Church, though the bishop and archdeacon were, naturally enough, perturbed by what I and my friends were doing. My visit to Peshawar had greatly disturbed the ecclesiastical authorities. Even the Indian Bishop of Dornakal wrote me a reproachful letter and the Bishop of Bombay, not dear Champagne Palmer but his rather dehydrated successor, wrote that 'I am sorry to be more and more unhappy about you. This is because it does seem clear that you are now an emissary of Congress rather than of Christ. I cannot otherwise account for your going to the NWF Province.' It did not occur to any of them that to attempt to apply Christian principles to a situation of misery and tension could be a Christian act.

But it became worse later, for when we decided to go to Karanjia in the Central Provinces we had to move out of Bombay, where I had a certain amount of support, into the diocese of Nagpur where I was friendless and unknown. I had to come to terms with a new Bishop. Shamrao and I met him in the house of the Deputy Commissioner at Bilaspur and at first (not having seen my police dossier) he was very friendly. But after we went to Karanjia there began a rather extraordinary correspondence from which I will give some extracts, for they illustrate the attitude of the Anglican Church in India at that time and also reveal the kind of struggle I had towards my own spiritual freedom. I will now turn to the letters and the goal to which they led.

In the middle of February 1932, the Bishop wrote to me at Karanjia:

> I fear there is going to be a lot of trouble about your being permitted to stay in the Mandla District. I wrote to Mr Irwin (the Commissioner), who promptly replied to me that he had already personally recommended that you should be deported from India for your activities in Jubbulpore. I have seen some of the evidence that was placed before Mr Irwin and really, on that, I do not wonder that he had made this recommendation.

The Bishop continued by insisting that I should take the Oath of Allegiance to the King-Emperor, an oath which even at that date was not constitutionally required from clergy of the Church of India, as well as the Oath of Canonical Obedience to himself. About the second, there was no question, but the meaning of the first was interpreted by the Bishop as follows:

> The meaning that I always attach to it is perfectly clear and straightforward. First of all I consider that the Clergy should belong to no political party. It is their duty to fit people to do their duty as good citizens in that state of life into which it shall please God to call them. They therefore should be prepared to support whatever is right and just regardless of political parties.
>
> The King-Emperor himself is not satisfied with the present methods of governing India and has directed that changes be made. Any priest therefore who takes the Oath of Allegiance is bound to separate himself from any party which adopts unconstitutional and illegal methods of political agitation.

In reply, I wrote to the Bishop to say that, although I would have no difficulty

> . . . in repeating the Oath of Allegiance in the Church of England, it would be wrong for me to take it in the Church of India which is free of state control and does not lay this obligation on its clergy.
>
> If no Congressman can be a member of the Church, you are yourself identifying the Church with a particular political party, and you are thereby closing its doors against the very flower of India, men and women who command the devotion and allegiance of the great bulk of people in this country, and into whose hands we shall have to transfer the reins of government in a year or two. I cannot see any meaning in the freedom of the Church of India unless it is to be the Church of the people of India, whose mouthpiece and representative is the National Congress. Congressmen do not forfeit the right to be members of Christ because they adopt the method of civil disobedience, which is the ancient and legitimate right of every people which cannot get justice by constitutional means.
>
> The Church, in the words of St Augustine, is a city which 'summoneth its citizens from all tribes, and collecteth its pilgrim fellowship from all languages, taking no heed of what is diverse in manners or laws or institutions'. It must enfold within its arms of love everyone in India. . . . There is nothing

in the Gospel of Jesus Christ to justify your Lordship's identification of the universal Church with party politics, or in penalizing me for my political opinions.

I am not a member of the Congress, and I do not understand your Lordship's reference to my liability to be arrested as being a member of an illegal Association. As a Christian, however, I naturally have the liveliest sympathy for an organization which has adopted into its political programme so much of the spirit and teaching of Jesus Christ, and which has taken as its weapon not armed force, but the truthful and non-violent method of Satyagraha which represents a transformation of the war-principle by the Sermon on the Mount. Nor need any Christian be ashamed of following Mahatma Gandhi, the most sublime and Christ-like figure now living on this planet.

I have never spoken as a party man, nor am I regarded as such by Indians. I do not remember giving a public lecture without proclaiming the Gospel of truth, love and sacrifice, that our first debt is to the poor, that we must forgive our enemies and that it is love which must in the future regulate the relationships of great peoples.

Shortly afterwards we were visited by the Bishop in person at Karanjia, and I will reproduce my own account of the interview which I wrote immediately afterwards.

The Bishop arrived in Karanjia, with two CMS missionaries, and, since we had no chairs, they had to sit on the floor, rather uncomfortably with their boots on. We had a long conversation which resulted more or less in a deadlock. The Bishop could not, he said, have anything to do with us, if we had anything to do with the Mahatma and his followers. Gandhi was the great enemy of Christ in modern India: C. F. Andrews was contemptuously dismissed as a 'recreant priest'; Congress was doing 'devil's work' and had substituted brute force for Satyagraha. The Bishop even took exception to khadi. If we did anything to promote spinning and weaving among the Gonds, he couldn't license me, presumably because the homespun uniform was the mark of a Congressman.

At this point, the younger of the two CMS missionaries, who had arrived in India a month previously, exclaimed in a very solemn voice, 'I do not see any use, my Lord, in discussing the affairs of Christ with a renegade. In fact, Mr Elwin is more than a renegade, he is a traitor: he has betrayed his country and his Lord and has thrown in his lot with their enemies. What profit is there in discussing the things of the Kingdom with such a man?'

This, almost too good to be true, was the sort of remark which compensates the sorrows of a lifetime, and my delighted smile was so obvious that I am sorry to say the poor fish blushed deeply, looking, as Bingo Little once did, like the Soul's Awakening done in pink.

'No priest of mine,' continued the Bishop, 'may have any political views.' I began to give some precedents, including St Thomas Aquinas and the Archbishop of York. 'I don't care about the Archbishop. In my diocese there will be nothing of the kind.'

'But if a Congressman wishes to become a Christian priest?'

'Then he must forswear the Congress.'

'But your clergy have the Union Jack in their churches. Isn't that politics?'

'Ah, but the Union Jack is the standard of the Cross.'

'A bloody Cross,' exclaimed Shamrao, unable to contain himself any longer.

I tried again, while the unfortunate Bishop shifted from ham to ham in an effort to get comfortable on our uneven cow-dunged floor.

'You, my Lord, were a Chaplain in the war. You lived among those whose hands were stained with blood, and whose profession was to kill others. You gave them your moral support (the Bishop nodded), and you did all you could to help your side to win. I have simply been a sort of Chaplain to men whose hands are not blood-stained but who are using the weapons of non-violence and truth. Why, if I am wrong, were you right? Haven't Congressmen souls?'

The Bishop looked incredulous, but could only say, 'Well, it takes a great deal to save the soul of a Congressman.'

There was a lot more, but the sum of the whole matter was that unless we were prepared to sever all connexion with Gandhi and his followers, even to the extent of dropping khadi work, the Bishop would have nothing whatever to do with us.

He concluded with these intimidating words: 'You are a

traitor to the cause of Christ. You are a traitor to the King-Emperor. You are doing the work of the devil.'

And he got up and went, only just turning to Shamrao. 'As for you, I will have nothing whatever to do with you.'

After his return to Nagpur, the Bishop wrote me another letter, pointing out what an undesirable and dangerous person I was, and explaining that he had asked me to leave the Congress . . .

. . . because I love the Gonds and I am not keen that through any act of mine they should be the people who should provide any part of the 'million lives' and the 'rivers of blood' that the Mahatma says he is willing to expend in the attainment of his political aims. Those aims appear to be the re-establishment of some form of the Vedic Religion and culture in India, when his party has the power.

If an Indian Christian desires to be a nationalist and to see India self-governing he has all my sympathy and, so long as his activities are constitutional, my support. But you have repeatedly told me that your sympathies are with Mahatma Gandhi and the Congress party—i.e., definitely Hindu and opposed to the spread of Christianity and that you put their political ideas above your duties as a priest to preach Christ.

In November of the same year, the Bishop wrote again.

As I wrote to you, the Commissioner in reply to my letter on your behalf stated that he had already applied to Government to have you removed from his Division and also from India. Honestly I do not blame him or Government. Your anti-Government and political activities have been very serious indeed—as I am now learning.

The only condition on which I can support you and approve of your working in this diocese is that you definitely sever your connexion with Congress. It is an illegal association and no priest of the Church should be connected with it in any way. It is definitely causing dispeace and hatred when all men of good will, who love India, are straining every effort to bring peace and progress. I urge you therefore to sever your connexion with it completely and to turn to your work—as a priest in the Church. So long as you keep your political opinions to yourself, you may hold what you please. One can only pray that you will outgrow your present opinions.

A fortnight later, I wrote to the Bishop to take my first important step towards severing my connexion with the Church, and declared that I proposed not to apply for a licence and realized that I would therefore be unable to function as a priest any longer. Three years later, I took the further step of surrendering my priesthood altogether and at about the same time I withdrew from membership of the Church even as a layman. I wrote again to the long-suffering Bishop.

My reason is that the Church of India, though nominally free, is still virtually under the control of a foreign government. While serving in the diocese of Bombay the extent of this control was less apparent, but my relations with you have raised the problems arising from it in an acute form.

I hope you will forgive me if I point out—in no spirit of hostility but in order to make my point clear—some examples of this. You address me on envelopes marked 'Government of India': your letters bear the imprint 'On His Majesty's Service'. You draw your salary from the coffers of Government: the Union Jack flies—illegally—over your Cathedral. When I asked you for a licence, you made no inquiries about my spiritual or theological qualifications: you demanded what you had no constitutional right to demand, an oath of allegiance to the King-Emperor. When we last met you concluded our conversation by saying that I was doing the work of the devil. When the private house of Seth Jamnalal Bajaj was declared illegal and occupied by the police a notification was sent to me; but this notification came, not from the Home Department of Government, but from your office. You have refused—on political grounds—even to consider one of my co-workers for ordination, although he has had three years' training in a religious house.

Neither you nor your fellow-Bishops have raised a word of protest against the ruthless and brutal policy of repression that in the last three years has attempted to crush the national spirit of India. Instead you have justified this repression, even claiming that flogging is a legitimate punishment for non-violent political offenders. In your dealings with me, you have played the part, not of a father in God, but of an agent of the foreign government.

Between this state-religion and the religion of the New Testament I can trace no connexion. It was not the disciples who cried 'We have no king but Caesar'. We never see our Exemplar sitting at ease at Caesar's table, but only standing in rags before his judgement-seat. I would feel the same if the Church allowed itself to be subservient to Mr Gandhi's government. Where the Government does not exist at the will of the people the position is even worse.

I have thrown in my lot with India. For the time being I am outside active politics, being bound by the restrictions laid on me by Government. I have never intended our ashram to be a centre of political agitation. But I am unwaveringly of the opposition. If I am silent, it is not because my heart is changed, but because I am a prisoner of honour to the Government, and until they release me I shall behave as such. But my heart and my spirit is with those who are suffering, in so Christ-like a spirit, in the jails. How can I work under one who is practically an official of the Government which I regard as hostile to the interests of the country which I love?

In November 1935, I finally wrote to the Metropolitan of Calcutta:

I am writing formally to announce to you my decision to be no longer a member of the Church of England either as a priest or a communicant. . . . I leave the Church of my baptism without a trace of bitterness and hostility, with nothing but love and reverence for the great tradition in which I have grown up. But it will be dishonest for me to remain longer.

This, however, was not enough. The position of an Anglican priest is not merely spiritual: there are social and legal implications. When I went to England in 1936, I consulted Archbishop Temple and in November of that year signed a Deed of Relinquishment stating that 'having been admitted to the office of Priest in the Church of England I do hereby in pursuance of the Clerical Disabilities Act 1870 declare that I relinquish all rights, privileges, advantages and exemptions of the Office as by law belonging to it'.

It may seem strange today in India to talk about bringing religion into politics, for one of our most important tasks now is to keep 'religion' out of them. But, of course, when Gandhi said religion he did not mean that communal religion which has constantly distracted and divided India and led to his own death. He meant, as I meant, the true spirit of religion, whether that be Christianity, Islam, Hinduism or Buddhism. Even today this essential spirit of love and tolerance is as necessary in the public life in India (and all countries) as it was in Gandhi's own day.

We may remember also that at this time we did not think of the Congress as a political party. This was one of the main points made by Gandhi at the Round Table Conference—that Congress was not a party, but represented the whole nation.

I think what really outraged me in my controversy with the bishops (for the Bishop of Nagpur was far from being my only opponent among them) was their attitude to war. Their opposition to the national movement was a temporary phase: since Independence some bishops dress in khadi and preach on Gandhi: on a recent visit the Archbishop of Canterbury laid a wreath on Gandhi's tomb at Rajghat. But war, violent war, was another matter. I became a pacifist in my Oxford days and have never swerved from my belief and it continually horrified me to find the official churches not only not condemning war but even actively supporting it.

I have put in these letters for they were part of my life. They are, of course, a young man's letters and behind them are the reluctant pangs of an abdicating faith. They are not bitter—they are too robust for that—but they are not kind. I had not yet learnt compassion for the rich and powerful. I am afraid I was a real headache to this and other bishops. It would probably not have been necessary to write today as I did then. India has changed and the Indian Church has changed with it. The Indian flag has replaced the Union Jack one the spires of Cathedrals. Even the Church of England has broadened.

Yet only recently when a beautiful child of three years died and was buried, not having been baptised, in consecrated ground, an Indian bishop made some sour remarks (which kindly persons at once passed on to the saddened mother) that this was most improper.

Even now what strikes me about conventionally religious people is the way they are tied up in spiritual red tape, and particularly new converts in India are apt to be very hard, fanatical in their beliefs, and cruel to those who stray from the strict path of what they consider morality. Some of the

Protestant Churches in Assam today excommunicate someone if he drinks rice-beer or takes part in a dance. For sexual lapses a whole machinery of public exposure and punishment is devised. A beautiful young tribal girl, a graduate, who showed every sign of going ahead in her profession, became pregnant before her marriage. She was so terrified of what the Christian leaders of her Church would say and do that she told no one until, when it was far too late, she tried to force an abortion and died of it. Had the Christian people been more gentle and more understanding this need never have happened. If only everyone had more love for love's failures!

My first conflict with the Church authorities was over politics. Presently this conflict resolved itself, for as I became more and more engrossed in literary and scientific work, I had less and less to do with politics, though my opinions remained the same. But a deeper issue remained and continues to this day, for the problem of religious conversion or cultural change is as interesting to the anthropologist as to the priest.

No one can withhold admiration from the Christian missionaries. They have brought to India the spirit of adventure and dedication. Hundreds of them have gone to live in the remotest places, denying themselves the comforts and amenities of life for many years. They have been the pioneers in the treatment of leprosy, championed the underdog, befriended the untouchables and taken a leading part in sponsoring the cause of the tribal people. They have done much for the languages of India, especially the tribal languages. In the fields of education and medicine their work has been distinguished by professional competence and human affection for children and the sick.

My own collision with the missionary movement did not depend on my estimate of the value of its work, but it went very far back to temperamental and intellectual attitudes of my Oxford days.

About half-way through my time there the influence of the mystical literature which I was then studying so eagerly began to make itself felt, and I began to think of religion not as a matter of saving yourself or your neighbour from sin and damnation or converting him to your own theological opinions, but as the quest of the soul for spiritual realities. The mystics have always been notoriously lukewarm about missions, and imperceptibly this attitude began to influence me, so that by the time I had left Oxford I was no longer interpreting my religion in terms of converting other people to it at all.

It is thus incorrect to say that I came to India as a missionary and then changed my mind. I was never a missionary in the ordinary sense. I joined the Christa Seva Sangh because I understood that its main interests were scholarship, mysticism, reparation rather than evangelism. Before long, however, I found a strong division of opinion among its members.

For example, Father Winslow had never really thought the problem through to its logical conclusion, with the result that he frequently made contradictory statements. He would tell Hindus of his horror of proselytization ; he would then explain to Christians the necessity for conversion. Proselytization to the European generally implies the taking of an unfair advantage of a victim. In times of famine many missionaries at one time undoubtedly took advantage of people's hunger to change their religious allegiance. But conversion, said Father Winslow, by which we mean sharing with others the best thing in one's own life, is a very different matter. It was the realization of this discrepancy which was one of the main reasons for my leaving the Society.

When I first went to Karanjia I was still thinking in terms of the Christian religion and my idea of reparation was a typically Christian one. But even then I did not have the least desire to preach my religion to anyone, still less to convert any of the Gonds to Christianity. It was enough that I should try to interpret life in Christian terms.

This was partly due, as I have said, to my Oxford studies in mysticism, partly due to the influence of Gandhi and my growing knowledge of other religions and reverence for them. Although I have never accepted the facile doctrine that all religions are the same, I did not feel it was my business to judge between them and to advocate one at the expense of others. I had also already developed my dislike of imposing on other people and especially on the tribal people. While I could see the point of a missionary entering into religious argument with a Brahmin, it seemed to me that to chase after a simple tribesman was rather too much like shooting a sitting bird.

Naturally this unwillingness to co-operate in the evangelistic mission of the Church was another point of conflict with the authorities, and even some of my more liberal friends continued to send me kindly rebukes for some time to come.

Father Winslow, for example, held the view that, although the spiritual and intelligent Hindu might well be left alone to live in his own community with nothing more than the inspiration of the Christian spirit, it was necessary, when dealing with the tribal people and untouchables, to bring them right inside the Christian community and Church.

No less a person than C. F. Andrews wrote to me several times in a rather similar strain. In a letter written on board s.s. *Maloja* and dated 12 November 1933, he says:

There is one thing that I think you should avoid and that is going too far when you take up a cause and thus losing the balance of judgement. I know that this is 'calling the kettle black', and I am quite aware of being the 'pot'; but all the same you and I have to learn by experience and we shall both lose a great deal if we lose our sense of proportion. For instance, while what you say is undoubtedly true about primitive people, there are hideous savageries which are unclean and diabolical, such as I myself have witnessed in Central Africa and Fiji. These may not actually exist among Gonds, but I wonder whether I am quite right in saying even this much. Such things as human sacrifice and witchcraft under the spell of religious dread and even cannibal orgies are common in Central Africa. And life in this primitive form becomes often a ghastly terror, impossible to describe. It would be difficult to over-estimate the freedom from these primitive terrors wherewith Christ has set us free.

And I cannot at all agree with Bapu that these forms of 'religion' which are really evil in their essence, are not to be condemned, and those who practise them are not to be converted. I believe in South India the devil worship is absolutely hideous in some of its forms and utterly unworthy of Man made in the image of God.

Once, at Muttra, I saw another sight which filled me with loathing and disgust. It was cow-worship in its most gross form —the literal lowering of the human spirit by *pooja* offered with all the ceremonial of worship to a cow, while frenzy increased every moment. Those who were present thought that I would rejoice in the scene because of my love of animals, and specially of the cow, but this mania on the part of human beings, who were otherwise perfectly sane, did nothing but disgust me.

I am writing all this out because I myself have gone to the utmost limits of toleration, bordering on weakness, and I can see the same danger in your own case.

Thus to turn back to yourself, while you will help the Gonds by revealing to us all their most beautiful characteristics, you will be doing no good at all to them or to us if you over-idealize them as I tended to over-idealize Hinduism at one time, with consequences such as I have hinted at in this letter. I was as young as you are when I did this. Now that I am much older I do not want in the least to lose my first love, but I do wish to gain wisdom and discernment.

And again, C. F. Andrews wrote on 31 March, 1938:

Have you not gone too far in following Bapu about 'conversion'? I fully accept that these hill tribes must be freed from the suspicion and fear that you have some ulterior motive. I would not wish you to take the ordinary standpoint with regard to them. But the joy which we have in our own hearts owing to the love of Christ must find its expression, because it is the one motive power in our own lives. Bapu would seem to suggest that even to wish in one's own heart to give to another that joy, which has been the strength and stay of one's own life, is itself wrong.

I cannot possibly go with him there; and if I could not speak quite freely about Christ in the Ashram at Shantiniketan, I should feel most unhappy: but everything there is as natural as possible and there are no inhibitions. At the same time, it is a matter of honour and trust with me there that I should never take any unfair advantage—which is what Christ meant by 'proselytizing' in the only sentence where He used the word.

I am afraid Andrews' reproaches fell on deaf ears and I have always believed that Mr Nehru's view (though not stated expressly in relation to missionaries) was the correct one:

I am alarmed when I see—not only in this country but in other great countries too—how anxious people are to shape others according to their own image or likeness, and to impose on them their particular way of living. We are welcome to our way of living, but why impose it on others? This applies equally to the national and international fields. In fact, there would be more peace in the world if people were to desist from imposing their way of living on other people and countries.

Mere politics, or even the more serious problem of spreading the Gospel, would not by themselves have driven me from the spiritual and material security of the Church. I think this book will show that I was an intensely religious person and was at one time almost passionately attached to one aspect of the Christian religion. My break with the Church was essentially a matter of belief. I once had a talk with Bishop Gore and told him that I had doubts about, for example, the truth of the Bible, the Virgin Birth and the Resurrection. 'All this, my dear boy,' he said, 'is nothing. The real snag in the Christian, or any religion, is the belief in God. If you can swallow God, you can swallow anything.' There came a time when I could not.

My experience in Gandhi's ashram made it impossible to believe in an exclusive form of Christianity and, whatever broadminded people may say, once you take the exclusiveness out of Christianity a great deal has to go with it. After several years of painful struggle about the relations of Church and State on one side and my own theological beliefs on the other, everything suddenly and quite naturally fell away from me and I was free. It was a dramatic conversion, but in reverse. It was such a great liberation, bringing so much freedom, that I look back to that moment with the greatest happiness and without a moment of regret.

5

Dear as the Moon

To me this little village is dear as the moon,
And from the great city it has dragged me away.
—Gond folk-song

I

A DELHI news-magazine recently referred to me as 'that freakish Englishman, the brilliance of whose eccentricities even Oxford could not dim', though it admitted that I had 'been able to discover poetry and art in strange places'. I do not resent this curious judgement, for there is nothing very discreditable in being eccentric, but I wonder whether it is really true. Is it eccentric to live in beautiful scenery in the hills among some of the most charming people in the country, even though they may be ignorant and poor? I would have thought that on other standards it was far more eccentric to live in the noise, the dirt and disturbance of a town, to waste one's time in clubs, playing silly games with cards or knocking little balls about on tennis court or golf course. To go to a village to find a cause that is worth living for, to escape from the infantile gossip and the tedious recreations of civilization may be unusual, but I do not think there is anything specially eccentric about it.

Even some of my own habits of that time still seem to me practical rather than odd. For many years I lived in villages and did all my long tours barefoot and thus saved quite a lot of money. I never wore a hat and that has not only suited me but has again saved me a little money. I have never used hair-oil. It is only recently that I have started using a mirror for shaving, though I am afraid I have never gone so far as to economize on razor blades and shaving cream by growing a beard. I seriously believe that simplicity in dress is far better, in view of the conditions and climate of the East, than to overload oneself with clothes.

All this may have been eccentric but I was comfortable and enjoyed myself. Nowadays I have become more conventional, though I have always been a little shaggy. Once, on arrival from tour in Howrah Station, I was approached by an excise officer who wanted to search my baggage for contraband drugs and, when I asked why he had picked me out from hundreds of other passengers, he replied, 'Because, Sir, you do not look like a first-class English gentleman.'

On a much earlier occasion my attire had caused trouble. Sir Mortimer Wheeler once invited me to dinner at one of the old-style pre-Independence clubs in Simla. It was bitterly cold and I had no coat. I did not see any point in catching a chill and so went to the club wrapped up in a blanket, which I deposited in the hands of a shocked butler in the hall. Wheeler was later hauled over the coals by the committee for inviting the wrong kind of guest into the club premises and I believe that even now, whenever my name comes up, he demands, 'What is Elwin wearing now?' I am told in fact that I resemble the P.G.W. character who looked as if he had been poured into his clothes and had forgotten to say 'When !'.

There is no doubt that I was often lonely on one side of me, in spite of the delightful company of the tribal people. One year in Patangarh during five months of the rains I saw just five people from the outside world. Often, on tour or in the village when Shamrao was away, I did not speak a word of English for three or four weeks at a time. This drove me in on myself, made me sometimes oversensitive, but it helped me to understand lonely people, and gave me a wonderful opportunity for writing and research. When we reflect on the enormous waste of time we all suffer in casual conversation, I think I am to be envied rather than condemned as eccentric.

From 1931 to 1953 I spent most of my time in houses of mud and thatch. I will shortly describe the beautiful mud house that I finally built at Patangarh. When we started we had very cramped quarters and in our first ashram, which included a small chapel, four living rooms and a veranda, there wasn't room to swing a cat, even if we had wished to indulge in such an unGandhian practice. The great advantage of a mud house is that when you get tired of it you can knock down a wall and rearrange your rooms. If necessary, you can knock the house down altogether and move the timber and bamboo to some other site. Even though a thatched roof often lets in the rain, it is cool in summer and does not make the terrific noise which is caused by the corrugated iron sheets which have become a fashion in parts of India. We had mud floors which were washed every day or two with cowdung. This may sound a little repulsive to anyone who has not tried it, but actually it is very pleasant and hygienic. If you once accept that it is a good and natural thing to live out of the way among tribal people in their own hills and forests, all the other things follow naturally from it.

II

It is easy to find the position of the little village of Karanjia even on a map of the world. Trace the course of the great Narbada river from its mouth on the west coast to its sacred source amid the eastern spurs of the Satpura Hills. Go a hair's breadth from its tail and there is Karanjia.

Here above the village where we had our original shed was a little hill, a *tikera,* overlooking the Pilgrim's Way that goes up to Amarkantak, eleven miles distant, where the Narbada rises, and on it we built the small huts of mud, bamboo and thatch which constituted the 'ashram'. In those early days all round us lay the vast mysterious forest, whose silence was broken at night only by the roar of the tiger or the high melancholy call of the deer.

The bulk of the people round us were Gonds, a great tribe, over three million in number, who are distributed all over central India. They will be found in the remote and malaria-smitten wilds of Chhindwara, by the wooded rivers of Betul, among the lovely hills of Seoni where Kipling's Mowgli hunted with the wolf-pack, in the great evergreen sal forests of Balaghat, in their ancient kingdom of Chanda, in

Bastar and Andhra, and amidst the spurs of the sacred Maikal Hills.

We have little knowledge of how they lived until, in the 14th century, we find them established as Rajas in different parts of central India, which at that time was known as the Gondwana. Their government seems to have been tolerant and kindly; the country prospered; forts, tanks and wells were built; the palaces were filled with wealth. Akbar found a hundred jars of gold coins, much jewellery and a thousand elephants in the fort of Chauragarh. The kings of Chanda built royal tombs, lakes and palaces and surrounded their city for seven miles with a great wall. Herds and flocks increased and even the peasants, it is said, paid tribute in elephants and gold mohurs.

But the Gond kings had no organization, no ability for war, and faced with the invasion of the Maratha chieftains in the eighteenth century their kingdoms collapsed almost without resistance, and they were driven deep into the recesses of the forest. By the beginning of the nineteenth century they had split up into a number of wild and warlike groups, making a living by plundering caravans and raiding the smaller towns from their mountain strongholds. Under British rule they grew pacific and settled on the land and took to their present occupation of farming. But now they suffered oppression and exploitation, for there soon came merchants and liquor-venders, cajoling, tricking, swindling them in their ignorance and simplicity until bit by bit their broad acres dwindled and they sank into the poverty in which many of them still live today. This poverty was not only material; at the same time there came a poverty of culture. For this reason it is not easy to speak of the culture of the Gonds, for it varies greatly from area to area and what there is today is only a shadow of what must once have been. The Gonds have few arts or crafts, they do not weave and only rarely carve in wood. Their pots and their baskets are usually made for them by others. They have adopted to a considerable degree the religion of their Hindu neighbours. Their language, which is a Dravidian tongue, is now spoken by less than half their people.

Their culture survives in their memories of the past, for they have an extensive mythology, in the legendary history of their old kings and heroes, and in the dance and song at which they are still expert. There is a story that long ago, at the beginning of all things, there were seven Gond brothers who made a feast in honour of Bura Pen, their great god. They spread sumptuous offerings before him, but he did not appear. Nothing could tempt him. Then they asked their youngest brother to make music for them but he refused, and it was only when they heaped gifts upon him, gold and silver, jewellery and all manner of ornaments, that he consented. Then with a gourd and a piece of wood and a strand of wire (some say it was a hair of his own head) he made the first fiddle and played so exquisitely on it that the god came down to bless the feast.

Gond poetry is simple and symbolic, free of all literary conventions and allusions. It is a poetry of earth and sky, of forest, hill and river, of the changing seasons and the varied passions of men, a poetry of love, naked and unashamed, unchecked by any inhibition or restraint. The bulk of the poems are songs of the dance and the most poetic of them are perhaps the songs of the great Karma dance which is common to many of the primitive tribes of central India. This dance symbolizes the growth of the green branches of the forest in the spring; sometimes a tree is set up in the village and the people dance round it. The men leap forward to a rapid roll of drums and the women sway back before them. Then bending low to the ground the women dance, their feet moving in perfect rhythm, until the group of singers advances towards them like the steady urge of wind coming and going among the tree-tops, and the girls swing to and fro in answer. They often dance all night until, lost in a rapture of movement, they surprise the secret of the Lila, the ecstasy of creation, that ancient zest in the glory of which God made all things.

This is the one great cultural interest of the people. A girl-dancer is compared by the Gonds to a lovely tree moving to the unseen power of nature, and one of their riddles asks, 'There is a dumb bird that sits on a beautiful tree; shake the tree and the bird awakes and sings.' The answer is, 'The anklets on the feet of a girl who goes to the dance.'

I have said that it is not easy to speak of a culture of the Gonds as they are today. And yet what is culture? Is it not something more than art, religion, language, tradition? There is a very true culture that depends mainly on character, and in this sense the Gonds are a highly cultured people. They have royal blood in their veins, and even the poorest and simplest of them has a strength of purpose, a dignity, a redeeming sense of humour, and a courage in face of the disasters of life that anyone may envy. The honest peasant in his field, the devotee of Mother Earth, drawing his strength from the elemental forces of Nature, is in this sense as truly cultured as the most sophisticated intellectual.

Besides the Gonds we had the Pardhans, the charming and romantic minstrels who have preserved the Gond epics, and the wilder Baigas and Agarias. None of those living in our neighbourhood were what tourists call colourful. They had all lost their own language. As compared with the people of eastern India, one would not call them tribal at all. Moreover, the population of Karanjia and some of the neighbouring villages was very mixed. There were Hindus of various castes, and even a few Mohammedans, and this meant that from the very beginning we did not take an exclusive interest in the tribes but were concerned with everybody who was poor or exploited.

III

As I have already suggested, our plan was to build up a small settlement to help the people and to base our policy and way of life on a mixture of Franciscan and Gandhian ideas. We gradually recruited a small body of workers which included two or three Christians, a Mohammedan, some Hindus and a few of the local tribal people. The idea was that each member should have complete freedom to follow his own religion—in those days we thought very much in religious terms—and that we should have regular prayers based on the Sabarmati model. We organized ourselves into a small Society, which we first called the Gond Seva Mandal. In 1949 we reorganized ourselves as the Tribal Welfare and Research Unit (TWARU).

The leading spirit of this little company was Shamrao, who in Karanjia became an entirely new person. He has always had an extraordinary warmth and humanity about him, and within a very short time of our arrival in Karanjia he had established himself as the Chhota Bhai, the little brother of the people, and as their guide, philosopher and friend. It soon became the custom for any tribesman who was in trouble to 'go to Chhota Bhai' for help. Once, when an old woman lay dying, she would not see any of her relations but called continually for Shamrao. One day a Gond friend said to him: 'Before you came here the moustaches of those who oppressed us turned up to the sky, but now they droop to the ground.' He has never been an outsider; he is never superior; never looks down on anyone or tries to 'uplift' him. To him every individual is a world and he accepts each child or growing youth or poor old woman, not as a 'case' but as a human personality, a sacred thing to be respected and loved, in whose sorrows and anxieties he himself must share. He is always accessible and in Karanjia used to be compared to a Hindu widow (old style) at the beck and call of everyone who wanted him, no task being too small, too humble or too unpleasant.

In the last eight years, he and his wife Kusum have carried on, with very little money and every circumstance of discouragement, by themselves but have continued to bring comfort and succour to hundreds of the poorest people. As someone said of Charles Lamb, Shamrao 'is only at ease in the old arms of humanity'.

The ashram looked exactly like part of the village which lay around and below it, for it was our policy from the first to build everything in the Gond style. All the houses were of mud and thatch, the walls covered with Gond decorations, and there was no furniture which could not be matched in the village itself. At the same time, the ashram was different, in that it attempted to demonstrate what a village might be like. The huts were clean and well-ventilated, everywhere there were flowers and fruit trees, proper houses for poultry and cattle, and pits for refuse and manure. The Gond visitor, therefore, found himself perfectly at home, and yet at the same time, even without a word being spoken, had the chance to learn something that he could take back to his own village.

To enter the settlement there was a long flight of steps which led you first to the little mud Chapel of St Francis, which was used by the Christian members. For this we had a fairly large court surrounded by a bamboo wall plastered with mud, and the chapel was in the middle of it, a little building rather like a Gond shrine. In front were some absurd rooms, in which I was just able to stand up, where we kept our books and spent most of our time. Outside the chapel was a flagstaff (essential to any place of worship in the Gondwana) bearing a saffron flag, which was fitted into a cowdunged platform on which grew the sacred basil tree. All round the courtyard we planted flowers in memory of St Francis's wish that gardens should be made that all who saw them should remember the Eternal Beauty. The tribal people are very fond of flowers and I have always done what I could to encourage them. In front of the whole building was a flat space on the edge of the hill, where the morning and evening prayers were held, and from here there was a wonderful view of forest, valley and hills.

The chapel and compound cost us a hundred rupees to build. At that time wages were two-and-a-half annas a day for women and three-and-a-half annas for men. We created a storm among the local officials and merchants by raising these to the pitiful rates of three annas and four annas. On the other hand, since paddy was at that time twenty-three seers to the rupee, an anna was worth a great deal more than it is now.

You went along the hill, which was sheltered by trees, many of them laden with sweet-smelling flowers, and reached the dispensary. This was well equipped with medicines, and villagers came to it from a radius of forty miles. It was the only dispensary along a main road of seventy-five miles, though there was a small Government dispensary across country, twenty miles away.

Next came a kitchen, built in Gond style round a small compound, dining-room and store-house, and a vegetable garden. Fruit trees were planted in the neighbourhood of all the buildings—mango, plantain, papaya, orange, fig, sour-lime, guava: we used to distribute seedlings and seed. Next door was a guest-house, where in-patients, pilgrims and other visitors could stay. Further along the hill was a small Museum, a very popular building which contained pictures, simple books, toy models and a Hornby train. Then came the largest of our establishments, the school and hostel. There was room for fifty boarders and a hundred others. The school was co-educational and a very fair proportion of girls attended. Here also was a carpenter's shop and a tailoring department. Beyond the school the hill became wild and thickly wooded, and a narrow path wound in and out of trees till it reached a gate beyond which no one might go without permission. This led to the Leper Refuge, where fifteen or sixteen lepers lived and received treatment in a beautiful little home, with a garden in which they took great pride.

This was the centre. Round it, hidden away in remote valleys or in the midst of the forest, there were eight branch ashrams within a radius of as many miles. Each of these had its resident worker, school, Hindi library and small dispensary, fitted with the simplest medicines. Once a week the workers gathered at Karanjia for conference. Model classes were given, and the plan of work for the coming week decided. This was necessary because the workers were themselves villagers without any very advanced education, and in this way they not only took their part in the fight against illiteracy, but also trained themselves to be leaders of their own people. There were between three and four hundred children in the schools, most of them belonging to the Gond and other tribes.

At that time in central India venereal disease was almost endemic among the tribal people. There was very little syphilis and what there was attacked the people in a rather mild way. I have wondered whether the fact that they suffered constantly from malaria might have had anything to do with it, for it has sometimes been supposed that malaria acts as a slight antidote. We were greatly distressed, however, by the way the villagers suffered from gonorrhoea. They got it very badly and it was a tragic thing to see young men and girls so full of love and natural happiness suffering from a disease which today, in view of the new treatment by penicillin, hardly matters at all but was then cruel and disabling.

There are still quite a number of people in the world who think that prophylactic measures against these diseases, and even their treatment, are morally wrong since they make sin easier. I think that if any of them could see what we used to see in Mandla they would change their opinion. A great deal of freedom was given to young men and women before marriage and it was ridiculous to imagine that Old Nobodaddy Aloft, as Blake once put it, was watching their delights with jealous eyes and punishing them for pleasures which he himself presumably could not share.

It was a very wonderful thing when first the sulphonamides, and then the antibiotics, came to bring relief to thousands of people. Even then the danger was that patients who were relieved of their immediate symptoms would stop treatment before they were completely cured, and we had to try very hard to persuade them to go on long enough.

Even among the tribes there was a great deal of hypocrisy about these diseases, as indeed about sexual morality generally. A girl was not looked down upon for any freedom which she might take, provided there was no public scandal, especially with an outsider, that she did not get a baby and that she did not contract a venereal disease. It is the same, to a large extent, in modern society, where the idea that the venereal diseases are a punishment for sin has led to a shameful attitude of scorn towards those who are so unfortunate as to contract them. Nowadays we generally speak of Hansen's Disease instead of leprosy because of the stigma which the older name carries. I have sometimes wondered whether we could not have another name for the venereal diseases. In actual fact, I believe that the WHO has suggested trepanomatosis for syphilis. The classic account of an attack of gonorrhoea is in Boswell's *London Journal* and 'Boswell's Disease' would be a very suitable name for this distressing complaint. I do not think that that charming and wayward lover would mind.

At this time we saw things very simply: we had to work for the health of the community; we had to see that there was enough food and that it was properly cooked; we had to help the people to get and save more money, and finally we had to give them sufficient knowledge to enable them to resist their exploiters and to widen their vision of the world. The first of these aims is secured by dispensaries, health propaganda, and the cleaning of villages; the second by the improvement of agriculture and the education of girls, especially if they can be given some training in the domestic arts and sciences. The third and fourth are also to no small extent the fruits of education. The educated Gond is less likely to be swindled when he takes his goods to market; if he has learnt a little carpentry or tailoring he can make a few things for sale, or at least mend his clothes and so make them last longer.

Above all, we had to rouse the people from their apathy. The prevailing attitude was that 'God has made us poor: it is no good trying to be anything else'. In a nearby village there was a very good pond where the people got their water. But one year heavy rain caused a breach in its bank and the water ran out. After that the village women had to walk two miles to the nearest river. A few days' work by the whole community could have repaired the pond and saved all the waste of time and energy. When we suggested it to them the Gonds said, 'We are poor men. What can we do?' In the end we had to mend the breach ourselves.

As time went on the people did become more alive to the possibility of prosperity and gradually a completely new spirit came to them. One day—but this was after Independence—a Gond woman walked into the dreaded police station and on being ordered out by the Sub-Inspector she said, 'But this is *our* police station, not yours. It belongs to the people.' And another day when a Brahmin Revenue official told one of the Gonds that it was useless to send his son to school, the Gond replied, 'Naturally you would think so, because you know that he would then get your job.'

I have described those early years at Karanjia in my *Leaves from the Jungle*, which originally appeared with a foreword by Romain Rolland, and was published by John Murray in 1936. It is not a book I have ever been very proud of, though it had a great success at the time and has recently been republished by the Oxford University Press. It does, however, give some picture of the strange, happy and exciting life we had during our first few years in the forest. The original success of this book was, I think, due to the humour of contrast, the idea of a clergyman, only recently away from Oxford, having some unusual experiences. Later, after I became part of the picture and both I myself and other people had got used to it, things were not so funny and by the time I reached NEFA I found very little humour in the tribal situation, though I continue to find plenty of it in life as a whole: in fact, Ranjee Shahani has said that I try to discover 'the cosmic through the comic'.

The best thing that *Leaves from the Jungle* did for me was to give me a link with Murrays, of whom I saw a lot during a two-months' visit to London in 1936. The beautiful old Murray house, with its memories of Byron and Thackeray, in Albemarle Street, is more like a very good club than an office, and I spent many happy hours there reading proofs, talking to Jock Murray who introduced me to Gerald Heard and through him to Aldous Huxley, and sometimes attending parties, at one of which I met the memorable Freya Stark. I did not get on so well with another Murray author, Axel Munthe, to whom I observed that I had greatly enjoyed his *Bridge of San Luis Rey*, a remark which for some reason did not go down very well. *The Baiga*, which Murrays published later, was rather strong meat for some of the Directors, especially for Lord Gorell, but he was always exceptionally nice to me about it.

IV

We were always fond of having pets and I remembered Byron's bear whom, he said, he was training for a Fellowship; Herrick's pig who learnt to drink beer out of a tankard; Wordsworth's goldfish, cold 'but pure'; Rossetti's opossum who died in a cigar-box. Though we didn't reach these heights, what we had were a great attraction to the local people. The most striking of them was a splendid young leopardess, whom we kept in a large specially-erected hut with wooden bars. She was so tame that I could go inside it to receive her affectionate, if rather intimidating, embraces. Thousands of people used to come and see her but, unfortunately, one day when we were away on tour she broke the bars of her house and escaped. She paid a visit to the Leper Home but, when she tried to embrace the lepers in the true Franciscan spirit, they took fright and one of them shot her with his muzzle-loader.

Then there was a beautiful chital stag, and a succession of barking-deer, small, timid, affectionate.

Among birds, a pair of turkeys, whom Margaret Moore, one of our early visitors, named the Macbeths, stood first in dignity and importance. There were a number of little Macbeths, but they all died, a fate incident to baby turkeys. There was a waddle of geese, but they all turned out to be ladies. The doves multiplied, but were always being eaten by cats or panthers. We built an aviary, a large well-lighted building with trees in it. There was a pair of blue jays, very pretty birds but with the expression of irascible dons. There were three solemn green parrots, several mainas, and three lovely golden-brown *titur*, a sort of partridge. The barking-deer lived with them and became very friendly with them, so much so that one of them sometimes licked the birds with his active little tongue and removed most of their feathers.

And then, chickens. The Rhode Island Red cocks certainly improved the local breed. Such of their offspring as survived were very good. But even the intra-oval existence of a chick in Karanjia was full of perils. Our hens seemed to have a passion for egg food. There was no more depressing sight than to watch Lady Macbeth lay an enormous egg (suggestive at the very least of triplets) and then turn round and gobble it up before it had even had time to cool. However, we hatched out a large number in course of time, of whom about half used to survive. Some died of heat, others of cold. Some were drowned in their own drinking-water, others trodden on by their parents. One night a gigantic cobra got into the hen-house. It devoured a chick and gave its mother a nasty bite. I attacked the creature with an antique Gond sword I had by my bedside, but it got away. The mother was paralysed for four days and then recovered, celebrating its return to health by pecking one of the other chicks to death.

We introduced pet rabbits and pigeons and gave some of them to the boys in our school hostel. The keeping of pets, so the Educational Department had recommended, was likely to have a mellowing effect on the boys' souls. The boys in Karanjia, however, did not seem to be so susceptible to the influence of simple natural things as Wordsworth would have expected. Little groups of them would get up at midnight, catch one of the unhappy pets, and cook and eat it in the jungle near the school. A grand time was had by all, and exciting stories of a tiger prowling round and killing the animals were put about, until we discovered the truth, and rescued the remaining animals and brought them back to our own charge.

All this made a great impression and one day we went with Mahatu the Baiga wizard to a neighbouring village and he gave a little talk on the ashram. 'They have a beautiful flower garden,' he said, 'and a leopard goddess, and a bird which goes gobble-gobble and another that says quack-quack and some deer.' 'That's all?' I asked. 'Yes, that's all. But'—after a little thought—'there *is* a school and hospital.' But you could see what really interested him.

Later, in Sanhrwachhapar, we had a magnificent brown mountain squirrel and a sagacious crane. It is a great satisfaction to tame some jungle creature. You feel you have stepped right outside your normal social orbit—it's like getting a nod from a head waiter at the Café Royal. The squirrel lived in a tree outside my house and came in regularly for meals. He would sit on my shoulder and share a cup of tea. The crane was even more friendly, and had a special devotion to Shamrao, whom he followed about. He once went into the dispensary and ate some ammonium nitrate, but he took no harm: it actually seemed to stimulate him. He was very fond of coming and standing beside me while I was typing, and often did a little himself. I rather encouraged him, because I've always wanted to test that bit about six monkeys typing all the works of Shakespeare in a million years.

One of our pet monkeys tempted me to a rather unfortunate encounter with Malinowski, the celebrated anthropologist, during a visit to London. I attended one of his seminars and went up afterwards to speak to him. An incurable levity, always stimulated by lectures, which I can never take seriously, prompted me to tell him a little story.

'I live', I said, 'in a mud house in a tribal village in India, and some time ago I got a pet monkey. This creature was normally very well behaved but one day he developed an appetite for literature and, searching through my shelves, found a copy of your *Sex and Repression in Savage Society*. He apparently liked the look of it, for he pulled it down from the shelf and began to eat it, whereupon he immediately went mad.'

I looked hopefully at the great man and the disciples that stood around, but there was not a flicker, just a ring of solemn sociological faces, and I made a rapid getaway.

Animals were, as a matter of fact, always dropping in at the Patangarh house for a snack of literature ; I recorded one such instance in the *Times Literary Supplement*, which Dr P. G. Wodehouse (taking it rather differently from Dr Malinowski) refers to in his *Over Seventy*. Mr Elwin, he says, 'speaks of a cow which came into his bungalow one day and ate his copy of *Carry On, Jeeves*, selecting it from a shelf which contained, among other works, books by Galsworthy, Jane Austen and T. S. Eliot. Surely rather a striking tribute.'

V

In 1936, after I had begun to be interested in research, we moved twelve miles away to a new village.

At Sanhrwachhapar, which consisted of three hamlets in a great valley with a small river running through it, we had plenty of land, timber and bamboo. We laid out the settlement very carefully, building our own houses on the side of a hill with a sort of studio for myself, high up, where I was able to write in peace. Below was a large field where we held a weekly bazaar and to one side was the school and hostel and, further down towards the river, a very beautiful little plateau where we built the Leper Home. Not far away we made a small village to accommodate members of the staff. We had no chapel in this new centre.

Here we were much more isolated than in Karanjia, though we did make our own road from the main highway which itself was out of action for about half the year. In two of our hamlets there were Gonds and Raj-Gonds and in the third was a community of what are now called Scheduled Caste people, the Meheras. We were nearer the Baigas and there were Agaria settlements all round us.

Here we came into much closer contact with problems of change and exploitation. We were on the fringe of the great forests and became more aware than ever of the great deprivation that the loss of their freedom meant to the people. They love the forest with a passionate devotion. It is to them, 'the forest of joy', 'the forest of sweet desire'. It is the scene of the early romances of their childhood, the arena in which they engage upon their most heroic struggles with nature. The Baigas regard themselves as the true *Pashupati*, the Lords of all wild animals; the magical protection of the forest is their charge; they have derived their material sustenance from it for hundreds of years. The reservation of vast tracts of forests, inevitable as it was, was therefore a very serious blow to the tribesman. He was forbidden to practise his traditional methods of cultivation. He was ordered to remain in one village and not to wander from place to place. When he had cattle he was kept in a state of continual anxiety for fear they should stray over the boundary and render him liable to what were for him heavy fines. If he was a Forest Villager he became liable at any moment to be called to work for the Forest Department. If he lived elsewhere he was forced to obtain a licence for almost every kind of forest produce. At every turn the Forest Laws cut across his life, limiting, frustrating, destroying his self-confidence. During the year 1933-4 there were 27,000 forest offences registered in the Central Provinces and Berar and probably ten times as many unwhipp'd of justice. It is obvious that so great a number of offences would not occur unless the forest regulations ran counter to the fundamental needs and sentiment of the tribesmen. A Forest Officer once said to me: 'Our laws are of such a kind that every villager breaks one forest law every day of his life.' This meant, of course, that the villager in relation to Government perpetually suffered from a bad conscience. He became both timid and obsequious, and it was almost impossible to develop in his mind a sense of citizenship, for he no longer felt at home in his own country.

The Meheras and even the Gonds of this area were rather inclined to litigation and we saw a great deal of the burden which police and court investigations placed upon them, as well as the physical distress and nervous exhaustion of long journeys to the distant courts, the demoralising contact of lawyers, lawyer's touts and petition-writers, and the bewilderment of dealing with laws they did not understand and which often ran counter to their own traditions. On one occasion we estimated that in a fairly simple registration case the applicant and four witnesses had to travel an aggregate of 3,700 miles before their business was finished.

The people at Sanhrwachhapar were a long way from shops, and commercial exploitation did not press on them very heavily. But in a remote area like this there was a lot of intimidation by the more sophisticated villagers, some of whom impersonated police or revenue officials and took money from the more simple.

I could fill a large book on this subject and I am afraid that part of it would be very up-to-date. Here I will give a few examples of the sort of thing that used to happen.

A merchant bought a couple of hundred rupees' worth of grain from a fairly well-to-do Gond and paid for it with two hundred-rupee notes. The 'notes' were coloured factory labels removed from bales of cloth. The Gond, who could not read, accepted them with pleasure, thinking he had a bargain, and only discovered the fraud when he took the notes to a police station—not to complain but to get change!

One day a loquacious petition-writer told us how he made a handsome living out of the unhappy tribesmen who found their way to the criminal or civil courts. 'I take them away quietly,' he said, 'and sit them down. The authorized charges are, of course, the first item of my bill. But I explain to my clients that they will not get very far with only that. Do they want their petition written with an ordinary pen, or a fountain pen? That is very important. They always choose the fountain pen, and that means a special charge of four annas. Then I have two books with me, a red and a yellow one—they are both law books. The red book is better: if I copy my stuff from that it is eight annas more than if I take it from the yellow book. They always pay. There is another little charge, anything from six to twelve annas, for putting *gur* or sweet-stuff into the writing, and finally a rupee or two to ensure the petition reaching the magistrate at all.'

But perhaps the most impoverishing factor for the lives of both the Gonds and the low-caste Hindus of this neighbourhood came not from outside but from movements for reform.

At that time there was an organization called the Raj-Gond Kshattriya Surajwansi Maha Sabha (to give it its full name) of Seoni and Mandla which had an ambitious programme of cultural change. Its propagandists went far and wide forbidding the Gonds to eat beef or even to yoke the cow to the plough, to abstain from pork and poultry, to avoid alcohol, and to prevent their women from dancing. When we took a party of Gond boys to demonstrate tribal dances at the Tripuri Congress in 1939, the Sabha wrote to Gandhi threatening to perform satyagraha if these children were permitted to give their show.

In Mandla a Gond reformer set up his 'court' near Dindori. At the end of 1936 he began to tour the district. He was accompanied by three or four 'chaprasis'—one of them was a hard-drinking Mussalman adventurer—and carried some large books, Hindu scriptures which he apparently had not studied. The party went from village to village holding meetings. The reformer stated that he had the authority of Government behind him and that failure to obey his orders would be punished by the police. He promulgated what he called the new Gond religion. He pointed out that the old life of the Gonds was altogether bad and caused them to be despised by their Hindu neighbours. Everything, therefore, that the Hindus despised must be abandoned. The great Karma dance, the one surviving instrument of Gond culture in that area, must stop. Men and women must not sing the 'immoral' Dadaria (the beautiful forest-songs) together. Pigs and chickens, the only tax-free domestic animals, must be destroyed—and an already insufficient diet be still further impoverished. The Gonds must become teetotal. Women should be put in purdah. The rules of untouchability must be strictly observed. Children must be married young in Hindu fashion. Cows must be honoured and not yoked to the plough.

Breach of these rules would involve the offenders in serious penalties, which would be enforced by Government. For dancing the Karma a fine of Rs. 50, for drinking liquor a fine of Rs. 50, for keeping pigs Rs. 25, for yoking cows to the plough Rs. 10

and so on. There was a regular tariff. A Sub-Inspector of Police gave his support to the movement and this corpulent futility started a story, which gained wide currency, that Government had recently fined a Gond Rs. 50 for shooting a crow; how much more then would it penalize the killing of chickens?

The movement spread rapidly through the district, and hundreds of Gonds donned the sacred thread and paid a four-anna subscription to the reformer. An unspeakable drabness settled down on the reformed villages. A 'Shiv-raj' was established at which the great dancer Natarajan would have shuddered. In the long evenings the men had nothing to do save quarrel with their wives, who were themselves greatly affronted at the restrictions on their liberty. The sick, who had hitherto turned in convalescence to the only tonic available to the poor, a little liquor, were now deprived of this remedy. The 'kick' went out of tribal festivals, the flavour from tribal feasts. 'What are we but animals?' said the Gonds. 'But in this life of two days, we used to have a few things that made us men, our beautiful dances, our songs, our drink, Now these are gone and we have sunk below the animals. Even our food is taken from us, and we have no other amusement than to commit adultery with one another's wives.'

Within two years, however, this reformer had been arrested and imprisoned on a charge of cheating, and many villages returned—though somewhat half-heartedly—to their old customs. But other propagandists are constantly on the move; it is an easy way of making money to improve your fellows; and the beautiful song and dance of the eastern Gond districts is probably doomed to ultimate extinction because of the pathetic notion that to abandon it is to rise in the social scale.

Later, I saw similar movements in Bastar, a few external and imposed, others springing up spontaneously. There had been spasmodic attempts from time to time on the part of Hindu State officials to check beef-eating; occasionally a social worker wandered across the border from Chanda or Jeypore and was scandalized at the freedom, the natural happiness, the lack of clothing of the Bastar tribesmen, and of course the simple and natural love-life of the Muria ghotul.

One year a rumour went through all the tribe of Koraput and spread thence into Bastar that a god had descended on one of the mountains of the Eastern Ghats and commanded all men to give up keeping black poultry and goats, wearing clothes or using umbrellas or blankets with any black in them, and using beads or articles made of aluminium alloy. Soon black goats, cocks, hens, umbrellas, blankets, and beads, were littering the roads, and were bought up for a song by local merchants.

In the latter part of our time at Sanhrwachhapar I found myself on more friendly terms with some of the liberal high officials of the local Government; I was relieved of police surveillance, and appointed an Honorary Magistrate. I still cannot decide if this was wise or not: what influenced me was the consideration that in point of fact I was unable to take part in active politics, being bound by my undertaking to the India Office, while on the other hand the opposition and interference by police, forest and other officials was seriously hindering our work for the tribes. My belief in India's right to independence never, of course, faltered, and my devotion to Gandhi as a person, though I saw little of him, never changed. And, in the long run, I am sure that I have been able to serve India better as a 'tribal man' than I could have done as an amateur politician.

It was Grigson, of whom more later, who introduced me to the few official families who were prepared to put up with me. Chief among them were John and the incomparable Pamela Stent, the judge Ronald Pollock, Pat and Maidie Hemeon, the policeman Ozanne, and C. D. Deshmukh, then serving in Chhattisgarh, who was later to rise to great eminence in the public life of India. Sir Francis Wiley, who was for a time Governor of the Central Provinces, once took me as a sort of adviser on a tour of the Dangs, an interesting tribal area in western India, the only time I have ever travelled in a special train. Sam Wiley was a big enthusiastic Irishman whom I liked immensely. I remember his once saying to me, when he had been telling me of the hostility I had excited by my political views; 'But never be ashamed, Verrier, of anything you have done out of love or enthusiasm.'

VI

We stayed at Sanhrwachhapar for four years and then moved again to our final home at Patangarh, partly on grounds of health, partly because I needed a place from which it would be easy to travel to other parts of tribal India and partly because we just liked Patangarh better.

Patangarh was a charming village on an abrupt hill in the midst of a wide clearing in the mountains. On every side were the hills, piled up on one another, of the Maikal Range. In the foreground was the magnificent symmetry of the Lingo mountain. The sacred Narbada was only half a mile away and we could see its bright waters. A fresh wind was always blowing. Patangarh was at least five degrees cooler than Sanhrwachhapar or Karanjia. Not only was the village beautiful, but its inhabitants were more delightful, more amusing, more friendly than any others. Most of our neighbours were Pardhans, the gay, romantic minstrels of the Gonds. 'Phulmat of the Hills' was a Pardhan.

At Patangarh we opened a dispensary, school, shop, guest-house and our main 'offices', continuing a school, the leper home, a small dispensary, the guest-house, and the bazaar at Sanhrwachhapar for some years. Gradually, however, we brought everything over to Patangarh and established the Leper Home on a flat-topped hill opposite ours.

The establishment of the new centre was rather complicated. The landlord first invited us to come, then gave us a notice to quit, then begged us to stay after all. An odd creature. Then we chose a really lovely site for the ashram round a group of ancient trees, and we started to build. But it turned out that one of the trees was the home of Thakur Deo, and another the haunt of the village Mother-goddess, for an unprecedented series of whirlwinds (which are evil spirits throwing their weight about) swept across our hill, and some of the leading villagers had dreams of the goddess, distracted, her hair dishevelled, tears pouring down her face, rushing wildly to and fro as our buildings were erected.

So we picked the houses up bodily and put them elsewhere, in a site commanding equally lovely views, but without the trees. Here too we bumped into a ghost, but we felt we had paid our tribute to local sentiment and could hardly be expected to move again.

In order to build at Patangarh we carried most of the houses at Sanhrwachhapar over to the new village. This saved us a lot of expense, for we were able to use all the timber and most of the bamboo walls, though, of course, we had to sacrifice the thatch. As I have said, this is the great advantage of living in mud huts.

I was in central India all through the Second World War.

When I meet someone like Arthur Koestler, I feel rather ashamed of the sheltered life I have lived. And yet it was not altogether easy in our remote villages.

It could in fact be argued that in the village we lived permanently under war conditions. There was a black-out every night, for the people could not afford lanterns. Even more deadly than the Messerschmidt, came a flight of mosquitoes with their load of parasites that killed thousands every year. We always had a rationing system, for the villagers never had enough to eat. For four months in the year the rains set up a great blockade of mud between our villages and the outside world.

A European, even at the seat of war, had a better expectation of life than a Gond ; and the diseases that ravaged our villages were every bit as deadly as bombs or gas. Against the ultimate enemies of man, hunger and fear, poverty and death, we were trying to construct a 'Line' of love and sympathy, and it would have been tragic if we had abandoned it because of the madness that had overtaken Europe.

The attitude of the Gonds and Baigas to the war was interesting. An old woman put it very well. 'This,' she said, 'is how God equalizes things. Our sons and daughters die young, of hunger or disease or the attacks of wild beasts. The sons and daughters of the English could grow old in comfort and happiness. But God sends madness upon them, and they destroy each other, and so in the end their great knowledge and their religion is useless and we are all the same.'

Some of the tribesmen, always excited by a quarrel, were anxious to help. A party of Baigas came one day with a bundle of bows and arrows which they wanted me to forward to the Government to aid in the war. When I told them that modern battles were no longer fought with these weapons they were much concerned. 'But if they use guns, people will really get killed,' they said. Some Gonds brought their old swords. A Baiga magician made what is called a *thua*—an essay in sympathetic magic. He buried a thorn-bush in the ground by a river and placed a heavy stone upon it. The thorn-bush represented Hitler and the hole in the ground his grave; the stone was to prevent him ever rising again. And once when I was going away somewhere, and a story went round that I was going to the war, I was seen off by a crowd of people shouting what they expected me do to Hitler's sisters and aunts, daughters and other female relations.

I kept Patangarh as headquarters until I went to NEFA, even during the period when I was working in the Department of Anthropology. It was, and still is, a village of great fascination, and I shall always miss it and its people. So will my wife Lila, for she was born there.

I specially miss our main house, to the construction of which I gave a great deal of attention. It was a large mud building with a thatched roof and I loved making it, for it had some special features. It had no outer door, though for the inner rooms I had some old carved Baiga doors that were most ornamental. This was a tribute to our tribal friends—you could not have a house like this in a town—and they could and did come in to see us at any hour of the day or night. Then the entire building was a sort of museum which had things collected from all over India in cases set in the very thick walls. And the building itself was an example of the local tribal art.

The chief surviving art of the Gonds and Pardhans of this part of India was to sculpt on the mud walls of their houses and you can still see many tiny hovels, devoid of every dignity save cleanliness, decorated with charming murals. We decided, therefore, to have all the walls of our own house decorated in this way. It was a big job and took nearly six months, for most of the artists were elderly women who had lots of other things to do, and tribal artists, like artists everywhere, are sensitive and temperamental and, unlike those elsewhere, had no tradition of doing anything for show or for pay.

One woman, whose work was really admirable, came for two days and then disappeared, for her relations had warned her that one of the local witches was jealous and might enchant her. She did in fact fall ill for a week or two—I think it was an entirely psychological illness—and then we persuaded her to come back and she completed some excellent designs. Another elderly woman came from a distant village; she was the most famous of any worker of this kind, a comfortable kindly person, intent on her work, taking a great pride in it. How we had to guard her! Almost every week a little deputation would arrive from her village; there was a wedding, someone had died, her cow had strayed into the forest, her granddaughter was crying for her: would she please come back. But she was so interested in what she was doing that she would not leave until she had finished. For she had the instincts of a true artist. Before starting a new canvas, as it were, she had an engaging habit of embracing the wall with her arms, as if she loved it and the beauty she was to create; which reminds me of a two-year-old tribal boy who never passed our radio set, which made the music he loved, without kissing it.

Soon the walls were covered with tribal heroes, birds, animals, scorpions, mountains, dancers, and deer with enormously long legs to symbolize their speed. In the dispensary, which formed part of the building, were representations of tribal medicine-men doing their stuff, and in contrast a model of the doctor with his hypodermic. In a bathroom were excellent mud water-girls, three feet high, with pots on their heads and a well at their feet.

This Gond art is characterized by symbolism and by a very simplified method of representation: a bird may be shown by its wings, a dancer by his legs. And the Gonds seem to have little idea of symmetry or straight lines. When I raised this point with one of them, she replied, 'But trees in the forest do not stand up straight, nor do the branches extend equally on either side. The pattern on the wall is like the forest.' And so in many cases it was, and the effect was not unpleasing.

The walls of the house did not go up to the roof, and the

artists wanted to put a sort of frieze right round the top. This was great fun. Everybody loved modelling mud animals and birds. A little boy of about twelve arrived one morning and revealed remarkable powers of imagination ; he made a splendid elephant with a crown on its head and a howdah on its back, a Ganpati which might shock an orthodox iconographer but which was interesting as showing the tribal conception of a Hindu deity, a most elegant camel, a mud motor-car, a tiger with a curling tail, birds so realistic that they looked as if they might fly into the air—and all in the clumsy medium of wet mud mixed with millet chaff.

Around this house and the other houses in which we lived there was a strong atmosphere of affection, not only on our side but also from the people who crowded in at all hours of the day and night in a completely natural and informal way as if the place was their own, as indeed it was. Outside, there was jealousy and even hatred, for some officials and other non-tribals resented the way that anyone could come to us ; they felt that we had let civilization down by being too accessible and thus making it more difficult for them to maintain their own barriers of superiority. But this was outside. Inside our walls we could forget everything in the warmth and simplicity of our tribal friends.

We often gave parties, which usually ended in a dance, and what was more important we were given parties in return. In the Mandla villages these were quite elaborate affairs—our hosts would clean their houses and spend all day preparing food, which was generally very tasty. When the time for supper came, a number of people would arrive to escort us. The strongest youth present would hoist me on his back, another would pick up Shamrao, and then, preceded by women singing songs of welcome, we would be carried to our host's house. In NEFA too, the hospitality of the villagers was generally almost overwhelming and I sometimes had to take lunch in half a dozen houses, for none of the leading people of a village liked to be left out. I have had strange dishes on some of these consoling occasions—roasted rats and mice in the Bondo hills ; chutneys of red ants among the Murias ; large white palm-tree grubs fried in their own fat, a little too rich, from the Marias ; a wonderful pilaff of dog's meat and mountain rice from the Kabui Nagas.

To accept tribal hospitality (provided it is not overdone) is a very good thing. It breaks the one-sided patronage of charity, the condescension of benevolence.

When you reach the point that people want to do things for you and are proud to do so rather than always being on the receiving end, you have made a big step forward. The goodness and kindness of my tribal friends, especially when I was ill, was, both in central India and on the frontier, touching and inspiring. Once in Patangarh I developed a very large septic boil which I attempted to cure by some antibiotic tablets from our dispensary. Unfortunately, these had got mixed up with tablets of Milk of Magnesia which they resembled in size, so they did not do very much good and I got steadily worse, until I was in acute pain and fever. It was the height of the rains, no motor transport was possible and I had to be carried thirty-two miles to a place where I could get a car to take me another ninety miles to the nearest hospital. I shall never forget the cheer and tenderness of the men who carried me in a sort of litter through pouring rain and partly by night. We had to cross flooded rivers into which my bearers plunged up to the neck, raising my litter above their heads to keep me dry. When I ultimately reached the hospital I was told that if I had delayed even a few hours I should have developed generalized blood-poisoning, but an immediate operation put me right. Yet it was my tribal friends who saved me.

I have said little about individual tribal friends. This I have done deliberately, partly because it does not do to have favourites (particularly among children) in a village and partly because in tribal society I found an entirely new kind of relationship with people. In a Muria ghotul, for example, you were friends with everybody: you might have more to do with the Sardar or Kotwar, but that was a matter of convenience: friendliness was universal. In all the tribes, some of the boys and girls stood out from the rest through their beauty, their intelligence or wit, their aptitude for games or dances. Some of the older people were distinguished by their appearance, their knowledge and willingness to share it, or by what they did for me. But generally speaking, though I have many names in my mind, they were all my friends—and this is the unique and rather wonderful thing about tribal life: you escape from the normal individualism, the possessiveness and jealousies of sophisticated friendships into something broader and more universal.

At the same time, in the Mandla villages at least, there were alliances into which one entered. You took someone as your Mahaprasad (mine was Mahatu the Baiga priest) or your Sakhi (Panda Baba, of whom there is a lot in *Leaves from the Jungle*), had several Jawaras and so on. But Shamrao and I acquired so many of these that they did not disturb the general relationship: a whole village was our Sakhi or Jawara.

This is why I have felt it better (as always searching for some sort of symbol) to write about the Saoras in general rather than the great Chief of Sogeda or the Bondos as a whole rather than the entertaining Miliya.

In our earlier years in the village Shamrao and I had a common purse. We did not take any salary and foolishly made no kind of insurance for the future. We drew what was needed for our expenses and tried to live simply. Anything we received went into the common stock. For example, for five years I received a research grant from Merton College and, later, a grant from the Leverhulme Foundation. Later, in Shillong, I had my official honorarium.

Although friends were very generous, finance was always a problem. I used to go out, generally in the rains, to hold meetings to try to raise money for the work and for a number of years we had an annual meeting in Bombay where people showed a great deal of interest in tribal matters. Without the help of the great Tata Trusts we could not have carried on. J.R.D. and Mrs Tata have always been very good to us and Rustom Choksi, whose friendship is like a rock, and his sister Pipsy Wadia, were most faithful in their support. Later in this book I describe the part that J. P. Patel played in our lives.

When Victor Sassoon joined us he contributed very generously to our funds. But Victor, of course, gave much more than financial support. He is a man who is equally at ease in the company of millionaires, dons or villagers and he was a wonderful success in all the tribal villages he visited and especially in Patangarh where we built a little cottage for him.

One result of my village experiences was that I developed a very strong sense of economy. For example, I still cannot bear to see water being wasted. For many years every drop of water I used had to be carried up a steep hill from a stream or well and now that I live in a world of taps I still do not like to turn them on fully or to allow the precious fluid to run away uselessly.

VII

Short of writing a day-to-day diary, as I did in *Leaves from the Jungle,* it is impossible to give a proper account of the many years we spent in the Mandla villages. There is not a great deal of variety in village life and our days followed a general pattern, which was interrupted from time to time by strange or dramatic incidents. There were the sick who crowded our dispensary. There were the schools or, after we settled in Patangarh the school, for, as Government began opening more schools, we thought it better to concentrate on one. There were the lepers who had to be provided for and cheered up. There was a host of problems and cases that poured in upon us every day. Shamrao dealt with most of the daily practical matters, and I spent a lot of my time writing. There were festivals, marriages and funerals to attend.

I can, therefore, only suggest a few incidents that will illustrate the kind of life we had and I will quote a passage written by my sister after a visit to Patangarh.

For example, the sort of strange thing that often happened is illustrated in the episode of the Mad Jackal.

One night a mad jackal came into the village and ranged round attacking everything it could find. It bit a dozen cattle, several dogs and seven human beings as they lay asleep on their verandas, before it was killed in the first light of dawn. Nobody came near us for at least twelve hours, so by that time there was little to be done by way of cauterizing the wounds. But we did what we could and then came the business of persuading the human victims to go to Jubbulpore for Pasteur treatment. After an immense amount of argument three of them agreed to go. Three others just did not believe that they were carrying in their bodies the menace of a hideous death, for the rabies from a mad jackal is said to be the worst of all: three of them did in fact die of hydrophobia. This was in spite of the fact that we offered to pay for the expense of the journey and provide them with food rations for a fortnight.

Later, a Gond girl, who had also been attacked in the same way, came to us from a distant village. In order to protect her baby, she had held out her arm and allowed the jackal to savage it until her cries attracted help. But this brave girl too refused to go for treatment, though we offered to take her in our own car.

The real reason for not going to hospital was probably that there is a tribal method of treatment in which everyone believed.

This is based on a fantastic physiological theory. When a man is bitten by a mad dog, the union of the animal saliva and the human blood causes puppies to be generated within his belly. They multiply rapidly and make a nest, from which they go, creeping along the veins, to possess the whole body. Soon there may be scores of them, and within four or five weeks they begin to quarrel and their barking can be clearly heard. At last the noise forces its way into the patient's throat and he himself begins to bark or cry like a dog or jackal. Then his relatives bind him hand and foot, and force emetics down his throat in the hope that he may expel the terrible intruders.

But, long before this, the medicine-man tries to banish the puppies. In Patangarh I was able to see how he did it. He caught a number of longicorn beetles, picked some leaves of the *Nyctanthes arbor-tristis* shrub, ground them up together and made them into pills with a little gur. These he gave one a day to his patients, who very soon began to purge and vomit. Within two or three days, two of the patients began to suffer what they called 'labour pains'—men suffer more acutely than women from these—and soon the tiny creatures appeared. They were, I was told, about the size of red ants, and when young

From a sketch by Maeve Wood

The author in 1942

With Gond and Pardhan children, 1942

had nothing but black heads and tails; as they grow older they develop bodies and feet 'like baby rats'. I was never allowed to see these creatures, perhaps because they are only visible to the eye of faith, but everyone was convinced that they were there.

If the puppies are expelled, the prognosis is regarded as favourable; if they do not appear, the patient is said to be in grave danger.

On one of my Saora tours I had a strange and moving experience which, like many of my experiences, had a symbolic value out of all proportion to what actually happened.

I was staying in a village high in the hills, which nobody dared to visit since it was the reputed home of black magic, and in fact some heavy deeds of murder and suicide had been done there. But I found it enchanting, with superb views and charming boys who played games till a late hour every evening in my camp.

One day a little Saora boy, an orphan, starved to a skeleton of food and affection, hardly able to walk, never a smile, came to my camp and attached himself to me. I gave him a bed beside me in my hut, and tried to look after him. His name was Raisinda. He was what the Saoras call *kodajang*, legged like a crane, and was evidently suffering from pneumonia and probably other things as well. He was, in spite of his weakness, a most charming child with beautiful manners. Though he could hardly stand he used to fold up his bedding in the morning and after drinking tea he always wanted to wash the cup himself. He was so ill that he could not lie down for, when he did, he said that he felt as if ants were crawling into his ears. When he came he was making loud harsh noises whenever he breathed: I gave him some antibiotics and he got better. He was a true Saora, for every morning he used to send for palm wine and preferred drinking this to any food we could give him. He also insisted on being provided with the little cheroots called *pikas* to which all the members of his tribe are greatly attached. He was fond of sitting on my lap and, towards the end, when his mind was not very clear, used to call me mother. Almost the last thing he did when he was sitting with me was to fumble at my pocket to put a precious half-smoked cheroot into safe keeping. He did smile just twice before he died and at the end he passed away very peacefully in his sleep.

Raisinda was infinitely pathetic, forlorn and remote in his boyish struggle to live. One night, while a sorceress in a hut nearby made the darkness uncanny with her conjurations, I dreamt that I was in a great cave, in utter darkness, and that Jammasum (the Saora god of death) had come as a vast Presence, inexorable and grim, to carry off the boy. I was trying frantically to get some light, striking match after match with no result, and then I woke with these words in my mind, 'Love is the true weapon, love is the dress, love is my gold.'

That evening had come the news of the UNO debate on Korea and the threat to use the atom bomb—hence love as the true weapon. I had found that after giving part of my bedding to the boy, I was actually warmer than I had been before—hence love as the dress. And too I had been very worried about money, and my dream rebuked me for this, reminding me of the hidden treasure.

It was a strange thing how this dying child affected my staff and all of us, as well as the other villagers. It was beautiful to see how much tenderness he excited in everybody. I wrote at the time: 'When I ask myself what is the use of a life like his, and why it ever was, coming to the world to be hungry and lonely and then to die without being any use—as one would say—to society, I can see dimly that his suffering, which reflects surely a greater suffering, has hallowed many people and spoken to them.'

There were other symbolic incidents. One day, long ago, a dear old Hindu sadhu came to us in the last stages of sickness and old age. He died bravely, for he was a true sadhu, courteous and detached and unafraid. Nobody would go near him and we laid him out and washed him and finally took him to the pyre in a beautiful little glade in the forest where some of our lepers had been cremated. The red flames leaping up to the rising sun and the peaceful trees and mountains all round made a picture that was in contrast to the horrid reality of disease and misery of the previous night.

Another time a barber, suffering from a very advanced degree of syphilis and entirely alone except for a deformed father, came for help and we did what we could, but he too died and his body was in a quite shocking condition. Here again, none of the Gonds would touch the corpse, not because he was syphilitic but because he was a barber. So Shamrao and I, with two brave men from the village, who risked excommunication for it, carried his body, which was very light from near-starvation, to the grave.

It was humbling to reflect that, at so little cost to oneself, it was possible to give some comfort, and the effect of the smallest such actions makes one wonder why one ever does anything else. Shamrao once showed his true insight when he immediately recognized the rightness of Blake's saying that, if we would do good, we must do it in minute and individual particulars.

When we were at Karanjia an elderly Pardhan who was suffering from leprosy in a very advanced form came to stay with us. Almost blind and hideously deformed, he could do nothing for himself. He had a young wife named Satula who became for us the symbol of all that was best in married life. She was outstandingly beautiful, graceful and charming, and many young men were anxious that she should divorce her husband and marry again. She could have had almost anyone she wanted and escaped from a life that held nothing but horror and misery. Yet she remained with her old husband, tending him devotedly and giving him her love, until he died. By then she herself had developed the disease and after a few years followed him to the pyre.

Nothing was more distressing than to discover signs of leprosy in young boys and girls. I remember another most beautiful Pardhan girl, only fifteen years old, full of life and happiness, already loved and in love, who one day came and showed us the anaesthetic patches which are early symptoms of the disease.

While I was in Patangarh I had a spell of writing verses, which I published privately in a little book called *28 Poems*. These 'secretions', which were as few as they were unexpected, soon passed and I have not written any poetry since. But what I wrote then put my feeling for the village and its people better than anything I could say today. Among these poems was one 'On the First Signs of Leprosy Discovered in a Young Tribal Girl':

How has your innocence deserved this fate,
    The subtle marks of doom upon your skin
So golden-fair in happy youth's estate
    That none would guess the traitor lurks within?

O my poor lovely child, I see already
    The lion-mask behind your oval face,
The clawing of the hands, the voice unsteady
    That now rings with so musical a grace.

The delicate fingers shaped for a caress,
    The careless feet that dance in joyous play,
The laughing lips apt for a lover's kiss
    Are doomed to mutilation and decay.

Still the Blind Forester goes through the glade,
    Enclosing or condemning as he wills,
And at his touch the bombax white is made,
    The ebony grows black upon the hills.

Why did he lay his calloused hand on you,
    Of all his planting the most tender shoot,
The young buds springing, leaves wet with love's dew,
    And fragile boughs alive with hope of fruit?

Another poem which expressed my feelings at this time was called 'Pity', a word which I used as Blake used it, to mean compassion.

O Pity, walk among our fields,
And touch the drooping ears of corn.
See how the scanty harvest yields
Its pittance from the tortured furrow,
And peasants fear to face the dawn.

And mingle, Pity, with the throng
That crowds the workshop and the mine,
Or in the jail where human wrong
Is punished with a world of sorrow,
Or where the broken-hearted pine.

And, Pity, come to visit homes
In villages remote, unblest,
Where death's sad step so quickly comes.
Regard that child with fever broken,
That mother with a cancered breast.

But first, make man's own spirit wise.
For only by the human hand,
And only through our human eyes,
Can Pity heal our desolation,
And spread compassion through the land.

VIII

My sister Eldyth came to stay with us in Patangarh for a few months just before the Second War. The people loved her and her little house was always crowded with visitors. I find it difficult to write about life in our village, and I will, therefore, give some extracts from letters she wrote at the time.

The Leper Home is close at hand and is a most beautiful place. Banana trees and flowers grow between the small white houses, which are very cosy, especially in the evenings with their little fires. There is the school and dispensary, where Shamrao stands radiating love and hope as he injects one after the other. They come crowding up on their poor swollen feet and as he talks to them and jokes with them, smiles split their distorted faces. The little leper children run to him, five tiny lovely children. A beautiful boy had just developed the disease and had his first injection while his father wept aloud. In such a place there is visible tragedy, but at least they are cared for, they have food and clothing, cows and doves and friends.

For all round us there is that flame of pain, that burns brightly in almost all whom we meet. Disease sunk in them in abysmal hopelessness, cold striking like a piercing arrow with a numbness that a strip of cotton cloth does little to cure ; and hunger is a stalking horse with thin arms and legs and wasted bodies. One sees this in the bazaar which gathers all over the ashram hill: the women who are really young look old and wrinkled, almost all are thin. The 'stalls' are tiny little heaps of beans and chillies, a few dried fish, some sweets and tobacco, some bangles and strips of cloth. But for all that it is a very social occasion and people come from miles around to buy or sell and meet friends.

I long to be able to make you see this village and its poor but loving courteous villagers, who refuse to 'improve', but who lodge in your heart. To show you Verrier and Shamrao, with all that there is to discourage them, ceaselessly returning good for evil and dispensing friendship with both hands.

There were many sick: pneumonia had followed measles. Crowds came to the Dispensary. Shamrao gazing over a selection of patients, all with strange and unknown diseases, cried 'I wish the masses didn't suffer so! ' And how difficult to know what to do even when the disease was diagnosed. We did what we could. There was one family where everyone went sick. The father, a magician, went thin as a bone with a terrible cough. The elder boy, deaf and dumb, became jaundiced and faded to a skeleton. The lovely daughter of about fourteen developed heart trouble, the little boys got bad fever and terrible pustulated itch, and the baby, a plump and merry little fellow, with a piece of the backbone of a snake round his neck to protect him from ill, looked like a famine waif, pitiful beyond words. The poor mother was desperate, and went from magician to magician for help, instead of coming to us. We went to them, however, and found them all sitting in a little inner room filled with smoke from the open fire. The skeleton boy was dragged out into the light for us to see, but we could do nothing for him and could only feel glad when he died. The others responded to Shamrao's injections, except for the baby, who, in spite of tinned milk, was too weak to survive. They had been terribly poor and undernourished all their lives.

Another little baby had been ill a long time, indeed ever since he was born he had suffered. His head was so big and his body so small, and he had great brown eyes. When he wasn't with his mother he rode on the hip of his small uncle aged nine, and was often put down for a game of marbles when he would wail in a thin little voice. His father was away and we thought the baby dying, but he got back and the baby laughed for joy and held out his arms and was held by his father till they came to tell us 'The child is dead'. We rushed round to find them all desperately weeping beside the still body of the child. The women weep in the most beautiful way; it is almost like singing, and as they weep they compose the words.

His mother wept, 'My little son, because you were so delicate I held you always on my breast, but now I must lay you all alone on the cold earth. Before you came I was so ugly, but you came and made me a queen. Your throne was between my breasts, but now I must be as I was before.'

They wrapped him in white cloth, and his father, taking him in his arms, led a party down the hillside to the field. Only men go to funerals but they let me follow a little way off. We crouched in the field in silence while the grave was dug with a little cave to one side. The father laid his child in this with most tender care, hovering over him till he felt sure the little body was comfortable, and then he covered his face. They all went to bathe ceremoniously at the well.

One day, startled by the boys' excited cries, we looked up to see, advancing over the plain like prehistoric monsters, twenty great elephants. They were journeying from Sarguja State to Tripuri for the Congress procession. We were all thrilled. Jai Gopal rushed to meet them crying to the mahout of the largest elephant, 'Here you are! Bara Bhai is here. Come along!' Verrier went out and invited them to spend the night in our village, which they did, spending the day eating large quantities of jungle rice laid in the heart of a ball of grass and ten great chapatis and ghee. How our peoples' mouths watered! All that food! People thronged the village and wherever the elephants went the entire Boarding School followed. At sunset the mahouts agreed to take us for a ride. I rode with the women on the Raja's elephant, a great beast nearly twelve feet high, and, with the rest of them laden with boys and villagers, we rode to the river two miles away and the huge creatures stood round drinking. Then we swayed back in the dark, all singing and piping, towering above the little huts. The mahouts were wonderful old men and each elephant had a special name. At dawn they were gone, leaving a treasured memory in the minds of us all. . . .

Anthropological committees are difficult if amusing. One night we had two Pardhans and a Panka to supper. They started off well with a fund of information that was irrelevant but interesting enough to make Verrier want to start a book on the subject. Brought back to the point, the small baby of the chief spokeswoman started to cry and she had to lie flat on the floor till he was soothed. The father, a bit of a wag, with a long piece of cloth wound round his face and head, sat sideways on a deck-chair commenting on the repast which he ate with relish. 'How much food you eat!' We gave them some coffee at the end to see how they liked it, and their faces were a study.

'After feeding us so well, you give us this bitter stuff to spoil it all,' he cried, but with looks of anguish he drank it.

It is rather terrible to see these people look at food. Whenever we gave the lepers a goat, while it was being cut up they used to gaze with devouring looks upon each piece. It comes from generations of hunger. We asked the boys what they would like for a farewell feast. 'Potatoes and chapatis' they said. That was all they asked.

Little pictures of village life stand out vividly. I remember walking through the village at Sanhrwachhapar on the way that leads down to the well. At the turn on the path you come to a great tree in which were dozens of green pigeons, with wings of mauve and green and feathers of bright yellow and dove-grey. At the top of the hill were two or three houses and they brought out a cot for us to sit down. The view was glorious—golden green forest behind and in front a sweep of plain and hill and close before us a long line of women with full water-pots on their heads coming slowly up the hill. I went on into the courtyard of one of the houses and sat down to watch the women grinding grain and tossing it in a fan to get rid of the chaff. Others were shaking rice and picking the stones from it. Little Indian hens and minute chickens pecked hopefully about, a calf wandered round bewildered, naked babies sprawled in the sun, and an old woman was making mud bins in the sun, patting the mud till it was smooth and round. There was companionship in this leisured simple toil though we could not talk to one another.

I can't write much about the parting from Patangarh; it was too sad. We all wept together and I left them a silent group with tears pouring down their faces. As we turned the corner of the hill there was the cook running hard to give us a last salute.

Just before Eldyth left us—Shamrao and I went with her to England—a young girl of about sixteen came from a distant village to the dispensary. She was singularly attractive but her beautiful young body was a thing of horror, covered with the secondary sores of syphilis. I have seen many such infections but nothing to compare with this. Eldyth gave her a bed in her room and looked after her, but there was not much we could do. Two days later we left and we took the girl in our car to the nearest hospital for treatment. I had never seen her before: I never saw her again, though I have never forgotten her.

On my return from England three months later, I found that she had been persuaded by some local gentlemen to go before a magistrate and declare that she had been my mistress for two years. The court did not find this very convincing and nothing came of it, but the incident illustrates the very real danger of working in a village if you have to make yourself unpopular by fighting vested interests. Unless you are determined not to be discouraged and are convinced of the paramount necessity of forgiveness which will not allow this kind of thing to embitter you, you will not get very far. But if it is possible to 'live happily indeed, not hating those who hate us; among men who hate us to dwell free from hatred . . . We shall be like the bright gods, feeding on happiness'.

IX

The years in the Gond villages taught me many things though, looking back, I am amazed that I did not learn more quickly. In this story of my life I have deliberately played down its difficulties. 'Being unhappy', said Sydney Smith, 'does no good,' and recalling, or describing, unhappiness does no good either. But memory is merciful to human beings, who cannot bear too much reality, for it censors the discouraging recollections of our darker moments. This does no harm so long as we recognize that they are there in the past and we can learn from them. On balance, my life in the villages was a happy, exciting and rewarding time, but I should give a false impression if I left the reader with the impression that everything was roses, thornless roses, all the way.

Without Shamrao I could have done nothing. If I provided thinking and ideas, he translated them into action.

The struggle from conventional religion into freedom was

very hard and, sensitive to other people's opinion as I was at that time, I dreaded opening my letters when I was in Karanjia. The hatred and jealousy I encountered distressed me and cast a cloud on my happiness. You cannot give yourself to a cause without opening the door to pain, and I have often been desperately worried, unable to sleep at night, over the tribes and their fate: whenever a friend went to jail or was deprived of his forest rights in hunting or fishing, or lost his land, it upset me intensely. The enemies of the tribal people became my enemies, and it was all the worse because so often I was powerless to help.

A lot of people were down on me in those days and, for an ordinary person, I had a rather disproportionate volume of notice in the press, some of it extravagantly kind and some bitterly hostile. At first I was very sensitive to this sort of thing, but gradually I learnt not to worry about it.

But my worst enemies were those of Everyman, inside myself. There was the weakness that comes from disliking people, the distraction that comes from being jealous of them, the resentment that inhibits love, that sick miserable feeling of uncertainty and apprehension that arises from bondage to oneself. And my greatest failure was in my first marriage.

Soon after we settled in Patangarh I married a very beautiful Gond girl, Kosi, who came from a village near Karanjia. She went with me on many of my early tours and gave me a son whom we named Jawaharlal, partly after the Gond Raja, Jawahar Singh, of Sarangarh, a very dear friend of mine, and partly after Jawaharlal Nehru. But he has generally been called Kumar, which is easier to say.

Unhappily, tragically, this marriage did not work out well and after some years I got a divorce. I cannot even now look back on this period of my life without a deep sense of pain and failure; indeed I can hardly bear to write about it.

Later, I married Lila, a Pardhan girl who lived in Patangarh itself and this, though undeserved and almost unexpected, has worked out very well indeed.

We are so accustomed to talking of the Indian villagers as miserable and unhappy that we are apt to forget that many of them, and especially the tribal people, where they are free.

are capable of idealizing their life, as the following Gond folk-song, which also reflects my own experience, shows.

> In all the world a village is the place for happiness.
> In every house are ploughs and bullocks,
> And everyone goes farming.
> When the villagers are working in the fields,
> It looks like a festival.
> With the consent of all, the fields are sown ;
> They are fenced with thorns to keep the jackals away.
> Slowly, steadily, the rain fills all the tanks
> and wells and hollows,
> While the clouds thunder through the air and
> frighten us out of our wits.
> Some sing Dadaria: some dance the Saila: those
> who are grazing cattle play on the bamboo flute.
> After the ploughing, the fields are thick with mud,
> but the women dance as they sow the rice.
> Friends play, throwing mud at one another.
> Some are smoking ; some are chewing *pan* ; some who
> are idle sit gaping at the workers ; while others sing.
> In all the world a village is the place for happiness.

6

Philanthropology

His anthropology might be called Philanthropology. His great service to science was to lay the foundations and to build the framework of anthropology well and truly on sound scientific principles ; his service to humanity was to show that ' the proper study of Mankind ' is to discover Man as a human being, whatever the texture of his hair, the colour of his skin or the shape of his skull.

—A. H. Quiggin, Haddon the Head-hunter

I

I WAS once introduced at a cocktail party to the wife of a British Colonel as an anthropologist. We sat down together on a sofa but I noticed that the lady squeezed herself into a corner as far away as possible and kept shooting furtive glances at me. Presently, however, after she had strengthened herself with three pink gins, she leant over and in a confidential and slightly guilty whisper asked me, 'Tell me, Dr Elwin, is anthropology very prevalent in your district? '

I am essentially a scholar, a research man. There are few greater pleasures than getting a footnote just right or correcting the items in a bibliography, no dismay more upsetting than to find uncorrected misprints in your final, unalterable, copy. I have had to live far away from libraries, but old friends like B. S. Kesavan, who has transformed the National Library in Calcutta, and gentle, learned Saurin Roy at the National Archives have kept me in touch and made available almost unobtainable books.

Had I not gone to the forest, I might have developed into the typical pedant ; even as it is, I take enormous pains over everything I write and, until I came to Shillong, I used to write or type everything over and over again myself. I took as my exemplar Addison hurrying all the way from his rooms at Magdalen to the Clarendon Press to correct a single letter in proof. I make mistakes, of course, but I try not to, and I check and recheck every item of information: I revised my book on Nagaland no fewer than thirteen times.

I have read a great deal of anthropology in the last thirty years. But unlike the professional anthropologists of today I did not begin with it. My interest in human beings began with literature and my first teachers were Jane Austen and Swift. What a wealth of sociological information and analysis can be found in *Pride and Prejudice* or *Gulliver's Travels*! And later, curiously enough, my studies in theology developed my interest in Man. The science of God led me to the science of human beings. I read a little history, philosophy and psychology: they too prepared the way.

My studies of Hinduism in Poona were also of great benefit. The majority of the tribal people outside Assam have been profoundly influenced by that great religion and it is not possible to understand them without knowing what it is about.

Anthropology is a very big subject, the science of man, man as a whole. We need different kinds of people to study it. We need the scholar trained in pre-history, archaeology, the exact measurement of physical characters, biology, statistics. But we also need some who come from a humanist background and I think it is unfortunate that nowadays what I may call the technical anthropologists look down on the humanist anthropologists, though I must admit that the latter fully return the compliment.

From the very beginning I was attracted by the practical application of anthropology and encouraged by the life of A. C. Haddon of Cambridge, than whom there could not have been a more exact scientist. The extract which I have quoted at the head of this chapter suggests that there is nothing whatever hostile to scientific inquiry in having an intense and affectionate interest in the people one studies, in desiring their progress and welfare and in regarding them as human beings rather than as laboratory specimens.

The essence and art of anthropology is love. Without it, nothing is fertile, nothing is true.

For me anthropology did not mean 'field work': it meant my whole life. My method was to settle down among the people, live with them, share their life as far as an outsider could, and generally do several books together. My Baiga book took me seven years, *The Agaria* ten. I spent ten years on my first collection of folktales and fourteen on the *Folk-Songs of Chhattisgarh*. And they were all going on at the same time. This meant that I did not depend merely on asking questions, but knowledge of the people gradually sank in until it was part of me.

And with knowledge came the desire to help. It was my realization of the psychological and economic impoverishment of the Baigas that led me to question the entire forest policy about shifting cultivation, which I have now examined in many parts of tribal India. It was initially the study of the Agarias that impressed me with the urgent need of encouraging the small cottage industries which were at one time in danger of disappearing altogether. A study of the Santals and Uraons equally impressed on me the importance of encouraging the few existing arts of the people. Some administrators were disturbed at the suspicious and even hostile attitude of tribes like the Bondos and Saoras towards outsiders. It was only when I had studied them very fully that I realized that they were not being merely bloody-minded, but that their apprehension was due to deep-rooted religious and magical ideas. Even the study of folktales and myths, which some people regard as unworthy of the notice of a serious scholar, brought home to me the importance of the fears and anxieties of the people and the need to ensure that we did nothing that would intensify them.

There are, of course, some fields of investigation which can and should be entirely academic, but in India at the present time, where, as a result of the great Five-Year Plans, the tribal people are being very rapidly changed and merged into ordinary society, I believe that we should put every possible anthropologist and sociologist into the work of guiding development and training its agents. This need not mean any lowering of the standards of research, still less a bias towards any particular theory. For it is the glory of science to direct the radiance of truth into the dark places of human life and transform them.

II

One of the things that roused great suspicion among the pandits was that I came to anthropology through poetry. I still cannot see what was wrong with this. The chief problem of the student of man is to find his way underneath the surface; he has to 'dig' people. Poetry is the revealer, the unveiler; by heightening a man's own sensitivity, by opening to him the treasures of the imagination, it increases his powers of sympathy and understanding. And when his people are (as they were in the Maikal Hills) themselves poets by temperament, there is a link between him and them; they talk the same language, love the same things.

Ever since I left Oxford poetry has been my inseparable companion. It has brought me 'in hours of weariness sensations sweet'; comforted and restored me in stormy weather; filled times of loneliness and illuminated all that has been dull and dark. Like Keats, I cannot exist without Eternal Poetry to fill the day.

Now, feeling as I did, when I first went to live in the tribal hills of India, with my Wordsworth, my T. S. Eliot, my Blake and Shakespeare burning like torches in my little mud house, it was natural that I should look about me for poetry. And I soon found it, for among these gentle and romantic tribal people, poetry jumps out at you. It is there everywhere, in their eyes, on their lips, even in some of their actions. And so now poetry became, from something external to be admired, part of me, a personal possession, and whatever I have done in the name of poetry comes from the work I have done with my tribal poet-friends.

I found the people talking poetry. An old woman speaks of fire as a flower blossoming on a dry tree, of an umbrella as a peacock with one leg. Children playing round the fire at night ask each other riddles which are sometimes real poems. Chillies are red and green birds sitting on a bush; a lamp is a little sparrow that scatters its feathers about the house. A man, speaking of his pregnant wife, says to me, 'She must be treated as a flower, or the light may fade from her blossom.' Young lovers sing poems to each other across the fields, arranging an elopement in verse, discussing their love in poetic symbols. The grain in the fields is beautified: the smallest of the millets is sweet as a lotus; tiny as it is, when it is cooked with milk it swaggers about. The forest herbs are personified; one has a shaven head, another long tresses hanging to the ground, a third parts her hair. The poorest cot has legs of gold and a frame of jewels when a lovely girl is sleeping on it.

My very first 'tribal' book was a joint venture by Shamrao and myself, called *Songs of the Forest,* which was published by Allen & Unwin with a kindly foreword by Sir Francis Younghusband. Although once I have finished a book I can rarely look at it again, I still read this one as well as my other translations with genuine pleasure, for many of the songs are beautiful by any standard. In the Mandla hills we had the immense advantage of talking a dialect of Hindi called Chhattisgarhi which proved very easy to learn and which we still talk at home. This meant that there was immediate and familiar contact with the people all the time.

Later, I published two other collections of folk-songs, one, (jointly with Shamrao)—*Folk-Songs of the Maikal Hills* in 1944, and another, *Folk-Songs of Chhattisgarh* two years later. Both were substantial volumes, one of 439 pages, the other of 527. I dedicated the first to W. G. Archer, and he wrote a long Comment for the second, which I regard as the finest statement about tribal poetry that has yet been made.

My method of translation was to be very simple and to be careful not to add any new images to the original. Arthur Waley says of his own method, 'Above all, considering images to be the soul of poetry, I have avoided either adding images of my own or suppressing those of the original.' A good example of the danger of breaking this rule may be seen in the work of Dryden, whose translations are really remarkable original poems suggested by classic models. In his famous stanza on Fortune occur the lines:

With Veddas in Ceylon, 1950

In the Bondo hills. *Above*, Shamrao, Kusum and Suresh Hivale
Below, Victor Sassoon

I can enjoy her while she's kind ;
But when she dances in the wind,
And shakes her wings and will not stay,
I puff the prostitute away.

This is supposed to be a translation of the twenty-ninth Ode of the Third Book of Horace. But the excellent line which was so much admired by Thackeray—'I puff the prostitute away'—is represented in the original simply by the words *resigno quae dedit.* Thus a new image is added to the poem, for which there is no warrant. Caution in this matter is all the more important when we consider the essential place that symbolism holds in village poetry.

I followed as well as I could the example of Arthur Waley and worked on the principles laid down by W. G. Archer, that is to say, to avoid rhyme and make no attempt to reproduce the form of the original. I tried to represent the meaning as literally as possible, within the limits of the demands of poetry, and was scrupulous in introducing no new image.

Bill Archer, in his book on Uraon folk-poetry, *The Dove and the Leopard,* makes many comparisons with my translations of Baiga, Pardhan and Gond poems. He considers that the poetry of these different tribes is of the same general type but differs remarkably in technique. There is in Uraon poetry no two-lined verse such as is common among the Baigas, nor do we find the custom (which was also common in Hebrew poetry) of rhyming thought, in which one line parallels the next. If we define a love-poem as the expression of rapture, Baiga poems are as obviously love-songs as Uraon poems are not. 'It is the necessity of sex rather than the charm of love which dominates Uraon songs.'

It is a very great pity, and I entirely accept any criticisms that may be made of me on this account, that we have not been able to publish the originals of these poems. It would have made the books far too unwieldy had we done so immediately, but we had an enormous pile of papers containing the originals in Devanagri script, which Shamrao was preparing for the printer. Unfortunately, in one of our absences on tour a great storm destroyed many of our things and these precious originals were among them. The songs were not of any particular linguistic value, for none of them were translated from the obscure tribal languages but, at the same time, they would have been of artistic and literary interest and as a result of their disappearance I cannot claim too much for the volumes of translations, although they contain a great deal of commentary which is of some sociological value.

III

My first large work was *The Baiga* which John Murray published with the help of a subsidy from the Dorabji Tata Trust. Previously Dr and Mrs C. G. Seligman, to whom I look back as my real inspiration in this field, had helped me to publish an article on Baiga dreams in the *British Journal of Medical Psychology* and I later did a second article for the same journal on the Vagina Dentata.

It was rather thrilling writing *The Baiga* and it had a remarkably good press, indeed the praise it received now seems to me somewhat extravagant. But like all the work we did at that time there was a certain atmosphere of enthusiasm and excitement which was, I think, infectious.

To be among the Baigas was like living in the middle of a fairy story. Of all the tribes I know they are the most possessed by their mythology. And these myths were not just interesting tales tacked on to the fringe of their life. They were alive ; every one of them was continually being put into action. When the Baiga was summoned to control a man-eating tiger, he faced this dangerous task with the more courage because he knew that the duty had been his from the beginning. When he performed magic on behalf of the Gond farmers, he recited the myth of the creation of the world and reminded his hearers of the unique share his tribe had in it. The myth breathed life into ancient custom ; it made the unintelligible real ; it turned the ancient heroes into contemporaries.

The founder of the tribe and its great hero was Nanga Baiga. Born on the Hill of Elephants, from the womb of Mother Earth, beneath a clump of bamboos, and nursed by the divine Bamboo Girl who gave him a golden axe to play with, Nanga

Baiga appeared just when he was wanted. The Creator had made the world, spreading it on the face of the primeval ocean like an enormous, flat chapati ; he had called the wind to harden its surface, but the wind is blind (that is why it is always knocking things over and banging against people) and did not finish the work. He called Bhimsen to put the mountains in place, but Bhimsen was always drunk and was so heavy that he kept on putting his foot through the thin surface. Nothing could make the earth firm and steady. It wobbled. It was like a broken spider's web.

So the Creator sent for Nanga Baiga. When he came and put his foot on the edge, the world tipped up—as they say the U S A tipped up when Bernard Shaw landed in New York. But Nanga Baiga soon put things right. He got four great nails and drove them into the four corners of the earth and after that it was firm and steady. Then Nanga Baiga helped in the creation of the rest of mankind ; it was through him that seed came to the world ; he instituted magic ; organized the social and economic life of man ; established control over the wild animals. He was the first real man.

No wonder that the Baiga, tracing his descent from such distinguished ancestry, has an air about him. A king (or perhaps I should say an archbishop) is always peeping through his loop'd and window'd raggedness. And still today he is *the* magician and medicine-man, the classic type, who acts as intermediary between the other tribes and their gods. He is sent for by the Gonds to charm fertility into their reluctant seed ; he is consulted even by Brahmins in time of sickness ; it is believed that he can divert hail from a treasured field ; he can detect with his divining-rod a stray bullock or a stolen goat far more efficiently than the police.

This tradition and pride of the Baigas brought them into conflict with Government in two ways. The first was that since they had been born from the womb of Mother Earth, they believed that it was a very wrong thing for them to lacerate her breast with the plough. The second was that, since they were the true Pashupati, lords of animals, they considered that they should have the freedom of the forest for their hunting. Nothing shows more clearly the evils of an administration ignorant of tribal mythology and indifferent to its custom than the way the old Government dealt with the Baigas on these two points.

From 1867 to the end of the century the unfortunate Baigas were pursued by zealous forest officers, determined to make them stop their axe-and-hoe cultivation and take to the plough. At the same time much of their hunting was stopped and some of them were even forced to make heaps of their precious bows and arrows and burn them.

Shifting-cultivation is a bad thing: unfortunately it is often the only possible thing. The Baigas used to cut down a track of forest, set fire to the wood when dry, and sow their seeds in the ashes. After repeating this for three years, they would move on to another patch of forest. Obviously, even where a tribe had a religious passion for this type of cultivation, it could not be permitted on a large scale and for ever. But where only a few tribesmen practised it—and the Baigas were a very small tribe—and where a regular rotation of at least twenty years was observed, the harm it did to the forest was greatly exaggerated. The Baigas have practised this form of cultivation for centuries in Mandla and Balaghat, yet nowhere is there better forest today.

But the Baigas were forced to the plough; many were reduced to poverty, for they hated the tabooed implement, and all suffered psychological disturbance deep in their souls. They have today sunk into the position of impoverished and inferior cultivators. Robbed of their bows and arrows, they are no longer lords of the forest, the great shikaris of former times. They have lost much of what used to make life so rich and enjoyable.

I had many Baiga friends and they were all pledged to inform me if anything interesting happened. So one day there would come news that someone thirty miles away had died, and we would be off within the hour to watch the funeral. Another day there would be a marriage; another we would have to climb a tall hill to see a Honey Festival, in honour of the bees, that occurs only once in nine years. Yet again the Baigas would come to my own village and protect it with a magic wall by driving nails along the boundaries.

It was in the very remote Bohi that I watched the strange and thrilling ceremonies designed to close the jaws of the man-eater and to frustrate the witch who had sent him. It was a desperately serious business ; seven of the most powerful magicians came to do battle with the forces of evil. The Tiger Spirit came upon one of the spectators ; he was transformed into a tiger and began to behave like one : there was an exciting tiger hunt ; and in the end nails were driven into rocks and trees.

The next morning, I was standing in the forest when a large pig lumbered up to me with a leaf in its mouth which it dropped at my feet. I was rather moved by this—sort of Francis among the birds touch, I thought—and then forgot all about it. But no sooner had I returned home than I went down with a violent attack of fever. The local magicians waited on me, and soon diagnosed the cause—the witch of Bohi, annoyed at my presence in the village, had put magic in a leaf and sent it to me by her pig. They immediately took the necessary measures, and I recovered.

The Baigas are very fond of pigs. One day a man came to me complaining that his wife had run away with someone else. 'That,' he said, 'I could have borne ; but they took away my favourite pig.' A pleasant picture—the happy couple fleeing through the moonlit forest glades, and on the lover's shoulder is a pole bearing a protesting, squealing pig.

Once when we were driving through the forest beyond Kapildara we met a large tiger on the road. It was an open car and personally I was considerably alarmed. But an old Baiga sitting by me did not turn a hair ; he began to mutter his charms and after a minute or two the tiger turned and went away quietly into the jungle. 'That is nothing,' the Baiga told me. 'There was a man called Dugru who used to be visited by three or four tigers at a time. They would lick his hands and feet and stroke him with their paws. Sometimes he got tired of them and would tell them to go away, and they always obeyed him.'

And he told another story of how once the Baigas, angry at some restriction of their forest rights, had warned all the tigers in their area that the Governor was coming for a hunt, and as a result His Excellency did not get a single animal!

It is very important that the anthropologist should come down from his perch and, as far as he possibly can, become what G. K. Chesterton once called 'the invisible man'. This was in one of the Father Brown detective stories where the murderer was the postman. All the witnesses declared that nobody had visited the house where the deed was done, but they forgot the postman who fitted into the picture so completely that he didn't count. It is not easy to reach this standard but I was always trying to, and one of the greatest compliments an ethnographer could be paid was once given me by a Baiga. I had visited his village and been received with great friendliness but none of the fuss and deference which the touring officer generally receives. One of my company was annoyed at this and said to the villagers: 'Here is a sahib: he must be someone important. Why don't you make proper arrangements for his reception?' The Baiga laughed at this. 'We know it's only Bara Bhai'—the usual name for me, by which I was distinguished from Shamrao, the Chhota Bhai: in fact we were often known by a portmanteau name, Bara Bhai-Chhota Bhai, Big Brother-Little Brother. 'He is such an ordinary man that when we see him coming we say, "Oh, it's only Bara Bhai, there's no need to bother!"'

IV

For my next book I turned to the Agarias, a small group of blacksmiths and iron-smelters, who are scattered all over the Mandla and Bilaspur Districts with cadet branches right across central India to Bihar. In this study I wanted to discipline myself and concentrated mainly on the techniques of craftsmanship with the mythology that vitalized them. I found it interesting enough and I felt it was good for me, but the Agarias are a dull people compared to the Baigas. Preparation of this book involved a great deal of travelling about and I kept on finding little groups of them in unexpected places.

Fifteen years later these early studies in iron resulted in my being invited to write *The Story of Tata Steel* for the jubilee celebrations of the Tata Iron and Steel Company, the only properly paid literary work I have ever done (they gave me ten thousand rupees for it) and the book was most handsomely produced.

All the time that I was working on these and other books I was collecting stories. I put some hundred and fifty of them in a book *Folk-Tales of Mahakoshal,* which was the first volume of my Specimens of the Oral Literature of Middle India. This included a fairly complete bibliography of the Indian folktale in English and was very fully edited with notes and comparative material. The second volume in this field was my *Myths of Middle India* which were not so good as stories, though of considerable significance for our knowledge of how tribal myths developed out of, and sometimes parallel to, the ancient Hindu traditions. Probably the most important section of this book was one, which some of my readers regarded as rather coarse, on the origin of the different parts of the human body and its natural functions. I was very pleased when the *American Anthropologist* described it as 'a landmark in the exploration of the intellectual history of mankind'.

Long afterwards I made two selections of folk-stories from my larger collections. The first was *Stories from India* in four small volumes published by the Oxford University Press ; the other was called *When the World was Young,* and was a National Book Trust publication. The best thing about them was the illustrations. The gracious and beautiful Leela Shiveshwarkar did the first, the brilliant and delightful Amina Jayal the second.

Another book, the preparation of which gave me great pleasure, was my *Tribal Art of Middle India,* but unfortunately I was so excited about it that I published it too soon. Had I waited another year or two I could have made it much better, for I discovered many new things as time went by and made, for example, a superb collection of wood-carvings from the Santal Parganas. I also found many Jadupatua scrolls, tribal comic strips as I call them, which tell the ancient stories of the Santals in pictures. Even so this book revealed a good many unexpected treasures and stimulated designers elsewhere.

At this time I also wrote two novels, both of which were published by Murray. The first, *Phulmat of the Hills,* was the love-story of a Pardhan girl whose beauty was finally destroyed by leprosy. The second, *A Cloud that's Dragonish,* was a tribal crime-story in which the detectives were Gonds and Baigas. Both these books got very good notices in England, though they were little read in India, but they have been out of print for over twenty years and have not been republished. Later, I wrote another novel, *Traitor's Gain,* which turned on the iniquitous exploitation of the tribal people, but I was unable to find a publisher. Later still, I wrote two thrillers which suffered the same fate. One was about a master criminal in India, which Mr Gollancz nearly accepted. The second was based on a visit to French West Africa that Victor Sassoon and I made in 1949. The failure of these books depressed me a little for, while I was writing them, I saw myself as a best-seller and all my financial problems solved.

Yet another novel, which Victor liked very much, though I never dared submit it to a more exacting critic, was about a girl—it really was—who became a prostitute for twenty-four hours and sold her favours to four different men, one of whom gave her syphilis. She had it very badly, it affected her brain and she was sent to an asylum. She escaped and devoted herself to tracking down her former lovers and, as she did not know which of them was responsible for her disease, murdered them all one by one. The series of crimes was naturally baffling to the police, for there was no apparent motive for them and nothing to link them together.

The discovery of penicillin has taken most of the kick out of stories about syphilis, and in any case I have now lost the manuscript.

The Baiga brought me many new friends, chief of whom was W. G. (Bill) Archer. The popular notion in India about the Indian Civil Service, that its members were stiff and arrogant, is not altogether correct. It also included some of the most friendly, sensitive and intelligent people you could meet anywhere, people like Bill himself or N. R. Pillai, V. Viswanathan (now Home Secretary), J. H. Hutton, the present Governor of Assam, and others whom I describe elsewhere in this book.

Shortly after the *The Baiga* was published, Bill wrote inviting me to Bihar. He was then Census Superintendent for the

Province and Shamrao and I went to stay with him and had the opportunity of touring in many Uraon, Munda, Ho and Asur villages. Later, when Bill was Deputy Commissioner of the Santal Parganas, I toured widely with him there and, later still, made a number of visits to the Santal and Uraon villages. These experiences enriched my book on the Murias and my first book on tribal art.

On this first visit I had the opportunity of meeting Sarat Chandra Roy, the veteran philanthropologist who not only wrote a whole series of books on the Bihar tribes but fought valiantly for the people both in the courts and outside. After his death Bill Archer and I, with the help of his son Romesh, took over the journal *Man in India,* which we edited for a number of years.

V

Lying to the south of what was then the Central Provinces was the State of Bastar, a territory the size of Belgium. The great plain of Chhattisgarh stretches down past Raipur and Dhamtari in hot and dusty monotony till it spends itself against the hills of Kanker. Thenceforward the journey is a never-failing delight ; as the traveller moves towards the Bastar plateau the countryside breaks into song about him ; he is greeted by hardy smiling woodmen singing at their work ; the skyline is broken by fantastic piles of rock ; all around is the evergreen sal forest. Presently he sees looming up before him a row of sharply-rising hills, the sentinels that stand on guard before the country of the Murias, and the long steep ascent of the Keskal Ghat has to be essayed. From the summit there is a magnificent view of the great sea of hill and forest below.

I was first attracted to Bastar by the late Sir W. V. Grigson, known to his friends as Frittles, one of the greatest men who has concerned himself with tribal problems in India, a witty, charming and faithful friend. From quite early days he had not allowed his attitude to me to be influenced by police reports. in the first place, I too had been to Oxford, and in the second, I shared his enthusiasm for all things tribal. He was

Administrator of Bastar from 1927 to 1931 and wrote a book about it called *The Maria Gonds of Bastar.* I first read this book in Frittles' own house when I was laid up with fever and was so excited by it that my temperature rose appreciably. It was, however, a long time before I had the opportunity or money to make any serious study of the Bastar tribes. In the earlier years the local Administrator was not at all favourable to my paying a visit to the State for fear that I would start a Congress rebellion, but ultimately he was persuaded to allow Shamrao and myself to make a short visit, when we drove about the State and saw as much as we could from the roadside.

Later, I took the late Mrs Marguerite Milward the sculptress there—she has described her visit in her book *Artist in Tribal India.*

Marguerite had studied in Paris under Bourdelle and she worked with him for many years. Her first visit abroad was in his company to Ceylon where she began her studies in the sculpture of primitive peoples, to which she devoted the better part of her life. She visited Tibet, Burma, Java, north-west Africa, French Indo-China as well as India for this purpose and used sometimes to lecture on anthropology. One of her sayings was that 'art unites where politics divide'. The Indian Government bought a number of her heads and they may still be seen in the Indian Museum in Calcutta. One beautiful head, however, of a Gond girl, which she made during her visit to us and which formerly stood in the window of India House in London, she gave to me shortly before her death in her eightieth year.

Marguerite, who was a most engaging person but of enormous size, along with her cases of cement and clay, was altogether too much for our old car and as we were passing through Kanker everything fell out through the bottom and we had to send to Jagdalpur to be rescued.

Finally, in May 1940, I went to Bastar with the idea of doing something really serious, and I was actually given an official appointment, that of Census Officer, which paid a monthly salary of a hundred rupees. Even at that time I was hardly educated in the ways of the world and was not aware that both one's travelling allowance and the respect in which one was held in official India depended almost entirely on one's pay. When I got to Bastar, however, Norval Mitchell, a very good type, who had then taken charge and gave me all possible support, changed this extraordinary arrangement and paid me a lump sum of 1,500 rupees for my work on the Census. Of course, all I wanted was some kind of official status without which in those days it was difficult to do any work in an Indian State. Later we again changed the arrangement and I became Hon. Ethnographer to Bastar. A local paper, boggling at the word 'ethnographer', announced that I had been appointed Hon. Stenographer.

My idea was to follow my usual technique and settle down among the people. We built a lovely little house of stone (which cost only 200 rupees) opposite the stupendous and beautiful Falls of Chitrakot and made small huts, quite habitable, at 40 rupees each, in two Muria villages. Our main centre continued to be at Patangarh, where Shamrao held the fort while I was away.

At that time Bastar was entirely delightful. The tribal people were poor but they were free and happy. There was a quality of enthusiasm and zest in their lives. Their dances were amongst some of the finest in India and they had not been corrupted by Puritan workers into a belief that their beautiful bodies were something to be ashamed of.

I travelled all over the State and collected a lot of notes and photographs of the Hill Marias of the Abujhmar whom we visited on elephants, the Koyas, Bhattras, Dorlas and others. But my main interest was in two of the tribes—the Bison-Horn Marias of the south and the Murias of the north. I did a book on the Marias called *Maria Murder and Suicide,* trying to discover what it was that drove these simple people to homicide, and I also studied the conditions in the Jagdalpur jail which I tried to get improved.

Of all the tribes I have studied, I found the Marias the most attractive and field-work among them the most comfortable and pleasant. The Bison-Horn Maria area was even in 1941 accessible in the open season by car, and every village had a well-built rest-house for visitors. The people were friendly, the climate was excellent, and I enjoyed my years there enormously.

It was in Bastar that I first began to use the gramophone as a means of breaking down barriers and creating a friendly atmosphere. I got some excellent Hindi comic records and also used to play a little Mozart and Beethoven which, I am sorry to say, did not go down very well.

And then, in the middle of one of my tours, a young man suddenly arrived in camp with a very large box, which had been sent up from Jagdalpur by the police. When we opened it we found it full of superb mechanical toys sent by two friends in Bombay. These toys must have given more pleasure over a wider area than any collection of toys that was ever made. Some of them lasted for eight years and I took one or two, their well-worn mechanisms still ticking over, with me on expeditions in NEFA. They were certainly a great help in making contact with the Marias.

Yet normally, anything unusual was dangerous. The Marias were very suspicious, for example, of the Census. They recalled that after the 1931 Census many tigers had appeared in the forest. It is always risky to count and measure, for 'the sin of numbering the people' may reduce fertility. So after the 1941 Census, in most villages, the house number-boards were carried out and sacrifices of pigs were made before them.

The Marias were a tough and rather formidable tribe, with a very high incidence of homicide, six times that of the neighbouring Central Provinces. The jail at Jagdalpur was always crowded with Marias serving sentences for murder. The administration was worried about this, and I offered to try and discover why it was. I was given the freedom of the Record Room and here, after turning over a great number of dusty files, I found a hundred that gave me the sort of information I wanted. I also wanted suicide records, but these were not so easy to come by, for they were not kept at headquarters but in the local police-stations. But the Superintendent of Police called in all the suicide files, and I was able to find fifty about the Marias.

Having collected the records I mapped out the villages where anything had happened and visited as many as I could. I talked to the relatives of the murderers and of their victims, got the opinions of village elders, studied the attitude of the other villagers, and frequently met the actual individuals who had served their term (for the death sentence was very rarely imposed) and had now returned home.

This was an extraordinarily interesting job. In Aranpur I stood beside the still warm ashes of the ritually-cremated clothes of Barse Chewa, who had recently been hanged in jail. At Khutepal, I watched Oyami's children playing on the very floor once stained by the blood of his murdered wife. In Rewali I was visited by a ferocious-looking youth, who had twice stood trial for his life and had twice preserved it.

Here too I talked with another youth who, in a fit of jealousy, had killed his wife and now—not unnaturally—found it hard to get another. In Doriras I saw the grave of the murdered Boti which had been desecrated by the Ghasias for the sake of the purse of money which had been buried to help the ghost on his journey to the other world. In the same village I visited the home of Kawasi Borga, then serving a life-sentence, and talked to his fine sons and his sad pathetic wife.

An analysis of the reasons and motives for these murders was revealing. Quarrels over property accounted for 15 per cent; family quarrels for 16 per cent; jealousy, infidelity, sex motives in general, for 17 per cent. Nineteen per cent were more or less trivial crimes committed when drunk. Only five per cent were caused by the suspicion or accusation of witchcraft and sorcery. There were six murders committed for revenge, and nine out of resentment at abuse or 'word-magic'. This last is an important and curious motive: to use the wrong kind of words may be a very risky thing, being not only insulting to the feelings but dangerous (magically) to the person.

One of the things which was a revelation, not only to me, but also (I have been told) to more than one Sessions Judge, was the discovery of the part played by fatigue in promoting acts of violence. There can be a sort of fatigue-intoxication, not unlike that caused at a certain stage by alcohol. Fatigue can cause dejection and irritability, worry, desperation and a desire to escape from a situation which seems intolerable. And the Marias, like other peasants, often get very tired. They return home in the evening; supper is not ready, the child is crying, and in a flash there is a blow and a dearly-loved wife is dead and a home is ruined.

I spent many hours in the Jagdalpur jail, talking to Maria prisoners, and what struck me most was the remarkable innocence of many of them. They felt that an inexplicable destiny had overtaken them. They did not feel like criminals ; in many cases their crimes were no more than tragic accidents. They were a very sad company.

I first became interested in prisons in the Satyagraha days when I made emphatic protest about the treatment of political prisoners. Then, later, my experiences with the police in Mandla gave me almost a horror of their methods and of the whole idea of punishment and retribution in the treatment of crime.

The descent of the police on a tribal village is a dreadful thing. For days the entire community is kept from its work and often has difficulty even in getting anything to eat. How often we watched it happen! The Sub-Inspector arrived and made his camp in the best house in the village. He and his constables had to be provided free of charge with food and drink of a kind that the people themselves could only afford at great festivals. Third-degree methods were often used before and, I am sorry to say, even after Independence to obtain evidence. No one felt safe. For days the shy and timid tribal people were distracted by anxiety. Large sums of money secretly changed hands and when the final arrest was made it was a heart-rending sight to watch the prisoner in his handcuffs escorted to the boundary of the village by a crowd of weeping relations.

I had the opportunity of visiting a number of prisons and seeing how the tribal people fared, and in Bastar my interest developed greatly. Dramatic incidents still further impressed on me the importance of revising our methods of investigation as well as our treatment of criminals. A girl in a village near Sanhrwachhapar was accused of poisoning her husband. The accepted routine was followed and though the villagers were convinced, as I was, that she was innocent—and villagers are seldom wrong about this sort of thing—she was arrested and sent to jail where she was capitally convicted. We did not think that there was any real danger of her being hanged, but one day I received a telegram from Frittles Grigson telling me that if nothing was done she would be hanged within a very short time. I have never driven a car so fast in my life as when I made the three-hundred-mile journey up to Pachmarhi, where the Government was having its summer session, in the hope of obtaining a reprieve. When I arrived I was told that it was too late. But I persevered and in the end succeeded in saving the girl's life, and she was reprieved to the terrible mercy of life-imprisonment.

On one of my visits to jail, I saw, and can still see, two young Gonds in handcuffs for murdering a Pathan moneylender who had driven them to the despair of hopeless poverty. With great eyes filled with bewilderment and fear, like frightened and beautiful deer of the forest, the two little Gonds were surrounded by enormous constables.

The tribesmen suffer out of all proportion in jail. 'If a Maria is sentenced to a long term of imprisonment,' says Grigson, 'he will beg to be hanged rather than be confined within walls: and few of the wilder Bison-horn Marias survive long imprisonment.' The grim forbidding walls, the stone beds, the rule of silence, the unfamiliar food and language, the attitude of suppliant and obsequious deference before officials, the absence of recreations, the lack of religious comfort, the denial of human companionship, the appalling monotony oppress and crush them.

This is particularly true of the frontier areas. The NEFA tribesman, who is taken down from the mountains and sent to prison in the plains, suffers, in addition to the inevitable sense of isolation, the affront to human dignity, the loneliness and despair that afflict all prisoners, special deprivations. The heat of the plains is almost unbearable to a hillman. It is probable that no one knows his language. He himself may only have a few words of Hindi or Assamese. In some cases tribal prisoners have been in jail for years without hearing a word of their families and they are too far away from them for visits.

Some of us have been very keen to have a special jail for our tribal people, which will be a place of healing and restoration and where the whole idea of punishment and revenge will be banished. It is, however, extraordinary how even today many officials think in very different terms. 'They put on weight while they are with us,' a Jail Superintendent told me. 'They do not feel things as we do,' said another, and many people have urged that even in the worst jail a tribal convict has a better time than at home.

There was a theory about the threshold of pain which was supposed to be higher among 'savages' than the civilized. In other words, if you pricked a bishop and a Maria at the same moment, it would be the bishop who jumped first. He was more delicate: it would hurt him more. I don't believe a word of it.

I have always felt ashamed that I did not manage to go to jail as a Satyagrahi but, as I have explained earlier, the British Government would not have given me this privilege: they would simply have deported me. When I was in Jagdalpur I did discuss with the Administrator whether I could somehow go as an ordinary prisoner into the prison there, but he thought it would be difficult to ensure that the local magistrate would not give me a sentence rather too long for scientific purposes.

VI

The Marias

The most memorable thing about the Marias is their superb marriage-dance when the men, wearing great headdresses of bison-horns and carrying their long drums, move in a large circle, while a row of women thread their way among them. It is probably the finest dance in tribal India.

One day a young Maria called Alami Mata returned home from the forest to find that the splendid horns and feathers of his hereditary dance outfit had been stolen. This was something more than the loss of a precious possession. In a neighbouring village was a beautiful girl, unmarried and growing to love him; Alami was wooing her in the dance, and indeed in his magnificent headdress, shaking his horns and prancing before his love like a young bison, he must have been hard to resist. But now, like Samson shorn of his hair, there was no strength in him; how could he go to meet his girl in the mean and undistinguished attire that was left to him?

An Agaria bringing ore from a pit

Muria cheliks of Bastar

As he stood brooding on his tragedy, his father came in and abused him roughly for wasting time. It was too much for the boy ; life without music, love or rhythm was not worth living, and he went out and hanged himself.

This incident illustrates the attachment of the Marias to their great dance and to the finery which adorns it. The headdress of bison-horns is the chief treasure of a Maria home. It is kept with the utmost care, dismantled, in closed bamboo baskets, and it takes nearly an hour to assemble.

This headdress, and the dance, is the sole expression of the Marias' aesthetic sensibility. They do not carve, or paint, or model images on their walls ; they do not, like their neighbours, the Murias, make attractive combs and tobacco-holders. Everything they have to say goes into the dance.

And what a superb spectacle they created! The women were less elaborately attired than the men, but they too were clothed in their own beauty, which was emphasized by the mass of bead and brass necklaces that almost covered the breasts, and the snoods and fillets of shining brass about their heads. I believe that officials have now taught them to put on white saris and cover themselves 'properly'.

The men, carrying their long drums, move in a great circle with a large variety of turns and changes ; the 'bison' charge and fight each other, pick up leaves on the point of their horns, and chase the girl dancers.

The girls, each with a dancing-stick in her right hand, form a long line and go round and through the men dancers with many different movements and steps. They do not usually sing, and indeed the tune would be lost in the thunder of the drums. As they go, they beat the ground with their sticks, 'dum-dum-dum, di-dum, dum-dum'. Masked mummers, clowns dressed in straw, naked acrobats carrying clubs, wooden guns and nets, add to the gaiety of the scene.

To witness this dance was an unforgettable experience. 'Whosoever danceth not, knoweth not the way of life,' and conversely these people, for all their poverty, found in the supreme ecstatic rhythm of their dance a way of life that raised them above mediocrity into a kind of splendour.

VII

The Murias

But my most important work in Bastar was to study the ghotul, the unique dormitory-club of the Muria boys and girls. The Murias live to the north of the Marias, all over a very large wooded plateau, in substantial villages many of which could, even in my day, be reached by car. The climate was good, the people friendly and responsive, the country was easy—and the whole business was exciting and interesting and new.

At this time the Murias enjoyed almost entire freedom. Once I was off the main road and away from the few administrative centres, I hardly ever saw an official. The people lived their own life, unhampered if unimproved, and they lived it well. But what I shall say about them is a part of history now and I must write in the past tense.

The ghotul was the central focus of Muria life, coming down to modern times from Lingo, the heroic ancestor of the tribe, who founded it.

The first ghotul is described as beautiful as the horns of bison, beautiful as a horse's throat. Its central pillar was a python, its poles were cobras. The frame of the roof was made of kraits tied together with vipers and covered with the tails of peacocks. The roof of the veranda was made of bulbul feathers. The walls were of fish-bones, the door was fashioned of crimson flowers, the door-frames were the bones of ogres. The floor was plastered with pulse. The seats were crocodiles.

The lord of the house wore a turban like a white gourd-flower ; his dhoti was coloured silk ; his shirt shone in the sun ; his clogs were made of sandalwood, his stockings of mongoose fur, his belt was a long thin snake ; as he walked he sparkled. In his hand he carried the eighteen instruments of music, heavy with the charms of love.

Such is the legendary picture of Lingo and the first ghotul.

Similar institutions are widely distributed among communities of the Austro-Asiatic cultures, but it seems probable that the Muria ghotul was one of the most highly developed and carefully organized in the world. For what was a village guardroom for the Nagas, a boys' club among the Uraons, a refuge for temporary sexual association in Indonesia, was for the Murias the centre of social and religious life. For although the ghotul was an independent autonomous children's republic, it had an all-pervading influence on the grown-ups, who could not manage any social function without its help.

All the unmarried boys and girls of the tribe had to be members of the ghotul. This membership was elaborately organized; after a period of probation, boys and girls were initiated and given special titles which carried with them graded ranks and social duties. Leaders were appointed to lead and discipline the society; the boys' leader was often called the Sirdar: the girls' leader was the Belosa. Boy members were known as cheliks and girls as motiaris.

The cheliks and motiaris had important duties to perform on all social occasions. The boys acted as acolytes at festivals, the girls as bridesmaids at weddings. They danced together before the clan-gods and at great fairs. They formed a choir at the funerals of important people. Their games and dances enlivened and enriched village life and redeemed it from that crushing monotony which was its normal characteristic in other parts of India.

It was natural that the ghotul, 'dear nurse of arts', should foster every kind of art, for here the boys and girls were all the time on their toes to attract one another and to make life what they believed it should be, beautiful, lively and interesting. And so the boys made and decorated charming little combs for their girls, and elaborate tobacco-boxes for themselves; the girls made necklaces, pendants and belts of beads and cowries. The boys carved the pillars and doors of their ghotul building, which was often the finest house in a village. They made exciting toys and masks. And above all they danced.

But this is common to many other cultures. What gave the ghotul its unique interest was the approved and recognized relationship between the boys and girls.

There were two types of ghotul. In the first, and probably the oldest, which was sometimes called the 'yoking' ghotul, the rule was that of fidelity to a single partner during the whole of the pre-marital period. Each chelik was paired off with a motiari; he was formally 'married' to her and she took the feminine form of his title as her own. Divorce was allowed, though 'infidelity' was punished.

In the second type of ghotul, which was probably a later development of the classic model, any kind of lasting attachment between chelik and motiari was forbidden. No one could say that such and such a motiari was *his* girl; his attachment was rationed to three days at a time.

Although outwardly both types of ghotul were the same and often only the most careful investigation could distinguish them, the customs and atmosphere of the modern type were entirely distinct. Here everything was arranged to prevent long-drawn intense attachments, to eliminate jealousy and possessiveness, to deepen the sense of communal property and action. There was no ghotul marriage, there were no ghotul partners. 'Everyone belonged to everyone else' in the very spirit of *Brave New World*. A chelik and motiari might sleep together for three nights; after that they were warned; if they persisted they were punished. If a boy showed any signs of possessiveness for a particular girl, if his face fell when he saw her making love to someone else, if he got annoyed at her sleeping with another chelik, should he be offended if she refused to massage him and went to someone else, he was forcibly reminded by his fellows that she was not his wife, he had no right over her, she was the property of the whole ghotul, and if he looked like that he would be punished.

This was sometimes called the 'changing ring' ghotul; because in it you changed from girl to girl just as you changed your rings from finger to finger.

The ghotul was very literally a night-club; it was only in the evening that there was 'a noise in the belly of the elephant'; during the day, except on festivals, it was deserted. The real life of the ghotul was in the firelight.

At any time after supper, the cheliks began to assemble. They came one by one, carrying their sleeping-mats and perhaps their drums. The little boys brought their daily 'tribute' of wood, 'clocked in' by showing it to the official responsible and threw it in a corner. The elder boys gathered round the fire; one took a half-smoked leaf-pipe from his turban and ignited it by placing a bit of glowing wood in the cup, another played a few notes on his flute, a third spread his mat and lay down. The Kotwar inspected the buildings to see if the girls had done their work properly. Gradually all the boys assembled.

Then the girls came in, with a rush, all together, and gathered round their own fire. After a while they scattered, some sitting with the boys, others singing in a corner, some lying down.

The others occupied the time in pleasant harmony; sometimes they danced for an hour or two; the smaller children played rampageous games; sometimes they just sat round the fire and talked; in the hot weather on a moonlit night they scattered all about the compound. Often they sang lying down, two by two, chelik with motiari, or in little groups. A boy told a story; they asked riddles; they reported on the affairs of the day; there was sometimes a ghotul trial; they planned a dancing expedition or allotted duties at a wedding. I shall never forget the sight in some of the larger ghotuls of sixty or seventy youngsters thus engaged.

After an hour or two of dancing, singing, games or story-telling, certainly not much after ten o'clock, the serious business of the evening began. The little boys went round saluting their elders, a ritual then repeated by the girls. One of them distributed finely-powdered tobacco from the ghotul store, to which all the parents contributed. Then the girls each went to her partner of the day and sat down behind him. First of all, she shook out and arranged his hair and then combed it. When this was done, she massaged him, sometimes with oilseed, sometimes rubbing his back with her comb, and then she cracked his fingers one by one.

By then it was fairly late and the boys and girls prepared to sleep. The little boys and girls slept in long rows, while those who had permanent or temporary partners lay down with them in each other's arms on their sleeping-mats.

Every night, when everything had warmed up, there came a moment when I had to leave the ghotul. I would have given almost anything to have stayed on, to have traced (having watched the process of tumescence) the story to its end, even if only as an observer. But the rules were very definite and I knew that if I broke them even once my chances of obtaining information might be lost. So I always went away to my cold and comfortless camp, nostalgic for the happy, exciting world I left behind.

In the very early morning the Belosa got up and went round the ghotul rousing her girls. They had to be out of the building before dawn. 'They leave early', a boy told me, 'because they come laughing from the arms of the cheliks and feel shy about it.'

At least at the time I knew them, the Murias had a simple, innocent and natural attitude to sex. In the ghotul this was strengthened by the absence of any sense of guilt and the general freedom from external interference. The Murias believed that sexual congress was a good thing ; it did you good ; it was healthy and beautiful ; when performed by the right people (such as a chelik and motiari who were not taboo to one another), at the right time (outside the menstrual period and avoiding forbidden days), and in the right place (within the ghotul walls where no 'sin' could be committed), it was the happiest and best thing in life.

This belief in sex as something good and normal gave the Murias a light touch. Their saying that the young lovers were *hassi ki nat,* in a 'joking relationship' to each other, expressed their attitude exactly. Sex was great fun ; it was the best of ghotul games ; it was the dance of enraptured bodies ; it was an ecstatic swinging in the arms of the beloved. It ought not to be too intense ; it must not be degraded by possessiveness or defiled by jealousy. It was believed that the best and most successful sex relations were to be had in the modern ghotul where partners often changed.

All this was, of course, very shocking to the conventionally-minded. Yet there is much to be said on the Murias' side. In the first place the cheliks and motiaris were wonderfully happy. Their life was full, interesting, exciting, useful. The ghotul was, as they often said, 'a little school'. The cheliks were 'like Boy Scouts', as I was told in a village which had a troop in the local school. There was no comparison between these children and the sad-eyed, dirty ragamuffins of villages at a similar cultural level elsewhere. In the ghotul the children were taught lessons of cleanliness, discipline and hard work that remained with them throughout their lives. They were taught to take a pride in their appearance, to respect themselves and their elders; above all, they were taught the spirit of service. These boys and girls worked very hard indeed for the public good. They were immediately available for the service of State officials or for labour on the roads. They had to be ready to work at a wedding or a funeral. They had to attend to the drudgery of festivals. In most tribal villages of the Central Provinces the children were slack, dirty, undisciplined and with no sense of public spirit. The Murias were very different.

With all this the missionary or social reformer would be in agreement. 'But', they would say, 'that is not the point. Our complaint is that these boys and girls sleep together.' It was at least one point in their favour that this sleeping together did not seem to do them a great deal of harm. There were no signs of corruption or excess; these bright-eyed, merry-faced boys and girls did not give you the impression of being the victims of debasing lust. They were living a life of fulfilment and it seemed to do them good.

They did (perhaps they still do) sleep together, but under conditions of discipline and some restraint. Children in other tribal villages also have sexual congress but without discipline and restraint. The tribal and semi-tribal boys whom I knew for so many years in other parts of central India all too often began their sexual life before the age of twelve and indulged in it freely till they were married and after. It is notorious that venereal disease has long been rampant throughout tribal India, and some of the most pathetic sights I have seen have been cases of young boys and girls afflicted by it. I have no hesitation in saying that for the areas that I know intimately, there was more sexual excess among young people in ordinary villages than in ghotul villages.

Another interesting and curious point is that there were few people with a stronger sense of domestic morality and conjugal fidelity than the Muria. Adultery was very rare, and was visited with supernatural punishment when it did occur. You could not find happier or more united families. One of the reasons for this was that the ghotul system discouraged the custom of child-marriage which was then rapidly spreading through tribal

India. Among romantically-minded tribal people, child-marriage means, inevitably, domestic infidelity. Boys or girls find themselves tied to partners in whom they have no interest and naturally leave them and seek others. Another reason for this remarkable fidelity among the Murias was that in many ghotuls boys and girls were 'married' and were taught the necessity of fidelity to their partners. In the other type of ghotul, they grew up from their earliest years to believe that, though change is the mark of the unmarried, stability must characterize the married. Once a girl was in your *haq* or 'right' she must stay there and you must stay with her.

Now one of the drawbacks of semi-tribal India is domestic infidelity. Divorce is universal, elopement common, adultery an everyday affair. The ghotul villages have a much higher standard in this respect. The incidence of divorce in Bastar was under 3 per cent. An examination of 50 marriages in Patangarh showed 23 divorces or 46 per cent.

We may also consider how the ghotul boys and girls were almost completely free from those furtive and unpleasant vices that so mar our modern civilization. There was hardly any masturbation ; where it was practised, it was due to the mistaken efforts of reformers to improve the ghotul. Prostitution was unknown, unthinkable. No motiari would ever give her body for money.

The village dormitory is a symptom of a certain stage of cultural development. We ourselves consider that we have outgrown it ; we may grow into it again. In the days when I shared the free and happy life of the Murias I used sometimes to wonder whether I was a hundred years behind the times or a hundred years ahead. I do not suggest that we should replace the Public Schools by ghotuls and turn our own children into cheliks and motiaris, but I do suggest that there are elements in ghotul life and teaching which we should do well to ponder and that an infection of the Muria spirit would do few of us any harm.

The message of the ghotul—that youth must be served, that freedom and happiness are more to be treasured than any material gain, that friendliness and sympathy, hospitality and unity are of the first importance, and above all that human love—and its physical expression—is beautiful, clean and precious, is typically Indian. The ghotul is no Austro-Asiatic alien in the Indian scene. Here was the atmosphere of the best old India ; here was something of the life (though on a humble scale) portrayed at Ajanta ; here was something (though now altogether human) of the Krishna legend and its ultimate significance ; this was the same life, the same tradition that inspired the Pahari paintings.

I wrote a big book of over 750 pages, *The Muria and their Ghotul,* about all this, studying first the whole life of the tribe and then going on to describe in great detail the life in the ghotul itself.

At the beginning of the book, I put three fine quotations. The first was from St Paul—'Unto the pure, all things are pure ; but unto them that are defiled and unbelieving is nothing pure ; but even their mind and conscience is defiled.'

The second quotation was from Hirschfeld: 'For thousands of years human folly has overwhelmed love with debris, pelted love with filth. To liberate love from this is to restore that vital human value which among all human values stands supreme.'

And the third was from Westermarck: 'The concealment of truth is the only indecorum known to science ; and to keep anything secret within its cold and passionless expanse would be as prudish as to throw a cloth round a naked statue.'

Even supported by this, I was not sure how the book would be received in India but in fact it was taken very well. A Bombay publisher tried hard to persuade me to put my discoveries of Baiga, Muria and other tribal intimate relations into *A Sexual Life of Tribal India,* but I resisted this, for my aim was never to titillate the reader's fancy, but to make a serious contribution to sexual knowledge, and this could only be done by regarding sex as a part of life as a whole: it could not be described in isolation, at least not by me.

My book was translated into French by Dr A. Bigot, a friend with whom I have often corresponded but never met, as *Maisons des Jeunes chez les Muria* and published by Gallimard. By this time, the English version had been long out of print and when an Italian translation was proposed, we could not find a copy and had to supply the publishers in Rome with the French version. This was actually an advantage since Dr Bigot had abridged the original and made a much more serviceable book. Descriptions of the *comportement sexuel* of the Murias go better in French than in English.

VIII

In December 1942 I paid my first visit to Orissa. The Darbars of the Bonai, Keonjhar and Pal Lahara States, at the suggestion of Norval Mitchell who had by then moved on to take charge of the Eastern States Agency, invited me to tour in the tribal areas of these States, inquire into the life and habits of the people and make reçommendations towards the solution of the problem of shifting-cultivation which was very widespread there at this time.

In view of the fact that it is frequently said that the British Government never took any interest in the tribal people, it is only fair to give my terms of reference, which incidentally give a programme for the philanthropologist.

Mr Elwin's task would be to show how best the people could be led away from shifting-cultivation into the settled life of the permanent cultivator after inquiring into their social, religious, economic, and physical conditions. In other words, the expert knowledge of an anthropologist would be added to the expert knowledge of Forest Officers. He would consider what elements of aboriginal life and culture should be preserved, and what should be regarded as anti-social. He should after his inquiry be in a position to advise what should be done to recompense and console aboriginals for the loss of their shifting-cultivation, with particular attention to arts and crafts, to see whether those could be preserved and developed in both the cultural and economic interest of the people. He would observe any other relevant features of aboriginal life, such as their need of medical services or education. The final result would be a full picture of the problem in all its aspects, which might be summed up as technical and humanitarian, against the background of which future policy and orders could be framed.

My charter of duties was once expressed more succinctly by another, very liberal, British official, who said, 'Your job is to make such a damned nuisance of yourself that we shall be forced to help your people.'

I found this tour, in the course of which I had some bad attacks of fever but was assisted by a couple of elephants, extremely interesting and I think my Report was useful. But this was the only time in all these years that I was met with opposition and for a very curious reason—that the villagers thought I had come to stop shifting-cultivation and rob them of their land whereas my Report actually made very different recommendations.

All sorts of rumours went about. An English official had gone with the Forest Adviser to the Bhuiya Pirh the previous year and the villagers believed that they were pursuing two European fugitives supposed to be hiding in the hills. Popular rumour had it that I myself was seeking to establish a place of refuge in the event of a Japanese invasion. In Bonai a belief that we were exporting girls 'for the war' meant that I hardly ever saw a woman who was not over military age. In the wilder Juang hills of Keonjhar, though some of the people remembered the former Administrator Macmillan (a popular, and then almost legendary, figure who married a Bhuiya girl), many had never seen a white face before and, believing me to be an evil spirit, fled into the jungle with shrill cries of horror and amazement.

But these suspicions soon disappeared and before long, specially in Pal Lahara and among the Juangs, there was a very friendly atmosphere—to which our elephants and Kumar, then a small baby, largely contributed. I soon found myself being called the 'Rusi Sahib'—Rusi being the name of the ancient cult-hero of the tribe. And once friendly, the Juangs were almost embarrassing in their attentions. They were full of interest about my way of life, invading the tent at all times, and even peeping into my bathroom (a very small leaf-hut) to study my techniques. Indeed, I often felt as if I was a museum specimen and the Juangs members of an ethnological committee investigating a creature of the absurdest habits!

One morning an aeroplane hummed distantly overhead. 'Do you see that?' said a Juang friend, 'It is Victoria Rani come for an inspection of her Raj, to see how it is getting on.' If she was really in the plane, I thought, and could see what was happening to her Empire today, she would probably fall out. But it started a discussion about aeroplanes. Somebody thought they ran on very thin wires stretched across the sky. Someone else suggested that there were men in them, special kind of men who did not eat ordinary food, but lived on air. The Saoras told us later that aeroplanes diffused a noxious vapour which gave fever to the children in the villages over which they passed.

This conversation illustrates how unusually out of touch with things were the Juangs, whom Dalton called 'the most primitive people I have ever met with or read of'.

At that time a visit to the Juang country was fascinating. The country was wild and beautiful. The journeys continually surprised us with the splendour of the landscape, and the palm-girt flat lands round darling Malyagiri, whose rocks caught the sun in ever-changing shades of colour, were unforgettable. In early December, the country had special charm, for all the hills were carpeted with fields of yellow sarson.

Two things about the Juangs stirred me very deeply. One was their poverty, the other their grace and beauty as displayed in their 'animal ballet'. To see a typical Juang village one had to go to the highest uplands of Keonjhar. Here were some of the most picturesque hamlets in peninsular India, comparable only to the enchanting Bondo villages of the Koraput Hills. Each village stood self-contained within a large fence in a site chosen not only for convenience but also for beauty. The houses, little huts of mud with red walls, were either in a huddle on top of one another or neatly arranged in narrow streets. Near by were well-kept sheds for goats and cattle. In the centre of the village was an open space used for a dancing-ground in front of the often imposing village dormitory or club, the Darbar, where the unmarried youths slept and the elders assembled on all important occasions. The people were comparatively prosperous.

The Juangs of Pal Lahara presented a melancholy contrast to those of Keonjhar. In the second decade of the present century, the forest round the slopes of Malyagiri was reserved and the Juangs suddenly found themselves cut off from their normal means of livelihood. They were given cattle and land in villages at the foot of the mountains, but they could not take to the unfamiliar plough, wild elephants destroyed the crops, and the cattle, 'which were old and decrepit', died in a year or two. The Juangs swiftly fell into the position of landless serfs in economic bondage to their neighbours, got more and more into debt, lost their fields and, when I saw them, were making a miserable living by weaving baskets—one of the most pitifully unremunerative of India's village industries. A man could make one large basket a day and got half an anna for it. He paid eight annas a year, or the equivalent of sixteen days' work, for the privilege of taking bamboo from the forest he regarded as his.

The economic condition of these Juangs was deplorable. I shall not easily forget going by night into a Juang village and seeing old women, naked but for a single rag about the loins, lying on the bare ground and trying to get a little warmth from a flickering fire. The physique of the people was poor and they were very diseased; the fine hard struggle with wild Nature in Keonjhar developed muscle and strength—but in Pal Lahara basket-making was a sedentary craft.

Even worse than their economic decay was their complete religious and cultural collapse. Gone were the fine Darbar halls, with their often remarkable carvings, of the Keonjhar Hills. Gone were the stone pillars to the village goddess. Since they had lost their own land, the Juangs themselves were unable to offer worship or sacrifice to their gods; they had to call in (and pay for) outside priests and magicians to help them. The beautifully fashioned combs, the elaborate smoker's equipment, the gay necklaces, which were so marked a feature of Keonjhar Juang life, were hardly known here.

The Juangs of Pal Lahara were the worst possible advertisement for a policy of stopping axe-cultivation or of moving people down to the plains. They underlined everything that the most captious critics have said against the forest administration. They were a pitiful instance of what happens when highlanders are dislodged from their mountains.

The traditional dress of Juang women was a mass of bead ornaments round the neck and a skirt of leaves fastened about the waist by a girdle of bugles of baked earth. This dress was established in the tribe's mythology and hedged about with the sanctions of religion.

The year 1871 was a bad one for the tribal people. In central India British officials were forcing the Baigas to commit the sin of lacerating the breasts of Mother Earth with the plough, thus throwing them into a psychological confusion from which they have never fully recovered. In Orissa other officials were persuading the Juangs to change their costume. A meeting was held and some two thousand pieces of cloth were distributed, after which the leaves were gathered in a heap and burnt. 'Persuasion' continued and a majority of Juangs took to putting on filthy rags instead of the beautiful and hygienic leaf-dress.

The futility of introducing the outward garb of civilization without doing anything to instil its spirit is seen in the effect this had on the Juangs, who still look back to the day when the sacred leaves were burnt as a conquered nation might recall the day of its defeat.

Since that time, the Juangs say, Sat—the spirit of truth and religion, the power to live safely in a world of hostile magic—has left the tribe. Tigers attack the cattle with impunity and the offended earth gives but a scanty crop.

This may seem odd today but to force improvement on very simple people without at the same time having an adequate programme of development to make their lives fuller, richer and happier can be disastrous and I was deeply disturbed by what I saw in the Juang hills and wrote strongly about it.

I have spoken of the extraordinary aesthetic experience of a genuine dance of the Juangs in the old style.

Long ago Dalton wrote splendidly about their 'animal ballet', and the dances which I saw again and again in 1943 were very like those he saw in 1866. Some of the women were still wearing their leaf-dress all the time, and they all put it on for ceremonial and special occasions. I do not know whether the custom still remains or how far they are maintaining their traditional ballet today, for one of the saddest things about the march of civilization into the forests is the way it kills so many forms of artistic expression. But when I saw it, the dancing was still adept and beautiful beyond words. The bright green leaves threw into relief the golden-brown bodies of the girls, whose beauty was so gracefully displayed. I specially remember the peacock and deer dances when the girls moved with the grace of the loveliest of all the creatures of the forest. They imitated the elephant and the vulture well too, and when they squatted on the ground like quails to peck up their food their movements were as characteristic as they were rhythmical.

At the end of my expedition, I wrote—among many other things: 'Today the Juangs are a small and impoverished tribe ; they demand great sympathy and knowledge for their administration. They live in forests capable of yielding great wealth ; surely some portion of that wealth should be made available to them so that they can enjoy fuller and happier lives.' It is only now that this is being done and, even now, I hope it is being done properly.

Christoph von Fürer-Haimendorf, always a most successful explorer, had paid a visit to the Gadabas and Bondos while I was in Bastar and had written to me with enthusiasm of the beauty of the country and the attractiveness of the people. Once I had finished work on my book about the Muria dormitory, and encouraged by my experiences among the Juangs, I decided to extend my interest to the Ganjam and Koraput Districts of Orissa. On my first trip I was escorted by a large, friendly, generous-hearted timber-man, Val Blackburn, who lived in Raipur. He took me into the very wild and almost unexplored country of the Kuttia Konds. A little later, we climbed the Nīmgiri mountain together and, later still, I made the first of several visits to the high Bondo plateau and at the same time made some study of the neighbouring Gadabas. Later, I moved across to the Saora country in Parlakimedi and Gunupur, quite the most lovely tribal area that I have ever seen anywhere. Here I found, in Gilbert Murray's phrase, 'the apple tree, the singing, and the gold'.

Touring, however, was already becoming more expensive, though not so ruinously so as it is today, and it became evident that to remain in the private sector would greatly hamper my work. I had made friends with some of the Orissa officials, who were very suspicious at first on account of my political opinions, but later evidently became convinced that I was not up to anything, and I was finally appointed Hon. Anthropologist to Orissa on an honorarium which covered my expenses. Long afterwards the late Mr S. Fazl Ali told me that when he was Governor of Orissa he had decided to invite me to be Adviser for Tribal Affairs for the State but, just as he was going to put the matter through, he heard that I had been sent by the Prime Minister to NEFA.

Out of my Orissa explorations came three books—*Bondo Highlander, The Religion of an Indian Tribe* (about the Saoras) and *Tribal Myths of Orissa,* as well as a special number of *Man in India* about the Juangs. I also wrote a number of reports for Government and made recommendations for the welfare of the tribal people. Had I been more energetic I could have done at least two more books, for I had a great many notes on the Gadabas and Konds and a large collection of photographs.

I will now give brief descriptions of three of the tribes I visited—the Kuttia Konds, the Bondos and the Saoras. They are not 'anthropological' descriptions and the reader who wants a detailed account must go elsewhere. It may perhaps be questioned whether what I say here and in chapter 9 on the NEFA tribes has a legitimate place in an autobiography. I think it has. The tribes were such an important part of my life and brought so much interest and pleasure into it that without them, without the Baigas and Murias, the Bondos, Konds and Saoras, my story would be incomplete. The Baigas introduced me to the wilder forests; the Kuttia Konds and Marias kindled and educated my sense of beauty. I thought about the Saoras, talked to and about them, loved them, was absorbed in them for years. I thought myself into the Murias, fascinated by not only the academic but also the human problems raised by their unusual social system. Only those who have some idea of them can really understand me. My entire attitude to life has been affected by the lovable NEFA folk. Apart from these tribes who, one by one, filled my life to the brim, there is not very much for me to talk about. Of the great events of my time I have only been a spectator; I have met very few important people. It is the tribes who have been my life and that is why I have had to put them in its record.

Bison-horn Maria girl in Bastar

Photo, D. V. Sassoon

Saora youths

IX

The Kuttia Konds

First let me describe the wild, remote and devastatingly attractive Kuttia Konds.

The Konds are a large tribe, speaking a Dravidian language akin to Gondi, who are scattered all over Orissa, but the Kuttia Konds are confined to the desolate hills and forests in the north-western corner of the Ganjam District. These Kuttias were very poor, very timid, strikingly good-looking and, once you got to know them, charming and loyal friends.

They had a good deal of cause for their timidity. They were grossly oppressed by Dom moneylenders and Patro landlords; they had a hard time from the officials of the Forest Department; their simplicity made them fair game for any rascally merchant or black-marketeer who adventured into their hills; and they lived in an area where wild animals made frequent attacks on their lives and property.

During my first visit to their hills, a Kond, who was carrying my mail down to the railway, was killed by a tiger and next morning, when we went to the spot, all we could find was a pool of blood and my letters scattered about the jungle. Wild elephants also were a constant danger and did great damage to the crops. Sometimes on tour we moved as a sort of convoy, all sorts of people joining our party for protection through a dangerous tract.

The Konds were constantly shifting their villages, which they built in such inaccessible places that there was often no level spot for us to make a camp. Like the Baigas, they were passionately devoted to the practice of axe-cultivation, though they were much more careful than the Baigas in observing a rotation so as not to ruin the forest permanently. Each village had perhaps a dozen traditional sites to which it shifted in turn when the available forest in the neighbourhood had been exhausted. Their houses were very small, often with tiny doors. Once when I was camping in one of their huts, the door was so low that I had to crawl in and out on my hands and knees.

The villages, however, were often very picturesque. They

were usually laid out in two long rows of houses, each joined to its neighbour. In the middle, standing up impressively against the sky, was a forked pillar of sacrifice with buffalo horns placed on its points. The stone of Mother Earth stood in front of three other stones which served it as a protecting wall. Often there was an elaborately carved pillar of sacrifice, decorated with such relics as a buffalo's skull, the tail of a barking-deer, sambhar bones or a buffalo's hoof. The villages were usually kept spotlessly clean.

Even in 1944 the desire for human sacrifice was fundamental to Kond psychology. It will be remembered that, about a hundred years ago, the Government put an end to the savage Meriah sacrifices—human beings, who were offered to the Earth Goddess in order to fertilize the soil. It was hard to believe that these simple inoffensive folk could ever have practised so barbarous a rite or could even now long so greatly for its restoration. But it was so. In almost every village, hidden away in a priest's house, were the old implements of sacrifice—the knife, the chains, the bowl to catch the blood—and the priests told me how at certain seasons when the moon was full they could hear these horrid tools weeping for the human blood which was now denied them.

There were still carefully treasured a few human skulls, perhaps a hundred years old, or bits of human bone, which were brought out at special ceremonies or used as amulets. A great hunter, who had a bit of finger bone, told me that he attributed all his luck in the chase to his possession of it.

Long ago, when the Meriah sacrifice was put down by Government, the Konds began to sacrifice buffaloes in place of human victims. When this was done, an old human skull or mask was brought out and laid before the symbols of divinity. There was, when I was there, an attempt being made by well-meaning but not very intelligent persons to stop even the buffalo sacrifices in the interests of vegetarianism.

The Konds were devotedly attached to that 'vile weed' of which Charles Lamb used to speak so eloquently. The boys made excellent tobacco-tubes, decorated with patterns of lozenges and triangles. Their legend of the origin of tobacco is told all over tribal India, even in NEFA. There was once a very ugly girl whom no one would marry. She did her best to get a husband, but no one wanted her. In despair she went to the Creator and begged to be allowed to die, and to return in her next birth as something which all men would love. He granted her request and after her death caused a tobacco plant to grow out of her despised body. And so the girl whom nobody wanted is now the desire of all the world.

The Kuttia Konds had nothing—and everything. Long ago I wrote some verses about them which puts it better than anything I could say now.

The True Treasure

They have no treasure as the world counts gain.
Some starving cattle ; a small bin of grain ;
Torn scraps of dirty cloth ; a string of beads ;
A mat, a broken bed, a pot of seeds,

A basketful of roots, a little meat,
The bows and arrows and a wooden seat,
Is all their low-roofed hovels boast of store.
Such is the sad accounting of the poor.

They have no treasure? Let us look again.
See how their courage triumphs over pain ;
How patiently they cast the annual seed ;
How steadfastly they bear their daily need.

These riches of the spirit are their power.
And then—the beauty like a perfect flower
That blossoms as the lotus from the mud,
The glory of the children in the bud.

See the fine bodies, unimproved by art,
The plum-black hair that twines about the heart,
The eyes that with the grace of fireflies move,
The shining teeth, the breasts that foster love.

Regard the features ravishing and dark,
And the gay song-filled voices. Hark, O hark,
To the sweet koel-music of their words
That dance and wanton with the coloured birds.

The breathing loveliness of human clay,
Though transient, transforms the hardest day.
How can we call them poor, whose wealth unbought
By contrast turns the rich man's gold to naught?

X

The Bondos

Some years ago Michael Huxley asked me to do a piece for the *Geographical Magazine* on 'My Worst Journey', part of which I will reproduce here. I began by saying that I did not find it easy to describe my worst journey, for I had never made a journey that was entirely bad. And I went on to summarize my experiences in the period before I went to Assam.

On the whole [I wrote] my travels in tribal India have been exceedingly rewarding. They have indeed often been uncomfortable; the marching and climbing has been arduous enough; I have had my share of sharp fevers with their dreary sequels, far from medical assistance; supplies of food have raised complicated problems. But in general, as I look back, almost all my memories are pleasant: the beauty of the countryside, the charm and friendliness of the people, the excitement of scientific inquiry, the support of devoted assistants, the alliance of true friends—these things have made a quarter of a century, the greater part of which has been spent far from the imagined comforts of civilization and the supposed stimulus of educated conversation, a period of singular happiness.

But of course I have had my troubles. I have been bored by delays, irritated by tedious officials, exasperated by puritans, padres and police, disappointed, frustrated, wearied, as every traveller must be. But not a single tour or expedition has been without its great rewards.

First visits to any area are difficult: you do not know the country or the language; interpreters are hard to come by and, until they are trained, are usually worse than useless; you yourself are unfamiliar and the people are not sure what you are up to: all the minor irritations of life are magnified. And of these first tours, I think the most difficult was the one I made into the Bondo country of Orissa in December 1943.

The Bondos are a small tribe of the type now often called Austro-Asiatic which—at the time of the 1941 Census—numbered only 2,565 persons. Their country, elevated, beautiful and remote, lies north-west of the Machkund river. Notorious for their violent and inhospitable ways, they have preserved themselves comparatively unaffected by the march of civilization. Indeed by plainsmen and officials the Bondos are regarded as entirely savage, almost as the classic savage type: the strange dress and appearance of the women with their exiguous skirts and shaven heads, the passionate and homicidal temper of the men, their unfamiliar tongue, the inaccessibility of their abode, have long separated them from their mild and conventional neighbours. I do not know what has happened to them in recent years, but when I visited them for the last time in 1947, the only change I found was in their reaction to myself: by now suspicion had given way to an almost overwhelming friendliness.

The end of 1943 was, of course, a bad time to get about. All maps were, very properly, controlled by the military authorities, and so I had very little idea of where anything was. Food, with equal propriety, was strictly rationed, and for a traveller to obtain the necessary permits involved endless waiting about in dreary offices. Rations were issued by the week, but I needed supplies for several months. There was no regulation, the matter would have to be referred to Cuttack, what was the real purpose of my visit?

Many things were not available at all. The absence of tinned foods did not worry me, for I detest the stuff, but condensed milk was a necessity in a part of the world where milk was taboo. And of course there was no petrol.

To reach the Bondo country, if there was no petrol to drive your car, involved a train-journey from Calcutta to Vizianagram, and then a ninety-mile trip by country bus through lovely scenery to Koraput. The road winds steeply through the hills, and many of the passengers were sick. At Koraput the chief official had been a contemporary of mine at Oxford, but did not think it necessary to look after me, and I was accommodated in a sleazy dak-bungalow with broken windows. Sitting among the rats and fleas, I recollected with satisfaction that my fellow-collegian had taken a poor Third in History.

In the India of that time, unless you were an official, rich, or had unimpeachable or intimidating introductions, no one took very much notice of you. This was evident when we continued our journey for the further fourteen miles. to Jeypore where a sumptuous guest-house was maintained by the Maharaja. Here everybody settled down to make my further progress as difficult as possible. In later years, I am glad to say, the local people were as helpful as they were then obstructive.

We first had to reach a place called Govindapalle, forty miles away. There was a bus, but it was not running that week: the proprietor's nephew was getting married. I waited several days and then put my stores and equipment on a couple of bullock-carts, a mode of travel which I have always rather enjoyed. Its one disadvantage is that it exposes you to interrogations: who was I, what was I doing, what was my aim in going to the Bondos?—everybody wanted to know. However, we reached our first Bondo village safely, but there discovered that no one was willing to go with us up into the hills. The Bondos were not used to carrying other people's loads—and who could blame them? It took a long time and much persuasion to get a dozen porters. But we did get them in the end, and one glorious morning climbed the steep hills to an enchantingly situated village, Dumiripada, on the top of the world.

It was beautiful, it was romantic, but it was not hospitable. There was no hostility: crowds of men, women and children thronged round as we put up a few leafy branches to make some sort of hut; they all beamed amiably, but no one would move a finger to help. Requests for wood and water, on extravagant payment, were met by charming smiles—but no action followed. The headman came, and he did his best, but Bondo headmen have little authority. At last, after tremendous argument and much shouting among themselves, a few boys brought just enough water for the kitchen.

The Bondos, in fact, are remarkably unwilling to oblige. They are prepared to sit round in the friendliest fashion, laughing, joking and chatting, so long as you do not ask them to do anything. They are always ready to give information. But they object very much to giving anything else. They have no apparent desire to earn money. At one village I offered some boys who had nothing whatever to do the equivalent of three days' earnings to catch some fish for me, but they refused. They dislike selling any of their possessions, and to live off the country here is a real problem. This was not a cause of irritation, for why *should* they do anything? But it was a practical difficulty.

Such help as we got came from an unexpected source. I have had the privilege of knowing a good many murderers, but hitherto most of these had been in jail. In the Bondo country, where the homicide rate is the highest in all India, murder is usually punished by a comparatively short sentence of five or seven years, and I found that the most affable and helpful people were those who had done time, even though I was sometimes apprehensive that one of them might feel the need of a little further practice. A further advantage was that these charming if ferocious ex-convicts usually knew some Hindi or Oriya, and we were therefore able to converse with them direct instead of through an interpreter.

Our next village, Bandapada, was very timid. As I went down the street, mothers seized their children and hurried them indoors, girls fled whimpering with fright, doors banged, fowls and pigs scurried to safety, one youth hastily got up a tree. Only a few old men, greatly daring, came to greet us. I can endure any hardship other than the realization that I look like a sort of ogre. Later I heard that it was supposed that I had come to take girls for the war, that I was going to send all the children to America to be baptized, and—most curious of all—that I was an Excise Officer who had come to introduce Prohibition. After a time, however, a delightful person, who had twice been to prison for successive murders and, as far as I could discover, was even then planning a third, turned up and with his help we got some kind of roof over our heads and a meagre supply of necessities.

I then brought out the gramophone, which is usually a great success. No sooner, however, had I put on a rather dreadful record entitled 'Fun with the Concertina', which I regret to say is everywhere in great demand, than one old woman fell down in a fit, several others flopped to the ground in an attitude of worship, and all the children ran screaming from the place. A deputation of elders quickly arrived to ask me to stop the music, if that is the correct word, as it was evident that there was something very dangerous inside the sound-box and they did not want to take any risks.

In the Bondo and Saora villages I departed from my usual custom of staying in someone's house and instead we made little huts for ourselves,

> Under the bam
> Under the boo
> Under the bamboo tree.

These were of leafy branches with a deep layer of straw underfoot and a rough thatch above. They were surprisingly comfortable but unfortunately they were edible and almost every night cattle would come and start eating the walls, which was a constant disturbance.

On later visits I had a very pleasant time with the Bondos. On one of them Shamrao with his wife and two small children, Suresh and Ramula, accompanied me and on my last trip I had Victor Sassoon, who enjoyed himself thoroughly and took a large number of first-class photographs, some of which I reproduced in my book, *Bondo Highlander*.

And the Bondos were well worth photographing, for on the whole they are a good-looking people. Boys and young men are often most attractive. Their fine carriage, magnificent physique, free and open countenance, delightful smile, are captivating. The way they do their hair is specially charming. As they grow older, however, they degenerate a little ; the face coarsens, the body is dirtier, the hair is done in a different, and less pleasing, fashion. Like most tribesmen above a certain age, the Bondos let themselves go. In jail, they look terrible.

At first sight a visitor may exclaim that Bondo women are the ugliest he has ever seen. But in a few days, after he has got over the first shock of their rather unconventional appearance, he may revise his opinion. The illusion of ugliness is largely created by the shaven head. But a young girl with something covering her head—a fish-basket or a sickle-curved bundle of bark—often shows the world a face of character and charm. Little girls, ten or twelve years old, are sometimes very pretty, especially when they decorate their head-bands with sprigs of greenery and white, mauve or scarlet flowers. The chief fault of the older girls (apart, of course, from the lack of hair) is that there is perhaps a little too much of them. They are apt to be plump, rather sleek and smooth, big-lipped, bagpipe-breasted, with large thighs, thick calves, 'thick as plantain stalks'. Older women are often very charming with good features and an indefinable attraction that speedily made one forget the oddity of their appearance.

Bondo boys have very definite views about feminine beauty and one day a group of them used some rather poetical expressions while attempting to explain the meaning of a love-song. The phrases are probably traditional or at least based on the highly condensed song-technique. They described a girl's body as 'beautiful as a white cloud', her arms and legs 'round and shapely as a bamboo', her breasts 'sparkling as two fishes'; her shadow 'broad and healthy as a buffalo'. Above all, the beautiful girl is 'useful as the leaf of a giant creeper'—from which leaf-cups and plates are made.

The Bondo sexual tradition was very different from the Muria. To the Bondos sexual experience was difficult, dangerous and expensive; while the Gond or Baiga often thought of intercourse as little more than a pleasant experience, the Bondo regarded it as a very serious matter. There were several reasons for this. The Bondo youth was bound by the most rigorous taboos from having anything to do with the girls of his own village; when he met the girls of other villages, he did so in public and under conditions of the strictest conventionality. This placed an effective brake on those casual everyday affairs which were the normal recreation of village boys in other parts of India. Then again sexual intercourse was a risky matter; it involved the introduction of the most precious of life's possessions into an unknown and alien world. This was something fundamental in the psychology of the tribe; the Bondo could not bear going abroad. That was his real torment in jail; that was why he was so unwilling to carry our baggage to another village—I once saw a group of women weeping in utter despair because a member of the household was carrying some of my things to a place only four miles away. Like other tribesmen, the Bondos had the strange and sinister legend of the Vagina Dentata, which is closely connected with the fear of castration. These legends, which I have found among many Indian tribes and which have also been recorded in North America and from the

Ainus, were entirely serious. They were not just dirty stories calculated to raise a hiccoughing chuckle in the dormitory ; they were the attempt of Bondo fiction to suggest the risk of sexual congress.

But the most potent influence against promiscuity was that the girls would not have it. It is generally admitted in other tribal societies—and I believe it is largely true—that it is the girls who lead men on. But this was not true of the Bondo girls. To them sexual intercourse in the pre-marital period implied a serious intention ; it was almost equivalent to a betrothal. The Saora youth drove an arrow between breasts carved in wood on the pillar of the house where his beloved lived ; after that she was his. But if the Bondo youth translated this symbolism into actuality, he was caught: he was hers.

All this was characteristic of the eastern group of tribes, who were remarkable for their sexual reticence. The Saoras had the same outlook, so did the Juangs, Gadabas and Marias. But the Gond group had a very different tradition. The Gonds, Pardhans, Konds and other allied tribes regarded the expression of sexual passion, however delightful it might be, as a comparatively trivial affair, to be indulged as a passing entertainment, unimportant (provided certain conventions were observed) in its effects. This does not mean that they do not fall in love ; they do, deeply and disastrously ; but they found it possible at the same time and in a different compartment, as it were, to enjoy sex without getting too much involved.

I came to like the Bondos immensely and made many personal friends among them. They were not only very lovable but unusually exciting. This was due mainly to their bad tempers, which meant that you never knew what was going to happen next. The Bondos were aware of this defect and had devised a curious and unique rite of mutual castigation, for the express purpose of teaching themselves to keep their tempers. Conducted with a mixture of ferocity and hilarity, it began with little boys. To the excited beating of drums they armed themselves with long switches, stood up two by two, and beat each other as hard as they could. It was no pretence ; soon backs were covered with weals, and the little fellows bit their lips as they went for each other with all their strength. When a couple had had enough they saluted one another with mutual respect, clasped each other in a warm embrace and retired in favour of another pair. When all the boys had completed this piquant exercise, the priest gave them a special kind of cake 'to stop their quarrels' and delivered a little lecture: 'Never beat anyone in anger. Let everyone treat his fellow as a brother. Never make other people angry.'

This was all right. The anxiety came when young men, perhaps jealous rivals for the same girl, or old toughs hardened by years in jail, began to beat each other: then there was a real sense of tension. I think that this unusual rite does to some extent succeed in its aim of training the Bondos to keep their tempers under the sudden stimulus of pain, and serves as a surrogate for the grosser emotions.

In spite of this there were a great many Bondo rows, some of which I was privileged to watch. I was once present at a violent quarrel when a Bondo attacked a Gadaba, who was supposed to have insulted him by exposing his private parts. The contrast between the ferocious Bondo, screaming abuse in three languages (including bits of English), and the meek Gadaba bowing before the storm with folded hands, was striking. Another day I saw a group of Bondo boys invade a Gadaba village, and rob its favourite sago palm of its juice. The Gadabas chattered with rage and anguish as they watched their precious wine slipping down the ample Bondo throats, but not one of them dared to interfere. When they had drunk their fill, the Bondo boys paraded the village with an electric insolence and charm. In spite of her rage, every Gadaba girl came out of her house and stood gazing fascinated. After executing a particularly obscene little dance just to put everyone in his place, the Bondos finally departed, leaving the village exhausted as a person through whose body has passed a powerful, but not quite fatal, shock.

It is indeed an extraordinary experience to witness a Bondo quarrel. There is first an exchange of words. Hints about a wife's chastity, allusions to a sister's virtue flicker to and fro. Then the Bondo suddenly comes to the boil; the waters rise and topple over. He twirls his moustache. He spits at his adversary. He pulls out a few hairs and throws them at him.

He chatters and bubbles with temper. And then he draws his knife or jumps for his bow and arrows.

Yet this is not the last word. Bondo life was marked by courage, freedom, equality, independence and industry. The defects of these qualities were equally evident ; courage became an indifference to human life, freedom and independence degenerated into ill-mannered aggressiveness, too strong a sense of equality could become bad citizenship. The Bondo drank too much ; he was often lazy and drove his womenfolk too hard ; he was not very clean ; he wasted a lot of time in the exact, and rather fussy, performance and repetition of ceremonial. But otherwise there was a great deal to be said for him. If he was a savage, he was at least a noble savage. If he was poor, he was at least patient and courageous in his poverty. If he was outside, and perhaps behind, the main stream of civilization, he was at least free of many of its debasing vices.

In a hotel where I stayed at Chiengmai in northern Thailand there was a notice announcing that young ladies and 'excessive persons' were not admitted into the rooms at night. The Bondos attracted me because they were excessive persons, and after all Blake once said that 'the road of excess leads to the palace of wisdom'.

XI

The Saoras

My study of the Saoras extended over seven years. I concentrated on one section of this very large tribe, the Hill Saoras of Ganjam and Koraput, and particularly of the villages in the hills above Gunupur, which at that time were almost completely untouched by missionary or other external influence and where it was possible to see the old life as it must have continued for hundreds of years.

To these I went from Patangarh to stay long periods and often made my camp in one village for two or three weeks at a time. I took my books and papers with me and settled down as though I were at home. In fact, I wrote a good deal of my book about the Saoras on the spot, and was able to correct or verify things as I went along. The people were very good to me and used to make me charming little two-roomed huts of branches and leaves, with good verandas. The quickest way to their hearts was by gifts of country-cigars called *pikas*. For these they had, and I hope still have, a passionate attachment. They were also very fond of tea and were constantly dropping in for a cup or two. I often had half a dozen people round my bed soon after dawn anxious to share my morning tea.

Yet in my day at least, the Saoras did not really want to have visitors. After any outsider had been to the village they made special sacrifices to purify the place from any possible magical defilement. In one area I found a regular tariff: for a Forest Officer they sacrificed a goat, for a Sub-Inspector of Police a fowl, and for an anthropologist a large black pig.

They had a god called Sahibosum, who was propitiated for the express purpose of keeping touring officials away. A sahib, of course, is anything in a hat and a pair of trousers. Wooden images were made and erected outside the village. There was also an image of the 'Memsahib' goddess, usually just a little larger and more formidable than her husband. She was always represented as wearing a sola topi.

There was nothing personal about this. Even your best friends would make these sacrifices and erect these images. It was simply that if you came from the outside world you might bring, clinging invisibly to you, some sort of spiritual infection; a spirit or demon might use you as a vehicle to get inside the charmed village boundaries.

In spite of this, I managed to visit almost all the hill Saora villages and in some of them I felt like an explorer, for those in the remoter parts of the hills had not been visited in living memory by any outsider, and for months at a time I did not meet any official: Sahibosum had clearly been effective. I was there in the cold and also when it was very hot, indeed at all times of the year except the height of the rains.

The beauty of the country was almost overwhelming. When I was younger I had a feeling for Nature akin to that of the young Wordsworth. Natural beauty haunted me like a passion.

It was 'an appetite ; a feeling and a love' that had no need for any interest 'unborrowed from the eye'.

But I think that from the very beginning of my time in tribal India I moved on to Wordsworth's further stage of hearing oftentimes 'the still, sad music of humanity' against the background of Nature. This was particularly true of my years in Bastar.

Later, in NEFA among the northern mountains, their mystery and grandeur disturbed me with the sense of the universal presence, 'the joy of elevated thoughts', of which Wordsworth writes again.

But in the Saora hills the appeal of Nature was largely sensuous. It was, it is true, always a setting for human beings and yet its impact was almost physical. I ached for it and when I had to leave it, it was always with a very heavy heart.

The Hill Saoras had large substantial villages ; they erected menhirs and sacrificed buffaloes for their dead ; their religious needs were served by male and female shamans ; they engaged in both terraced and shifting cultivation ; their men put on a long brightly-coloured loin-cloth and their women wore a handwoven brown-bordered skirt and did not usually wear anything else ; the women also greatly enlarged the lobes of their ears and had a characteristic tattoo mark down the middle of the forehead. They retained their own language and very few of them spoke any other.

Saora houses were well-built and in long streets, and some Saora chieftains were comparatively wealthy. Indeed, they might all have been fairly well-to-do, so laborious and careful were they, had it not been for the shocking exploitation to which they were subjected by their landlords and moneylenders.

It was a heart-breaking sight to stand by a Saora's threshing-floor and watch his creditors and parasites remove in payment of their dues so much of the grain which he had laboured so hard to produce.

The great achievement of the Saoras is their terracing. They build up the hillsides for a thousand feet, terrace rising above terrace, perfectly aligned, so carefully done that not a drop of water escapes uselessly and all erosion is checked. Sometimes a great stone wall, 15 feet high, will hold up a ridge of cultivable soil only three feet wide. These terraces have been rightly praised as works of great engineering skill.

The main subject of my study was Saora religion, for the Saoras are quite the most religious people I have ever met. Happily, they did not resent my inquiries but were rather flattered by them. Where other tribes postpone a festival or ceremony if a visitor comes to the village, the Saoras used to insist on my presence at everything. They took me into their houses, made me sit on the floor near the officiating priest and explained it all in great detail as the long ceremonies took their course.

In fact we used to have a saying that there was never a holiday for the anthropologist in the Saora country. Every day something happened. You were just settling down to a quiet siesta when you would hear the roar of gunfire echoing in a neighbouring valley, and you knew there was a funeral which you simply must attend. Or someone would arrive at dawn with news of a most exciting ceremony in a village five miles away and due to start in half an hour.

I was rather often ill in the Saora country, for malaria was a dangerous scourge there and I had some very bad bouts of toothache. Even this worked out well, for the priests and even the priestesses used to crowd in to my little hut, sit by my bedside and attempt to cure me by their own techniques. And cure or relieve me they often did, for their methods were extremely soothing and their affection and interest was reviving. I also learnt by personal experience a great deal about their ideas that I might otherwise have missed.

During this happy period I found that my old Oxford studies in theology, which at one time I had written off as wasted, were of unexpected value. Heiler's monumental book on prayer, for example, William James on the varieties of religious experience, Otto on the numinous element in religion as well as many other books helped me to understand the Saoras better.

Saora life was completely dominated by their religion. Beyond and around this life and this visible world is an unseen realm of vital reality, peopled by a host of spirits whose activities impinge on normal existence at every turn.

The ghosts live in an Underworld, which is something like

this world of our own, but everything is on a Lilliputian scale. The houses are very small ; the clouds lie low upon the land ; it is always twilight under the infernal moon. The ghosts live a sad half-life, ill-fed and poorly clad, until they themselves die again and, if they are cremated in proper form, vanish from the misery of existence forever.

But the rulers of the Underworld, the tutelary spirits, do themselves well. They have large houses, the best of food and clothing and many servants. They keep tigers and leopards (as men keep dogs) as pets. The bear is the priest and the porcupine the medicine-man of this strange world.

It is the great desire of the tutelary spirits, both male and female, to find partners among the living. They come to them in dreams and beg them to marry them. There is a special class of girls who at the age of puberty have dreamt of these unearthly lovers and after a turbulent period of wooing have agreed to marry them.

The marriage is an elaborate affair, quite as elaborate and expensive as an ordinary marriage, and when it is over, the girl is a Kuranboi, a priestess who henceforth will be able to do the work of divination and healing with the aid of her unseen husband. The Saoras believe that the girls can have children from these husbands, and I met many Saora women who had families both in this and in the other world. Sometimes, listening to the way they talked, I used to wonder which was the more real to them.

But in spite of the realm of fantasy in which they lived, these women were practical and devoted servants of their tribe. They were always ready to hasten to minister to the sick and console the sorrowful. Men also were subject to these experiences, and they became, as a result, the all-important medicine-men of the tribe.

The work of these simple 'doctors' had great survival value. It gave the patient the sense that someone cared about him. It made him believe that he was going to get well. It settled his conscience and gave him the will to recover. And the medicine-men took their profession seriously and worked very hard at it.

To the research man there is no greater happiness, no deeper love, no more thrilling excitement than to work in such a field

Bondo girl picking castor seeds

Hill Maria boys in dancing dress

as this. I have found not only among the Saoras but other tribes too that there comes a moment when everything falls into place and you suddenly see the life of a people as a harmonious whole and understand how it works. This decisive moment, which can only be achieved after arduous study, is one of the greatest experiences that a scholar can have.

But it always took a long time. A friend of mine who read this book in manuscript, unlike my other friends who wanted me to put in more about my vices, told me I should say something about my virtues. 'That would be very nice,' I said, 'but what virtues have I?' He was a little stumped by this but after some thought he said, 'I think your greatest virtue is patience.' There may be something in this, for I have always been content to go forward without reward or recognition and in my search for the truth to take any trouble and to spend any amount of time in finding it. Things take me a long time, and I have always been content to wait.

Sometimes people wrote about the sacrifice I made in going into tribal India. But that is certainly not a virtue I can claim. What sacrifice could there possibly be in living in the beauty of the Saora hills or in the heart-warming atmosphere of Patangarh? There has never been a moment of sacrifice in my life; for everything I have given I have been repaid tenfold, and of myself I can say:

> Love had he found in huts where poor men lie;
> His daily teachers had been woods and rills,
> The silence that is in the starry sky,
> The sleep that is among the lonely hills.

My memories of life in Bastar and Orissa are, like my memories of Oxford, inconsolable. I shall never see, no one will ever see, the Muria ghotul as I saw it, or the Saoras as I saw them. It may be that I myself helped by my very presence to destroy what I so much admired. But all over tribal India the old freedom is disappearing and with it something of the old happiness. Change is inevitable and I have no doubt that the great schemes of village welfare have brought some profit to some of the people already and in time will bring new life to them all. How far this will in the long run result in their happiness is a problem that vexes all those who think seriously on the subject.

But however this may be, one thing is clear. The old romantic exciting days, the beauty and the zest have gone for ever. I would not recall them if it meant loss to even a single child, yet it is hard not to feel nostalgic for what used to be.

> I heard a voice that cried,
> Balder the beautiful
> Is dead, is dead.

XII

A special, and very important, aspect of research is photography: this led me into many adventures, especially in the early days and the remoter regions, where it was by no means easy.

The camera to many tribal people is an object not only of embarrassment, but of fear. That mysterious aperture which points in their direction in so sinister a manner, the almost inevitable fuss and preparation that precedes the taking of even the simplest photographs, the fixing of the tripod, the manoeuvring for position, cannot fail to alarm them. In a bazaar in Mandla District I saw a rather photogenic blacksmith—it was when I was writing my book about the Agarias—but when I pointed my camera at him I was startled to see a wave of fear pass over everybody within sight. The local constable came up to me, saluted smartly, and said, 'I can get you a much better man than that,' but before I realized what he meant the whole bazaar was on the move. People leapt to their feet upsetting the stalls, throwing baskets of vegetables to the ground, trampling on bales of cloth, and in a few moments they were all streaming away into the jungle. I later discovered that even the constable supposed that my camera was a sort of anthropometric instrument by which I could measure the stature of likely recruits for the Army. Another time in the Raipur District, people trembled with fear while I was photographing them and afterwards one of them said, 'You have taken all my strength and shut it up in that little box.' In another place I found that the people supposed the camera to be a sort of X-ray instrument with which I could see right through their clothes and bodies down to their livers. Everybody knows, of course, that the liver is a very important thing in black magic. You try to affect the person's liver as a preliminary to murdering him by witchcraft. If you can get hold of a bit of the liver of a dead man or even a picture of it, it is a very potent source of supernatural power.

In Bastar, when I was making a documentary film of the Murias and Marias, I found, on the whole, that they were very good about letting me photograph them and I was often astonished at the willingness of even the children to come before the camera. But sometimes the luck was bad. I once went to photograph a Muria wedding; in fact, I was invited to go by the father of the bride, who was an old friend. For the first day everything went swimmingly. We exchanged presents: we were allowed to see everything that went on: I have seldom been in a more friendly company of people. I was able to get a number of excellent pictures. Then, on the morning of the second day, the bridegroom had a fit. I was standing nearby with my ubiquitous camera in my hand. My heart sank. I knew what would happen. Gradually, inevitably, the eyes of the entire company turned to me. I knew what they were thinking: that queer little box had brought the wrath of the gods on the bridegroom. After a few minutes the boy's mother, a very forceful woman with a mass of false hair curled up and up on the top of her head (she was said to be an incarnation of the god Mahadeo), declared to my face that it was the camera that had troubled her son. There was nothing to be done. The atmosphere was ruined. After that, even though I put the camera away, whenever people saw me they looked embarrassed and awkward. I felt as though I had indeed a black monkey sitting on my back.

Once when I was touring among the Bison-Horn Marias in the beautiful mountains of south Bastar I had with infinite trouble arranged to take a photograph of boys and girls fishing in a river. As always, of course, the people had first of all declared that they did not know what fish were. Then, when they had gone so far as to admit that there were fish, they said they never actually caught any of them (they probably thought that I was making an inquiry to take their fishing rights from them—a thing which has been done in some parts of India). Then they said they had no fish-traps and we had to go and search for them in the village. When at last we got the boys and girls carrying their traps down to the river bank, a sinister-looking old man appeared and said something in a loud voice. Immediately, before you could count ten, the place was deserted. Everybody disappeared into the jungle, leaving the traps and fishing-tackle on the ground. I then discovered that the old gentleman was the village priest and had announced that it had been revealed to him by the gods that anyone who allowed himself to be photographed would die forthwith.

I dealt with this by making the priest himself pose for his photograph. At first he presented a large and obstinate back, but I ultimately made him face me, and so was able to declare that if anybody was going to die he would be the first. I then showed the villagers photographs of the Maharaja and my own wife and myself and pointed out that we were all alive and happy in spite of the way our 'souls' were plastered on these bits of paper. On this occasion it was possible to make a certain impression and I shortly afterwards got an excellent picture of a cock-fight, the villagers presumably supposing that even if my lethal weapon did slaughter the cocks they could always eat them; but I was unable, with all our persuading, to recapture the same happy natural atmosphere which we had had before and which is, of course, essential to the making of a successful film.

Sometimes local subordinates or helpful friends can be equally embarrassing. Once in Sarangarh I had succeeded, with a lot of trouble, in getting a group of villagers natural and at ease, just ready for a good picture, when a zealous chaprasi rushed up exclaiming 'How dare you sit in that casual manner in front of the Sahib!'

I had similar experiences in NEFA, and among such highly photogenic people as the Boris and Wanchos I had to put my camera away entirely when I visited most of their villages. I never had any difficulty, however, among the Buddhist tribes along the frontier.

XIII

Composing books is one thing. Typing them out and getting them printed is quite another. Until I came to Shillong, except for a brief period, I never had a stenographer or typist and I myself typed out all my larger books. My practice was to type out a rough draft, then retype it again filling in the gaps and finally to make a fair copy. This involved an enormous amount of work but it was worth it, for I am convinced that you can do much better when you write yourself than when you dictate.

Then there is the business of proof-reading. My publisher, Roy Hawkins of the Oxford University Press, who undertook the profitless task of producing a whole series of my books during the war-years when paper was hard to obtain and printers were overburdened, used to tell me the way to read a proof before you sent your typescript to the printer. The Oxford Press impressed on me, among many other things, how careful you must be if you are going into print. What used to happen was that soon after I sent them a manuscript I would get a letter with a long list of queries. I have never been very good at spelling and the Press usually discovered that I had spelt words in different ways on different pages. Sometimes there were mistakes in grammar, sometimes in punctuation. When I began publishing I had the idea, so common among young authors, that somehow or other the printers would 'put it right'. I now learnt that, particularly in India, the printers would reproduce exactly what they saw in the text. Many compositors, in fact, do not know English but are simply trained to follow their copy exactly.

Then proofs would come and go ; I would read them two or three times ; the office of the Press would also read them ; and finally Hawkins himself reads, I believe, every book he publishes at the final stage before it is struck off.

Sometimes we had amusing problems, particularly when I wrote about more intimate matters. There was one compositor, clearly suffering from a little complex about it, who, whenever the word 'sex' came in my manuscript, set it upside down. Nearly all compositors, I found, set up the expression 'public hairs', which is one of the curious things anthropologists sometimes write about, but this is, of course, exactly what they are not. When my book on the Murias was half ready there was a crisis because the mission press which was doing it suddenly realized what it was about and wrote to say that they could not possibly print such a shocking work. Hawkins, however, was firm and told them that they should have read the typescript before accepting the contract. Fortunately, the manager of the press was an exceptionally liberal Baptist and he himself thought the whole business rather funny. I estimated that by the time we finished, the Oxford Press and I between us read the proofs of this book no fewer than eight times, with the gratifying result that in three-quarters of a million words only three misprints have been found, an achievement to which the Baptist Mission Press of Calcutta notably contributed.

7

The Earth is Round

Ceaseless travel meant continual meetings. One day Pierre Teilhard came across a friend in some remote corner of the globe. He greeted him so warmly that the other expressed mild surprise. 'Why am I so happy?' said the traveller, 'Why, because the earth is round.' —*Claude Aragonnès*

I

IN the twenty-two years of forest life before I came to Shillong, I tended, I think, to isolate myself a little too much from the outside world. I dodged conferences and committees, though I corresponded fairly widely with other scholars in the same field. I did, however, go fairly regularly to Bombay, once a year in the rains, in order to raise funds for our tribal work and, as I love travelling, I made a few trips abroad. People in Bombay were extraordinarily generous and kind and I had a large number of friends there, chief of whom was Jehangir Patel.

J. P. Patel is a Mr Pickwick of a man. When I first met him he was a businessman beginning to do well in cotton. Then he came in touch with Gandhi and entertained him in Juhu after one of his fasts. Later, not content with helping us in our work in Patangarh, he started an admirable institution for the very oppressed Warlis in the Thana district. He organized a number of Forest Cooperatives and opened dispensaries and schools. He finally crowned his achievements by marrying Sophie, a Spanish lady, whom one day he brought home in triumph to Bombay. During the past fifteen years he has helped me in every possible way to collect funds for Patangarh, to publish my books, and to introduce me to a wide circle of friends. His sane and wise advice has always stood me in good stead.

Perhaps my earliest friends in Bombay were the Macleans, who had a house in the Gowalia Tank Road where I used to stay in the Christa Seva Sangh days. John Maclean was a professor of mathematics at the Wilson College, and he and his wife kept open house for Indians: they were both strongly sympathetic to the national movement. Another missionary friend was the late Margaret Moore, a devout but very witty woman: years afterwards she paid us a visit at Karanjia and enjoyed it.

The Inter-Religious Fellowship often met in the Macleans' house, and here I got to know C. J. Shah, who produced a fine history of Jainism but later went into business. He accompanied me on my mission of inquiry in Gujarat, and we have now been friends for over thirty years.

After going to Karanjia I came to know the Davids: Meyer the eldest; Wilfrid who wrote the sensational *Monsoon* and stayed some days with us in Karanjia; the lovely and always entertaining Florence, and their mother Mrs David herself. Like the other old Jewish families I have known intimately, they were generous and hospitable to a fault, and gave us a great deal of support and encouragement in those early days.

Bombay is for me a place of many friendly memories, and I had contacts of very varied kinds. Among the politicians were M. R. Jayakar, a great lawyer and orator: Bhulabhai Desai, of whom I was very fond; K. F. Nariman, Purshottamdas Tricumdas, B. G. Kher and others. Among journalists were D. F. Karaka with whom I had Oxford ties; Shamlal of the *Times of India*; Shaun Mandy, the delightful Irishman who edited the *Illustrated Weekly of India* for many years; and above all Frank and Beryl Moraes. I have known Frank's son Dom since he was a baby and as he grew up he used to give me copies of his early poems.

I never went to Bombay without making a pilgrimage to Bandra to see Hilla Vakil. One of J. P. Patel's closest friends, whom he shared with me, is Wasant Velinkar, whose gift for humorous conversation makes him a joy to know.

There were many people connected with Bombay House and

the Tata enterprises in general, some of whom I have already mentioned. I have always had a special link with dear Pilloo Vesugar. I got to know Jamshed Bhabha and his wife Betty very well when I was working on the history of Jamshedpur, and other honoured friends are Jamshed's brother Homi, the nuclear energy expert, and K. A. D. Naoroji. Homi Mody, and the late Ardeshir Dalal; each took the chair at our annual meetings as did another old friend, M. C. Chagla. J. A. D. Naoroji, Soona Batliwalla and John Matthai were close friends whom death has taken from us.

For many years I have stayed during visits to Bombay with my publisher Roy Hawkins. An open-hearted and thoughtful host, an entertaining companion, he has always made a special appeal to me by his gifts as a listener. Too often, when I meet people, I can't get a word in edgewise, but Hawk not only leads one on with appropriate questions, but even listens to the answers. And, as a result perhaps of going through the proofs of so many of my books, he has become really interested in the tribes. His affection for me has even stood up to reading all the unfavourable reviews which, as publisher, he forwards to me, the worst passages carefully marked in red pencil. 'I like my friends to have plenty of faults,' he once told me, 'for then I don't feel oppressed by them.'

An earlier host was Evelyn Wood, a very old friend who has always had a cathartic effect, helping me to clear my mind of cant. His first wife Maeve did a drawing of me in 1942 which is reproduced in this book.

II

Later, I also had experience of life in Calcutta. Until 1946 anthropology was a subsection of the Zoological Survey of India —man prostrate at the feet of the other animals—and there was a Special Officer, Dr B. S. Guha, who worked as Anthropologist attached to the Survey. In that year, however, an Anthropological Survey (later to be known as the Department of Anthropology) was established by the Government of India and Guha became its first Director. He invited me to join him for a time as Deputy Director to help to get it started. It was agreed that I should retain close relations with Patangarh where Shamrao would carry on, and accordingly I went to Banaras where the Survey was then stationed.

I lived in Banaras for over a year and had I not been able to go out frequently on tour in the tribal hills, I doubt if I could have stood it. The atmosphere was academic in the worst sense—there were quarrels and jealousies ; very little work was done ; Banaras Cantonment, where we lived, was devastatingly tedious—and it was a great relief when the Survey was shifted to Calcutta.

In Calcutta we got a pleasant flat at the top of a house in Park Street, No. 64. The Survey's office was in the Indian Museum in Chowringhee and conveniently near at hand. This was the first and only time in my life when I have gone physically from a house to an office. I spent just about a year in Calcutta with a good deal of time out on tour in the Bondo and Saora areas of Orissa, in South India and in Assam. At the end of my contract Guha was anxious for me to stay on but I was not happy in the atmosphere of the Department and I longed to return to the village. Two or three years later I was officially asked to return as Director but I still felt that this was not my job and everything that has happened since has convinced me that I was right.

Calcutta, however, gave me some lifelong friends. I have never had a friend quite like Victor Sassoon, affectionate, liberal, witty, a man of exceptional quality. He is the best of companions and brought a great enlargement into my life. It was due to him that I was able to see something of Europe and make two visits to Africa and it was due to him also that I was able, for once in my life, to eat good food while it was still possible to obtain it.

His brother Joe was another good friend and the beautiful house that the Sassoons owned in Middleton Street was almost an extra home to us.

Then there were Minnie and Lindsay Emmerson, association with whom has meant more and more to me as the years have passed. Ever since I knew him Lindsay has been on the staff of the *Statesman* newspaper (other special friends on this paper are Desmond Doig and Niranjan Mazumder) and later, Minnie became Principal of the Bethune College ; they have been my generous hosts on many occasions. They always have the latest books, the most recent information and the most amusing stories, and to go to their house is a treasured experience. Minnie's sister Sheila, the artist, and her husband John Auden (brother of W.H.) were other friends, and in Bombay there was another sister, the delightful Indira.

While we were in Calcutta Victor was running a picture agency which he called Tropix. He did the writing and Sunil Janah, whom I do not hesitate to call the greatest photographer in India, used to take the pictures. At that time Sunil was unmarried but later he was lucky enough to win the beautiful and talented Sobha. Then there were Jamini Roy, Gopal Ghose, Ratin Moitra and other artists, poets like Bishnu Dey and, above all, Sudhin Dutta, his wife Rajeshwari, and his charming brother Subul. Sudhin's comparatively early death (he was only fifty-nine) robbed India of a major poet and me of a precious friend.

During my year in Calcutta I became a member of the Council of the Asiatic Society (which was then called the Royal Asiatic Society of Bengal) and was elected a Fellow, one of the most jealously guarded honours in the country. It brought me in contact with many Indian scholars, among whom I particularly treasure Suniti Chatterji, a unique character among India's learned men. I was also elected a Fellow of the National Institute of Sciences of India and was twice member of its Council.

Since coming to Shillong, I have often been to Calcutta but nearly always on my way somewhere else, with the result that my visits have been brief and overcrowded, with little chance to make new friends. But among the few I did make, the chief were Bob and Margot Gilkey and their lovely children, David, John and Sharada. Bob was in the USIS, a learned man (he has written, in French, a large treatise on comparative literature) with the kindest eyes you ever saw ; and Margot, a shy and too-modest poet, has in addition to her gifts of heart and mind a breath-taking beauty. Lila and I stayed with them in their air-conditioned flat in Calcutta and they stayed with us and completely won the children's hearts. But now they have gone away, as people in official positions always do.

III

At the end of April 1949 I said goodbye to the Department of Anthropology and a week later set off with Victor on a visit to Europe and Africa. We flew by Pan American to Brussels and then travelled about Europe (Paris, Venice, Rome) for a fortnight, finally reaching England, where I stayed with my mother and Eldyth for a couple of months. At the end of this time, at the beginning of August, Victor and I went to French West Africa (AOF).

The trip required elaborate preparations. Geoffrey Gorer gave us advice; Daryll Forde (a great charmer but with the habit, common to Africanists, of talking about cliteridectomy at the top of his voice in crowded restaurants) fixed us up. We studied photos at the International African Institute, read books at the Royal Anthropological Institute. Victor went over to Paris to see Professor Monod who agreed that his Institut Français d'Afrique Noire (IFAN) would give us every assistance, and obtained a gracious letter from Marcel Griaule who recommended the *érudit* Dr Elwin to the *bienveillante attention* of the Governor-General of the AOF. I myself got a rather cold letter from the British Colonial Office, asking the local officials to give 'whatever assistance may properly be afforded to you', should we go into 'British' Africa.

For some time we wondered if we would be able to go at all, but at last there was a copy of a document from the Ministre de la France d'Outre-Mer to say that our request had received *une suite favorable*.

We left London on August 1st for Paris, where the formalities went on and on, and four days later flew in a Skymaster, not one of my favourite aircraft, to Dakar and got seats (as we say in India) in a hotel at midnight. Here the IFAN people were very helpful; we interviewed Ministers, Commissioners and police. The British Consul, apart from his view that anthropologists were only interested in 'tits and temples', was kind.

From Dakar we went to the Haute Volta, flying to Bobo-Dioulasso in the heart of the bush, where we started our adventures.

We were late in arriving, and the sun was going down. It was drizzling a little. The airport was crowded with enthusiastic Frenchwomen in shorts and topis welcoming their husbands back from Dakar, and African chiefs greeting a party of Deputies on their way to Ouagadougou.

We stood drearily under a wing of the plane waiting for something to happen and at last we saw our baggage being piled into a decrepit bus with the words 'God is My Refuge' painted above the windscreen.

'I suppose we'd better get in,' said Victor, and so we did.

There was another pause, and then a young policeman approached and inquired our professions. He did not, I thought, seem altogether satisfied with the word *ethnologue*. He had no pencil, so I had to lend him mine and he went off with it.

There was another wait, but finally a handsome fellow in a deerstalker's cap shook us by the hand, climbed into the driver's seat and took off at a great pace towards the town.

After calling at an interminable number of places, where the driver appeared to have personal affairs to settle, the car stopped abruptly outside the Hôtel du Cercle, where we had wired for reservations. Our baggage was hastily dumped on the side of the road, the driver with a beaming smile shook hands all round, and drove off into the night.

The hotel was brightly lit and looked rather attractive. There was a large palm court in front of the building and waiters were busy setting out tables, for it had now ceased to rain. For the moment my spirits rose. But when we met the apple-cheeked proprietor, who might have come straight off a farm in the Médoc, he protested that he had never had any telegram about reservations. I suspect that even if he had it would have made little difference. For already we could see our fellow-passengers, most of whom had arrived long before in private cars, in full possession; the hotel had, I think, some contract with Air France to give priority accommodation whenever one of their planes was benighted, as it was that day.

There was not a room in the place, explained the proprietor. No, there were no other hotels. But it was the Feast of the Assumption; there would be dancing all night; and the *ethnologue anglais* and his party would be most welcome to dinner. Regard, he spread out his hands, what a *repas,* what *vins,* what an *ambiance*!

Our bags had by now been heaped into a small mountain under a tree to one side of the court. I could see nowhere to sit, so I put myself down on Victor's bedding and gazed mournfully at the gay scene, while Victor himself continued to protest in his most idiomatic French.

I sat on. Presently a small French child hugging a golliwog came up and stared at me in a most offensive manner, as if comparing me unfavourably with her toy. I was meditating a protest when fortunately a dog-fight broke out among the tables. Women screamed, bottles were upset, Victor jumped to safety on his chair.

In the end, we got rooms of a sort. Very fortunately, one of the Administrateurs Adjoints des Colonies was there, having an aperitif in honour of the Assumption, and overheard a reference to the Directeur-Général de l'Interieur, for Victor—having failed with his Haut-Commissaire's letter—was firing off even his secondary armament in his despair. Monsieur Dubonnet, for such was the improbable name of this pleasant, capable if bullet-headed young official, soon had the matter settled. The entire hotel was rearranged and a room was put at our disposal.

Dinner, moreover, was not too bad. The *repas vin non compris* was only a hundred francs, and there were over forty *supplé-ments.* We made a fair meal of fish soup, braised tongue and ices. There were even *escargots* (one hundred francs) which I insisted on having, though I left most of them when I found they were tinned.

Such was our introduction to Bobo-Dioulasso. Next morning we were up early and went out to try and make arrangements. Just outside our door two of the hotel servants were engaged in skinning a monkey, which must have died of some nameless disease during the night. They grinned at me as I went past, but fortunately did not offer to shake hands. After a breakfast of lukewarm coffee and rolls, Victor and I walked down one of the long red streets—rather pretty with flowers growing everywhere—towards the shops.

After a lot of palaver, we were able to make a programme, hire a car, and set out to explore.

Our first destination was Gaoua, a small town some two hundred kilometres along a road *en bon état* from Bobo-Dioulasso, which is the centre of a district which the guide-book describes as *région très accidentée,* and specially interesting for *le particularisme de ses habitants.* We left, fairly early, in two cars—a large station-wagon and a jeep. The drive through the bush was, frankly, rather dull.

The road went on and on and on, through a green desert of low trees and thorny shrubs. There were very few people about, and we saw no animals. Sometimes there was a sudden activity of people assembling for a bazaar, women tramping along in file, great strapping creatures, many of them, their height accentuated by piles of baskets on their heads.

An occasional scarlet bird flickered and flaunted its beauty across the way.

From time to time we would pass a village ; the car would stop and we would tumble out to have a look. The mud houses, built like fortresses in the middle of their fields, were impressive. The lines of battlements appeared as rocks rising above a green sea of vegetation.

In this way we spent a week visiting some delightful Bobos, a Dian village, saw Fulanis tending cattle and at a place called Coule had our first sight of the extraordinary Lobi *femmes aux plateaux* who at first seemed the most unsightly women we had ever seen, though it was strange how quickly we got used to them.

We returned to Bobo-Dioulasso and left for Abidjan on the Ivory Coast by train. With our memories of the Blue Train and the Grands Express of France and impressed by the sonorous name of the railway company, we had been looking forward to comfort if not luxury. In fact la Compagnie Internationale des Wagons-Lits et des Grands Express Européens had arranged for us wooden benches, four to a compartment, with straw mattresses and very narrow straw pillows. They had covered the windows with a thick gauze to keep out the showers of sparks which blew in from the wood fire of the engine. This also protected the passengers from any inconvenient *courant d'air* and indeed from any air at all. They had provided one lavatory for the entire bogie, and this was small and dirty; when I turned the single tap not a drop of water came out.

A train in Africa is less a means of locomotion than a great slowly-moving bazaar. At every wayside station there was a long halt. Peasants crowded round with flocks of goats, baskets of eggs, headloads of yams, calabashes of rice-beer. The more enterprising railway servants and many of the third-class passengers bought these things in large quantities to resell at a profit on the coast, and when their own compartments were full, piled them up in the first-class corridor. There was a great deal of handshaking everywhere. At each station the staff drank a little beer, with the result that by nightfall the train was proceeding in a most unusual manner. Sometimes it would go so slowly that you thought it was going to stop; then suddenly it would wake up and presently be pounding along at a tremendous rate, the furnace erupting clouds of fiery particles. Then, with loud cries of excitement, the brakesmen would rush at wheels fixed at the rear of each coach, and turn them excitedly until the train slowed a little.

But the highlight of our expedition was our visit to French Togo to which we had been attracted by Geoffrey Gorer, who had been there in 1933. He had told us that the Cabrais were the only group of 'uncivilized' Africans he had met who were not mad. We flew from Abidjan to Lomé, the pretty little capital on the coast, and then worked our way north. Togo is a long slender finger poked into the ribs of Africa and our destination was somewhere near the base of the nail, the hill country where the Cabrais had their villages. On the way we visited the Konkombas and at Sara, where for once we got a comfortable Chief's house to live in, we had a wonderful time with attractive and friendly people and a dance, lasting all night, which I shall never forget.

We had an interesting, and exciting, journey, up and away from the coast. It was a sort of geographical striptease, for the people wore fewer and fewer clothes as we went north. We passed through lovely wooded country and were greeted all along the road by smiling men and women who raised their hands in salute. We were told that they raised an open hand to show that they held no weapons.

Finally we reached Lama Kara where M. Pierre Aubanel, the Commandant de Cercle, was very good to us and made some admirable arrangements. These were necessary, for we proposed to walk and did walk right across the Cabrai hills just as if we had been in India. Our first two or three villages were dull and sophisticated and we began by cursing Geoffrey for misleading us. But once we were in the heart of the country we found something that I had never found before, entirely fascinating.

The Cabrais are good cultivators and build excellent houses which are kept as clean as their own attractive persons. When we were there, there was still a great deal of disease in the country, especially goitre, umbilical hernia and sleeping-sickness. But many of the people were fine specimens of humanity. The Chiefs and other important gentlemen were rather overdressed but the others (and especially the beautiful younger ones) lived at this time completely naked; even the Catholic girls had nothing but a crucifix pendant between their splendid breasts. Some of the men had bought bowler hats which an enterprising French businessman had imported and they looked very quaint with them and nothing else. One day I met an old man dressed in nothing except a beard and a large sun-hat. He swept it off and bowed with a gesture worthy of a Marquis, saying 'Bonjour, Monsieur'.

I think what most impressed me was the mental freedom of the Cabrais who, as Gorer pointed out long ago, had very little religion and were not haunted by the fear of their dead ancestors. They were also free of shyness and prudery and gave one an unusual sense of innocence. In each village Victor and I used to be given separate mud cabins and lovely creatures 'naked as cows' would come in at any time, day or night, and sit beside us with no trace of self-consciousness. Gorer says that 'women enjoy great sexual licence' and the men are 'much addicted to pederasty'. Neither Victor nor I saw any sign of this: perhaps we were so preoccupied with preserving our own virtue that our powers of observation were weakened. I think that Gorer was speaking of a rather different area, for he did not go, as we did, into the deep interior.

There were two special villages, Phauda and Aneida, in each of which we spent several days and I shall never forget them. I had several attacks of malaria and a bad throat most of the time but even these could not take away the excitement and pleasure of this wonderful visit.

Victor took some of the best photographs that he has ever made and a number of them were later reproduced in the *Geographical Magazine.*

Then, finally, with regret, we left the country of this happy, uninhibited and carefree people and went down to the coast whence we went by boat to Dahomey, and from there by car to Lagos.

Our departure from Lomé was sensational.

On the pier stood a row of curious wooden seats, rather like those in which one sits when one is rash enough to ascend a giant wheel at an English fair. An official motioned to us to put ourselves and our baggage into one of them, and we did so.

Suddenly with a shrill blast on its siren and a shrieking of rusty machinery a crane leapt into life. A great hook descended above us out of the darkness ; with shouts of excitement our porters jumped for it and attached it to an iron bar which was fixed to our seat ; there was another blast on the siren, and we were swung up and out over the dark Atlantic forty feet below.

At this moment all the lights went out.

There seemed to be some kind of boat beneath us, for harsh cries in an unknown language came up from the depths. But we could see nothing, and remained swinging to and fro.

After five or six minutes the lights came on. The siren screamed, and we went down towards the sea and hit the deck of a small boat tossing and heaving on the rollers with such force that all the lights went out again.

This time they stayed out for half an hour.

The waves seemed enormous and our little boat stood alternately on head and tail. I should have been very sick indeed had I not been so anxious.

'Good god! What's that?' suddenly exclaimed Victor, clutching me by the arm.

Out of the darkness a boat piled high with cases of copra appeared almost on top of us. I shut my eyes. A collision seemed inevitable. Everybody shouted at once, our boatmen leapt to their feet and with their oars just managed to fend off the intruder, which vanished into the night as suddenly as it had come.

When the lights did at last come on, another mammy chair (as these abominable contraptions are called) came down into our boat. This one contained a ship's officer and two almost hysterical French girls who had been ashore for a few hours. A steam launch fussed up beside us, a rope was slung, and we were tugged at a rapid speed out into the Atlantic.

Our boat heaved and swayed, clouds of spray broke over us, the ship's officer chattered, the girls screamed, Victor and I, green of face and sick with apprehension, clung to our seats.

At last we saw the great sides of the liner looming up before us, and we were pulled round to a point where high above us on a brightly-lighted deck we could see its cranes. But we were not to be released yet. It was rougher out here, and there were perhaps a score of other boats clattering and banging against the liner's side. An exceptionally big wave lifted them up and it seemed that they must inevitably crash down upon us. It was a terrifying sight, this mass of crude wooden boats with their gesticulating shouting crews lifted above our heads and ourselves in the trough of a swirling mass of water.

But at last we saw to our joy a hook descending. To my annoyance our boatmen sent the other chair up first, though in view of the fact that we had been in the boat for at least half an hour longer, we should have had priority. But the hook came down again and we were drawn up to lights and a steady deck.

Then we were very comfortable—a good cabin, French food, wine. But the mammy chairs were not easily forgotten.

In British Nigeria things were done much better: the roads were straighter, the hospitals bigger, the schools cleaner, but by comparison it was cold. There was no handshaking: it was no longer French.

After a few days in Lagos, we flew back to Paris, and thence direct to Calcutta and home to Patangarh.

IV

Our visit to French West Africa had one serious drawback, that I was unable to get, anywhere, a cup of tea.

The shops and hotels all over that great area had only the vaguest idea of what it was. In place of the reviving and 'wink-tippling cordial' to which long habit had attached me, I was given messy cups of bad coffee. At last, after several frustrated weeks, in the great market of Lomé in Togoland, I found a very fly-blown packet of the divine leaves tucked away between one stall selling the impedimenta of black magic and another stocked with chamber-pots. It was then that I realized Dr Johnson's devotion to 'the infusion of this fascinating plant', 'whose kettle has scarcely time to cool; who with tea amuses the evening, with tea solaces the midnight, and with tea welcomes the morning'.

Tea, and to a less extent coffee, is the background. But there is also food.

I am perfectly content, really content, with the simplest Indian vegetarian food—it is hard to beat a plain dish of well-cooked pulse and rice—and in Patangarh my menu was often a simple *mélange* of:

Riz pardhan
Plat de lentilles Esaü
Poulet au safran à la facon de Patangarh
Purée de légumes forestière

At the same time I am greatly attracted to the more elaborate and exotic foods, though I hardly ever get them. In India I like Gujarati vegetarian food best of all, such as I had from Anasuya Behn over thirty years ago. And another hostess of whose dishes I would say

Art could not feign more simple grace
Nor Nature take a line away

is Indira Luthra.

My knowledge of other kinds of food is inseparably associated with Victor Sassoon. I had long wanted to eat a meal at the Tour d'Argent with its view of Nôtre-Dame in Paris, for although A. E. Housman thought the cooking at the Café de

Paris was better, he had a great opinion of its *Canard à la presse*, and they had devised a dish, *Barbue Housman*—fish cooked with cheese and served with new potatoes, very small—in his honour. Victor took me there on a lovely May morning. The maître d'hôtel had never heard of *Barbue Housman*, so instead we began with a little smoked salmon, went on to the *Canard au sang* (No. 199549) and ended up with some artichoke bottoms, the whole washed down by an aristocratic Montrachet.

During those days with Victor, I ate my way across Europe and even French Africa, where we were able to get wonderful brandy in little shops far away in the bush and many simple but exquisite French meals. We did not aim at the highest flights but for the only time in my life I had things which I have never forgotten. One of our most memorable meals was, unexpectedly, in Brussels at a little place in the Rue de la Violette called L'Ecu de France, where much of our enjoyment was due to a very human and competent waiter. He brought us *Escargots de Bourgogne*, followed by cold lobster and *Coq au vin de Savigny*, and ended up by setting fire to our *Crêpes flambées* with quite reckless contributions of Grand Marnier.

Another admirable lunch—I greatly prefer lunches to dinners—was at Lugano: *Nouillettes à l'oeuf au beurre* with *sauce bolognaise* and *Fraises des bois Romanoff*. Another day we had cold artichokes, with *sauce Gribiche*, which were delicious.

In Venice and Rome, we fed well but not exceptionally. For the best Italian food I have ever tasted I had to wait for Shillong and beautiful Inez (wife of our very special friend Jiten Ghosh), who used to give us a *ravioli*, with all the trimmings, which had to be tasted to be believed.

We naturally let ourselves go in Paris. I had first visited the Reine Pédauque fifteen years before with the novelist Wilfrid David and Shamrao; now Victor and I had a good but rather unbalanced lunch, stupidly not accepting the maître d'hôtel's advice to take the famous *Coq au vin au Château de Corton André*. Instead we had

Champignons sautés á la Bordelaise
Truite sautée fines herbes
Rognons de veau flambés Reine Pédauque.

In Montmartre we found the delightful Auberge du Sanglier Bleu, whose grilled lamb chops took one into another world, and to whose lobster soup we returned more than once.

I also liked the Restaurant de l'Escargot, of whose *menu très soigné* the first prize goes to the snails which give it its name.

However, I can manage with perfectly simple dishes. If it were to be my last meal on earth I would start with a dish of *escargots* with a *sauce vinaigrette*, go on to a dozen oysters, some asparagus with *sauce hollandaise* and end up with *crêpes Suzette*. It is no good thinking of the wine, for there probably wouldn't be any in India by then.

And afterwards, when it is all over, I agree with Sydney Smith who once said that his idea of heaven was 'eating *pâté de foie gras* to the sound of trumpets'.

I may sum it all up by going back twenty years to Patangarh, where our very rustic cook one day startled us by announcing a 'Buttocks Savoury' for supper. He was very proud of the few English dishes he knew and by 'buttocks' he probably meant *batak* or duck. Another day there was a discussion in the village as to what kind of sahib I was. The Commissioner had recently visited us. There was no doubt about him—he was a *pakka sahib*. A minor Indian official had also been—he was a *dal-bhat sahib*. But what was I? Our cook solved the riddle. 'He is a *savoury sahib*,' he declared.

V

In the following year Victor and I went again to Africa, this time with the idea of visiting the Belgian Congo and French Equatorial Africa. We went by boat to Mombasa which I did not enjoy, for if air-travel inspires me with the fear of death, sea-travel fills me with the desire for it. We went up to Nairobi and were just making our arrangements to go into the heart of Africa, when I developed gall-bladder trouble and the specialist we consulted said it would be dangerous for me to go into the wilds remote from the possibility of medical attention. This meant that we had to rearrange our programme, though Victor in the end did go to AEF and saw something of the Congo, for which I have always envied him. We spent some time based on Nairobi where there was an old friend, Dr L. S. B. Leakey, with whom I had grown up as a little boy, for both he and I are renegade sons of pious missionary parents. He enabled us to see something of the Kikuyu and Masai. The Mau-Mau movement had not yet begun but the British residents were busily digging the foundations of their own destruction and we could already feel the growing tension.

We then made a quick visit to Tanganyika where we stayed at Arusha and Moshi below Kilimanjaro. In a place called Voi we saw the usual animals and went up into the Teista hills to see something of the people. At Mzima Springs we were charged by an enraged female hippopotamus.

After this we flew to Entebbe and thus to Kampala. We liked Uganda best of all, for racial distinctions were much weaker there, and we were fortunate in being able to hire a good car with a first-rate African driver. In this we drove up to the north of Gulu, went boating on the Nile and during our wanderings saw something of the Acholis and Lugbaras. We actually went for two hours into the Belgian Congo, after an incredible lot of fuss about passports and permits, characteristic of the impenetrable hinterlands of red-tape everywhere, and had lunch there.

'Africans dance,' says Geoffrey Gorer, in his classical book on the subject. 'They dance for joy, and they dance for grief; they dance for love and they dance for hate; they dance to avert calamity; they dance for religion and they dance to pass the time.'

But even in 1950 African dancing had become sporadic. There were still areas—East as well as West—where these words of Gorer were true. There were many other parts where they were already out of date, where a change of religion, or a general economic and cultural malaise had robbed the people of their passion for the dance. Nor was it always easy to witness a dance in Africa: you had to be at the right season, find the people in the mood, above all you must not be in a hurry.

As we drove north through the pleasant fertile country of Uganda, we at last reached the Acholi district which extends almost to the Sudan border. The Acholis are a Nilotic people, who at one time were distinguished by their beautiful headdress and clothes of leopard skin ; today, however, many of them have adopted the outward garb of civilization.

On our way back to Kampala we found ourselves one warm midday at a little town called Atiak. Here were a few Indian shops, and to our surprise and delight we were received and most hospitably entertained by a Gujarati family. It is astonishing how the Indian merchants of East Africa have penetrated to the remotest places, and with what enterprise and courage they ply their trade. Their importance is indicated by the fact that East African bank-notes are printed in Gujarati as well as English. After a delicious lunch of *puris,* mango chutney and other delicacies, the thunder of drums outside proclaimed that the Acholis had assembled for a dance.

This dance was one of the most splendid and exciting that I have ever seen—and for thirty years I have been watching and recording tribal dances. It roused in me the same feeling of delight that I have had when witnessing a Naga war dance or a Bison-Horn Maria wedding dance. Imagine a vast crowd of shining glistening bodies of a beautiful jet black gyrating, gesticulating, now moving in ordered rhythm, now breaking into individual ecstasy, stamping, thumping, jumping with enormous enthusiasm and zest. That is, I think, the first thing that strikes the onlooker about an African dance—its zest.

To these people a dance is not just an extra, a luxury to be indulged in or not as one feels inclined ; where it has remained, it is an essential force in life, as natural as breathing or eating, and always done with passionate delight. The Acholi dancers never smiled ; they were too intent, too keyed up ; they were at serious business, they were entranced.

The dancers entered the field in a succession of processions, leaping and dancing like war-horses. They moved roughly round a tall pole, but they did not observe any special order, and indeed the area soon became so congested with hundreds of dancers that it began to resemble the dance-floor of a popular Parisian cabaret. Unhappily very few of the people were dressed in traditional style, but some had the old headdresses of feathers, and most of the men had a curious label attached to their bottoms, on which they inscribed their initials or some such caption as H E, A D C, and in one striking case, U S A.

To witness a dance such as the one we saw at Atiak was to realize the deep elemental power of Africa, its capacity for enjoyment and display, its overmastering love of rhythm. 'The discovery of the dark races,' said Karen Blixen, 'was to me a magnificent enlargement of all my world,' and anyone who is not blinded by prejudice will agree with her.

There are, in fact, two ways of seeing the African villagers at their best—at a dance and at a market. The great markets of Africa are still exciting spectacles, where every stage of civilization, every degree of economic progress meet and mingle.

On the eastern boundaries of the Belgian Congo lies the West Nile district of Uganda, a remote and lovely part of the world, with its astonishing variety of big game and its friendly, almost bewitching people. Here lives the large and comparatively prosperous tribe of the Lugbaras. There are about two lakhs of them and they are reckoned to be some of the best cultivators in Africa. That means they have money to spend in their markets.

Thirty years ago most of them went entirely naked, but today the men wear clothes, often rather regrettable European clothes, and the women dress in leaves for the most part, though some have begun to put on skirts and blouses. This means that there are things they want to buy.

I visited three great markets in a single morning. Under the lovely flowering trees—the Uganda tulip with its glorious red tubular blossoms, the yellow cassia, a beautiful acacia with fluffy spikes—was a sea of black bodies, diversified by vivid splashes of colour: gay silk turbans, bright wimples round the head, flowers in the hair, strings of variegated beads. To me black is a lovely colour, and when it shines and dances in the sun, and is set off by the bright reds and greens and blues of art or nature, I find it entrancing.

Each market had a great fenced-in enclosure and there was a small entrance fee. Inside, it was hardly possible to move. On every side groups of chattering people sat on the ground beside their wares, and the wares were as varied as the people who sold them—mats, baskets, pots, grindstones, food (raw and cooked), fruit, ornaments, tobacco, sugarcane, beer (these happy people can make beer out of almost anything; there is honey-beer and banana-beer). It was in a way—except for the beer—much like an Indian bazaar out in the mofussil. There was a lot of trade by barter, but money was used and I did not see the cowries which are common in French West Africa.

The most memorable thing to my mind about those Lugbara markets was their friendliness. Beaming smiles greeted me everywhere, and for once I found people clamouring to be photographed and I had to pretend to take many pictures which never actually went on to the film!

There is a great potential store of friendliness and goodwill in Africa, but there is hate there too—and one of the great factors of the world-peace of the future will be whether goodwill or hate prevails.

VI

I was invited to visit Ceylon by Suzanne Karpeles and G. P. Malalasekara and spent an exciting and profitable three weeks there. I got landed in rather a lot of public appearances and have never received so much attention from the newspapers. I held an exhibition of my photographs which was visited by over a thousand people, which was not bad for Colombo, and lectured at the University, the Royal Asiatic Society, Young Men's Buddhist Association and so on. I also made three expeditions. The first was with Suzanne and the Director of Archaeology in Ceylon, a most learned person, S. Paravatana. We went to all the right places, to Sigiriya, Dambulla and Anuradhapura, but of all the ancient cities we visited, the one that stirred me most was Mihintale. I had, of course, visited northern Ceylon before but it was on this occasion that the impact of the old Buddhism hit me most strongly.

Then I made another excursion with Dr R. L. Spittel, a very old resident of Colombo and an authority, perhaps the only living authority, on the Veddas, whom I had long wanted to see. He took me out into the wilds, to two of the only remaining primitive Vedda settlements, and it was an experience of a quite different flavour to any I have had either in India or in Africa. I had no idea, of course, of telling the Ceylon Government their business but the reporters were so persistent that I did express myself rather strongly on the lack of attention paid to the Veddas who were completely neglected. My remarks had their effect and Dick Spittel wrote to me after I left: 'Believe me, your comments in the press stirred the hearts of our Ministers. They felt the sting pretty badly, as more than one of them confessed to me. I have now drawn up, at their request, a Vedda Welfare Scheme, with a V. W. Officer and V. W. Advisory Committee and suggested as an immediate necessity, that the Pollebedde folk at least should have food rations and guns. *Mirabile dictu*—this has already been put into effect. You can well picture the result on some of those sad starved faces you saw.'

I believe that Spittel himself was finally appointed Adviser for the Veddas to the Ceylon Government.

My third trip was with my old Oxford friend Bernard Aluwihare. He took me out to Matale where he had a house right up in the hills in very beautiful surroundings, and I paid a visit to what was in some ways the family temple, a superb shrine cut in the rock and decorated with many paintings.

VII

Probably of all my visits abroad the most exciting was to Thailand. When I was at Oxford there was a boy, somewhat junior to me, at University College, called Arthur Braine-Hartnell. He was a poet and created an atmosphere about himself that very few could equal. He was a dear, excessive person and, when he died recently at the age of 56, I was very sad about it. I often used to go to his rooms to drink beer and he told me long afterwards that I met Graham Greene, Evelyn Waugh and W. H. Auden there. The trouble was, of course, that when I met them (if I really did) they were just intelligent young men. They had not yet become what they are now. But Harold Acton was already a vivid and original personality.

Later B.-H. migrated to Thailand and became a professor in

the University. Something recalled me to his recollection and he wrote to invite me to stay with him in Bangkok, and Shamrao and I had a wonderful month there and in the north.

A great deal has been written about Thailand and a good guide-book will really tell the reader most of what we saw. We looked at temples till our eyes bubbled and I took some remarkably successful photographs, particularly one of Wat Arun with three aircraft flying round the spire in formation, a picture one might get once in a thousand years.

Unfortunately, I wrote very little about this visit while it was fresh in my mind, just a few articles for newspapers. I did what I could to meet Thai scholars and visited their Asiatic Society. But actually we were there on holiday and Thailand is a place where you can have a real holiday. There is nothing here to excite your idealism. In Africa there was the race problem to make you miserable. In Ceylon there were the neglected Veddas. In India, of course, one has no rest. But in Thailand I felt that we were with a people who were perfectly adjusted to their setting and that even where they had wrongs they were so happy that they could forget them.

We stayed for some days with Braine-Hartnell and then moved to the Norfolk Hotel. There we met a remarkable English lawyer who had been President of the Cambridge Union and Legal Adviser to the Thai Government, Gerald Sparrow, who was extraordinarily good to Shamrao and myself.

One great thing he did for us was to take us to Chiengmai in the north and provide a car for us to get about. Chiengmai is a striking contrast to Bangkok. Where that is crowded, this is comparatively open. The people, who have much Lao and Burmese blood, are fairer of complexion and even more charming in manner than the southerners. The temples are built in a different style ; they are less elaborate, less gaudy, yet with a dignity and beauty all their own. The climate is better, considerably cooler than Bangkok, and roses—which do not succeed in the capital—grow here to a wonderful size and colour.

Gerald took us fifty miles to the north to a little monastery hidden under a great hill whose jagged fingers of rock pointed to the sky. This was Chiang Dao, one of the most peaceful and romantic spots I have ever visited. There is a great cave thronged with silent images, and many little pagodas built on the rocks; some of them look down on a pond full of fishes which are fed by the gentle monks. It was delightful to drive here through the fields where the peasants were gathering the rice-harvest; Siam is so full of water that they often transport their crops by boat instead of by bullock-cart, and most of their houses are built up on piles to avoid the universal damp. The people looked picturesque in their blue dresses with large straw sun-hats.

Siamese religion owes a great deal to India. The story of the Ramayana (with not a little of its piety extracted) has been a universal inspiration to architecture, sculpture, woodwork and mural paintings, and it has dominated the theatre. Court terminology, dress and festivals also owe much to Indian tradition. But religion is less obvious in Siam than in India; it does not go so deep, it is less fanatical, it is not so strong a factor in public life.

An American anthropologist, J. F. Embree, once compared Thai culture with that of Japan and Vietnam, and suggested that while the social structure of Japan and Vietnam is 'close' —that is, the behaviour of the people conforms closely to the formal social patterns of human relations—that of Siam is very loosely woven. The Thais are individualists, and Embree speaks of the 'almost determined lack of regularity, discipline and regimentation' in their ordinary life. There is little respect for administrative regularity and no industrial time-sense. While the Japanese regard work as a virtue, and the Chinese accept it as a rule, the Thais do not consider it to be a thing good in itself. And this temperamental attitude shows itself in Thai religion. The chief end of Siamese Buddhism is happiness. One of the first things I was asked by a Thai friend in Chiengmai was: 'Are you happy?' To a visitor from India, where we do not think about happiness very often and certainly do not use it as a yardstick of success, the question came as a shock, a very pleasant shock. Not 'Are you well?' or 'Are you good?' or 'Are you making money or getting promotion?' but 'Are you happy?' There is a Siamese word *sunuk*, which means something pleasant, absorbing, delightful, tolerant—it is one of the primary values. It is *sunuk* to travel hopefully, *sunuk* to enjoy a game or a dance or someone's company. Buddhism is *sunuk*: other religions are a little dull. It is said that the Siamese respect those who can make them laugh; to make a Siamese like you, you must make him feel happy.

Of all the places I visited in the happy land of Siam, Chiengmai was the most *sunuk*.

I have mentioned the poor murdered Bella Wright who, though I never saw her, had such an influence on my life. Rather similar was the lovely Rada, the Siamese girl with whom I spent rapturous days in Chiengmai. She had been educated in America, spoke English 'slowly and easily', with a trace of the accent found among 'the very smart young ladies who had been to the most exclusive finishing schools in the States or in Paris'. We ate sucking-pig together and drank Black Label. One evening she did a superb lampoon on American and Siamese dancing and I declared, 'I did not know men could be so happy.' But at last we had to part. 'Most reluctantly we waved farewell to our lovely and gifted Rada. As we became air-borne, we saw her waving a little lace handkerchief until we were out of sight.' How wonderful it was and that little lace handkerchief still tears my heart. Gerald Sparrow tells you all about it in his *Land of the Moonflower*.

The only trouble is that Rada never existed. Gerald invented the whole thing to make me more interesting. It never, I am sure, occurred to him that the story might go, as it did, to a high level in the Government of India with the suggestion that I was not very nice to know. Gerald was genuinely fond of me as I was of him and, in fact, he did me proud in this book: 'Verrier was as untidy and as delightful as ever, a genial bear of a man, with long hair, searching eyes and a gentle voice . . . a great man, judged by any standards other than mercenary ones . . . a saint, not a pale historical saint reeking of purity and unction, but a modern saint, fallible and human, yet with an infinite compassion.' You can't be cross with someone who says such nice things about you.

But what are we to do with Rada? For hundreds of readers she exists as firmly as any other historical character we know only from books. She is part of my own life now. Dear Rada, how nice it would have been . . .

One result of our visit was that I wrote such enthusiastic letters to Victor about Thailand that he left India for good and went to live in Bangkok where he was appointed to a professorship of English in the University.

VIII

Since 1928 I have been to Europe four times, staying on each occasion for about two months. Eight months in thirty-four years is not very long, and the result has been that my links with Oxford have been impaired, old friends have fallen into neglect, but worst of all, it meant that I inevitably neglected my mother (though I wrote to her every week without fail) who died a few years ago at the age of 89.

But there were some friends with whom I never lost touch. Closest of these was the late Laurence Housman who gave me a lot of help when I was working for Gandhi in the early years. Later, just before the Second World War, he invited Shamrao and me to England and made the visit financially possible. I carried on an animated correspondence with him for many years.

Laurence was a strong pacifist, an admirer of Gandhi, and at the end of his life joined the Society of Friends, in which, he told me, he had the only religious comfort that was left for him. Blake's poem 'The Divine Image' stated the whole of his religious beliefs. He had, he said, 'become very anti-theological'.

In the last letter I had from him, written shortly before his death, he wrote:

> I am almost in despair about the world's future. Our acceptance of War as a remedy for wrong has produced the Hydrogen Bomb which, if we stumble into another World War, will mean suicide and extinction for friend and foe alike. . . . There is no one in the political world whom I can put much trust in—except Nehru who, to my mind, is the greatest man alive. I hope you love him.

During all these years my sister Eldyth had been living with mother and, though she would never admit it, losing much of what life had to give in consequence. I have never met anyone so completely unselfish as Eldyth. Her whole life has been devoted to other people. Fortunately, even when mother was alive, since they lived in or near London, she was able to find interesting work as one of the Secretaries of the Church Missionary Society, a job she has now been doing for many years. Eldyth visited us in Patangarh in 1939 just before the War, and again spent a very happy two months with us in Shillong during an official tour which took her all over India visiting mission stations and hospitals.

In her own person, Eldyth illustrates one of Gandhi's sayings: 'True love is boundless like the ocean and, rising and swelling within one, spreads itself out and crossing all boundaries and frontiers envelops the whole world.'

Basil became a schoolmaster and for some time taught at the famous Cheam School, where one of his pupils was a boy who was later to become the Duke of Edinburgh. Since then he has taught at two or three other schools. He married an outstandingly beautiful girl called Helen; they now have three children who are, I am told, enchanting though I have only seen one of them and that when she was a baby. I have seen little of Basil and we seldom write, but I feel very close to him, for he is a man after my own heart and, when we do meet, we get on exceptionally well together.

8

Passage to NEFA

Great things are done when Men and Mountains meet ;
This is not done by Jostling in the Street.

—William Blake

I

THE years of research in Bastar and Orissa were happy and rewarding. Yet for a long time I had been thinking of Assam and Dr J. H. Hutton wrote me a detailed letter far back in the early forties about the possibilities of research there. In June 1947, just before Independence, Bill Archer, who had been transferred from Bihar to the Naga Hills, invited me to visit him at Mokokchung. He told me to come to a station called Nakachari and said that he would send someone to meet me. Bill, of course, is a poet and did not think of telling me where Mokokchung was.

Accordingly Shamrao and I set out by road and rail—the air service was not yet operating—on the long journey to Assam. The heat was almost Promethean. After some days of constant travel we arrived at Nakachari and were greeted by two affable Nagas. I asked them to take me to Mr Archer's bungalow, which I assumed would be a mile or so from the railway station.

'Well actually,' they said, 'Mokokchung is forty-seven miles away.'

This was a good deal further than I expected, but I was not unduly perturbed, for I supposed it would not take very long. 'Where,' I said, 'is the car?'

'I am afraid,' replied one of the Nagas, 'a car wouldn't be much use, for there's no road. We shall have to walk. It takes four days.'

So walk we did, a very strenuous expedition in the great heat, but there were good dak bungalows along the way and Bill came down one stage to greet us.

We spent a few days in Mokokchung itself and visited a number of Ao villages in the neighbourhood and then went across to Kohima, where we met the famous Sir Charles Pawsey and were taken by a very charming and efficient Naga official, Mr Kevichusa Angami, to see a number of Naga villages. I had already begun collecting material for a new book on tribal art and I took many photographs of the old village gates, so strikingly carved, most of which have been destroyed by now. I also met Phizo, who was then developing his zenophobic policy which was to bring so much suffering and discredit on his people.

Then Shamrao returned to Patangarh and I went down to meet Bill at Jorhat and we went together into the Konyak country, up to Wakching where Christoph von Fürer-Haimendorf had once spent a year. Bill, of course, was very busy about his official duties, and during our few days' stay in Wakching many of the Konyak and Phom Chiefs from Tuensang came to visit him. We both made useful collections of carvings, hats and other trophies.

On our way up, we arrived completely by chance at a village called Kongan just as it was celebrating the capture of a human ear from a remote village near Burma. The British Government was then doing what it could to check head-hunting and this particular village had accepted a well-meant suggestion to hunt monkeys instead of human beings. Unfortunately, immediately after they had done so, they had a disastrous outbreak of cholera and decided that substitutes just would not do.

The custom at this time was that if you could not get a complete head you could buy part of one, such as an ear, from a more successful village. The people of Kongan had done this and, when we arrived, were celebrating the purchase just as if they had conducted a victorious head-hunting expedition themselves. I have seen many Naga dances since then but nothing ever to compare with this, for this was the real thing, not something 'laid on' for a visiting official. In fact, the people had no idea that we were coming and would certainly not have done the dance had they heard in time, for Bill in his official capacity had to impose a heavy fine, though with great reluctance. The villagers, however, took it very well and said that after all it was worth it, as they would now get good crops and better babies.

From Mokokchung I went by myself, with my assistant Sundarlal and a completely delightful Naga interpreter, into the Konyak country. Now we saw the last of the old life. The missionaries had not yet penetrated into the villages we visited and everything was going on as it must have done for hundreds of years past. Next to my Cabrai expedition it was one of the most exciting adventures I have ever had.

II

My next visit to Assam was in 1952 when the Governor, Mr Jairamdas Daulatram, invited me. This time Shamrao and I drove all the way from Patangarh by car along roads that were not then as good as they are today. It took us nearly twenty-four hours to cross the Ganges in a country boat. In Shillong I had some long talks with the Governor and called on N. K. (Nari) Rustomji who was then Adviser for Tribal Areas, including the great tract of what was then little-explored territory, the North-East Frontier Agency (NEFA). Today we both remember with amusement that almost the first thing Nari said to me was, 'I am sorry to tell you that NEFA is *out*.' For I was not yet (though by no fault of mine) officially an Indian citizen, and foreigners were not normally admitted into the area.

Actually my idea was to visit the hills of Manipur, of which I had heard enthusiastic accounts. We drove from Shillong to Dimapur and then, through Kohima, down to Imphal where we found to our dismay that there was only one small dak bungalow, which was so crowded that it looked like a bazaar, and no hotel. We went to see the Deputy Commissioner, a pleasant person called M. N. Phukan who had a guest-house in his garden, allowed us to stay in it, and arranged all 'facilities'. We drove about the beautiful valley and then Shamrao returned home and I went with Sundarlal on a hundred-mile trip by foot through the Kabui hills.

The Kabuis of eastern Manipur are among the most attractive tribal people in India. Graceful, hospitable and industrious, they combine a delicate sensitivity with an impeccable taste for design and colour. Although they have no wood-carving or painting, their women weave very pretty cloth, and the young men excel in personal adornment, making splendid head-dresses, armlets and necklets of bone and ivory, and unusual decorations for the ears and throat.

When I was staying in a village called Haochang, I noticed a number of little wooden cases stuck in the rafters of the house where I was being entertained. My host took one of them down and, slipping off the cane bands which kept it closed, opened it and revealed, nestling between leaves and scraps of silk-cotton, a lovely ornament made of the brilliant blue feathers of the Long-Tailed Broadbill. In the other cases there were similar ornaments of different shapes and sizes. The following day, the villagers were observing a festival for a child's ear-piercing ceremony and for the dance that followed the boys tied these ornaments to their ears, and covered their heads with horns and feathers. One boy had a glittering pendant made of beetle-backs; the girls, waving their arms in the air, fluttered like butterflies, and the young warriors paraded with their spears. The dance, I was told, had no special meaning: 'it was for beauty and happiness.'

Fortunate are those who, even in this utilitarian modern world, can place beauty and happiness first among their concerns!

The Kabui trip was a wonderful experience, but poor Sundarlal developed acute arthritis in the latter part of the tour and walking was agony for him. When we got back to Imphal I put him in the hospital, where he had to remain for three weeks. Phukan, however, was going on a tour in the Thangkhul country and I accompanied him as far as Ukhrul but afterwards went by myself, as Phukan is the fastest walker I have ever met and I could not keep up with him. Instead I had a young Thangkhul Christian as my guide and interpreter through the wide and open glories of the country round the Sirohi mountains, to the top of which we climbed. He dressed in an American bush-coat and a jockey's cap, but he was good company and an excellent guide. He tended, however, to talk rather a lot about Salvation and sometimes I felt as if I was walking with the ghost of my own lost youth.

III

I returned to Patangarh and made another visit to the Santal country but all through 1953 I found that I was getting a little stale. I felt that I had explored central India rather thoroughly. I had been violently excited and equally frustrated by Assam, and the constant rise in prices and wages was making it very difficult for any private person to carry on research.

Suddenly at the beginning of December, like a call from heaven, as I was sitting in our house at Patangarh, a mysterious telegram arrived from New Delhi signed by somebody called FOREIGN, asking me to come immediately to sit on some Selection Board for NEFA. I knew nothing about the capital and my only knowledge of NEFA was that it was a place I was not allowed to visit. The telegram had been delayed a week on the way, so there was very little time, and there was no letter to explain what it was about. After some agitated consultations with Lila and Shamrao I thought I had better go, and Lila and I went off together to Delhi as soon as we could.

We got a place in Constitution House. Most of the rooms in this attractively inexpensive hostelry have common bath-rooms. You went from your room into the bath-room and bolted the door which led into the room on the other side. This gave you temporary privacy which you surrendered by unbolting the other person's door when you went out. Unfortunately, Lila began by forgetting the unbolting ceremony with the result that our neighbour, a young and rather violent journalist, got extremely annoyed.

A few days later we were invited to breakfast by the Prime Minister and our neighbour saw his chance to take revenge. As breakfast was at 8.30 we naturally got up at 5.0, only to find that the door on our side was firmly locked and all our bangings and entreaties failed to make the slightest impression. We were both almost frantic, for one does not have breakfast with a Prime Minister every day, and Lila naturally wanted to look her best. Even I wanted a shave. We ran about trying to find some other bath-room but every room was full and it was not until a quarter past seven and after I had humbly apologized, that our young neighbour agreed to open the door and allowed us to get a wash.

But this is by the way. Early in the morning, the day after we arrived, there was a summons from my mysterious friend Foreign, who turned out to be a Joint Secretary in the Ministry of External Affairs, T. N. Kaul.

Tikki Kaul is the kind of person whom you like at first sight, and within five minutes I felt that I had known him all my life. He told me that it had been decided to form a new cadre of officials (which was ultimately called the Indian Frontier Administrative Service), that I should help to select them, and that the Prime Minister had suggested that I should join the NEFA Administration to advise it on tribal problems.

The idea was so new to me that at first I did not know what to say. I felt like someone who, after being refused a sandwich, is suddenly offered a seven-course dinner. It would mean pulling up my roots in Patangarh but, on the other hand, it would open a very wide new field of work both for the welfare of the tribes and in research. I wired to Shamrao to come to Delhi, and Lila, he and I had a long discussion and finally decided that I should accept the NEFA proposal, even though from Shamrao's point of view this was a very serious blow, for it meant that he would be left to carry on alone in Patangarh. But Shamrao has always been a person of singular unselfishness and he felt that this would be a good thing for me to do.

The move to NEFA, though I think something of the kind was a logical development and perhaps inevitable, meant a reversal of many of my original ideals. It meant going from a village that was over a hundred miles in the interior to live in a town, a small town it is true, and one in the heart of a tribal area, but still a town. It meant a regular income with comforts and amenities that I had never known before, and a corresponding loss of my former intimacy with the realities of poverty and exploitation. It meant a loss of freedom; one could no longer say exactly what one liked; one had to work to a programme: there were rules. It meant a decline in 'eccentricity', for since coming to Shillong my life has been tediously conventional.

All this raised the problem: which was more important, to have elevated ideals operating over a restricted field or to be useful on a wider scale? I have no doubt in my own mind that coming to NEFA greatly increased my usefulness to the tribes: it widened my own horizons; it strengthened my personal influence on many individuals. It decreased my own opportunities for research but made it possible for me to stimulate and direct research by other people. The restraints and discipline were doubtless very good for me. On the whole, I think it was the right thing.

IV

In Delhi, therefore, I took my seat on the Selection Board to help choose the foundation members of what was to be the IFAS. In the last eight years I have sat on a good many Selection Boards and they are much more interesting and amusing than they sound, though I frankly doubt the possibility of making a decision affecting a man's entire life in an interview of fifteen minutes. Indeed, an official from England, who had a good deal to do with such Boards there, told me that they had worked it out statistically that thirty per cent of their selections were unsuccessful.

On one Board a candidate came in looking exactly like a gorilla, with a great prognathous jaw and hands hanging down to the floor on either side of his chair. We asked him his record and he claimed to be a champion boxer and weight-lifter. When I asked him if he had any academic qualifications, he replied that he did not think these would be needed on the frontier.

One of the important things in selecting candidates for the frontier is to discover their attitude to the tribes, and the examiners would sometimes ask whether the applicant would be willing to marry a tribal girl.

'Certainly,' replied one of them, 'provided a suitable candidate presents herself.'

I was so keen on getting to NEFA and starting to tour during the winter months that I asked Tikki Kaul to let me leave the Selection Board early and I went back as quickly as possible to Patangarh and packed up. I had a feeling, a right feeling as it turned out, that this was going to mean drastic separation from the people I had known for so many years, and of whom I had grown so fond, and it was a real wrench to break away from Patangarh. But it had to be done and I went down to Calcutta where Victor Sassoon joined me, for he had offered to come and help us settle in Shillong, the beautiful but now overcrowded town in the Khasi Hills of Assam where the NEFA Administration has its headquarters. We flew up to Gauhati on 31 December 1953 and got to the Pinewood Hotel in Shillong just in time for the New Year Eve dinner. The next day I went to see the Governor and Rustomji, who was still Adviser, and began my new life. I was at first called Anthropological Consultant but after a year this was changed to Adviser for Tribal Affairs, which was more appropriate. I was not a regular Government servant, but was paid an honorarium and was at first on a three-year contract: this was renewed for another three, and then for another five, years. The post carries no pension but, though I may have to leave NEFA one day, I cannot imagine myself ever actually retiring.

Nari Rustomji is a unique character, one of the friendliest and kindest people you could meet in a lifetime, a man of great imagination and sympathy, with brains and an infectious vitality. On that first day he took me for a walk for several miles, most of it uphill, which meant that I was so breathless that I could not say a word, which was, I think, exactly what he wanted, for it gave him a chance to brief me, without interruption, at considerable length. Nari has a profound and essentially practical affection for the tribal people. He has an extraordinary flair for them as persons and his great love for and knowledge of music has helped to endear him to these music-loving folk. I do not think anybody has done more for Naga individuals or felt more deeply for them. His mother, 'Mummy Rustomji', who kept house for him for many years, is a warm, generous person. Very recently, just in time to get her into this book, Nari married the bewitching Avi Dalal.

A person who played a very large part in my life during my first few years in NEFA was the Governor, Mr Jairamdas Daulatram. We did not always agree, but our discussions added a spice to life and we were always held together by our common absorption in tribal problems. The Governor was specially interested in tribal religion and never tired of asking questions about the people's attitude to the Supreme Being.

One day, for example, a Tagin Chief from the wild north of Subansiri was brought over to Shillong. He was a ferocious-looking person, bristling with weapons, with a very long pipe sticking out of his mouth. The Governor asked me, with an interpreter, to come and hear what he had to say. The Tagin marched into Raj Bhavan and to my admiration (for I myself always put out my cigar when I met the Governor) kept his pipe firmly in place. We all sat down and Mr Daulatram began his questions. After about half an hour's interrogation the Tagin showed signs of restiveness; the clouds of noxious smoke from the pipe grew blacker and his hand began to move, to our great alarm, towards his long razor-sharp sword. When at last the Governor reached the critical point and asked for his views on the nature of the Supreme Being, the Tagin replied, 'I don't know anything about that; what I want is a drop of beer.'

The Governor always used green ink. He rarely went to bed before two in the morning and studied every report and tour diary, even of the most junior officers, in minute detail, making notes on every possible point. He had the idea of writing a large book about NEFA which he might well have done, for his knowledge and love were unsurpassed. Perhaps he still will write it: I hope so.

V

I was at first completely lost in Shillong. Apart from discussions with the Governor, of which there were a good many, and listening to Nari, there was not much to occupy me: nobody quite knew what to do with me. There was virtually no literature to study but I was given copies of old tour diaries. My very first 'case' concerned the library in the great Buddhist monastery at Tawang, which I suggested should be catalogued; three years later it was.

Nobody seemed anxious to become my stenographer; I could not even get a chaprasi. Had Victor not been with me, I doubt if I would ever have got anything. The two fundamental problems were a house and a car. We went house-hunting everywhere, for a long time without success, but finally discovered a large building on the outskirts of the town in a part called Nongthymmai. It was on a little hill and agreeably isolated among the pines. There was a cemetery opposite, which kept it quiet, and the approach-road was difficult, but this rather suited me. Here I could feel back in the forest.

After a lot of hesitation and strong prompting by Victor, who pointed out that there was room in this remarkable house for my museum collections and library as well as an office, I decided to rent it and Victor went down to Calcutta to fix up everything with the landlord, a distinguished barrister, A. C. Ganguly. For years we have had the happiest relations with him and his family, and his recent death was a real blow to us.

Victor also got us a car, a very old Rover. It once actually did the journey to Gauhati, when I went to fetch Lila and the children who joined me in Shillong when things were in some sort of order.

So, by the end of January, I had a family, a house, a car and even a telephone, a thing I had never had all my life before. Our phone-number was a little unfortunate, for it was 420 which in the Indian Penal Code is the section which deals with Cheating. On the other hand, most people in Shillong, where the telephone exchange has not yet reached four figures, have numbers with some relation to the IPC and we consoled ourselves with the reflection that at least we were not 302 (Murder) or 397 (Adultery). And, as a devout Baptist said, we were lucky that our car number was not 666.

About this time I became an Indian citizen which I had been trying to be for a long time past and which I had been *de facto* from my early days in Sabarmati. The order was issued by the Assam Government and friends have sometimes raised the question whether this made me an Assamese. Actually, of course, when one becomes an Indian citizen one becomes a citizen of India as a whole. One day I hope it will be possible to become a citizen of the world. Yet this has given me a special affinity with Assam and I have a great liking for the gentle, artistic Assamese people. Constitutionally NEFA is part of Assam and from my earliest days in Shillong I felt how important it was that these two areas should be in amity with each other and know each other well. The old days of tribal raids on the inoffensive plains and of military retaliation are happily long over, for NEFA at least, and the fortunes of the frontier hills are obviously bound up with those of their immediate neighbour Assam.

VI

By the end of January I had collected my staff and started the office. We had even got a cook, whom Victor named 'the gourmet's dream'. My Khasi steno, who was a good scrounger, got me a comfortable chair and an office clock. For the first time in my life I began dealing with files. When I was in the Department of Anthropology I was engaged entirely in research work and I do not think that a file ever came my way. It was not easy to adjust myself to the atmosphere of an office, to deal with audit objections or even the mechanical business of endorsing documents.

NEFA was fascinating for someone like myself who had lived a sheltered life in the forest for so long. There were contacts with the Army, Air Force, the whole official world, and the Assam Rifles, that very special force which polices the frontiers of north-eastern India.

In the middle of January a new Adviser, K. L. Mehta, arrived. For a long time I called him Ken, vaguely supposing that the 'K' in his initials stood for Kenneth. Later he told me that I must write Kan, short for Kanhaiya Lal, and I remarked that a single letter could change a name from one hemisphere to the other. Rustomji was transferred to Sikkim where he spent five very successful years as Diwan, returning to Shillong in 1959 for a second term as Adviser, and going on in the middle of 1963 to Bhutan.

Kan Mehta will be remembered as one of the great administrators of the tribal areas, and the idea of the 'single line administration', which was developed during his time, has excited the admiration of all visitors to NEFA. He had no previous experience of the tribal people but his quick and lively mind soon grasped their problems, and his intellectual generosity was such that he did not automatically oppose a policy simply because it was commended by someone else. This meant that we were able to work together harmoniously and *A Philosophy for NEFA*, which I worked out, owes a great deal to him. Kan's wife, Gisela, is a lovely person. In the five-and-a-half years that she was in Shillong I never once heard her say a nasty thing about anyone, and she was ideally fitted to hold together the various elements in the administration.

Another very fine man, with whom I have been closely connected for many years, is Pran Luthra who succeeded Rustomji as Adviser in July 1963. An exceptionally good field officer, he later came to Shillong as Development Commissioner and, after a time in Delhi, played an important part in the solution of the Naga problem as the first Commissioner of the newly-established Naga Hills-Tuensang Area. Highly competent, driving everybody hard, but always very good to his subordinates, he at times reminds me of Sydney Smith's description of someone as a 'steam-engine in trousers', which is, of course, just what we want, for he gets things done. At the same time he is human and witty and once, travelling from Gauhati to Shillong, he kept the whole carload of people in constant chuckles with descriptions of his various experiences. But the strongest link I have had with him is on a deeper level. Some years ago he was appointed to escort the Dalai and Panchen Lamas round the Buddhist holy places in India. This, I suspect, had a profound effect on him and as I too had come under Buddhist influence about the same time, our minds began to move in the same direction. Whenever I have been ill or depressed he has always been a great comfort and support. His wife, Indira, is equally charming and her knowledge and good taste inspired her to a splendid bit of work in reviving the cottage industries of Kohima. She arranged a first-rate exhibition in Delhi, which I had the honour of opening. An extra pleasure was to find my admired friend Kamaladevi Chattopadhyaya in the chair.

Yet another friend and counsellor for five years was Brigadier D. M. Sen. Formerly Judge-Advocate in the Army he has, throughout the time I have known him, guided the legal policy of the Administration in NEFA, and later in Nagaland, with great wisdom. What we call our Kebang policy (by which nearly all disputes and even criminal matters are entrusted to the traditional tribal councils in NEFA) owes everything to him and its success can be judged by the fact that at the time of writing there are only half a dozen NEFA tribesmen in jail. Gentle and affectionate, Sen has brought a tolerant and sympathetic philosophy into our dealings with the tribal people.

I cannot possibly do justice to my friends and colleagues in Assam and NEFA. There are so many, so many to whom I owe much or to whom I have owed much—at a crisis, on an expedition, in conference. But I cannot omit Major-General Ajit Guraya, head of the Assam Rifles, his wife Prem—and specially young Vijay, Nakul's special friend. And just one more: dear Diying Ering, Member of Parliament for NEFA and now a Parliamentary Secretary, who symbolizes the way the tribal people are coming forward to help in shaping their own destiny.

After an initial period of not having very much to do, once we had moved into the new house I found myself extremely busy. A training course was started for the newly recruited Political Officers and for two or three weeks we met daily in Raj Bhavan to hear lectures and hold discussions. I had to give four lectures on 'the tribal approach' which went over quite well. I noticed with gratification that at least one of the officers was taking me seriously, being assiduous in taking notes. I mentioned this to him at the end of the lectures and he said, 'Well, as a matter of fact, what I was really doing was composing dubious limericks.'

Then we also had the Hills and Plains Festival which for some reason was never repeated. For somebody new to Assam this was very exciting, for the tribal people from most of the Hill Districts attended it and parties from all over NEFA came down to dance and enjoy themselves. The Governor, Jairamdas Daulatram, gave a big lunch party on the lawns of Raj Bhavan and I was greatly struck by the way all the visitors mixed up together and the Governor himself sat on the ground between two of the NEFA tribal ladies. There was nothing of the atmosphere which I have met elsewhere, when at a party the officials are given chairs while the tribal people sit on the ground or where different kinds of food or cigarettes are given to the two classes of visitors.

At the end of January Kan and I snatched two days away from Shillong to make a first very hurried tour of NEFA. We left Shillong at four in the morning of a Sunday and got back late at night on the Monday, flying round to a number of places. This journey by air impressed on me the grandeur of the frontier mountains and the magnitude of our task.

Before we left on this trip Nari pulled my leg unmercifully. He pointed out the extreme danger of flying in NEFA at all and particularly of flying to the places we proposed to visit. The landing-ground at one place, he said, sloped downwards to the river and, whenever a plane landed, Assam Rifles jawans had to stand on both sides of the air strip and catch hold of its wings in order to bring it to a halt before it plunged into the river. Elsewhere aircraft crashed into the sides of mountains and bumped against football-posts on the ground. In any case, there were no doors on these very old Dakotas, for they were removed to facilitate air-dropping, and one never knew what sort of fellow-passengers one would have. In actual fact, I have travelled with cows, goats, sheep and, on this particular tour, with a large pig.

Flying in NEFA is always exciting, for if anything were to go wrong there would be little chance among the mountains. One of the most memorable flights I have ever made was in a light Auster, which has a seat for just one passenger, down from the hills. It was a rough day and we had to go very high. In this little aircraft you sit inside a sort of plastic bubble and you really feel that you are flying. That day the views were superb, for there were dark clouds everywhere with occasional bursts of sunshine lighting the savage hills that seemed to be clawing up at us.

For a long time I disliked flying, though I have done so much in the last few years, including a good deal among the mountains of NEFA and landing in the most unsuitable places, that I am getting used to it. My first trip in a Viscount, curiously enough, was one of the most alarming. Of all the things I dislike is the pilot's habit of switching on an orange-lighted notice to tell you to fasten your seat-belt in mid-air; this means that you are in for turbulence or worse.

I was sitting about half-way up the aircraft, reading a little book of meditations on sudden death. That meant that I had my reading-glasses on and could not decipher anything at a distance. After we had been in the air for about an hour, I noticed that the orange light was on, and hastily with trembling fingers fastened my seat-belt, and lay back with eyes shut waiting for the end. Presently, taking a peep at the panel I saw the light was off. Splendid fellow, our pilot, I thought. 'He's gone over or round it' and I undid myself. But ten minutes later, on went the light again. Once more I fastened my belt with unsteady hands and lay back concentrating on tender images of my wife and little ones. A few minutes later the light went off again. We are safe after all. By now I had given up reading and put on my other glasses. When a few minutes later the light went on yet again, I was able to see the notice. It read ENGAGED.

VII

From this time onward I divided my time between touring, research and evolution of policy. I discovered a completely new form of literary activity—noting on files—which is interesting, but has the drawback for a professional writer (when, as so often in NEFA, the noting has to be Secret or Top Secret) of confining one's readers to one or two people. In fact, I achieved the Miltonic ideal—'Fit audience find though few', though sometimes I have wondered whether there was any audience at all.

The most important and the most enjoyable part of my work during these years has been the touring, to which I devote a separate chapter. Until very recently I was in the mountains for six or seven months every year.

The character of my research work changed, as it was bound to do. Formerly I had a great deal of time, freedom from preoccupations and I was able to settle down for long periods among the people. In NEFA I had to survey a vast tract of mountainous territory, some thirty-three thousand square miles in extent, and help to look after thirty or forty tribal groups. What I did, therefore, was to go out on tour for periods varying from three to six or seven weeks far into the interior, collect what sociological facts were possible, write reports on the general condition of the tribes and make suggestions to the Administration. I have continued my interest in folklore and art but my main concern has been in what is called applied anthropology.

The first book I wrote was at the instance of the Governor, Mr Daulatram, who wanted a small book on Gandhi which would appeal to the tribal people. Most of the books about him stress aspects of his life and teaching which are not only unfamiliar but tend to put off or puzzle the tribal reader. For example, Gandhi took a vow not to drink cow's milk. The tribesman could not understand how, in view of this, we were doing all we could to persuade him to break his taboo on milk and give it to his children. Gandhi regarded alcohol and tobacco as bad, an estimate with which the people emphatically disagree. So I wrote a little book emphasizing those aspects of Gandhi's life which I thought would appeal to the tribes. It has now been translated into Hindi, Adi, Ao Naga, Monpa, Apa Tani, Dafla and other languages.

For several years I collected folktales on my tours, many of them strikingly original and nearly all quite unlike those in my other collections. When I had enough, I published a book, *Myths of the North-East Frontier of India,* which contains about four hundred of these stories.

I had also gradually been making extracts from the old literature about NEFA, of which there is a great deal more than is generally supposed, though most of it is buried in rare books which are very hard to come by. In my *India's North-East Frontier in the 19th Century*, therefore, which was published by the Oxford University Press, I made a book of about five hundred pages containing a large number of extracts from the old explorers, missionaries and administrators who wrote between 1800 and 1900. Many of these extracts are of the greatest interest and some are amusing. The book had an unexpected success and has now been reprinted.

Since then I have done a similar anthology. *The Nagas in the 19th Century* which will be published before long.

I had for some years been thinking of writing a sequel to my *Tribal Art of Middle India* and had collected a fairly large number of pictures, which I still have. In NEFA, however, I found a storehouse of treasures, far beyond anything I had made elsewhere, and from my very first visit to Tuensang, where I collected many authentic head-hunting relics, I managed to add to my collection during every tour I made. I also took a large number of photographs, some of which came out fairly well, and finally had sufficient to make into a book which I called *The Art of the North-East Frontier of India*. The Administration agreed that we should publish it ourselves and I found this great fun. It was printed by the Saraswati Press, Calcutta, which is managed by some very competent people who are most pleasant to deal with. We had an excellent artist, R. Bagchi, and the preparation of the lay-outs and so on was an absorbing task. Finance was very good to me, for my friend Nirmal Sen Gupta, himself an artist (he did a charming sketch of Wasant), was then in charge of Finance and we were able to bring out an impressively printed book which, in spite of being rather expensive, has had a very fair circulation.

The most widely-read of my books, however, was *A Philosophy for NEFA*, now in a third revised edition. Later I wrote a rather short book, about a hundred pages, on Nagaland, of which I was again both author and publisher. This was not a sociological study but dealt with the history and politics of this interesting part of the world. As a publication, it won a President's Award.

I was asked to give general direction to the work of a small Research Department. This had different sections—one for cultural, one for philological and a third for historical research. The department has since produced a number of books in all its different subjects. One of the things that distinguishes it and has greatly contributed to its output has been the fact that we have posted Research Officers in the interior so that they have to live among their people, relax in their company and spend virtually their whole time studying them. Outstanding among our officers in B. Das Shastri, a philologist, a brilliant scholar and a man of wide and unusual interests whose friendship has come to mean a great deal to me.

As time went by the scope of my work enlarged. I had a lot to do with the establishment of a Tribal Research Institute for Assam State. I was appointed Hon. Adviser for Tribal Affairs for both Manipur and Tripura, to which I pay occasional visits though not as many as I would like. I have never been appointed to any official post in the Naga area but, in practice, I have paid a number of visits to it both before and after the foundation of Nagaland.

This naturally widened my circle of friends. In Imphal there were J. M. Raina and his brilliant wife Vimala. In Shillong I found many friends—Mr and Mrs Duncan, wise leaders of the Khasi people ; other tribal leaders like Mrs Khongmen, Stanley Nichols-Roy and L. K. Doley ; Ahmed Kidwai, R. B. Vaghaiwalla and P. H. Trivedi, men of wide reading and ready wit ; R. T. Rymbai, with whom I worked for the Assam Research Institute ; S. Barkataki, whose knowledge of the tribal areas is profound and whose caustic pen is always stimulating ; and many others.

VIII

Then in 1959, the Home Minister, Pandit G. B. Pant, asked me to be chairman of a committee to study the progress of development in selected tribal areas throughout the country. Under the Second Five-Year Plan the normal Community Development Blocks had been supplemented by a scheme, sponsored and paid for by the Home Ministry, for what were then known as Special Multipurpose Tribal Blocks, the main point of which was that each Block was given twenty-seven lakhs of rupees instead of twelve. This came in for a good deal of criticism, for it was said that the money was not spent properly and sometimes not at all, and my committee was set up to investigate and report on what was really happening.

My colleagues were all men of wide experience in the tribal areas, and one of the very best of the younger men working in this field, O. K. Moorthy, who had for many years been concerned with tribal affairs in the Home Ministry, was Secretary.

We took about a year to complete our report and its preparation gave me opportunity to revisit some of my old haunts and discover others. For the first time I was able to go to the tribal districts of Andhra Pradesh, Chanda and Mokada-Talasari in Bombay, the Autonomous Hill Districts of Assam, and later to Rajasthan.

When we had finished our inquiries I felt the only possible way of getting a report written was to do it in Delhi, and the Home Ministry accommodated me in a pleasant room in the main Secretariat where I spent a couple of months. As this was holiday time for the children I took them and Lila with me and we all stayed with the Rathees, which must have been a tremendous burden on them but was very delightful for us.

Khemlal Rathee was Financial Adviser to the NEFA administration and when he left there were extraordinary demonstrations of regret. Himself a Jat, he had an instinctive feeling for the tribes and made it his business to understand them thoroughly. In honesty akin to men like Jamnalal Bajaj, universal in kindness, accessible to everyone, deeply religious in the right way, an excellent administrator, he has played a unique part in my life. His family and mine came very close together and his wonderful wife is a great friend of Lila's.

One day while I was working in Delhi, I wanted to make a quotation from *King Lear* to emphasize a point in my report and I sent my assistant over to the Secretariat Library to get a copy of Shakespeare, as none of my friends had one. When he asked for it, the Librarian said sharply, 'What is the Home Ministry doing reading Shakespeare in office hours? I certainly won't issue a copy.' My assistant replied, 'But this is for Dr Elwin.' 'Oh, Dr Elwin? I know he does read that sort of thing. All right, he'd better have it.'

There was also the problem of how to put things.

The Community Development people are devoted and intelligent. The only trouble is that I often just cannot understand what they are talking about. And, what is even more disconcerting, they cannot understand me.

For example, where I would say, 'How do you do it?' they say 'What is your methodological approach?'

In one note I remarked that 'when tribal girls go to the towns, they sometimes become tarts'. This caused a lot of trouble. I was hauled over the coals at a very high level for using the word 'tart' in an official document. The sentence was then revised for my instruction to show me how one ought to write. 'When females belonging to the Scheduled Tribes become acculturated to the socio-economic conditions of urban society, they become psychologically maladjusted and adopt anti-social practices.' That is what is necessary: that is what people understand.

However at last, after toning down my English suitably, all the members agreed to sign the report which ran to about 550 pages, most of them written, or at least rewritten, by me, and I presented it to the Home Minister, Pandit G. B. Pant, at the end of March 1960.

Our report dealt with all the varied aspects of development. We had chapters on staffing problems and training; on land, forests and agriculture with special attention to the vexed question of shifting cultivation; on animal husbandry, communications, health services, education, women's programmes, arts and crafts, housing, cooperation and research. We also supplied detailed and specific accounts of twenty of the Special Blocks in different parts of India.

I myself felt that the most important part of our report was an introductory chapter called 'The Fundamentals of an Approach to the Tribes' for, as I have said on many occasions, it is not so much what you do, still less the amount of money you spend, as the way you will do it that makes the real difference to the tribal people. One of the criticisms of these Special Development schemes had been that they lacked any 'tribal touch', for stereotyped plans had generally been taken over as they stood for the tribal areas and there was no serious attempt to adapt the budget to tribal needs or the policy to tribal life. The idea of a 'tribal touch' caused a certain amount of ridicule, for unsympathetic officials interpreted it as meaning that we wanted the people to put feathers in their hair and go about with nothing on. This was not, of course, the idea at all and we explained what it really meant.

A 'tribal touch' or 'tribal bias' means that we must look, if we can, at things through tribal eyes and from the tribal point of view. We must find out what means most to them. We must see that they do in fact get a square deal: we must save them from the exploiters who still invade their villages, and ensure that in the future they will be in a position to administer and develop their own areas.

A tribal bias means that we recognize and honour their way of doing things, not because it is old or picturesque but because it is theirs, and they have as much right to their own culture and religion as anyone else in India. It means that we must talk their language, and not only the language that is expressed in words but the deeper language of the heart. It means that we will not make the tribes ashamed of their past or force a sudden break with it, but that we will help them to build upon it and grow by a natural process of evolution. It does not mean a policy of mere preservation; it implies a constant development and change, a change that in time will bring unbelievable enrichment, as there is ever closer integration in the main stream of Indian life and culture.

We concluded by suggesting a great expansion of properly-adapted development schemes during the Third Five-Year Plan, and asked for what we called a 'trivial' thirty crores of rupees for new Tribal Blocks. This, we pointed out, when spread over difficult and widespread areas, was actually a very modest sum. We went on to say:

The fear has been expressed that this will involve too rapid a progress, too complicated a programme, the employment of inferior men. This need not be so. We agree that we should 'hasten slowly', advance with caution, give the tribes a breathing-space to adapt themselves to the new world. Whatever we do, that world will come upon them and they must be ready for it. Hunger, disease, exploitation, ignorance, isolation are evils whose cure cannot be delayed; they must be treated rapidly and efficiently.

Each man is his brother's keeper and we must all atone for our long neglect and our wrong attitude. Mankind is one and the tribes are a very precious part of mankind.

The report was well received and discussed at a number of conferences and meetings. The Government of India did not accept some of the administrative proposals but did, by and large, accept practically everything else. I think that our fundamental ideas of tribal development have now won very general acceptance.

IX

The work on this committee took me away from NEFA a good deal and I was looking forward to returning to my main job when it ended, but in April 1960 a Scheduled Areas and Scheduled Tribes Commission, as provided in the Constitution of India, was appointed. Mr U. N. Dhebar was the Chairman and I was one of the members. There were nine others, most of them Members of Parliament, and the terms of reference were very wide indeed, much wider, of course, than those of my own committee.

Dhebar had been Congress President and a Chief Minister; he is a persuasive and attractive man, with a boundless capacity for work and a passionate belief in social and economic justice. I got on well with him and we agreed on most of the major policy matters that came before us. Dhebar kept the Commission down to earth and was essentially interested in obtaining justice for the tribal people who had been so long neglected and so grossly exploited. The Commission's report has made its chief contribution by its insistence on a fair deal for the tribal people politically, economically and in the field of administration. We discovered that the Fifth Schedule of the Constitution, which set up special areas all over tribal India in which the Governors were expected to take a special interest, had been an almost complete failure. Land was still being alienated on a staggering scale. Millions of tribesmen were in the clutches of the moneylenders. The great industrial projects have led to the dispossession of vast tracts of tribal land and, although proper compensation was provided, this had often not been paid. On the question of development the Commission had nothing very new to say and in a sense it was a duplication of the work of our earlier committee and other committees.

Unfortunately just when I should have been in Delhi to assist in the writing out of this report I was taken ill and from June 1961 onwards I was not allowed to travel. Dhebar himself was good enough to come over twice all the way from Delhi to see me and to discuss a large number of points that arose from the evidence we had collected, and he made an arrangement that the rest of the Commission would sit in Delhi and prepare drafts of the different chapters, which they would then send down to me by air-freight. My own staff was strengthened by two additional stenos and another typist and for about two months, during part of which I was in bed and during all of which I was supposed to be having complete rest, we lived in a state of constant excitement. The parcels would arrive, I would get to work on them immediately, revising, amending the English and so on, dictating additional or alternative passages, and then everybody would get to work retyping and we would dispatch again, always within forty-eight hours, by the Chief Minister's special bag that went direct to Delhi. In this way I worked right through the entire report. Unhappily when the day came for the ceremony of signing it, I was still unable to travel but someone flew down from Delhi with thirteen large printed volumes and I signed them in my room in Shillong.

X

During this year I was invited to give the Sardar Vallabhbhai Patel Memorial Lectures. This is an annual event in Delhi, arranged by All India Radio. Previous lecturers were Mr C. Rajagopalachari, Dr J. B. S. Haldane, Dr M. S. Krishnan and Dr Zakir Hussain. I was very pleased about this for two reasons. I took as my subject 'The Philosophy of Love' and this meant that I had to re-read a great deal, which I was able to do for at the time I was confined to the house under doctor's orders. This did me a lot of good. It forced me to study again Gandhi's ideas on Ahimsa in all their beauty and profundity; it fired me afresh with my old enthusiasm for Plato and Augustine, though it confirmed me in my original impression that Aristotle was a dull dog. I felt much more charitable towards C. S. Lewis after reading his *Allegory of Love* for (I am ashamed to say) the first time. I discovered Father M. C. D'Arcy and some of the writings of Bengal Vaishnavism.

The other reason was that I have always had a very affectionate memory of Sardar Patel and he had a considerable influence on my life, since it was he who had originally insisted that I should go to tribal India.

Normally I dislike lecturing: I feel nervous beforehand and disgusted with myself afterwards. I never write out anything, for it is only when you speak off the cuff that you can get *en rapport* with your audience. So I was rather apprehensive about these lectures, which I had had to write, for I should have to read them out (each an hour long) to an audience and be recorded at the same time.

But in fact it worked out very well. After twenty minutes or so I felt quite at home and I found that having to speak into a microphone was rather consoling. I had, of course, to use my reading-glasses and this meant that the audience was reduced to an unfocused blur and I lost interest in how they responded, even though the AIR auditorium was crowded with people, many of whom I think expected me to talk on those aspects of love about which I had been so explicit in some of my books. Two truck-loads of lady sociologists, I was told, came for the first lecture but were somewhat disappointed at the elevated character of my remarks, and did not come again. I did, of course, touch on sex but since the lectures were recorded and broadcast in chunks of half an hour a time on six successive Wednesdays, I obviously could not say very much. Even so one of the Delhi papers came out with headlines: ELWIN SAYS CARNAL LOVE IS GOOD, and so it is, though I did not put it quite so baldly.

I enjoyed this visit to Delhi, for these lectures brought me in touch with a good many new people and particularly with the very fine group at Akashvani Bhavan, the AIR headquarters. Long ago I had known the first Controller of Broadcasting in India, Lionel Fielden, fairly well. I stayed with him in Delhi and he invited me to represent India (for two-and-a-half minutes) at the last of King George V's Christmas Eve broadcasts—recently the BBC asked me to do a short piece on a similar occasion when the chief speaker was Queen Elizabeth.

Now I came to know B. P. Bhatt, Director-General, a delightful person with a sensitive knowledge of English poetry; Gopal Das, the Station Director at Gauhati; a younger man, J. D. Bhaveja, who has a wide knowledge of tribal music; and several others. They all gave me a very pleasant time. I was particularly glad to renew my friendship with P. C. (Tiny) Chatterji, whom I had known since my first visit to Assam. Learned as he is in the philosophy of aesthetics, he keeps a light touch on everything, and shares my interest in cigars.

XI

I do not go to Delhi very often, but I generally enjoy myself there: to a provincial like me a visit to the capital is an adventure: one can do a little lion-hunting; interesting things happen. I am not specially excited by important people, but I do like meeting unusual or significant people who have something to say. Let me now describe a few such encounters.

When I go to Delhi the Prime Minister sometimes calls me and I have had many talks with him. On one occasion I had nothing very much to say and did not want to bother him. So I was carefully keeping out of the way. But one morning as I was going to see someone in the External Affairs Ministry I was suddenly taken short and slipped into one of the VIP lavatories along the corridor. When I came out I ran slap into the Prime Minister himself. He said, 'Hallo, what are you doing here?' I didn't quite like to tell him, but he went on to say, 'Come and see me tomorrow.'

I had just published *India's North-East Frontier in the 19th Century*, and my friends insisted that I should take a copy with me to present to Mr Nehru. I raided the Delhi bookshops and with some difficulty found and bought a copy and on the following day took it with me and presented it to him. He took it and turned over a few pages, grunted a little, then looked at me and said, 'What do you think of *Lolita*?'

All I actually thought was that, with the competition there is nowadays in the field of literature, it is hardly worth while going on.

When Malcolm MacDonald's book *Borneo People* was published I wrote to him saying how much I liked it (incidentally I gave it an enthusiastic review in the *Statesman*). MacDonald, who was then High Commissioner for the United Kingdom in India, wrote back inviting me to come and see him when I next visited Delhi. Accordingly, at the next opportunity I rang up his office, and he asked me to come round for lunch.

When the time came I took a taxi to the High Commissioner's residence and went in. I had never seen MacDonald and had no idea what he was like. I was greeted by a dignified, indeed distinguished-looking, person whom I grasped by the hand and said how much I had enjoyed his book on Borneo. This was rather coldly received and it turned out that this gentleman was MacDonald's Secretary. However, he took me to the drawing-room where there was a nice Englishwoman drinking gin and I allowed myself to be given the same stimulant. Presently a tall elegantly dressed Englishman, who seemed very much at home, walked into the room. I leapt to my feet, seized him by the hand and said how much I had enjoyed his book on Borneo. He seemed a little taken aback and hastily changed the subject.

Five minutes later, yet another tall, distinguished-looking Englishman came in and I again leapt to my feet, seized him by the hand and said my little piece about how much I had enjoyed his book on Borneo. 'Never been there,' replied this individual and rushed for the gin-bottle.

By this time I had come to the conclusion that I was in the wrong house and that these English people, always so polite, were wondering who the devil I was but did not like to say so. But at last MacDonald himself, short, not distinguished-looking at all, completely charming, bustled in, apologizing for being late and in five minutes we were examining Iban textiles and comparing notes on head-hunters we had known.

During their visit to India in 1958, I had the honour of meeting the Dalai Lama and the Panchen Lama in New Delhi, and was invited to Rastrapati Bhavan to a lunch which was attended by the President, the Prime Minister, the great Lamas and their entourage of about seventy monks and a number of Ministers and high officials. The invitation came rather late and my clothes were not quite in order. The only available socks, for example, were a little seedy and one of them had a huge hole in the heel. My shoes, however, appeared to cover it and suppress the rest adequately and, since I knew that at Rashtrapati Bhavan one either sat at table or stood round a buffet, I thought I was safe enough.

We arrived—Khemlal Rathee was with me—and wandered through the splendid rooms sipping our aperitifs of tomato juice.

I met one or two nice people and all was going splendidly until we were asked to go into the great dining-hall for lunch. And then to my horror I saw that, for the first time in history, it was to be a sit-on-the-floor lunch in traditional Indian style. It was superbly arranged; long rows of little seats or *asanas*, with piles of flowers everywhere. How pretty it was, how altogether suitable! But naturally, for an Indian-style meal everybody has to remove his shoes. I got as near the door as I could and then furtively removed my shoes and shuffled in, keeping the toes of one foot covering, as far as possible, the revealing hole in the other.

Happily, the excellence of the food diverted everyone's attention and I think I got out unobserved.

XII

When India became a Republic she abolished all civilian titles, to the agonized regret of those who had them and the disappointment of those who hoped to get them one day. But it was soon found that some sort of honours were necessary even in the public life of a democracy and accordingly four Orders, as they would be called in England, were established—the

Bharat Ratna, Padma Vibhushan, Padma Bhushan and Padma Shri. These are awarded by the President to scientists, doctors, philosophers, musicians, men of letters, leading athletes, artists, social workers and a carefully restricted number of officials and administrators.

On 26 January 1961—Republic Day—I was in Along with the Tribal Commission. Someone had a transistor radio and I was listening to the news when I heard to my great pleasure that I had been awarded the Padma Bhushan.

Three months later, on 27 April, the investiture was held in New Delhi, and I arrived looking reasonably smart in white khadi trousers and short black buttoned-up coat.

For the ceremony recipients were arranged in two rows: I was just behind the late Dr B. C. Roy (who got the Bharat Ratna) and beside me was a veteran and distinguished Congressman. He was dressed in a slightly off-colour shirt and dhoti and his first remark to me was: 'What are you dressed up like that for?'

I murmured something, and he said, 'I dressed like this while I was earning this Padma Bhushan and I'll dress like this while I receive it. Let them turn me out if they don't like it.'

Presently, he asked, 'You are an Englishman?'

'I used to be,' I said.

'Then you will know. This Padma Bhushan would make me a Lord in England?'

'Not quite, I'm afraid.'

'But at least I would be a Sir and my wife a Lady.'

'Something like that.'

'But this is India, so it wouldn't be.'

'It won't be.'

On our chairs were the cases in which the decorations were to be put after we received them. The Bharat Ratna was naturally much bigger, better polished, in every way better than ours. My companion noticed this.

'Why has Dr Roy got a bigger one than me?' he demanded.

I told him why.

'Ah,' he said, seeking refuge in traditional Indian philosophy, 'what does it matter? After all'—raising his voice and directing a cautionary look at the broad back of Dr Roy—'what will these honours matter in a few years' time? And in any case, most of us'—another look at Dr Roy—'deserve them no more than millions of others. Full many a gem'—he went on, now really getting into his stride—'of purest ray serene wastes its sweetness on the desert air. We are just lucky: we have caught someone's attention.'

And then, more seriously, and I thought rather charmingly: 'I have never sought for or expected honours: my only ambition, as I pray to the Lord, is, Do what thou wilt with me, so long as I may be somewhere near thy feet.'

After this I had so many congratulations from all over the place that I am afraid I rather got into the habit of expecting them. One day when I went to the cinema, the ticket-vendor, who was rather a friend of mine, held out his hand after I had bought my ticket and I grasped it firmly and said, 'Thank you so very much.' It turned out, however, that all he wanted was another twelve naye paise on the entrance-fee.

One day shortly afterwards, I read an amusing leader on the new Companions of Literature in the *Times Literary Supplement*, which quoted Erik Satie as saying that 'To have turned down the Légion d'Honneur is not enough. One should never have deserved it.' Housman refused the C.H. because Galsworthy had been awarded it. I had no such temptation. I actually have never thought I deserved the Padma Bhushan—I had never expected it or anything other than entirely academic awards: I just didn't think in those terms—but I was certainly very pleased, for I felt it was really in recognition of our NEFA policy for the tribes.

XIII

This policy faced its severest test when in October 1962 a long-gathering storm broke over the NEFA hills. The Chinese swept over the frontier in great strength, overwhelming the defence forces in parts of Kameng, Siang and Lohit. First to fall was Tawang, the place of pilgrimage which Lila and I had visited six years previously. Then after a deceptive lull the invaders bypassed the Se La, occupied Bomdi La and came south towards

Tezpur. In Lohit, Wallong fell after heavy fighting and the Chinese threatened the valley below it. At about the same time they thrust their way into northern Siang, invaded the lovely Mechuka valley and occupied some of the little villages where I had once made my camps. The fact that I knew most of the places, except those in the far north of Subansiri, so well made this very real to me. My blood pressure went up twenty-five points after the fall of Tawang, came down during the lull and then went up again thirty points after the collapse of Bomdi La. This was not due to fear or anxiety, for I always had complete confidence about the final outcome of the struggle, but to real sorrow. I felt as if parts of me were being torn away: those days of crisis will never be forgotten by any of us who were closely associated with NEFA.

In Shillong there was some alarm and a number of people sent their families away. Friends put a good deal of pressure on Lila to go away too with the children, but I took the line that we all belonged to the tribal people and to Assam and since it was obviously impossible for the whole population to be evacuated we should remain where we were. Events proved me right, for the cease-fire came and the Chinese withdrew.

Then came the task of re-establishing administration in the areas that had been invaded and of restoring confidence in the people. Happily there were a number of brilliant Frontier Service men available for this exacting duty. Pran Luthra, Bob Khating, U. Chakma, Krishna Johorey, Bernard Dougal and others did a wonderful job, in which they were assisted in every way by the tribal leaders. In a remarkably short time the frontier, so grievously disturbed, had settled down to its normal life again.

9

Travels in the NEFA Highlands

His country lies beyond and beyond, forest and river, forest, swamp and river, the mountains of Arakkaboa—leagues and leagues . . . —*Walter de la Mare*

I

ALTHOUGH nothing has ever compared for sheer academic excitement with my investigations into the Muria dormitory in Bastar and the religion of the Saoras, touring in NEFA has been something completely different to anything I had ever experienced before. Except in the Kuttia Kond and Abujhmar Hills the physical exertion demanded was comparatively easy elsewhere in India. Now in NEFA I had to face vast distances which had always to be done on foot, mountains of a height which I had hardly even seen before and, at least in the early days, tracks were very bad. Although, specially in Orissa, I often visited villages which were practically unexplored, untouched even by minor officials, now in NEFA I aimed always at the most isolated and difficult areas and I had, on a number of occasions, the thrill of being almost an explorer. As a local paper, discussing the possibilities of research, once pointed out: 'NEFA is a great field of virgins for the Elwins of this world.' Friendly as the central Indian people usually were, there was nothing to compare with the enthusiastic hospitality shown to the traveller in the remoter parts of NEFA. The difficulties were great but the splendour of the countryside and the charm of the people were altogether exhilarating.

On my tours I moved as a self-contained unit, taking with me almost all my food and what little camp equipment was needed. I very rarely had a tent and nearly always slept either in the men's dormitory or in somebody's house. I used, however, to take a couple of tarpaulins with which we would build an open shed somewhere in the middle of the village where I sat during the day. This was rather like having a good seat at a theatre, for from it I could watch the whole varied panorama of village life. I always took a gramophone with me and found it of great value in attracting the people: some tins of sweets quickly created friendship with the children: and my box of mechanical toys, some inherited from Bastar days, quickly broke down any shyness or suspicion.

The great thing was that I was forced to travel on foot or occasionally by pony. To tour in a jeep is to get a completely superficial picture of the people. When you have to walk slowly from village to village you have a chance of getting to know them. On several tours I did not see a government official for weeks at a time. I was entirely on my own and I always travelled without any kind of escort. In fact, I have found, in all these years, that I have never needed one.

Although I love touring, I do puff and pant a bit going up the hills, and this amuses the tribal people with me.

One day going up a mountain in Manipur, a kindly English-speaking Naga boy who was a little ahead of me, turned round and said, 'This must be a frightful ordeal, sir, for a fat old man like you.' And Membas up in Gelling, near the Tibetan border, described me as going along making a noise like an aeroplane. We must remember that among the tribes words like fat or old are complimentary. Fat implies potency and substance; age is always venerated—and anyone over forty is old.

Once, travelling in the Sherdukpen country, as I was going along a lovely wooded valley, my pony suddenly leapt into the air for no apparent reason and hurled me to the ground. I was smoking at the time and everyone was impressed by the fact that I kept my cigar in position and alight. I came down rather heavily, but nothing was broken, though I got an enormous bruise on my rump and had to be carried to the nearest outpost. When I asked what had frightened the pony, the Sherdukpens beamingly explained that there was a ghost living in a tree under which I passed and that he usually threw people off horses when they went below it.

'But you might have warned me,' I complained.

'No,' they said, 'we wanted to see whether he would dare to frighten you just like anyone else.'

Later it was suggested that the place should be named Elwin's Fall, but I discouraged the kindly thought for fear that it might be misconstrued.

Another time Lila and I once flew to Pasighat and, as the plane came down, I was gratified to see a very large crowd waiting and thought to myself what a proper spirit this showed. We landed and came out to face an enthusiastic mob of all the local officials and many Abors, but when they saw us there was an appreciable drop in temperature.

'We thought,' they told us, 'that you were a load of Yorkshire pigs.'

I will now give brief descriptions of a few of the more important of my tours, for they gave me the things I most cherish—affectionate, friendly people ; the beauty of mountains ; excitement and variety ; and a sense of doing something worth while.

II

A Pilgrimage to Tawang

Tawang, with its great monastery in a beautiful upland valley in a corner between Bhutan and Tibet, came into world-news as the first place of importance visited by the Dalai Lama, when he sought political asylum in India four years ago. It came again, more tragically, into the headlines when it was captured by the Chinese and yet again as the scene of rejoicing when it was reoccupied by its Lamas and the Indian administrators a few weeks later.

Tawang is a long way off, and when I went there the journey had to be made on foot or pony: now a wonderful mountain road makes it accessible. Lila and I went there in May 1956 and, since we covered the exact route taken by the Dalai Lama and his party when they travelled down to the plains, I will describe our experiences, for he saw the same places and met the same people that we did, though in reverse order.

From Tezpur, where over two hundred journalists gathered to greet the Dalai Lama when he arrived there, we drove through Charduar at the foot of the mountains, and then up the new road towards Bomdi La. The Dalai Lama was able to make the entire journey between Charduar and Bomdi La by jeep, but when we went we were only able to drive about twenty-eight miles, in the course of which we climbed 8,000 feet, to the road-head, after which we went on foot and pony along a rather narrow bridlepath. It was not an easy journey, for to those unaccustomed to riding on the little mountain ponies, their habit of walking on the extreme edge of precipices (and there are many of them) is somewhat alarming; we were badly bitten by dimdam flies, horrid insects whose bites leave poisoned and itching sores; and before long our leg-muscles began to ache excruciatingly. But the path led us through such lovely scenery, valley and stream and hill, with sacred shrines to bless us on our way, that we quickly forgot the discomforts. The dust and tumult of mechanized transport were left behind us; ahead was pilgrimage among the snow mountains and the holy places.

This is, in fact, one of the most memorable adventures that NEFA has to offer.

There is first the beauty of the countryside—the distant mountains white with snow, the nearer hills dressed in pine, oak and fir; the smell of the pines; the waterfalls and streams; the banks carpeted with wild strawberries; the great displays of rhododendrons and a score of other multicoloured flowers. The journey over the Se La is unforgettable; haunted, mysterious, remote, the great Pass gives the authentic thrill—distance and height are forgotten in wonder. And as you descend, there are the flowers. If there is a Paradise in NEFA, this is it, this is it, this is it.

At Bomdi La, which we reached after a two days' journey, we bought dress suitable for our pilgrimage. I had a brown silk shirt and a long dark coat to the ankles with a red sash and a fine fur hat; Lila had a red shirt, a black coat, an apron

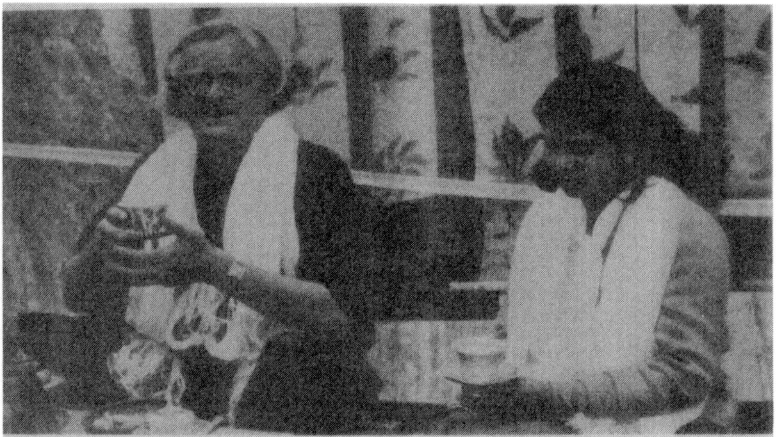

The author and Lila entertained on the way to Tawang

Lila with Mishmi girls high in the Khamlang valley

TRIBAL PEOPLE OF
NORTH-EASTERN INDIA

Top left. A Tagin from northern Subansiri

„ *right.* Son of a Konyak chief

Bottom left. Digaru Mishmi girl

„ *right.* Tapang Taki, a Minyong Abor

decorated with gay brocade, ornamental boots, and a charming, brilliantly coloured little hat which was perched on the side of her head—she looked enchanting.

From Bomdi La, escorted by a very dear friend, R. S. Nag, who was then Political Officer, and a fine young anthropologist, Sachin Roy, we went along a river valley to Dirang, eighteen miles away, which is one of the prettiest places I have ever seen. Monpa houses are substantial two-story stone buildings, and here they are perched picturesquely on a number of small hills between which runs a lovely little stream of crystal-clear water. There are several Buddhist temples and other buildings which house prayer-wheels and grindstones worked by water. The great prayer-wheels, like the flags fluttering in the breeze, repeat endlessly (if inaudibly) the sacred words OM MANI PADME HUM.

In the middle of the village is an imposing old fort (*dzong*) and above it is a temple where we made our camp. This is a fine building with an upper story containing many small images of the Buddha and a little library in which Lila and I were accommodated. Below there was another room with some large images where the rest of our party stayed. It was refreshing to be in a really natural religious environment, in a temple where you could put up your camp-bed and sleep under the gentle and compassionate gaze of the statues. In Buddhism religion is not a thing apart from life: it is a part of it.

At Dirang we first met the Abbot of Tawang who happened to be staying there on his way to his monastery. This Abbot is one of the few real saints that one may meet in a lifetime. Looking at him, the phrase 'the beauty of holiness' came into my mind. Gentle, courteous, simple, luminous with inner joy, he is a completely charming personality and every time I met him I felt the better for it.

A mile or so outside Dirang we experienced the first of the welcomes with which the local people greet visitors. There were the Head Lama and his band of trumpeters (some of the trumpets were seven or eight feet long) and drummers, and with him was a large crowd of local officials, Chiefs and delightful school-children, all in their own attractive dress, very pretty and charming children too. At every village along the way the procedure was the same. We were met by the local dignitaries, generally with a band. Each garlanded us with a white scarf and we gave scarves in return. Then they led us in procession to a small tent, tastefully decorated with flowers, in which a number of seats covered with brightly-coloured carpets or saddle-cloths awaited us. There were low tables and on them silver, china or wooden cups. Sometimes there was a bowl of walnuts or wild strawberries. Then the wife of the leading inhabitant filled the cups with butter-tea—an alarming concoction of tea, salt and butter—and raised them one by one first to my lips and to my wife's and then to the rest of the company in strict order of precedence. I myself usually only touched the cup with my lips, for I found the smell of the often rancid butter overwhelming, but everybody else enjoyed it and some drank as many as eight cups in succession. After the tea, we were often offered rice-spirit, one of the strongest drinks you can get, rather like vodka.

This was sometimes a real embarrassment, especially when offered early in the morning and then repeated in village after village throughout the day. But we learnt that if we dipped one finger in the bowl and sprinkled a little of the spirit three times in honour of the Lord Buddha, it was not necessary to drink it. Occasionally, however, the woman offering the drink would catch you by the ear and, tilting up your head, force the fiery spirit down your throat; sometimes she would sit in your lap to do so. I had heard that this was done by the prettiest girl in the village but, in my case, perhaps because I was chaperoned by Lila, I always got old ladies.

These Monpa people are singularly courteous, gentle and friendly. They take off their hats and, holding them between their hands, make a little bow at every word you speak. They still, in some places, put out their tongues by way of greeting. In my whole tour I never heard a child crying and I do not remember hearing a single angry word.

As we continued our march from Dirang the country got more and more beautiful, the mountains became higher, snow peaks appeared, and now as we approached any village people lit fires of aromatic leaves and branches to greet us. At Senzedzong, where the Dalai Lama halted on his journey, we had a wonderful reception on a broad plateau under the towering Se La mountains. It was a perfect day and the colour, the beauty of the scenery, the picturesque delightful people, the trumpets, the dignified ceremonial were unforgettable.

Now we had to cross the Se La Pass, over 14,000 feet high. We had been warned that the way was steep, that we should not be able to breathe, that it was sure to rain. And alas, rain it did, both on our way up and our way back but, though we could not see the distant views, it was a memorable climb. At the top, where we had a picnic lunch, there are twin lakes or tarns which are called the 'Eyes of God'.

When we reached our little camp by a stream, half-way down the other side, we found our tent had been made by the Monpas into a sort of bower of flowers, most beautifully done.

But flowers do not keep out the cold. It was the smallest tent I have ever been in; it was pouring with rain, and at about 12,000 feet we had the coldest night I had known for a long while. But at sunset Lila and I had a wonderful time picking wild strawberries.

Then we went on for another twenty miles to Tawang. From a distance of fifteen miles we got the first view of the great monastery riding like a ship on its hillside, 10,000 feet above sea level, and as we approached we had a dozen receptions in little villages along the way. As we drew nearer Tawang, the Prior and some of the senior monks in their splendid robes and impressive hats of yellow cloth came three miles out to meet us. The following day, May the 24th, Buddha Purnima, 2,500th anniversary of the birth of the Buddha we visited the monastery: there could not have been a more auspicious moment.

We were met at the entrance of the monastery by the Prior and other monks; scarves were exchanged; trumpets were blown, and we walked slowly through a fantastic medley of buildings into the great courtyard and the main temple, which with its great statue and hundreds of smaller images is the centre of an ardent devotion, of the Mahayana type of Buddhism with strong Tantric elements. Fantastic images of demons, dignified images of great saints and Rinpoches (holy men who have been reincarnated in another birth), scrolls, flags, temple-hangings, bells and lights, human thigh-bones used as trumpets, rich carpets, give the temple, which tradition decrees should always be illuminated by artificial light, a rich and sombre magnificence.

As it was Buddha Purnima day, most of the monks were sitting in long rows in the temple chanting prayers. We went round offering scarves to the principal images. The temple on this day was lit by a thousand lamps and decorated with some remarkable pictures made on the ground with coloured butter. There were also a thousand little Buddhas made of butter round the walls.

Later we went to the very fine library whose great treasure is the Getompa, eight large volumes, three of which are lettered in gold. There are also copies of the other main Buddhist scriptures, some printed and some handwritten, over seven hundred books in all. This may not sound very much, but a monastic book is a real book, about the size of half a dozen ordinary books of this careless modern world. The Lamas have a great reverence for knowledge, even though many of them are not themselves learned. Every temple has its sacred books which are carried in procession round the village on festal days. Books are worshipped, even if they are not read. In the library we were entertained to some strange-tasting but pleasant dishes and, of course, the butter-tea, and from the balcony we watched the dances performed in honour of the festival. The most moving of these was the Thutotdam, the dance of the king and queen of death, which reminds the spectators that death awaits every man and that they must not, therefore, be too much attached to worldly existence.

The monastery awoke nostalgic memories of Oxford or even, for I am a broadminded person, of Cambridge. There was the same casual atmosphere which conceals so much dignity and protocol. There were the little narrow streets dividing the tall houses where the monks had their cells. There was the dignified common-room where the leading Lamas met to decide monastic policy and affairs. There was a great kitchen, and I especially noticed the enormous tea-pots in which the Lamas make their butter-tea. The courtyards were paved and there were many horses about. In a basement below the library was a large room in which were kept the great boxes containing the masks and elaborate dresses used for ceremonial dances, and even a printing-press. Printing was a laborious business. Books here are in the shape of long narrow rectangles and every page had to be carved separately on wooden blocks.

This pilgrimage, as I have always called it, meant something much more to me than the ordinary official tour. I had always been interested in Buddhism and inspired by much of its teaching: now it became real to me. These few weeks brought a definite change in my life, a step forward in spiritual realization.

III

A Scramble among the Tagins

Shortly before I came to Shillong the Tagins of the far north had attacked a detachment of Assam Rifles and their porters at a place called Achingmori and killed many of them. Military operations had to be mounted against the turbulent tribesmen, but they were soon over, and the people settled down fairly quickly. In March 1955 I decided to visit the Tagins, although their country was then difficult and wild.

The tour began rather inauspiciously. We had to fly from Jorhat to a remote place far away in the hills and the morning of our departure was lean and hungry, overshadowed by great clouds. We were to go in the usual old Dakota which was fortunately driven (as our people say) by the Wing-Commander himself. When we arrived at the airstrip we found him already in a rather bad temper. The aircraft was overloaded, there was something wrong with the battery and the engine was making a queer noise, as if the sprockets were not running true with the differential gear. 'She wheezes like an old woman,' he muttered, reducing my already low morale. When we got in we found that half the aircraft was full to the brim with sacks of rice, tin boxes and so on, all of which looked as if they would slide down on top of us if we tilted up. However, we strapped ourselves in and the Wing-Commander took off. As we went down the airstrip someone retracted the wheels while we were still on the ground and our momentum was still weak. The pilot just managed to get us into the air and, flying very low, slowly turned and circled three times over the airport. I thought that this was because we were too heavily loaded but he thought that the right tyre had burst. The radio-operator came in hurriedly and scrabbled at our belts. 'Tighter, tighter,' he said, just like my headmaster when he bent me over before a beating.

We came down safely, however, and for a few moments there was complete silence. Then the cockpit door swung open and such a stream of profanity poured out that I thought the fuel would catch fire. As I was listening to this with reverence, the pilot appeared, his face bathed with perspiration, and said, 'That's the nearest to death you bastards have ever been.' Later, one of the crew told me that on such occasions, though the crew may escape, the passengers were *always* killed.

The pilot now took a firm line and insisted on transferring to another aircraft and this time we had a good quick flight to make a perfect landing at our destination.

From there I went first into the lonely and almost unvisited Sipi valley. The track north at the time was so bad that we sometimes had to go on our hands and knees and, unlike other parts of NEFA, there were no dormitories and the houses were so small and crowded that, although I did sometimes stay in them, I found that my presence was rather an embarrassment. I had no tent and only two tarpaulins. We used to make a little hut, sometimes having to cut away part of the hillside to get a flat piece of ground, and with one tarpaulin on the floor and the other above me I used to crouch like a frog in the pouring rain which even in March fell upon us relentlessly.

Our first march of twelve miles, which took us over eight hours, up to a little camp by the Sipi river, was an appropriate introduction to what we were in for. We pushed our way up and down, down and up, along a narrow slippery track, part of it on a slant so that you could not put your feet comfortably on the ground, along the right bank of the Subansiri. There seemed no end to it, the slither down, the clamber up. Twice I fell through the track up to my waist. Hundreds of leeches reared their lithe bodies on the ground baring their anti-coagulant jaws, great spiders the size of your hand hung from above, dimdams buzzed like jet fighters round our heads. On this first day I picked forty-eight leeches off my person, finding them inside my socks, deep in my boots, on my arms and even in my hair.

The Sipi river flows through a narrow valley, flanked by steep, heavily-wooded hills, and the Tagin villages are mostly in hollows well below the summits, and those I visited were well watered. They were small, with not more than six to eight houses, though each house had at least four hearths and accommodated a fairly large number of people. The granaries were built a short distance away as a protection against fire.

There was at first some apprehension that I had come to make further inquiries about the Achingmori tragedy. At a remote village at the very end of the valley, the leaders did not come to see me for a considerable time, though I was immediately surrounded by a large crowd of ordinary people. But presently the Chief, dressed in fine handwoven robes and attended by a small bodyguard, marched up in grim silence. The crowd scattered and we were left face to face. It was an electric moment: for the first time the Chief's eyes rested on, shall we say, a regular subscriber to the *New Statesman*. Here, he said to himself, is civilization. He obviously did not care greatly for what he saw. I could feel him drinking me in—the undistinguished features, the spectacles, the worn-out coat, frayed and baggy trousers, the muddy boots. Is that all, he seemed to say, that they have to offer? He stood upright, motionless, and glowered at me, while he fingered, rather suggestively I thought, his formidable sword. I tried a smile—there was no response. I offered the customary gifts—he waved them aside. I tried the few words I knew—and with a gesture of dignity and scorn he handed me a present, a solitary egg: white and chill it nestled in my palm. I smiled again but even I felt that my smiles had become a thought mechanical. There was obviously nothing for it: I would have to put on my little act, which in my opinion is worth a whole platoon of Assam Rifles as a safety measure. I removed my dentures. There was a roar of interest and excitement from the crowd. I put them back. Another roar. After I had conducted this humiliating performance several times, there was at last a reaction. The Chief's lips began to twitch, and he finally broke into a hearty laugh. Pointing to his greying hair, he declared, 'I am an old man too,' and soon he was sitting beside me very affably.

But even now not altogether at ease. The Tagins, he knew, had misbehaved and he had clearly made up his mind not to talk. So to every question, he had but one reply: 'I know nothing, I didn't do it.'

When our conversation came round to theology, a subject on which I was hoping, rather optimistically, to obtain some information, this attitude became a little embarrassing.

'Tell me, who is the Supreme Being?' I inquired.

He leapt to his feet, raised his hand to heaven. 'It isn't me, I swear it.'

'But who created the world?'

'I have no idea. But I didn't do it. It was before my time.'

'And what about the Sun and Moon?'

'Not me, not me. I did wipe out a village in my youth, but that was a long time ago. I have done nothing since.'

But I think that by the time I left he was happy and content, and he was certainly almost vociferous in his demands for a fuller development of the area.

One of the most distressing features in the life of these people was a form of dermatitis, which begins as a patch of ringworm and develops into a generalized scaly desquamation of the skin of the entire body. The skin turns a white or silvery colour and flakes off: I saw men scraping themselves with knives to remove the scales; they were always restless with the constant itch and irritation. This disfiguring and distressing affliction has now been diagnosed as *tinea imbricata,* and the NEFA doctors are making it their special care to treat it.

After my visit to the Tagins and the northern Gallongs I returned to Daporijo and then, leaving the regular route, set out on a fantastically difficult cross-country journey down to Ziro, over the great Kamla river and then along the Pein valley.

Although the marches were as hard as anything further north, I found the people much more attractive and cooperative. They were what have long been called Hill Miris, Saraks or Panibotias. They were free of the disturbing skin disease that afflicted the Tagins; many of them were very good-looking. Some of the women were still wearing their traditional cane-brassières and all had elaborate cane-belts, very carefully woven. They did their hair in rather the same way as the Daflas, with a knot in front and very attractive little cane-hats, sometimes decorated with porcupine quills.

An interesting feature of many villages were the tombs. Some of these had rows of stuffed monkeys with gaping mouths, paws extended, baskets on their backs with tobacco and bits of food which were placed there to assist the ghost as he marched down to the underworld.

My interpreters had their wives with them and we went along stimulated by the constant crackle of matrimonial discord. They were all polygamous. One of them had three wives with him in the camp—he had four altogether, three, he said, to work in the house and one for sex. He hoped for eight and explained that he actually wanted twelve but, owing to the new-fangled ideas of Government, he supposed he would have to be content with less.

This part of the world impressed me with a sense of extreme desolation which was emphasized by the pouring rain and the mist that went with us for almost the whole of our way. The Kamla river, which would ordinarily have been very pretty, looked awe-inspiring as we climbed down the hill to cross it by a rickety cane bridge. And the last lap of the journey was through a great forest with rain dripping drearily from the branches of its trees.

This was perhaps the most exacting tour I have ever done. I can't say that I had enjoyed it, but I shall always be glad that I did it.

IV

Promenades in Siang

There is nothing to compare with Siang, and the four long tours I have made in this delectable Division stand out beyond comparison with any others. On the first of them, in January

1955, I went from Along down to Pangin and then up the left bank of the Siang river to Shimong, crossed by bamboo bridge to Karko and then back to Along along the right bank.

This was my first long tour in the non-Naga part of the frontier and, though it was physically exhausting, I found it stimulating and exhilarating. In the villages we were as usual accommodated in the boys' dormitory, a long and very draughty building with a low roof. Down one side was a series of pigsties, with little platforms above them, for use as lavatories: rich men value the privilege of keeping their pigs in places where they receive such ample nourishment. In the dormitories we were surrounded by a perpetual crowd ; boys climbed into the rafters and looked down, in some places we were even watched by people peering up through cracks in the floor. Every evening the girls assembled for a dance, which often went on till long past midnight.

Victor was with us, and my eldest son Kumar, and the invaluable Sundarlal. Bhajan did the cooking and we had Haricharan as chaprasi. A very good domestic team. For interpreter I had two of the Political interpreters in their red coats, Tapang Taki and Orin Modi, two charming people who added much to the success of the tour.

Kumar, then about fourteen, was in tremendous form ; he had his Abor dao (a sort of hatchet) and a spear and made great friends with Tapang and Orin, as well as with many of the villagers. He looked after the first-aid, tying up many wounds and distributing simple medicines. He played the gramophone to frequent and admiring crowds. And all the time he was in the highest spirits. He was able to watch an interesting airdrop and was very excited at seeing the parachutes billowing down, and thoroughly enjoyed balancing himself across Abor bridges. He fell a dozen times on every march, but was light enough to do himself no damage. Victor, however, had a number of nasty falls, but on the marches I got through unscathed. One night, however, I went down into a deep ditch among rocks and sprained my ankle. Fortunately we only had forty miles more to walk.

My next visit, now six years ago, was to the very isolated Bori area.

After flying part of the way, with two dozen goats as fellow-passengers, I set out on foot with my little party into the Bori villages, a very interesting and picturesque part of the world, about which nothing has so far been written. The Boris are Abors in the sense that they speak the same language, but in dress and appearance they are distinctive. They are enthusiastic weavers and they make an attractive skirt, coat and cloak of wool which is brought down from the north. Both men and women cut their hair in a fringe across the forehead and keep it long behind and it looks unusually attractive. The children, and especially the little girls, were some of the most beautiful I have ever seen.

To my mind, the most alarming things on this tour were the suspension-bridges. These are bamboo tubes which are slung across the rivers, sometimes strengthened by a couple of wire-ropes supplied by Government and sometimes not. You have to balance on a narrow strip of cane or wire and support yourself by cane-ropes on either side. The entire tube is enclosed by bits of cane or bamboo but there are many gaps and the whole thing looks extremely fragile. When there is a strong wind, a bridge may wriggle like a snake. In this part of the world it is as important to be an acrobat as an anthropologist!

Above the valleys rise the splendid snow-covered peaks of the Pari mountains and in many places we had fine views, almost like Switzerland. Unhappily, after a few days the weather turned against us and the beauty of the country was lost in constant cloud and mist. It also began to rain.

In the Bori country we made our camp as elsewhere in the boys' dormitories, which here are called bangos. The bango is a long draughty building with a floor that feels as if it may collapse any moment, and has a series of hearths down its length. It is used by the villagers as council-house, dormitory and club and all day long there are people sitting round the fire and talking at the top of their voices: the Boris, when excited, speak in a high-pitched monotone and generally three or four of them hold forth at the same time. When they do the din is terrific. 'A Bori's tongue', they say, 'is four yards long.' All the unmarried boys and men sleep round the fire. I generally had my bed in one corner.

We were the first visitors who had stayed in the bangos in this way, in fact only two officers had visited this area before us and they travelled with escorts and halted in well-protected camps. It was interesting that the Boris hardly took any notice of us. There we were among them and they sat all round shouting and yelling, making baskets, getting drunk, quarrelling, without troubling about us at all. This gave us some idea of how they really lived.

Another remarkable thing was how we could, even in this kind of crowded atmosphere (for sometimes there were over a hundred people in the house at once) leave all our things about in perfect safety. There were tea-leaves, sugar, cigarettes, all sorts of things the people would have liked to have, and yet there was no need to lock anything up, for nobody would dream of stealing.

All my life I have had the misfortune to incur the displeasure of the clergy. It was the same in the Bori country. There was no apprehension that we had come to take away their land or impose taxes, as I have found when visiting other remote areas in India. Here the suspicion and fear of us was not political but theological. On entering every village I was greeted with rows of sharp bamboo stakes and gates adorned with a number of symbols—sometimes it was the head of a dead dog—designed to frighten away the evil spirits whom we were certainly bringing with us. I and my party in fact were spiritually toxic—we carried with us the infection of another world. When I tried to buy specimens for my museum the priests announced that if anybody allowed us to take something belonging to him out of the Bori country he would die. There was the strongest possible objection to being photographed, for fear that the subject's soul would be removed by the camera. In one case, when an old man had been sitting with me for some time, his little daughter came screaming that he would be devoured by a Wiyu-spirit if he remained with me longer. She emphasized her remarks by throwing a heavy piece of iron and a block of wood at him. In some villages we were warned that the names of gods and spirits must not be taken inside a building and so our inquiries had to be conducted out of doors.

Such fears have now largely disappeared. Here were people

who were still in the childhood of the race. Many of them had never struck a match ; they had not seen a watch and did not know what it was. They had the most intense curiosity about everything we had, examined with great care the construction of a chair or table and were fascinated by our cooking arrangements. The one thing in which they had lost interest was the aeroplane, the 'Government cart', so often passing overhead that they no longer bothered to look up.

There was still slavery in this area, though the Administration was gradually liberating the slaves and has now succeeded in liberating nearly all of them. The slaves were often well treated, and I got to know a number of them and wrote down their stories. I brought back with me a dear old Tagin woman, who had been captured as a slave when very young and had been sold again and again to members of different tribes. She had a dream about her deliverance, that she went into a hole in the ground and travelled in the great darkness for many weary miles 'until she came out into a place of light, to the presence of the Sun-Moon God'. I brought her back to Along and she was liberated ; I have told her story in *A Philosophy for NEFA*.

At the beginning of 1958 I went, with Kumar and my usual small party, to Tuting in the extreme north of Siang for a wonderful seven weeks' tour. We went first down the right bank of the Siang river, visiting the villages of the Ashings as far as lovely Bomdo where we crossed the river on an improvised bamboo raft, and then worked north again through the Shimong area to the east, and finally up the sacred, fertile and beautiful Yang Sang Chu valley as far as Mankhota. On our return to Tuting we were held up by bad weather for ten days and used part of the time to visit Gelling and the Kepang La which forms the boundary between India and Tibet.

This is one of the most fascinating and exciting parts of NEFA ; the scenery, when it is not hidden by cloud and rain, is superb ; the people are charming, hospitable and photogenic : tribal institutions still retain their vitality. It is a country of song and dance, of hard enthusiastic work, of fine spinning and weaving, and of laughing, pretty children.

We crossed the Siang river on bamboo rafts, a greater adventure than it sounds, for the Abors are afraid of the rivers that are one of the most notable features of their territory, for they are believed to be haunted by dangerous spirits, the Nippongs, who drag men down into the water, and a number of drowning tragedies in the past had discouraged them from either fishing or crossing the river by boat or raft. It was, therefore, by no means easy to persuade the Ashings to help us make the raft at Bomdo and only one or two of them would venture on it, although scores of people gathered at the bank to watch the hazardous crossing. At Tuting, however, a very fine raft was constructed by a Memba who had learnt to use a primitive kind of oar. It could accommodate eleven persons and there was a comfortable seat with a prayer-flag at the prow. On the bank the Abors busied themselves in offering sacrifices for our safe crossing and the Membas and Khambas erected a sapling decorated with prayer-flags.

In October of the same year I made another long tour, of six weeks, in north-west Siang, going first to Mechuka and then working down through the Ramo, Pailibo and Bori areas back to Along.

The valley here is of great beauty. I had visited Mechuka before for a few hours but a visit only to the outpost gives no idea of the scenery and the possibilities of this lovely valley surrounded by pine-covered hills which give way to the snow-covered high ranges beyond.

We went on to the Ramo-Pailibo area, a strange and unique part of the world. The mountains are formidable and the tracks in the main are very difficult. The Niying Shi river between Mechuka and Tato is so hemmed in by steep and towering hills that the traveller feels as if he is passing through a deep gorge and after a time has a sense of claustrophobia. This is a country where formerly there were human sacrifices, where slaves were captured and sold, hostages kept in the stocks, and suspicion and hostility ruled the day: but it is a very friendly part of the world now. In one village, a kindly Pailibo presented me with a piece of monkey meat, but to my disappointment my cook rejected it indignantly. He gave it to one of my interpreters who fell seriously ill after eating it, for it had been killed with a poisoned arrow, and was insufficiently cooked to counteract the aconite.

My great love in the Abor country was the Siang river. This marvellous stream, which rises as the Tsang-Po far away in Tibet, enters India in the extreme north and then flows down to enter the plains at Pasighat and then merge in the mighty Brahmaputra. I have often flown along the course of the Siang and have at different times walked its entire length from Komsing to Tuting and beyond. I have also travelled along two of its enticingly beautiful tributaries, the Yang Sang Chu in the far north and the Siyom.

If all the pens that ever poets held were to get to work on it, I doubt if they could digest into words the fascination of this wonderful river, so exquisite, so mysterious, so varied in its charms, at one point flowing through gently sloping woods, at another forcing its way through high gorges. Its colour is always changing and when you see it shrouded in gentle mist against a background of snow-mountains towering in the distance, it is one of the loveliest sights that can meet the eye of man. The Siang is a hard mistress and sometimes exhausted me so completely that I came to think of it as the river of no return. Indeed, I would be happy one day to lay my body beside its waters.

V

The Strange Fascination of Lohit

The people of Lohit have always fascinated me and I do not know why I have not spent more time among them, even though I did make two long tours among the Mishmis. I never, however, made my way on foot up the Lohit valley to Wallong although, as I shall describe, I went up by plane. I also visited the Khamptis several times and particularly my 1959 visit to their villages (when Wasant came with me) was most rewarding. It was there that I saw village Buddhism at its simplest and best. I took a number of bronze Buddhas to present to the little temples and everywhere was welcomed with most touching enthusiasm. I was given the honorable title of Phradayaka by the monks of Ningro.

My very first visit to the Division was with Rashid Yusuf Ali, one of the most remarkable (though as yet unrecognized) men that I have ever met. We went at the height of the rains, plunging on elephants through trackless jungle in search of a ruined copper temple. This slightly lunatic, fruitless yet altogether worthwhile adventure was typical of Rashid—I would like to think it was typical of me also, but I am not sure: on my own I am afraid I should have waited for the rain to stop.

My first Mishmi tour was across country from Tezu to Roing, nothing very adventurous, but at that time, in November 1955, it was possible in three weeks to see real Mishmi life there without marching hundreds of miles and climbing impossible mountains, though the country was very rough.

There is always a special thrill in one's first visit to a new tribe, and in this case I was a little apprehensive, for all previous travellers had stressed how 'difficult' the Mishmis were and how unpleasant and unattractive. I can only say I fell in love with them at once. Our first village was inhabited by Taraon (or Digaru) Mishmis and the men wore their hair tied in a knot on the top of the head and the women had theirs in a fantastic piled-up style which would attract admiring attention anywhere.

I stayed throughout the tour in Mishmi houses, some of which are very large, containing a number of related families. You must imagine a long low building raised on poles above the ground, with an entrance and veranda at each end. A corridor runs down one side and off this open a number of small rooms, each for a separate family or, where the owner of the house has several wives, each for a different wife and her children. Visitors enter by the eastern door, and it is correct for you to go and sit by the fire in complete silence for a few minutes before doing anything. Then you are given the first room as you enter, for this is maintained as a guest-room: it even has its own lavatory above the pigsty. The rooms were always clean and tidy and for the first time since I came to NEFA I managed to avoid the bites of fleas, though there was an alarming number of hornets. The only disadvantage for a tall person like myself was that the roof was so low that I had to stoop the whole time I was indoors. My guest-room was always crowded with people, young and old of both sexes, and I had as much privacy as a rare fish has in an aquarium. But the Mishmis have no idea of privacy ; at night husbands and wives lay in couples all round us and no one seemed to be embarrassed.

Some Mishmis are so lazy that they do not bother to clear the ground even round their houses and the jungle comes right up to the door. In front of the house is often an elaborate tomb, with a spire and flags flying, and on the walls inside are racks of the skulls of animals. Every animal ever taken in the chase or offered at a ceremonial feast is represented here. The Mishmis never did head-hunting in the ordinary way: what they went in for was hair-hunting and thumb-hunting. When they killed an enemy, they cut off the thumb of the right hand, 'the hand with which you eat your food', and a tuft of hair, and brought these trophies home in triumph. After a special celebration, the hair was hung above the door and the thumb buried before it.

The first ten days of the tour was among these Taraon Mishmis, who are the most picturesque and handsome. Their weaving is good and I was able to collect a number of beautiful textiles. They are devoted to tobacco and both men and women always had very long brass or silver pipes in their mouths. They are almost the only people in NEFA who do not tattoo and do not chew betel, and most of them had lovely white teeth.

The second ten days was spent among the Idu Mishmis, a tougher and more warlike group, separated from the Taraons by the Paya river. At our first village we were a little disconcerted ; the people did not seem friendly ; our interpreter was lying dead drunk out in the jungle ; the local Chief did not come near us. But things warmed up later, and I was soon liking the Idus almost as much as the Taraons. They are rather like Baigas, very wild and shaggy, real jungle folk, with their poisoned arrows and a cross-bow which they fire by a trigger like a gun. The weaving of the Idus is also good and one day a party of them came to our camp from a village many days distant towards the frontier selling cloth of excellent quality and pattern. Some of them wear bright-coloured woollen coats adorned with crosses, a circumstance which in the last century had made Father Krick believe that they had been converted to Christianity long ago and had then reverted.

This is the country of wild elephants, who sometimes kill people and often spoil the crops. I saw a man in the Tezu hospital who had been tossed by one of them two years before and had not yet fully recovered. Anyone killed by a wild elephant, however, goes to the Land of the Sun, not the ordinary subterranean Land of the Dead, and has every comfort there. It is, therefore, a not undesirable death.

One year Lila went with me on a long and very arduous tour of the Khamlang valley. We were seen off at Tezu by the Political Officer, Uma Sharma, one of the best of men, courteous, gentle and courageous, and we first passed through a few Khampti villages and then went into the lonely valley running up into the mountains.

The Khamlang valley is a thinly populated and little-explored area of great beauty running eastward from Wakro up to the snow-line. It is sparsely inhabited by the Miju or Kaman Mishmis; there are fewer than fifty houses in the entire valley and I estimated the population at about five hundred. I was able to visit every village except two, most of the settlements consisting of only one to four houses. The tracks were as bad as anything I have met in NEFA, and most of the villages are placed high on the hills and there are long and steep climbs up to them. The countryside is further divided by many streams which in the rains become impassable for days at a time.

The Kaman Mishmis are an attractive people, quiet and friendly, and in this area, where they have largely retained their own beautiful dress and ornaments, they look delightful. Their weaving is among the finest in NEFA and is of extraordinary variety; we hardly ever saw two articles with exactly the same pattern. Their legends attribute the origin of these designs to butterflies, fish and snakes, whose markings they have copied, and there are other designs representing houses, human figures and even aeroplanes.

Our first halt was at Choukham and we then continued our journey on elephants up to the lonely outpost of Wakro at the entrance of the Khamlang valley. This first part of the journey was rather dreary, but we saw one or two Buddhist temples on the way, tumbledown buildings housing carvings of surprising beauty.

Looking up the valley we received an impression of incomparably wild scenery shrouded in mist and cloud. We had Tapan Kumar Barua, who has gone with me on a number of tours, to escort us and an excellent Mishmi interpreter, Somiya, and as we had been warned that the villages were very small, we for once took a tent. We sent the elephants home and proceeded on foot.

Our first village was rather discouraging, for we found it under a taboo and were not allowed to go in or see anybody. We camped outside in the jungle and were kept awake by the screams of wild elephants during the night. The next village, however, was high up among the hills, with a superb view of snow-clad mountains rising into a blue sky. The camp was ideally placed on the side of a hill and had views on three sides, and here the people, dressed in a fantastic variety of textiles, nearly all beautiful, were most friendly.

Here, Lila began to indulge her lifelong passion for washing people. There was a small waterfall and a pool nearby, and Lila collected the children (who were quite exceptionally dirty) and began a tremendous soaping and scrubbing. Presently some older girls and boys came to be washed too. Later, one of the boys said that it was an interesting experience, but not one that he would like to have repeated.

We travelled almost to the end of the valley, at least as far as we saw any people living, and then crossed the river, Lila washing people along the way and catching fish in the streams—she got some very fine three-inchers. Everywhere we went we found goitre and the Mishmis here were much poorer than those I had seen before.

At a village called Glao we found a fine lake among the hills. By now I was feeling rather heroic, for there was no evidence that anybody had been before us. But at Glao we discovered that Kingdon-Ward had long ago camped there for a whole week. In fact, in spite of exploring some very wild places, I have never been able to feel really heroic in NEFA. I have always been put down by either Kingdon-Ward or Peter James, a very popular Political Officer, now in tea, of the old days.

No matter where I went, or how many miles I heaved myself over the mountains in northern Siang, everywhere I found that James Migam, as the Abors called him, had been before me, and not only had been before me but had been very much better. 'James Migam', they would say severely, 'gave us a mithun. James Migam danced all night. James Migam drank all the rice-beer we gave him.' I had to say that I was afraid I was not James Migam and just couldn't keep up with him.

The lake at Glao was full of fish but none of the Mishmis were willing to try to catch them. For eleven years before two boys and two girls had gone out on a raft and had never returned. It was said that they had been dragged below the water by the goddess of the lake.

On this tour I was, in addition to my general study of the needs of the people, specially interested in collecting textiles and discovering the meaning of their patterns. This was not very easy, for the Kaman Mishmis are not very free in their information. Everyone, however, told me that if I would persevere, I should find a very great authority, an old Mishmi, who knew everything. When we did finally discover him, I was thrilled, collected my assistants and rushed to greet him with my little note-book. Unfortunately he turned out to be deaf and dumb.

The only time, I am ashamed to say, that I went up the Lohit was by plane. Khemlal Rathee went with me and it was most exciting. From Jorhat there is first a quiet trip to Tezu when you pass over a large number of tea gardens and you realize how beautifully laid out these are. The country below looks like a chess-board. We flew over Tezu fairly high and then went up the Lohit valley to Haiyuliang. The scenery got grander and grander as we went along and more and more snow-mountains came into view. The path from Haiyuliang to Changwinty did not look difficult and I wished that I was walking along it and meeting the people instead of flying above it, even though I would have missed the scenery. We passed Changwinty and looked up the desolate valley which stretches to the snows beyond it and then turned towards Wallong and Kibithu. The landing at Wallong is very tricky and at one moment it looked as if we were flying straight into the hillside. The airstrip had been used for air-dropping and was pitted with holes so that when we came down we bumped along like a kangaroo. We were in some apprehension as to how we were to take off, but we managed it by revving up violently and going almost straight up into the air.

VI

Visits to Tirap

I have made many visits to Tirap, the most south-easterly of the NEFA Divisions, but two of my tours remain specially in my memory, for they were of four or five weeks each and took me into what was at that time little-explored territory. I first went to the Wancho area in November 1954, and was received everywhere with great friendliness and hospitality, though some of these villages had not been visited for a long time. At Pomau, a song was sung about my coming:

The sahib who lives in Shillong
Has flown like a maina bird to these high hills
And has perched on a tree in our village.
Our minds are full of happiness.
As the fish swim up the little streams from the great river,
The sahib has come from the plains to our high hills,
And our minds are full of happiness.

Although very few visitors, at that date, had gone into the Wancho hills, the nearer Wanchos themselves had for a hundred years been visiting the plains and this had led to a greater degree of acculturation than, for example, in the neighbouring Tuensang, now part of Nagaland. Dress had changed to some extent, though not as much as might have been expected: many of the men wore black coats, and some women had abandoned the characteristic and very pretty hand-woven skirt and were putting on a slightly broader piece of dirty mill-cloth. But many others in the interior retained their traditional, very becoming, dress and ornaments; most of the young boys and girls lived naked, except for their beads, their headdress and their flowers. The chief effect of contact with the outside world had been to make the people self-conscious, and when we entered a village all the women, and some even of the men, hastily draped themselves from head to foot in bedsheets. At Longphong, the women covered their heads and most of their faces, leaving only their eyes peeping out: one might have been in Arabia. This habit is not only most unaesthetic, but the moral effect of self-consciousness cannot be good.

There were many quaint and incongruous things—such as a trilby hat perched above a splendid array of beads. The Wancho men always wear something at the back of the head, round which the hair is wound. This, traditionally, is a piece of wood, which may be carved with human heads or other designs, or in the shape of a hand, if one is a warrior, or be made in various geometric patterns, and gaily coloured, if one is not. The custom survives, but you may see an old electric torch, a tablespoon, a pencil now used instead. Cartridges are commonly used in the ears, and plugs faced with mirrors: it is amusing to see a boy remove his ear-mirror, do his hair in it, and then replace it. Wancho warriors, who took heads long ago, still wear brass or wooden heads round their necks. On two occasions I saw, on either side of a large brass head, a pair of pink plastic heads, wrenched off dolls purchased in the bazaar: the effect was grimly horrible.

In a house in Lankao, I saw a long string of train-tickets hung up in memory of daring journeys to distant bazaars. In the house of the Chief of Senua, there were decorations of strings of monkey's paws, the beaks of the Great Indian Hornbill and old batteries from an electric torch.

The Wanchos are passionately attached to tea. They had heard that tea is made with a kettle. So they solemnly pour water from a bamboo container into the kettle; then they put the leaves into another bamboo, and pour the water from the kettle back into the bamboo to heat it. The tea emerges stewed and black, and is taken without milk or sugar.

On the other hand, although they brew rice-beer, they were remarkably moderate in their use of it. I did not see a single drunken man, not a single person who was even slightly high, in the course of a month.

But many people were smoking opium. I saw dozens of little poppy plantations, and in some places every house was festooned with bundles of ganja hanging up to dry. The older people were making some attempt to stop the younger generation from opium, but they were not prepared to set an example. The Administration has since made a lot of propaganda to reduce the opium habit.

The memory of my first tour in the Wancho hills of Tirap is of hard climbs over clean open country with great bare hills swept by the wind. Most of the Wancho villages are sited at something like three thousand feet on the tops of hills and for every march we had to climb down to the valley below, walk anything from five to ten miles along the lower ground and then climb up, when we were really tired, another three thousand feet to the next village. But there was magnificence and splendour about this country ; you could stand on the top of a hill and see your whole programme mapped out around you, with the grey roofs of the villages you were to visit clustered on the top of the surrounding hills.

Some of the villages were a little dull, but there were two which I shall always remember. The first was Senua, where I had the good fortune of being able to watch the ceremony when the Wanchos send a girl to her husband's village. A party of boys and girls had come to fetch her and they all were decorated in their elaborate finery. They had head-bands of orange beads, brightly coloured cloth, and their hair was full of waving feathers and flowers. The bride was a very pretty little creature, with a fine bead-crown, and obviously happy. She was fortunate enough, they explained, to have slept with her future husband already and so it was not as if she were going to a stranger. I watched her put on her ornaments, while her friends made little parcels of presents. Finally, there was a great procession headed by two old women and followed by the bride and a long line of handmaidens.

Another delightful village was Lonkao. What struck me about this village was its innocence. Most of the boys and girls had very little in the way of clothes and were not in the least self-conscious about it. The morung was commodious, comfortable and clean and we were surrounded night and day by children, as well as by older boys and girls, some of them very attractive to look at. All day long they played round and in my camp. They did the tug-of-war, using a long creeper, with great gusto and loud cries of excitement. Some of them hopped about on one leg singing little songs. The babies were most attractive with their brass bracelets, cane-armlets and tails of squirrels hanging from their ears. Throughout the Wancho country the children of the great Chiefs had unusual character and, as I have noticed elsewhere, I was struck by the fact that I hardly ever heard children cry. They are very rough, they fight, tear each other's hair, roll in the dust, are dragged along in the tug-of-war, fall headlong to the ground, but they don't cry. I remember two boys fighting, each with a baby tied to his back, and then it is true that the babies screamed in fright.

On our last day in this captivating village there was a great dance. We were woken very early by the thunder of the drums and all the morning the boys prepared their special decorations. At midday, the dance began. It was an attempt to recapture the old days of head-hunting, to which they all looked back as the time when they were really men. Three groups of gaily decorated Wanchos, armed to the teeth, crept up through the surrounding forest, put out scouts, came forward, retreated, then advanced and discharged their guns. One man got a wooden head which he put in his basket with shouts of triumph. Then they started dancing in a great circle, jogging about and waving guns and spears in the air. Every now and then the boys would let off their guns just behind me to see me jump. This caused pleasure to one and all, though I myself was perhaps less amused than some.

Later I made another long tour (this time Kumar was with me) right along the formidable slopes of the Patkoi mountains up to Wakka, then across the Laju through the Hatut Nocte area and the Tangsa villages. Since then splendid roads have been built in the face of almost insuperable difficulties, but at the time of my own tours mechanized transport was not available and to my own great benefit I was forced to walk.

We first went into the Nocte country. The Noctes are a rather detribalized group, who have been in contact with the plains for centuries, and their dress was deplorable. But their villages were as interesting as any. Here were the skulls ranged in the morungs (village guard-houses), grim reminders of a day when head-hunting was the chief occupation of the people, and many stone pillars in memory of battles long ago.

After passing through the Nocte area, we marched eight miles over very steep and rough hills to Longkhai and were at once in a different world, in the beautiful and highly-coloured land of the remote Wanchos. Now, instead of trilby hats, sleazy singlets and dirty shorts, the pathetic symbols of 'civilization', we had waving plumes, the 'eternally dressed nakedness of the brown skin', ornaments, hand-woven cloth, gleaming brass waist-bands, and the most lovely scenery everywhere.

This is the country of the great Chiefs, who have vast houses, pitch dark inside, containing many wives and handmaidens, and people who are not quite slaves and who have to keep their heads shaven,

In certain parts of Tirap I found that the expression 'Jai Hind' (the common greeting of independent India) was being used as a proper noun to indicate what the simple tribesmen regarded as a person of importance. It would be used, for example, for a visitor from Shillong or Delhi. 'Has the Jai Hind arrived ?' the people would inquire, or they would say, 'Please tell this to the Jai Hind.' I thought this was a rather pleasant variation on the usual 'sahib'.

As we went along, the country grew wilder and wilder until we reached the Patkoi mountains which divide India from Burma.

For nearly three weeks we marched along the slopes of the Patkoi rising from eight to nine thousand feet in a grim unbroken wall against the sky. For almost the whole of this period the mountains were shrouded in cloud and mist, and life got rather dreary with the incessant sunlessness and raw bitter wind. It was not so much the discomfort that was depressing as the fact that the people in such weather draped their beauty in dirty sheets and sat about miserably.

I shall never forget these inhospitable hills, lonely and desolate, with great valleys running up to the main wall between the bluffs and spurs that descend to the Tirap river. One such valley, which I never saw touched by the sun, was dominated by a village on a forest-clad spur—like something in *Dracula.* This was the fabled home of the dreaded Rangpangs, who until twenty years ago are believed to have practised human sacrifice. We went there and found them quiet and amiable, though rather cagey when it came to discussing their past history.

In the final lap of our journey we entered the Tangsa hills. Tangsa means 'children of Burma' and the people here have traditions of immigration from Burma and still have a decidedly Burmese look about them. They wear their hair in a top-knot and dress in sarongs of a pattern resembling a Scotch plaid. I greatly enjoyed the days spent in their company.

It was a long and interesting tour, full of contrasts—the sophisticated Noctes near the plains, then the delightful Wanchos full of colour and zest for living, then the opium-taking and impoverished people of the Hatut confederacy, and finally the handsome, picturesque Tangsas.

In some of the frontier villages the people had no interest in money, and we had to get our supplies by barter; a box of matches for an egg, a string of beads or hank of yarn for a fowl; tea-leaves for rice. Kumar was specially expert at this and at one time kept a regular shop where we got specimens for our museum when the people would not part with them for money.

It was a long tour, about 160 miles, and we got a little tired towards the end. The last two marches were done in the rain and we finally arrived at a place called Changlang which was on a road, one of our development centres, in a marvellous state of damp and dirt. But we cleaned up and were preparing to spend a quiet night there when suddenly there was the hoot of a car—what a wonderful sound after all those weeks: I remember kissing the bonnet, the rough male kiss of motor transport—and out got Lila with Khemlal Rathee who had come up by Land-Rover to fetch us back. So there was hurried packing and at sunset we went down a very winding road, including a dozen hairpin bends, for Margherita and thus back to Shillong.

VII

On these and other tours in north-eastern India I covered approximately two thousand miles, of which about two hundred and fifty were on elephant and pony and the rest on foot. The physical exertion required was sometimes a little severe, for I was from fifty-two to fifty-seven years old at the time and, though I love getting to the top of things, I am no athlete. I sometimes thought it might have been better if I had come to NEFA when I was thirty and spent these later years among the indulgent hills of Orissa or Bastar. And yet had I done that, I should not have been able to write the books I did about the central Indian tribes, for soon afterwards they changed.

In NEFA I always had to push on. It was difficult to stay, as I used to stay in Orissa, for long periods in one village at a time; there were difficulties about supplies and porters: I was possessed by the desire to explore. It was difficult also to be the Invisible Man which I have always tried to be, for now I was regarded as an official and a rather senior one; altogether too much fuss was made of me and I was an oddity which everyone wanted to observe.

These long tours meant leaving Lila and the children behind. My very first tour of seven weeks in Tuensang was a great strain on Lila, for we had only just come to Shillong: she had few friends in those days, and when I returned I found her weak and ill: nobody had sent me the news that there was anything the matter with her.

I learnt a useful lesson from these tours which underlined something that a wise old Forest Officer had said to me long before. 'I never,' he said, 'send a rebuke to any member of my staff while he is on tour or posted by himself in a lonely place.' I myself have had disturbing letters from time to time, as we all do, when I have been travelling alone, and these upset me far more than they would have done had I been able to discuss them with friends who knew the background. This is another of the dangers of loneliness; if an administrator finds it necessary to give one of his subordinates a rocket it is far better to wait until the latter comes into headquarters. Isolation makes everything more acute.

I enjoyed these tours in NEFA tremendously and learnt a great deal from them. On the way to Tawang I felt purified and strengthened by the beauty of the mountains and chastened by the gentleness and quietness of the people. But I think it was the Tagins who affected me more than any other tribe. I have always tended to romanticize the tribal people, whom it is so easy to love and admire. But among the Tagins there was little but misery and emptiness. Gandhi developed the idea of Daridranarayana, the God of the Poor, the God who appears in each poor man in whose service his worship is fulfilled. Among many tribes, for all their poverty, Daridranarayana appears as a God of beauty and enchantment, but among the Tagins He took the form of the Starved Buddha or the Suffering Servant of Isaiah in whom there was no beauty that we should desire him.

How much we romantics have to learn! To have compassion on the rich and successful, who are often so unhappy; to love and care for the conventional and ordinary; to recognize the importance of the ugly and the dull. For me this was a hard lesson, for my poetic soul delights in the exotic and surprising, and beauty draws me with a single hair.

10

Growth of a 'Philosophy'

What more felicity can fall to creature
Than to enjoy delight with liberty?
—Edmund Spenser

I

WHEN Shamrao and I first settled in the Maikal hills we were singularly ill-equipped to be of use to anyone. Shamrao knew something about medicine. I knew a little about gardening but our knowledge, say, of chicken-breeding, which was based on P. G. Wodehouse's *Love among the Chickens,* was typical of our experience of practical realities. At that time, of course, there were no Five-Year Plans, no great schemes for the all-round development of India. Even the handful of social workers who specialized in tribal matters thought mainly in terms of opening small schools and dispensaries.

Our original idea was a mystical rather than a material one, though we hoped to express it in practical terms. We thought that simply by living among the tribes, sharing their life as far as possible and, to some extent, suffering with them, we would make reparation for their long neglect and their treatment by a hard-hearted world. It was a way of becoming part of 'the whole human condition'. It was not, of course, possible for us really to identify ourselves on the physical plane with the poorest Gonds. Even the possession of a wrist-watch or a fountain-pen put us far away from them. On the other hand, we did live, not as a temporary gesture but for a very long time, in houses like their own very simply indeed, suffered from the same anxieties, were bullied, as they were, by Government officials, and were tormented in typical village fashion by malaria. We felt that even this small attempt towards identification would mean something and I think that there is no doubt that it did touch the hearts of many thousands of tribesmen who realized that, impractical as we were, we were thinking about them and showing them affection.

Psychologically at least, I think we were able to bring them a new spirit and a new hope, for they were very crushed when we first settled among them.

We were not, of course, content with this. We opened schools and started a dispensary where Shamrao in time became famous, people coming fifty, even a hundred, miles to consult him. We were able to help a large number of individuals by acting as peace-makers in their disputes, assisting them when they got into trouble with officials and by our advice when they were dragged to court. We did what little we could, and slowly began to learn the practical needs of village life.

One of the things that meant a great deal to us was the opening of our refuge for lepers, small as it was. At that time the chaulmogra medicines available for the treatment of leprosy were not very effective, but we thought that at least we could make a place where these unfortunate people could live fairly comfortably and in security, and at the same time we might check the spread of the disease by containing it in one colony. Even at this time leprosy was regarded with something of the horror that it inherited from the Dark Ages, and the opening of this home was for us ourselves a special symbol of concern and love. We kept it going for about a quarter of a century and, as time went on, learnt the new method of sulphone treatment.

In those first years our policy, if we can dignify it by that term, was partly to encourage the people by simple everyday acts of kindness, but also to rouse them to a sense of their rights —for we early saw that any real progress was in their own hands. We fought many battles with the police, forest officials, merchants and others on their behalf, and so taught them in time to fight for themselves. This made us very unpopular with most of the non-tribals, who did not hesitate to spread every sort of scandal about us and, what was even more dangerous, told the villagers that our medicines were diluted with water drawn by untouchables, that we were planning to convert them to Christianity and that we would send their boys and girls away to institutions in the cities. It was only when, fortunately, a Sub-Inspector of Police got gonorrhoea and Shamrao cured him, that the officials began to come round.

At this time we were mainly concerned with problems of economics and as early as 1934, in an article on the Baigas in the *Modern Review*, the first that I ever wrote on the tribal problem, I pointed out 'the appalling poverty, destitution and ignorance of this heroic and fascinating people'. 'You are certain to be enchanted by them', I wrote, 'but you are equally certain to lie awake at night—and for many nights—haunted by the scenes of suffering that you have witnessed, and wondering what judgement must be passed on society that can calmly allow such things to continue from generation to generation.'

Poverty and disease were the fundamental problems, but the need for protection against every kind of exploitation was also constantly before us. I wanted to save what was beautiful, what was free: I have always opposed those who try to inject a sense of guilt into love, especially the love and happiness of simple people: I wanted to save them from anxiety—about their land, their forests, their next meal. I was absurdly misunderstood, but the poets and artists were always with me. W. G. Archer, for example, in his book of poems *The Plains of the Sun*, addressed one of his pieces (written during the war) to me and I put it in here, not just because I was flattered by it, but because it expresses exactly what I was trying to do.

> Among your burning hills, the lonely jungle
> Roars in the summer. The sterile land
> Rests; and news comes up like clouds
> While you are active in the needs of peace
> Saving the gestures of the happy lovers
> The poems vivid as the tiger
> Faced with destruction from the septic plains
> And with your love and art delay
> The crawling agony and the death of the tribes.

Another very important aspect of what I was trying to do was to make the tribal people known. At that time in India, in spite of the work of a few anthropological pioneers who were seldom read, the tribal people were regarded either as tiresome savages who caused trouble or as colourful and picturesque folk engaging themselves in sexual orgies, human sacrifice and head-hunting. As a result, although a few people tended to sentimentalize them, the general idea was to regard them as a different kind of human being, who might excite our condescending pity but could hardly arouse any kind of admiration.

I felt that if the tribes were to make any progress, it was essential that the rest of the country should treat them properly and regard them with affection and respect.

II

My views on the protection of the tribes caused a regular flutter, and for many years, indeed right up to the present time, I have been accused of wanting 'to keep them as they are', to hold up their development, to preserve them as museum specimens for the benefit of anthropologists. This is, and always has been, nonsense.

Some of the attacks upon me have been the result of deliberate misrepresentation, and generally my critics have not bothered to read what I have actually written. For in fact there was nothing very extraordinary about my policy. I thought the tribes had discovered secrets of living under hard conditions that the rest of us needed, and that their development should be a matter of careful timing. I wanted to ensure that they should only be 'civilized' (for it was obviously inevitable that they would be) when they could be civilized properly and I wanted to give them a breathing-space to build up pride in their own life and become economically self-sufficient so that they would not be completely overwhelmed when the outside world came upon them. I wanted them to make terms with their past and go forward in a natural evolution from it.

In the early years, however, I was greatly impressed by the urgent need of protection and in my book *The Baiga*, published in 1939, I advocated some sort of National Park in a 'wild and largely inaccessible' part of the country, under the direct control of a Tribes Commissioner. But this did not mean that nothing was to be done.

Inside this area, the administration was to allow the tribesmen to live their lives with the 'utmost possible happiness and freedom'. Wide powers were to be given to the traditional tribal councils and the headmen of the villages would have their old authority re-established. Non-tribals settling in the area would be required to take out licences. No missionaries of any religion would be permitted to break up tribal life. Everything possible would be done for the progress of the people within the area, provided that the quality of tribal life was not impaired, tribal culture was not destroyed and tribal freedom was restored or maintained. Economic development would be given high priority and schools should be on the lines of what is now called Basic Education simplified and adapted to local needs. Fishing and hunting were to be freely permitted. The dictatorship of subordinate officials was to come to an end.

As I wrote a little later, we should, even for the wildest and most isolated groups, 'fight for the three freedoms—freedom from fear, freedom from want, freedom from interference. We may see that the aboriginals get a square deal economically. We may see that they are freed from cheats and impostors, from oppressive landlords and moneylenders, from corrupt and rapacious officials. We may see that they get medical aid . . . We may guard them against adventurers who would rob them of their songs, their dances, their festivals, their laughter.' This was not a policy for the isolation of the tribes: what I wanted was planned and controlled contact—which is a very different matter.

My suggestion in *The Baiga* was badly put and I should have realized the unfortunate connotations of the expression 'National Park'. But in 1939 what on earth was one to do? It was not a question of preserving Baiga culture—for the Baigas had very little culture: it was a question of keeping them alive, saving them from oppression and exploitation, giving them a simple form of development. In actual fact, the Government of India has now appointed a Tribes Commissioner and established Tribal Welfare Departments in several States, as well as

Scheduled and Tribal Areas, which in practice are not unlike what I suggested so long ago.

III

During the years preceding Independence there was not much scope for working out policies or philosophies, though there was a good deal of rather unrealistic academic discussion on the future of the tribes. The reason was that plans for the tribal people obviously had to keep pace with plans for the country as a whole. At this time *everybody* was neglected. The great majority of Indian villagers were still illiterate ; they were still attached to antiquated and economically injurious social, religious and agricultural habits. They had little medical assistance, meagre educational facilities, bad communications ; they were exploited and oppressed just as the tribal people were. The latter, however, were even more neglected than the rest and their lot was complicated by the anxiety of the British Government to prevent the independence movement from spreading among them. Congress workers were often not allowed to go into their hills, and when I myself first began work for the tribes I was kept under police surveillance for several years, perhaps naturally, for I certainly had a 'programme of discontent'. I was not allowed to open schools for the Baigas. Visits to forest villages were carefully supervised, if not prevented. There were hardly any roads, hospitals or dispensaries ; there was little interest in the improvement of agriculture and there was no real protection against those who then preyed on and impoverished the tribal people.

This did not mean that nothing could be done but we had to be content to work at specific cases and within restricted limits. I used to draw the attention of the authorities to any outstanding abuses which I discovered, made suggestions for improvements in detail and studied such special subjects as the conditions of the tribal people in jail, the problem of shifting-cultivation and so on. At the same time, I and others continued to keep the tribal people in the public eye.

But then came Independence and with it a great awakening

throughout the country. The tribal people found their place on the map; they became news; great schemes of development were proposed. It quickly became clear that the timid and grudging programmes of British days were entirely unsuitable in free India. Although things still moved slowly, there came a new stress on the need to bring the tribes out of their long isolation and integrate them with the rest of India. Although before Independence I myself had accepted the position that some of the smaller and remotest tribes would have to remain out of the picture for the time being, this was never what might be called a 'philosophical' position: it was due to the necessities of the situation. Later, even for so remote an area as NEFA, I made it sufficiently plain in, for example, the second edition of *A Philosophy for NEFA,* that even there our policy was neither to isolate the tribes nor to freeze their culture and way of life as it was. During the Five-Year Plans large sums of money have been and will be spent on the tribal people throughout India, and I have been one of those who have advocated spending a great deal more than was originally proposed. You do not keep people 'as they are' or as a picturesque enclave by building roads into the very heart of their territory and by taking up very widespread schemes of development. I want change. Even in 1932 I wanted change. But what I want, and what those who think with me want, is change for the better and not degradation and decay.

There is endless talk nowadays about tribal development: if even a quarter of it were translated into action the position would be transformed. And in every conference, at every committee, in every speech, people feel it their duty to discuss over and over again the old controversy of Isolation, Assimilation or Integration, forgetting that it has been put completely out of date as a result of one major circumstance—that the whole of India, including tribal India, will be covered by Community Development Blocks in a year or two's time. This is a decision, this is going to happen, and it is therefore meaningless to discuss whether it is desirable to bring the tribes into the stream of modern civilization or whether it is good or bad to open up their country. Whether we like it or not, whether they like it or not, they are going to be 'civilized'; their country will be opened up. There is, of course, still plenty to discuss, but such discussions must henceforth concern themselves with the details of programmes: the fundamental policy is settled. The conclusion of my committee appointed by the Home Ministry to study how these plans could be implemented, and my own view, was that, in the context of modern India, development in the tribal areas must be much more intensive than elsewhere to enable them to catch up with their neighbours, that special emphasis must be laid on economic programmes and on health, and that very large sums of money must be spent on roads to make the people accessible. 'The unity of the hills and plains', I wrote, 'is as essential to the general national interest as it is to that of the hill and forest people themselves. We may indeed look forward to an enriching process of mutual fertilization: we have much to give the tribes and they have much to give us.'

IV

With the coming of Independence and the birth of the Community Development movement I felt more and more that my own task was to emphasize attitudes and methods rather than to draw up programmes at which I could only be an amateur, and in the first five years after Independence I wrote and spoke mainly about the attitude that should be taken towards the tribal people and the psychological and social adjustments that had to be made both in ourselves and in them. I also pointed out the need for caution, the danger of overwhelming the people with too many schemes, of depressing them by our technological superiority and of creating an inferiority complex and anxiety about their land by importing too many outsiders into their villages.

It was also clear that, with the great schemes of development coming into being, a twofold policy was necessary. One was to ensure that the people were not culturally emasculated in a way that would rob them of their identity and character. India's is a rich and varied tapestry, as Mr Nehru has said, and the tribes had to be encouraged to maintain their own personality, their own culture and their own language. But although in the earlier years I had thought in terms of *preserving* tribal culture, I came later to think in a less static way. Culture obviously must be a living, moving thing always subject to change, and Mr Nehru's formula of developing the tribal people along the lines of their own tradition and genius seemed to put what was needed in a nutshell.

At the same time I emphasized, writing in 1944, that 'it would be deplorable if yet another minority community which would claim special representation, weightage and a percentage of Government posts were to be created'. I wrote again five years later in the *Statesman* that 'the special care and protection given to the tribesmen must not cast any shadow on the unity of India. They must be educated to feel that they are full citizens of the Republic, with real rights and still more urgent duties.'

In most of tribal India the problems were comparatively simple. The people needed protection, development and social justice. But in a few places the problems were more complex. In the Saora hills and among the Murias, for example, there was still a strong, vigorous and very happy tribal life, and when I came to NEFA I found that here and in other parts of the frontier the tribes had retained their ancient culture and were developing their arts in a way that was rare elsewhere in India. Tribal life was still vigorous. It still meant something. It was not a question of reviving anything: it was more a problem of introducing change without being destructive of the best values of the old life.

Nari Rustomji had been thinking about these problems for a number of years and his ideas were already being put into practice on the frontier, though unfortunately I did not get copies of his notes until much later, and as a result did not do him justice when I wrote *A Philosophy for NEFA*.

As long ago as 1948, for example, we find him advocating very sound policies which would apply to the advance of civilization anywhere in the world. He condemns 'reckless' talk of 'uplifting and civilizing' the tribes. Officials or social workers must go to the people not as 'masters who dictate but as elder brothers who have suffered themselves and wish through their experience to spare others the pains they have had to endure'. They must not try to impose a uniform machinery of administration everywhere and certainly not try to bring the traditional judicial system of the hills into line with that elsewhere. They should not dream of 'imposing a system, notorious for its abuses and its delays, over areas where a sense of justice is, one might almost say, inherent amongst the people, and where the law operates both speedily and effectively'.

And a later note, which Rustomji wrote in 1953, anticipated so exactly what I was to think and say later that I will quote it in full.

'Much of the beauty of living still survives in these remote and distant hills, where dance and song are a vital part of everyday living, where people speak and think freely, without fear or restraint. Our workers must ensure, therefore, that the good that is inherent in the institutions of the hill people is not tainted or substituted by practices that may be "modern" and "advanced", but are totally unsuited to their economy and way of thinking. The hillman has, essentially, a clean, direct and healthy outlook; he is free, happily, from the morbid complexes induced by the unnatural life of the city folk.

'The greatest disservice will be done, therefore, if in an excess of missionary zeal, our workers destroy the fresh creative urge that lives, strong and vital, within the denizens of the hills. For if we wish to serve, we must show that we have respect for the hillmen and their institutions, their language and their song; and, in showing such respect, we shall secure their confidence in the work that lies ahead.' For this reason, everyone should make it his first task to familiarize himself with the local language, 'take an interest and come to understand the customs and usages of the people and share fully in their life, not as a stranger from without, but as one of themselves.'

V

My first contribution to a philosophy of tribal change and development in NEFA was contained in a report (unfortunately marked SECRET) that I submitted to the Governor, who sent it up to the Prime Minister, after a seven-weeks' tour in Tuensang. Almost everything that I later elaborated was contained, at least in germ, in this report, on which Mr Nehru wrote a long note giving his general support to what I had proposed.

After this I worked with my colleagues in the NEFA Secretariat for two or three very interesting years thinking out in great detail all sorts of problems and policies. Sometimes we met in Raj Bhavan to discuss tribal religion with the Governor. More often we met in my own house. The very first seminar we held was on the subject of tribal dress, and this was followed by a good many others. The Administration embodied our conclusions in a series of directives and later asked me to prepare a book which I called *A Philosophy for NEFA*. The first edition was short and plain but it earned an encouraging foreword from Mr Nehru and aroused sufficient interest for me to rewrite it entirely; I doubled its length, inserted plenty of illustrations and republished it in 1957. Mr Nehru gave a new foreword to this edition in which he laid down his famous Panch Shila (Five Principles) for the tribal people. The book was reprinted two years later, and has now been translated into Hindi and Assamese.

The fundamental basis of this philosophy goes back to the attitude of my Oxford days; even then I had a dislike of imposing things on people and this naturally developed into an aversion in the religious sphere to proselytizing and converting people or, in the social sphere, to forcing one type of civilization on another. So in this tribal policy, nothing was to be forced or imposed on the people, who were to be encouraged to develop (the key word is 'develop') along the path of their own traditions. They should come to terms with their past and grow from it by a natural evolution. This, of course, imposed considerable restraint on officials who, in all countries, are apt to feel superior to so-called primitive folk and to think that they have a god-given right to teach them better and do them good. But Mr Nehru said:

The problem of the tribal areas is to make the people feel that they have perfect freedom to live their own lives and to develop according to their wishes and genius. India to them should signify not only a protecting force but a liberating one. Any conception that India is ruling them and that they are the ruled, or that customs and habits with which they are unfamiliar are going to be imposed upon them, will alienate them.

There is no room here to summarize the closely-packed argument of *A Philosophy for NEFA* which dealt with tribal problems under the heading of material needs, psychological adaptations, and social, religious and cultural problems. Perhaps the most fundamental aspect of this idealistic policy was actually a material one—that, as Mr Nehru said, 'tribal rights in land and forest should be respected'. Another was that we should build up and train a team of the tribal people themselves to do the work of administration and development. Indigenous social and cultural institutions should be regarded as allies and not as rivals. Many tribes have very old youth clubs or dormitories which provide an excellent foundation for building up educational training institutions. The development of tribal councils, to which in NEFA very wide powers have been given, has proved of great importance in establishing the people in their own self-respect.

Then we were anxious to preserve the good taste of the tribes. Businessmen were not permitted to settle in NEFA; instead, the people themselves were encouraged to go in for trade, a policy which has proved very successful. The arts—the beautiful textiles, the music and the dance—were not to be corrupted but encouraged. There was no idea of keeping anything static and, in actual fact, there is continual creative development in all these fields. In architecture the idea was that even official buildings should be built so that they would grow out of the landscape and not appear as strangers in the rural scene, though unfortunately this has not proved very successful. Above all, the attitude of the official or social worker, whoever he might be, was to be based on a feeling of complete equality and friendship.

The ideas of this book were in the first place evolved in the NEFA context, but many of them can be, and have been, adapted also to other tribal areas. Some of these have very different problems—indebtedness, for example, or the impact of industrialization—but the essential attitude is needed for them all.

My own policy is expressed, perhaps most clearly, in *A Philosophy for NEFA*. But it appears also in two other works. The first is in the Report of the Committee for Multipurpose Tribal Blocks, of which I was Chairman and for the writing of which I was largely responsible. The second is in the Report of the Scheduled Tribes Commission, generally known as the Dhebar Commission, of which I was a member. I was asked by Dhebar to prepare a shortened version of this rather formidable report (which ran to over 750 pages) and the little book that I did, *A New Deal for Tribal India,* should be read along with *A Philosophy for NEFA* by anyone sufficiently interested to know my wider ideas about what could be done for the tribal people throughout India.

In the Scheduled Tribes Commission Report Dhebar's emphasis on social justice led us to stress protection side by side with development. In essence, the report of this Commission, which was exhaustively debated in Parliament and accepted by it, is a justification of the stand I have made for thirty years and shows that the attacks upon me for stressing the importance of the war against exploitation have hardly been justified.

VI

My 'philosophy' has had its critics. At a conference in Ranchi one of the Development Commissioners present got up and asked plaintively, 'How can we develop the tribes along the lines of their own genius when they haven't got any genius?' It is true that many of the more sophisticated tribes have lost nearly all their culture and individuality, but there are others which have retained a great deal that is good and they all reveal to the sympathetic and intelligent observer certain things on which to build.

Another criticism is made in the interest of integration. It is said that, if we allow the tribal people to retain their own languages, dress or social institutions, we keep them separate from the rest of India, and if we want to integrate them properly we should assimilate them as quickly as possible and smooth them out, as it were, so that they will be exactly like everybody else. The fallacy in this is that the people of India as a whole are marked by great variety and that there is no standard of culture, religion or language to which we can adapt the tribes. In practice, too, it is just those tribesmen who have smoothed themselves out and adopted a way of life that is indistinguishable from that of their neighbours who have been most clamorous for separation from the rest of the population. They have realized that they are losing their identity and are desperately anxious to preserve it. Many of the Naga rebels have taken to a Western way of life and dress in Western clothes. The hill people of Assam proper who want a separate State are just those who have been most completely assimilated. It may well be that in the long run all the tribes will lose their distinctiveness and sink into a drab uniformity, possibly dominated by the overpowering American civilization that is so rapidly spreading across the world. But it seems to me foolish to try to accelerate this process in the interest of integration, for this does not and will not work.

The Chinese invasion of NEFA set everyone thinking about the frontier but, instead of acclaiming our policy which had ensured a loyal and even enthusiastic local population to support the Defence Forces, a number of critics made it the subject of bitter and extravagant attack. For weeks it was impossible to open the newspapers without finding some denunciation of the 'philosophy' of NEFA or even of myself.

Not one in a hundred of the people who so readily denounced *A Philosophy for NEFA* appeared to have ever read it. The main reason why it was believed to have failed was that I was supposed to have advocated a policy of isolation, to have urged the separation of NEFA from the people of Assam, and naturally the old cry of keeping the tribes as museum specimens was raised again, though no one could point out how any of this had affected the course of the military operations. Generally my critics attributed to me views which were the exact opposite of what I had advocated. In actual fact, I had not supported any policy of isolation of the NEFA people but had devoted several pages of this book to condemning it. The Inner Line, as it was called, by which the frontier is kept as a restricted area only to be entered by authorized persons, was established eighty-five years before my book was written and though I realize I am getting on, I am not as old as that. As for the Assamese people, for whom I have great affection and respect, I had included in my book the suggestion that every scheme of development, progress or welfare in NEFA should be submitted to the test whether it would help to integrate the tribal people with Assam and, of course, with India as a whole.

At the same time there were many supporters of our policy and Christoph von Fürer-Haimendorf, for example, wrote enthusiastically after a very recent visit to NEFA:

The 19th and early 20th century policy of *laissez faire* of provincial and state governments favoured exploiters and land-grabbers and the voices of the few devoted civil servants who spoke for the rights of the aboriginals remained largely unheard. There is only one region where a really bold and sympathetic approach to the problem of tribal development has saved the tribesmen from exploitation and the domination of outsiders. In the North-East Frontier Agency an administration has been instituted which develops the country solely for the benefit of its tribal inhabitants, and all those who have had an opportunity to visit this area in recent years must have been impressed by the skilful combination of a modernization of external living conditions with the retention of tribal traditions and values. Here the tribesmen have lost neither their dignity nor their *joie de vivre*, and they know that they themselves and their children are going to profit from the economic development of their country. The lessons learnt from the decline of many of the tribal communities in other parts of India have here been applied, and it is an encouraging thought that the *Philosophy for NEFA* has borne such splendid fruit.

VII

Let me then summarize my ideas for the tribal people as a whole, all twenty-five million of them (of whom the NEFA tribes are a small but significant part). To my mind, the five most important needs, in the context of many-sided schemes of development of agriculture, communications, medical facilities, education, and so on common to the whole of India, are these:

1. That their land should be guaranteed to them and that any further alienation of it to outsiders should be stopped.

2. That their rights in forest should be respected and that an entirely new attitude should be taken towards them by the forest authorities throughout India.

3. That the problem of indebtedness should be solved without delay, partly by legislation and partly by a great intensification of the co-operative movement and the availability of easy credit from official sources.

4. That the problem of the industrialization of the tribal areas must be regarded much more seriously and that where the tribal people are dispossessed of their lands and settled elsewhere, intelligent and generous measures should be taken to compensate them.

5. That the long isolation of the tribes should come to an end, that they should be welcomed everywhere with warm affection and on equal terms, and that they should be given every opportunity of public service.

I stress these points because they have been badly neglected in the last ten years, because they are simple and obvious, and can be solved if there is a real will to solution in the Central and State Governments.

But there are five other points which are more complex.

1. We must help the tribes to come to terms with their own past so that their present and future will not be a denial of it but a natural evolution from it.

2. We must fight the danger of pauperization, the creation of a special class called 'tribal', who will want to be labelled 'backward' in order to get material benefits from Government. Unintelligent benevolence can be as great a danger as intelligent exploitation.

3. It is essential to avoid creating a sense of inferiority in the tribal people. This means that we must not impose our own ideas upon them. We must not create a sense of guilt by forcing on them laws and customs they do not understand and cannot observe. We must not make them anxious and afraid: we must not make them feel ashamed of their own natural ways.

4. We should lay much greater stress on the possibility of the tribal people helping us. At present all the emphasis is on our helping them. Let us teach them that their own culture, their own arts are precious things that we respect and need. When they feel they can make a contribution to their country, they will feel part of it: this is therefore an important aspect of their integration.

5. We must try to ensure that the people do not lose their freedom and their zest for living. I have put at the head of this chapter words that to me are the heart of the matter:

> What more felicity can fall to creature
> Than to enjoy delight with liberty?

Although my final conclusions were present in my thinking thirty years ago, the emphasis changed as I gained experience and as conditions changed in the country as a whole. At first my ideas were limited but intense, and I saw the problem as basically a spiritual one, investing every act of kindness with symbolic value. Gradually the harsh realities of the time caused me to emphasize the need for protection. It was only much later that I became concerned about the preservation and development of tribal culture. In north-eastern India protection was already assured and the important problem was how to give the tribes the good things of our life without destroying the good things of theirs. Internal political issues and international affairs generally have recently turned our thoughts to the importance of integration, although many of us had been thinking of this ever since Independence. And finally, I see a large, difficult, almost majestic, plan which includes on one side schemes for food, health, mobility and knowledge and, on the other, respect for and encouragement of tribal culture in the widest sense—religion, language, self-governing village institutions, social polity. To reconcile these two aims, to develop, yet not to destroy, is not easy but I believe it can be done.

11

Ultimate Ambition

To be happy at home is the ultimate result of all ambition.
—Samuel Johnson

I

FOR the past nine years we have lived in Shillong and, though I have been frequently away on tour, often for long periods, it has become a real home. Kumar, who has joined the Assam Rifles, is not now with us here but the smaller boys have just reached the right age to make a nice, obstreperous, untidy establishment.

The children practise, or rather claim to hold, different religions. Kumar became a Roman Catholic when he was seventeen and in a position to choose for himself. Wasant claims to be a Hindu and refuses 'to eat cows'. Nakul declares himself a pagan. Ashok is a Buddhist, can recite some of the sacred verses and makes flower-offerings at our shrine. Lila and I profess no particular religion, though I have a strong 'feeling' for Buddhism.

Lila is the centre of this home; key of the house; store of happiness; Heaven's best gift to all of us. In Congreve's words, she is the moon and I the man in the moon: I am still slightly lunatic about her. In fact, I love her even more today than when I first met her. What Arthur Koestler calls 'the normal, neutralizing effect of habituation' has had no effect on us.

Marriage and the family are central to Indian life. As Dr Radhakrishnan has said, 'There is little in Hindu thought to support the view that one has to attain spiritual freedom by means of a violent rupture with ordinary life. On the other hand, it lays down that we must pass through the normal life

Photo, Sunil Janah

Lila

Kumar on the Tibetan frontier

Ashok and Rani

Photo, P. Pal

conscientiously and with knowledge, work out its values and accept its enjoyments. Spiritual life is an integration of man's being, in its depth and breadth, in its capacity for deep meditation as well as reckless transport.'

On the other hand, some of India's spiritual leaders have taken a rather poor view of marriage. 'The love for our children and our wives is mere animal love,' says one of them. 'Man finds out that human love is all hollow.' 'Ordinary love is mere animal attraction.' 'I do not think', says another, 'that in our conception of marriage our lusts should enter.' And a third, widely renowned as a very great saint, declares that, 'The feeling which a woman feels for her husband is not love, for her feeling is based upon self. She loves her husband because he is her property.'

Yet surely, far from the need to prevent our lusts entering the marriage bed, passion is what modern marriage needs and its absence is the reason why so many marriages fail: art, technique, adventure, passion are the ingredients of happiness. Sex is good and lovely; all the extravagant phrases that the poets have ever used for it have not exhausted its beauty and delight: and the most important thing about it is not the pleasure it gives (though personally I enjoy it immensely) but the sense of identification with another person, the going out from oneself into someone else. 'Love', says Tagore, 'gives evidence to something which is outside us but which intensely exists and thus stimulates the sense of our own existence. It radiantly reveals the reality of its objects.'

I am a very lucky man—to have a young and exquisite wife who keeps me young. If Lila regards me as her property I am all for it: the mutual sense of selfless possession is one of the many precious treasures of a happy marriage.

> She is my field, and in her furrows run
> my ways like rain, and the crops of her shadows
> are pools, are a wild sea—and she has mountains
> stranger than feathers, hard as fishes. There
> fall in her hollows shadows of orchard trees
> that follow the moon's circle like a tide—
> grassy nets that move on the dropped apples.

Someone who married a tribal girl said he had done so to

further the cause of national integration, and some politicians have seriously advocated a policy of intermarriage to bring the tribal people closer to the rest of India. I did not marry Lila on any theory, but simply because I loved her. Not all such marriages turn out well, as I know from my own first sad experience, but in this marriage we have both been very happy. This surprises some of our friends, for it would be hard to find two people more different in background, education and temperament. Yet I find in Lila the truest companionship, and while it would no doubt be amusing to have a wife with whom I could discuss the symbolism of Ezra Pound or Toynbee's theory of history, her loyalty, compassion and a rare capacity for understanding are much more precious. There is no sense of difference between us, and in practice we find we can share all the really important things. It is harder for Lila than for me, for I often have to go away on exciting missions and I am sometimes preoccupied with urgent problems. The 'office' appears sometimes as a rival, but she has adapted herself to it and takes a lively interest in everything that goes on. The love of man and wife is constantly re-created in their children, renewed by joy, strengthened by anxiety and sorrow. A 'love-marriage', where the impetus of love is strong, is the nearest thing to pure happiness on earth.

One difficulty we had at first was that many people found it almost impossible to believe we were legal. How could a lovely young creature who at that time, as Minnie Emmerson put it, looked at you like a startled deer from the woods, and who is so well described in the above lines by Alex Comfort, be actually *married* to a tumbledown, dilapidated old bear like me?

And other people ask how I could have married her. 'Sex,' they say, and dismiss the problem. But in reply I ask how it is that it is just the sort of women I like who like her. Amina Jayal, as she is now, daughter of the late Sir Akbar Hydari, humorous, gay and understanding, was the first of them. We saw a great deal of her delightful children, Pimmy and Laddu, while her youngest boy Akbar, who died so tragically when he was only three years old, is buried within sight of our house. When, after her divorce, she married Nalini Jayal, the Hindu ceremony was performed in our house and I acted as the bride's father. Then among Lila's friends there was the kind, gentle Kanta Dhar ; the graceful, elegant and witty Pankaj Kakati, whose recent death was a great shock to us, and her daughter Cuckoo ; Pushpa Sharma, the wife of a distinguished officer in the Assam Rifles ; 'Channi' Dougal, whose husband Bernard has been a friend of mine for years ; Ellie Duara, highly literate but not a bit of a blue-stocking ; Gita Krishnatry ; many beautiful and talented Khasi and Lushai ladies who give distinction to Shillong ; as well as others mentioned elsewhere in this book.

Lila has extraordinary powers of adaptation. She came to Shillong almost direct from a remote tribal village, yet within three months was proving an admirable hostess at parties, and even when our few VIPS came to visit us she was thrown off balance less than I was.

But Lila remains, I am glad to say, a villager at heart. She is always wanting to be growing things and loves animals, and especially our young Alsatian, Rani. She works very hard in the house and has become an expert at knitting. She has, as they say, great 'character', can be very determined and, like most tribal folk, quickly sees through humbug and pretence. I myself tend to enthuse too quickly after meeting people but she is a better judge and much more cautious than I am. She is very kind ; she is strict with people but at the least trouble her heart melts, and if she finds that anyone associated with us has not had a square meal she cannot eat herself until this is remedied.

II

Ashok was born in Shillong on a Sunday. From the early morning Lila began to get contractions, but she said nothing about it for, as she explained, 'No one labours on a Sunday in Shillong, so I can't labour either.'

I thought she wasn't very well, and made her lie down a good deal, but I was not actually expecting anything for another week. Fortunately, a nice girl called Gita Mehta (now Trivedi), who was a doctor, came to tea. It was Victor's birthday—he was staying with us at the time—and we had a chocolate cake with HAPPY BIRTHDAY VICTOR on it. Phukan came, the man who looked after me so well in Manipur, an authority on P.G.W. Then this girl Gita arrived with Aporbo Chanda, once Director of Public Instruction for Bengal, now retired, a great character. And on top of all there was dear old Ganpat Rai, a Forest Officer, with a present of an outsize bunch of green bananas.

In the middle of this, Phukan talking about Lord Emsworth's pig, Aporbo holding forth on T. S. Eliot, Victor lecturing on the decline of the West, and dear old Ganpat describing how he had 'trampled two hundred serpents under foot' during his travels in NEFA, all talking at once, Gita came in and said that if we didn't get Lila to hospital immediately she'd be having the baby in the drawing-room. So we all got busy. Gita tried to telephone the hospital: the entire staff was at church, no one could do anything. At last a Sister turned up who said, couldn't the lady come tomorrow, they didn't like doing things on Sunday. So we decided to go ahead, packing, finding blankets, getting the ayah ready, calming the children, while all the time Aporbo boomed on indefatigably, now about Dylan Thomas.

Finally we got into the car, Lila, the ayah, Gita and me, with Victor driving. The car wouldn't go very well, and I said Victor was like a pilot carrying an atom bomb in an old Dakota. But we reached the hospital at last, found a Sister, got a very nice room, put Lila to bed, and then came back for dinner. At 10.0 we returned, we being Victor, Kumar and me, with blankets for an all-night vigil. We were put in a waiting-room, where Victor got hold of one of the hospital Bibles, a book he said he had often meant to read but had never got round to, and we waited. To our astonishment, at 11.10 p.m. dear Dr Hughes, looking exhausted and dishevelled—he at least never gets a Sunday off—peeped in and said, 'It's a boy.' After some time we were admitted to the Labour Room and there was Lila looking a bit worn on a stretcher which I helped push down to her ward, with the baby screaming away, looking rather charming. Lila was full of dope and sleepy, so we said good-night and came home at midnight. And that is how Ashok got his start.

III

Of all the delightful things in the world, children are the best and of them all tribal children are incomparable. It is they who have made life bearable for me at times when life was hard to bear, whether in the Mandla villages, where they were the best of company, or on many tours, or at home in Shillong. Their liveliness makes our gloom absurd, their beauty is reviving and since they are the very symbols of hope and expectation, they are a cure for anxiety and disappointment. Children have always been among the chief loves of my life.

In Patangarh, our house was always full of Gond and Pardhan children. I had a very large writing table which made an ideal place for hide-and-seek and other games. At any time of the day you could find children underneath it playing quietly or climbing about on top of it. This must, you will say, have been rather disturbing to a writer, but in the course of time it helped me to develop very strong powers of concentration. When I myself see somebody writing anything I approach on tiptoe and speak in a whisper. Nobody in a village or in my own family has ever done this for me. In time I became so practised in concentrating in the midst of turmoil that I could carry on my writing without any disturbance or irritation, except, of course, when I was pulled away from my desk and made to go on hands and knees with a couple of children on my back. At first I was a horse but later as I swelled a little they decided I was an elephant and Kumar once insisted that I was a hippopotamus.

Again on tour, whether in central India or the frontier, my camps have always been crowded with children, for I think they feel instinctively that I am on their side. Some of the most attractive young creatures I have seen anywhere were the Bondo boys, of whom I could say with Dr Johnson: 'I love the young dogs of this age.' Other children became so intimate and at-home that they would pull my cigar out of my mouth, take a puff or two themselves, sometimes handing it round from friend to friend, and then return it between my lips. In some villages, particularly the Saora villages where children used to drop in at meal-times, I sometimes had a regular battle to get any food at all, with a group of boys and girls stretching out eager hands for what there was on my plate and even helping themselves.

In NEFA one of the things that used to depress me was the habit of the village elders driving away children from my camp because they thought that the sahib would be annoyed. It generally took a little explanation before they could believe that he really enjoyed the company of children. The tribal people themselves, however, have a very great love for their children and some of my most heartbreaking moments have been at children's funerals or sitting helplessly by when a child was dying.

To turn from this great family to the more immediate one of our own children. Kumar, the eldest, was very charming as a small boy and a good companion when he got older—he did two long tours on foot with me, a couple of hundred miles each time, in northern Siang, and also went to Tirap. Wasant also, at eight and nine years, went out twice with me, and Nakul and Ashok joined him when we all went to Lungleh, an exciting drive through the remote and lovely Lushai hills.

It is always fun taking the children by air. One day great clouds rolled up and I was looking at them with apprehension when Wasant said, 'Daddy, the clouds look like angels. There's nothing to be afraid of.' When we went into them and it got very bumpy, the orange lights flashing on, he said excitedly, 'Do you think we can have a crash?' And afterwards, when I asked Nakul if he had been afraid, he said, 'Why should I have been? I had my seat-belt on.'

The children have developed their own vocabulary of essentially amiable denunciation. Ashok is the most original. 'You nonsense,' he says, an admirable adaptation. 'Get out, you fat English,' he attacks me if I refuse to 'pass him' four annas. When he was about three years old, my sister Eldyth came to stay with us. A few days after her arrival Ashok got annoyed with her about something, and a stream of four-letter Hindi words poured from his baby lips.

'What is the sweet little darling saying?' asked Eldyth.

I explained hastily that he was telling her how much he liked her and how glad he was that she was here.

Photo, P Pal

Nakul, Ashok and Wasant
at a party, 1962

The Siang river

When Eldyth went away, Nakul—then about four—squeezed her arm and said, 'Very good meat.'

My Patel Memorial lectures on 'A Philosophy of Love' were broadcast: Ashok heard bits of them, and made his own contribution. 'When I grow up,' he said, 'I'm not going to marry a pretty girl, for then hundreds of mens would run after her to do loving and would say, "Come, come to me, my girl-friend".'

Of the younger boys, Wasant is sensitive and affectionate; Nakul is sensible, hard-working, very popular at school and a wonderful patient when he is ill; Ashok is full of ideas and excels as a businessman.

Wasant is the one to whom things happen. One evening when he was very small an almirah, full of books, toppled over on top of him, but fortunately was caught on a stool and although he was badly frightened by the cascade of books he was not injured. One year in Delhi I took Lila and the children to watch the Republic Day parade. There were a million people there and when it was over and we were going out, Wasant, then eight years old, got lost in the crowd. We had been hearing frightening stories about child-kidnappers and Ashok described how he had seen Wasant walking away with an old beggar woman, which greatly added to our anxiety. It was an agonizing experience, for we felt helpless, almost paralysed as we thought of this tiny child from quiet Shillong in the vast crowds that thronged the great city. There were police camps for missing children and we went to them, finding in each twenty or thirty small boys and girls crying for their mothers. But though we looked eagerly into their faces, there was no sign of Wasant. Khemlal Rathee brought his car and sent for his astrologer who worked it out that Wasant would return after about five hours, though I must confess this did not greatly console me. We drove round and round Delhi, our apprehension increasing each hour that passed. I got hold of one of our younger officers, Tapan Kumar Barua, then in Delhi, who had accompanied me on tour when Wasant was with me, and he went out on an independent search. By 5.30 poor Lila was almost hysterical and I do not think I have ever felt quite so despairing, for by then most of us and even the Rathees were afraid that the child had been kidnapped.

And then at just about the time that the astrologer had prophesied, a taxi drew up and out got Tapan Kumar with a beaming Wasant. For the first time in my life I burst into tears, the relief was so great. Wasant was full of his adventures. He had wandered through the crowds, not specially frightened, for he was sure we would find him, until he was discovered by a kindly policeman who had given him biscuits and shown him his revolver. But it was a long time before Lila fully recovered from the strain of those few hours.

Whenever I am ill, Wasant gets very worried about me, looks after me and constantly inquires how I am. Like many Indian children, he confuses 'yesterday' and 'tomorrow', since they both translate the same Hindi word, and every day for months he used to say, 'Are you better than you were tomorrow, Daddy?', which gave me a pleasant science-fiction sensation as if I had got out of the time-space continuum. One day I had a slight relapse and I shall never forget how Wasant, observing this, began to scream in panic, tears pouring down his face. The love that moment of anxiety revealed was one of the precious things in my life.

Ashok is the businessman of the family. When he was only four years old he exclaimed, 'Daddy, I do love money.' He often refuses to go to the cinema when the other boys do and demands compensation instead. If he has to have an injection, he charges a suitable fee. He makes little portable shops and sells things to everyone. He collects stamps, which has great commercial possibilities. He has a special interest in medals, or at least in their monetary value, as all the family has. I have been lucky in getting a number of them from academic societies in India and England. The attitude of Ashok to them is simple. If they are bronze, like my Rivers or Wellcome medals, he is not interested: they won't fetch anything. But anything in gold is another matter. I have three—the Roy and Annandale from the Asiatic Society in Calcutta and a nice heavy one, the Campbell, from its opposite number in Bombay. There is a rush to get the letter-weight machine from the office, and Ashok and the others weigh them and make elaborate calculations to discover how much they are worth at present prices.

I am not ferocious enough to be a good father. My attitude to children is Thomas More's in his epistle *To his sweetest children*:

> I have given you, forsooth, kisses in plenty and but few stripes.
> If ever I have flogged you 'twas but with a peacock's tail.

IV

Part of the family about whom I must say a word is my personal staff, in whom I have been very fortunate. My stenographer, Someswar Lahiri, who has been with me now for eight years, is loyal and efficient; my two Khasi typists, Higher Land Syiemlieh (now promoted) and Lockhart Jyrwa, are as good as anyone could desire. My field-assistant, Sundarlal Narmada, has been with me now for over thirty years, my two chaprasis—Haricharan and Bhajan—for about twenty-five. Sundarlal has gone with me on nearly all my tours and is an able and effective organizer. My usual practice on tour is to send Sundarlal and Bhajan ahead—they walk twice as fast as I do—to prepare camp, and Haricharan goes with me to help me over bridges and sometimes to pull me up very steep ascents. The result is that when I reach camp, I find a little shed erected, my things laid out in dormitory or house, and a hot meal nearly always ready. How they manage to cook, and cook well, under the most difficult conditions has always been a mystery to me.

Both Haricharan and Bhajan are tribal Pardhans but they sometimes find it a little difficult to put up with their more primitive brethren and their habit of crowding the little kitchens on tour, fingering and examining everything with absorbed interest. There was once a heated dispute when Bhajan opened a tin of ham and some Wanchos insisted that it was human flesh. Once, when a group of 'naked' Bondos was rude to him, Haricharan exclaimed, 'May tigers munch their bare bottoms *kirach karach*!'

Sundarlal, who is not tribal, has a tender and sympathetic attitude: his trouble has been with what Bertrand Russell has called 'the insolent aristocracy of jacks-in-office' and one day, when he was in Patangarh and I in Calcutta, he sent me a telegram: HAVE KICKED POLICEMAN COME AT ONCE. Victor and I hastened to the rescue, and it was just as well for, though the kick was eminently justified and didn't really hurt, one could hardly expect the police to appreciate it.

V

I brought to Shillong a lot of pictures and some big boxes of trophies with the idea at first simply of building around me a comforting tribal atmosphere. I brought, for example, the very fine Santal wood-carvings and Jadupatua scrolls which I had collected in Bihar, Gond and Muria masks and my early Naga specimens of a kind which were already becoming very hard to get. The house was large; I had display-cases made and, as I travelled about NEFA, I gradually added to the original collection until it became a rather overcrowded but interesting museum which belongs to our little society TWARU and will in the end go to the nation. I could write an entire chapter about my adventures as a collector—every specimen has its story—but I have no room to do so here.

The Buddhist images, masks and pictures—some of which I brought down from the extreme north—made a particularly charming room, and one result has been to attract a number of very interesting people to our house. One of the earliest of these was Mr Nehru.

Hours before the Prime Minister was due to arrive, the police and CID appeared. They were very doubtful whether he should be allowed to come at all since our house is, thank goodness, in a lonely spot and surrounded by trees and bushes, any of which, they pointed out, could give good shelter to an assassin. In the end no fewer than thirty-five plain-clothes policemen were assembled in and around the house. They were there in the kitchen, in the bedrooms, and Lila had the pleasure of entertaining them all with tea and sweets.

Before Mr Nehru arrived, the chief topic of discussion was what kind of refreshment we should offer him. I personally, having heard his views on Prohibition for the tribes, was in favour of some sort of stimulant. Others thought this was going too far, so we compromised with a bottle of good sherry which we placed on a tray with some suitable (borrowed) glasses, in the bath-room adjoining one of the museum rooms. At the same time we arranged to have a tray with coffee and cups more obviously on a table in the room itself.

Mr Nehru, accompanied by the Governor, Mr Jairamdas Daulatram, went all round and looked at everything with great interest and made a number of remarks which I still treasure. I myself was in a state of nerves, not because of our illustrious visitor who, as always, was delightful, but because there were so many gate-crashers outside the building trying to get in and I feared that they might cause a disturbance. When the suitable moment, therefore, came I was hardly in a position to offer a Prime Minister anything, let alone something alcoholic, and in my agitation I said, 'Sir, will you have a cup of sherry?' Quick as lightning the P.M. replied, 'No, I think I will make do with a glass of coffee.'

Another very distinguished visitor was the Home Minister of the time, Pandit G. B. Pant, who showed great interest in my collections and said something which I have always treasured and will risk the charge of vanity by repeating. He said: 'It has been the great work of Dr Elwin to raise the status of the tribal people in public opinion all over India. He has shown us that they are not just backward people but have an art and a culture of their own, and so has influenced the policy of the whole country.' Pandit Pant in fact was always very good to me and I saw something of him towards the end of his life and developed a deep affection for him. I shall always be grateful that I had the opportunity of knowing him and working for him.

There also came the Chief Minister of Assam, Mr B. P. Chaliha, a gentle kind man with an exceptional affection for the tribal people. On one occasion before he became Chief Minister, he visited the Naga Hills and went, without any kind of protection and at night, to contact some of the rebels in the heart of the forest. On his return he wrote one of the most understanding reports on the Naga problem that I have ever read. I once asked him what magic he had used towards the solution of the many human and political tribal problems of his State, and he replied, 'A little understanding, a genuine respect, a lot of affection. That is the real magic that works wonders in human hearts.'

VI

A few years ago Arthur Koestler stayed with us in Shillong for a week. He was on a visit to India and, since he is an incurably controversial person, he had been pursued by journalists and sniped at by Communists wherever he went. He wanted a little peace and I think we gave him that, while unexpectedly he brought such an atmosphere of serenity and strength into our house that, when he went away, Lila—who is not easily impressed—said that it was as if some great sadhu had been with us. Arthur has said of Vinoba Bhave that he has 'that curious gift of radiating peace which is physically felt like a laying on of hands: of making people feel enriched by his mere presence' and, though Arthur is a very different kind of man, his effect on me was something of the same kind.

Arthur came to India and Japan in the mood of a pilgrim, to discover whether the East had any answer to the perplexities and deadlocked problems of Europe. He wanted to look at the predicament of the West from a new perspective, a 'different spiritual latitude'. His 'reluctant' conclusion was characteristically forthright: 'neither Yoga, Zen, nor any other Asian form of mysticism has any significant advice to offer.' *The Lotus and the Robot*, which, to my great pleasure, he dedicated to me, describes his Indian tour and, perhaps naturally, annoyed a number of people, especially orthodox Hindus, in India, who do not take criticism very well. There were meetings and protests, some of which, I suspect, may have been instigated by Communists disguised in saffron robes.

It is true that Arthur says some hard things about India and her religion, but some of them badly needed saying and in most of them he had actually been anticipated by modern-minded Indians. Three hundred years ago, of course, had Arthur written about Christianity as he did about Hinduism, he would have been burnt alive. But we have moved forward a little since that time. Christianity has endured and survived every sort of attack upon it: it has even grown and improved as a result. A book which makes a rather similar psychological analysis is Leuba's *The Psychology of Religious Mysticism*, which is far more damaging to Christian mysticism than Arthur's comments to yoga, because it is much more thorough. A work like Frazer's *Folk-Lore in the Old Testament* undermines the unique character of the Bible in a far more devastating way than anything Arthur did for Hinduism. Indeed, the obscurantist attitude of some people in this matter reminds me of the story of the two old ladies of the last century who were discussing the shocking theories of Charles Darwin. 'Descended from apes, my dear?' said one of them. 'Let us hope it is not true. But if it is true, let us pray it does not become too widely known.'

I do not, of course, agree with everything in *The Lotus and the Robot* and I wrote to Arthur, soon after I received my copy, to suggest that his account of Gandhi's experiments in brahmacharya gave a wrong picture. Arthur depended far too much on a rather bad book, *My Days with Gandhi*. He does not seem to have seen the remarkable study of the same subject by Pyarelal in his *Gandhi: The Last Phase*, which brings out Gandhi's conception of himself as the Mother and gives a different and much more intelligible interpretation of the famous experiments. I had the book on my shelves when Arthur was staying with us and I am ashamed that I did not bring it to his attention, but the matter was not one that we discussed.

Nor do I altogether agree with Arthur's disappointed estimate of Hinduism. He drew, I think, a little too much from the professionals, though it is hard to see what else he could have done. If a Hindu were to go to England to study Christianity he too would have to meet the experts. I myself have learnt a great deal from Hindu and Buddhist mysticism, though I would not like to affirm that I could not have found much the same message in the mystics of the West.

What has so impressed me has been the effect of these oriental religions on ordinary and simple people, from whom I have learnt much more than from the books. I think, for example, of the man I call the Good Hansenian. He was a Bhil who had adopted the Hindu religion. He made a great journey on foot—what is called in India a *pradakshina*—which involved walking right up the length of the sacred Narbada river from its mouth in western India to its source near our house at Patangarh by one bank, and then all the way back by the other. But he was a leper, and by the time he had reached Amarkantak and was on his way home, his disease had advanced to a stage where he could go no further and he took refuge with us. In this deformed and terribly afflicted tribal sadhu I saw the Hindu religion at its best. For all his sufferings he was unfailingly cheerful and patient. I do not remember his ever complaining about anything. So far as he could, he helped his fellow-patients in little ways. When they were bad-tempered he brought peace and when they were unhappy he cheered them up. He was possessed by heroic charity. He died, as he had lived, in confidence and serenity.

As I say, I do not agree with everything in Arthur Koestler's book, and I am quite sure he would not want me to, but a work of this kind, which makes people think, which stimulates and challenges them, is surely to be welcomed rather than denounced. At the height of the Pasternak controversy, Mr Nehru declared that 'a noted writer, even if he expresses an opinion opposed to the dominating opinion, according to us should be respected and it should be given free play'.

Among anthropologists my closest friends have been J. H. Hutton who has been a sort of god-father for many years; that most liberal of scholar-missionaries, Edwin Smith, who visited us at Sanhrwachhapar; and above all Christoph and Betty von Fürer-Haimendorf. Christoph is a man of exceptional courage and perseverance, an intrepid explorer, with an astonishing flair for the unusual and significant: I followed in his footsteps to the Bondo-Gadaba country, the Konyak villages and the north of NEFA. He possesses a charity and generosity all too rare among anthropologists; high-spirited Betty has a tremendous zest for life: both are very lovable people.

Recent visitors in Shillong were Otto and Juliana Kadlecsovics, and their entrancing little daughter Magdalena. Otto is from

Austria, an artist and photographer, and Juliana is English. They were travelling round the world in a Land-Rover, an original and exciting family. While he was with us Otto painted the (for me) thought-provoking portrait which is reproduced on the jacket of this book.

VII

Although in the earlier years in central India I had a long struggle to keep going, for I often fell ill, since coming to Shillong I have generally enjoyed excellent health and so have Lila and the children. But when we do fall ill we make the most of it. I have given a lurid description of a three months' stay in a Bombay hospital in my *Leaves from the Jungle*.

When I was in East Africa I began to develop mysterious pains. I went to a specialist in Nairobi who subjected me to the usual indignities. When he had completed the drill he produced a report which I secretly considered highly offensive. Among other things, this is what it said:

> The stomach is of high transverse type. Its mucosal pattern is coarse, particularly in the distal third where it appears almost polypoid.

At that time I was getting a little stout and, being rather sensitive about my corporation, to have it called polypoid was the last straw and I went on a diet immediately and this was a great strain. Alexander Woolcott once said that all the things he really liked were immoral, illegal or fattening.

The cholecystogram revealed that I had no fewer than two gall-bladders and my specialist wanted to operate at once and urged me to go into the very fine hospital in Nairobi and have it done. I discovered, however, that this hospital, at least at that time, would not admit coloured patients and I probably saved my life (for I heard afterwards that it would have been a very tricky operation) by refusing to go into a place to which Africans and Indians would not be admitted. When I returned to Bombay I had to go through an entire fortnight of further examination but, apart from a few pills and a quite ferocious diet-chart, the doctors there decided that it would be better not to operate. In the past ten years, these two gall-bladders, which my specialist told me were at that time only the twenty-eighth recorded in medical history—there was great excitement in a Bombay hospital when my X-ray picture was developed—have given me little trouble. By a policy of masterly inaction, I hope I have got them in hand.

In June 1961 I had an exciting attack of coronary insufficiency, and was rushed to the Military Hospital in Shillong, where there is a staff of brilliant Army doctors and sisters. I was allowed no visitors for ten days, which made me feel very important, but Lila of course came and Nari Rustomji, who is an angel when one is ill, slipped in twice a day and brought me most of Somerset Maugham's stories which, curiously enough, I had never read.

I had begun six months previously with high blood-pressure and the *rauwolfia serpentina,* one of India's oldest drugs, given for this made me feel as if I was perpetually detumescent after an unsatisfactory performance. But the tranquillizers I got later were delicious.

They had little bits of paper wrapped round them saying what they did for you. One, I was told, saved me from mental and emotional disturbance, another cured my dysmenorrhoea, morning sickness and bed-wetting: a third enabled me to have a baby in comfort. I was soon free of anxiety and nephrogenic hypertension. I also got some injections that the doctor said would make me a new man. The phials were filled with nor-androstenolene phenylpropionate dissolved in oil, which sounded as if it would make a new man of anything, but I was mortified to read a note saying that it was indicated for the 'treatment of men when increased libido was undesirable'.

The doctor told me that I should ration myself to 'one peg of gin a day', for gin is a coronary dilatant and does one good. He forgot, however, to mention whether it should be big or small, and I didn't pursue the matter. In fact, I have drunk very little for a long time now. Alcohol I would not miss, tobacco is a much sterner tyrant. The trouble is that I *believe* in tobacco: it has made me a better man. I like the old story about Samuel Butler.

He was once invited to Peterborough by Bishop Mandell Creighton, and was a little doubtful whether to go or not. As usual he consulted his clerk Alfred, who said,

'Let me have a look at his letter, sir.'

Butler gave him the letter, and Alfred said, 'I see, sir, there is a crumb of tobacco in it; I think you may go.'

Butler, inspired by this favourable omen, and borrowing a prayer-book to pack in his portmanteau, went to stay with the bishop and enjoyed himself very much.

At meetings of the Tribal Commission, Jaipal Singh and I used to sit together at the end of the table blowing cigar smoke over the other nine members who were all non-smokers and some of them protested. But our chairman, Dhebar, was always very kind about it and once endeared himself to me by taking a bottle of ink out of its cardbord box which he passed to me to use as an ash-tray.

But to be serious for a moment. Pain, which Schweitzer calls 'a more terrible lord of mankind than even Death himself', yet does not deny some blessing to a family: it holds it together in strong bonds of compassionate affection. One year Lila was tormented by a stone, another year she had an acute appendicitis, and it was when she was in hospital that we all realized how much we loved her. It was when I myself was ill that I in turn realized how Lila and the boys felt about me. It is in sickness that we see how love, and all the beautiful things that come from it, can not only make suffering bearable and bring out of distress the possibility of spiritual growth, but can itself act as a healing force.

I have experienced the healing power of music. Long ago when I was very ill in a Bombay hospital, I was kept alive, stimulated to go on living in a world which had such beauty, by having Beethoven's Fifth symphony (the only one I had) played over and over again by my bedside. And recently when I was suffering agonies of toothache, another of Beethoven's symphonies, the Pastoral, drew the pain out of me. I could actually feel it being drawn away in the joy of the music.

I have often been treated by tribal medicine-men, whose methods are strange but do express their affection and concern. I have always found them singularly comforting. And to the many doctors who have looked after me, too many to mention by name, I must express my gratitude for their professional competence and human affection.

I recently had a second bout of trouble with the one organ I had always thought was tough and durable: I did not have the distinction of a thrombosis, but was on a lower level altogether, only some myocardiac insufficiency. But the doctors take even this seriously: 'your life,' they said, 'must now be regular, moderate, cautious'—what depressing adjectives these are! In fact, of all the things that have happened to me, more even than leaving the Church or changing my nationality, this has demanded the greatest mental adjustment.

'The tragedy of age', said Oscar Wilde, 'is not that we are old, but that we are young.' To some extent too, the tragedy of illness is not that we are sick, but that we are well. They tell me I shall be perfectly all right and have still plenty of work in me: in fact, almost as soon as I got out of hospital and long before I was supposed to be doing anything more than lying back in bed and enjoying my tranquillizers, I was very fully engaged in editing a popular version of the Tribal Commission Report, *A New Deal for Tribal India*. But I doubt if I shall be able to clamber about the high mountains very much or lose myself, as I used to, in the wilds. There could be no greater blow than this, for my loves are the remote, the lonely, the unknown.

Yet I and thousands of others have to accept this, live with it, find happiness and usefulness in spite of it, perhaps even through it. The real life of man, which no one can take from him, is within, and neither poverty nor disappointment nor change of circumstances can harm him if he has learnt to guard his spirit well.

12

The Elusive Treasure

To abandon the struggle for private happiness, to expel all eagerness of temporary desire, to burn with passion for eternal things—this is emancipation, and this is the free man's worship. —*Bertrand Russell*

I

IT would be presumptuous for me to give a summing-up of my ideas on life, God and eternity at what I will call the early age of sixty, though it might be said that I should have made up my mind about these things by now. But it is just at this stage of life that a man really begins to learn, and I am learning so fast now that what I have to say in this final chapter can only be tentative.

Looking back across my life and over what I have written in this book I see that, although I am not really a clubbable man, it has always been people that have mattered. I can tell the story of my life most easily in terms of my friends.

All my life I have been in love with something, a cause, a tribe, a person. I fall in love in turn with every tribe I study. On the whole, I find the world a very lovable place and human beings, once you get to know them, very lovable creatures.

I have also loved a few people in a more intimate fashion. I have written a lot, and in great detail, about sex and some of my friends have supposed that I must have drawn my knowledge of the Murias' erotic life, for example, from personal experience. Indeed, a well-known anthropologist once said that the only way to break down the barriers between the investigator and his tribe was to speak the latter's language, eat his food and sleep with his women. In my own experience eating tribal food may be helpful in creating confidence on a brief visit, but otherwise does nothing but ruin your digestion. And it is a fallacy to suppose that by sleeping with a tribal girl you will find a way to the discovery of tribal secrets. For sleeping with girls is not an anthropological experience and to do so does not even give an insight into traditional sex techniques.

The professional research man, therefore, must be strict with himself on his expeditions. Among the Marias (to whom I would give the first prize), the Konyaks, Kuttia Konds, Mishmis and the Cabrais of Africa, there were girls of devastating beauty and fascination. They lit up their whole tribe for me—but I admired them at a distance.

People often say, even Bernard Shaw has said it, that dress is more exciting than nudity. Not for me. The complete Cabrai nudity thrilled me with its beauty and freedom and even the semi-nudity of Marias, Konds and Saoras (as they lived in the old days) seemed to me aesthetically and morally good. A woman's breasts are sometimes regarded as symbols of compassion rather than of sex, and to see them bravely and innocently exposed has always delighted me, not because they excite me sensuously (I hope I am not humbugging myself over this) but because they speak of freedom, health and naturalness.

I suppose a man never forgets his first intimate relationship with a girl ; in my case, I am glad to say, it was no purchased furtive pleasure, but the culmination of a long period of romantic love and was not unrequited. The forest setting was as lovely as my 'girl of furious gold' herself.

I have had one overwhelming experience of love which could not be fulfilled, that malady which the medieval physicians so rightly classed with madness, frenzy and hydrophobia. The torment and wonder of this, disastrous and impossible as it was, gave a quality to living that I have never known before or since ; it heightened all my sensibilities ; and made many things real that I have only known in books. Our lives 'so truly parallel', though infinite, could never meet.

> Therefore the love which us doth bind,
> But Fate so enviously debars,
> Is the conjunction of the mind,
> And opposition of the stars.

But love of a less dramatic kind, love tender, precious, reciprocated, I have sometimes known, and I count these moments as among the finest in my life. I am not in the least ashamed. I am proud that I was capable of them.

Today, and for many years past, my old loves have been concentrated on my beloved wife, in whom I have found the essence of them all. I am a better lover now for those experiences.

And, moving forward and outward (I will not say upward) from the passionate, enthralling love of treasured individuals, I have found a wider love for people generally. I am very serious about love—sexual love, spiritual love, love as a substitute for quarrelling and war. It is, as I shall urge at the end of this chapter, the final solution of our problems.

II

To change one's nationality is, unfortunately, still a very serious matter. In my own case, however, the formal legal act was only the culmination of a very long process which had begun twenty-five years before, the fruit of an intense desire for identification. Denis de Rougement says: 'The love of Tristan and Iseult was the anguish of being *two*: and its culmination was a headlong fall into the limitless bosom of light, there where individual shapes, faces and destinies all vanish: "Iseult is no more, Tristan no more, and no name can any longer part us".' I have always felt this need of identification—with a loved person, with a loved tribe, with a loved country. I cannot bear to be a mere spectator: I want to be involved. So becoming an Indian citizen was a spiritual experience, involving every part of me, as a love-marriage would.

I did not give up my British nationality in a fit of pique. I have always been very fond of Britain and proud of her. It is true that in the thirties I was greatly concerned about British imperialism and, more specifically, about the way the British Government handled things in India. The treatment of Gandhi's followers and of Gandhi himself is an old story now and I would be the last to revive it. Perhaps one of the most remarkable things about modern India is the way she has forgotten and forgiven what happened at that time. But then it was very real, and the superior attitude of both State and Church officials, even though there were notable exceptions, made it more and more difficult for me to feel at ease with my fellow-countrymen. But my becoming an Indian was not a negative thing, a reaction against something. I fell in love with India when I was with Gandhi and he accepted me. Later I had an even stronger intense and specialized attachment to India's tribal people.

For very many years past I have never thought of myself as an ex-Englishman. It just does not occur to me unless somebody mentions it and then it is always rather a shock. I do not know whether my Indian friends regard me as part of the picture but I myself feel so much part of the Indian scene, and I have felt like this for so many years, that I am not self-conscious about it. I am here and everything is entirely natural. Ours is an Indian home, and my children look on themselves as Indian and are proud of their country. One day during the Chinese invasion, young Wasant came to me and said very seriously, 'Daddy, I want to talk to you about our nation'. A Delhi paper described me the other day as 'a British-born Indian', which puts it very well.

My former countrymen, although at first they regarded me as someone not very nice to know, have accepted me since Independence as a sort of phenomenon who might be regretted but could not be helped. Occasionally I meet people whom I distress. One day in Calcutta there was a South African who said pleadingly, 'However extraordinary your opinions may be, there is one thing that can never be taken from you. Your blood is white.' And an American from Texas, who was rather sensitive about the race problem and said he could never bring himself to touch a Negro, said much the same thing that, however I might try, I still remained an Oxford man. Well, after all, there are a number of distinguished born-Indians who are even more 'Oxford' than I am.

I want then to make this clear, that my becoming an Indian citizen did not involve any real break with Europe. I realize that the roots of my culture are there. I am not one of those exceptional Europeans who have been able to assimilate Hindu or Buddhist culture into the very texture of their thinking as well as into their way of life. I lived for many years in the forest in a rather odd way, not because it was 'Indian' but because I liked it. If I eat Indian food today I am not making a gesture but I have it simply because I enjoy rice and curry and Indian sweets. I have learnt much from my studies in Indian philosophy, art and literature, which have opened out an entire new world to me, but down at the bottom there is still the foundation of European culture. I do not say that this is good or bad but simply that it is a fact.

India shook me out of convention and acceptance. She destroyed my religion and gave me a working faith.

She has given me wonderful friends—scholars, administrators, journalists, poets, artists, and plenty of nice ordinary human beings. The Indians are a warm-hearted people who respond to affection; a people with whom you quickly get on terms; a kind, generous, thoughtful people. Long ago Voltaire, writing with rather similar enthusiasm about England, added: 'not but there are some fools in England'. And in India too, I am afraid.

All the same I am incurably optimistic about India. Her angry young men and disillusioned old men are full of criticism and resentment. It is true that there is some corruption and a good deal of inefficiency; there is hypocrisy, too much of it. But how much there is on the credit side! It is a thrilling experience to be part of a nation that is trying, against enormous odds, to reshape itself.

One day on a visit to Nagaland I went to Ungma, a very large Ao Naga village near Mokokchung. When I arrived I saw, to my horror, a notice outside the great church there that there would be a service that afternoon and that Dr Elwin would preach the sermon. I had had no warning and I couldn't imagine what to say. So instead of talking to the congregation of at least four thousand people about conventional religion (which I would have been in any case unfitted to do) I told them why I had become an Indian citizen. Some of the Naga leaders had told their people that they were not Indians and, though most of them had by then accepted the idea that they were, I thought it would interest them to know how someone coming originally from another strong and independent country could regard it as the proudest day in his life when he became an Indian citizen and how happy he was to belong to India and to be accepted by her people.

One of the reasons I gave was that in India, gentle, tolerant India, it is possible (despite the Puritans) to live your own life more freely and with less interference than almost anywhere in the world. There are irritations, as there must always be if one wishes to live in society, but these are not so heavy as to depress one unduly. Dr Radhakrishnan said recently that it was much more important 'to safeguard the unfettered freedom of the individual to pursue truth and seek beauty' than to pass laws.

Secondly, in India there is real freedom of religion. At one time there had been a lot of rebel propaganda among the Nagas that the Christians among them would not be permitted to practise their faith and that some form of Hinduism would be imposed on them. I reminded the congregation that India's Constitution guaranteed liberty not only to believe and practise, but also to propagate, one's religion. A man is, of course, equally free to have no religion at all.

And thirdly, I told the Nagas that I do not think there is any country where there is more warmth and affection. I anticipated, in simpler language, what I later elaborated in my Patel lectures:

India, throughout its history which has been assailed so often by forces inimical to love, has in its metaphysics, its social customs and the temperament of its people always been dominated by love. It has believed that all life is sacred and among its ideals are those of Ahimsa which will cause no injury, Karuna which has compassion on all beings, and Maitri which gives itself in practical love and charity. The love deep in its heart has made men tolerant and liberal towards the beliefs and customs of others. It has inspired its people with the desire for integration and harmony. The future of India depends on the degree in which its traditional love-energy can continue to dominate its civilization. It is only through love that all the diversities of language, race and custom can be transcended.

III

Most of the essential values of my life have grown and developed out of my contact with the tribal people. They have influenced me far more than I have influenced them. They have taught me the importance of happiness, the importance of simplicity. Their own attachment to colour and rhythm has found an immediate response in my own mind.

My opposition to any kind of imperialism or colonialism has been made clear in the earlier part of this book. The change that has come over the world in my lifetime, whereby even little Sierra Leone, my father's diocese, has won its self-government, is wonderful. But there is a long way to go and great nations still show signs of wishing to impose their own ideas and at least economic domination on others.

Ever since I went to Oxford I have been a pacifist and I believe very strongly that the use of violence and force is no way of solving the disputes of mankind. This is so particularly in the tribal areas, where affection and understanding is the only way to achieve their integration with the rest of the country. The wrongs of Africa, the memory of Jomo Kenyatta in jail and the excesses of apartheid in South Africa have haunted me.

Among the tribes I came to see that war was not only a betrayal of life but a waste of life-saving resources. In my Sabarmati days pacifism was an ideal. It was only among the tribes that it became a reality. It seemed intolerable then that, when so many people were living in poverty, the men and money that might succour them should be diverted to so foolish a purpose as war. Nor is this enough: we must, as the Buddhists put it, suffuse every quarter of the globe with the gentle and creative spirit of love.

The problem of punishment and revenge became very urgent in the tribal hills. I need hardly say that I am an opponent of capital punishment and I feel rather ashamed that India, which leads the world in so many humane causes, should not yet have abolished it. It is futile and unfair to continue to regard attempted suicide as a crime. I remember seeing a poverty-stricken Gond in jail sentenced to a term of imprisonment for trying to kill himself. He told me: 'My wife had died. I had no food. My whole body was full of pain. What was the point of going on living?' So long as society allows suicide-conditions to exist, it cannot rightly penalize those who try to escape them.

I am astonished that we have not made greater progress in prison-reform in India, where so many of our leading men have themselves spent many years in jail. The philosophy dominating our police-system and prisons is still that of punishment, the reaction of an outraged society towards trespassers against its code. Whatever may be done in other countries, we are certainly not paying enough attention to this in India.

When I was at school I was rather often subject to corporal chastisement. Masters used to beat us with a cane and the prefects used the heel of a walking-shoe. This was very painful, inflicted a large bruise that lasted for days, and gave a real shock to the nervous system. These beatings had the worst possible effect on me, made me jumpy and resentful, and I am ashamed to say that when I myself became a prefect I was energetic in administering them myself. Corporal punishment in schools should be abolished altogether and especially in the tribal areas where the people are extremely sensitive to any kind of physical indignity.

I will not, however, say anything about education, which is an inexhaustible subject, except to make one point, that we should not impose on children outdated religious ideas which the general sense of mankind has now abandoned and that we should begin from a very early age to teach the folly of war.

The tribal people awoke me to beauty in a way that even the paintings of my favourite Gauguin had not. Beauty is part of youth and the central crime of the exploiter is that he makes people old. Not disease alone but economic stress greys the hair and bends the shoulders of the peasants of India.

Looking back through my diaries I see that one of the things that has always haunted me is the importance of keeping people young. On one occasion when I had been greatly disappointed I wrote: 'It is most important that failure in one thing should not mean failure in everything. The essential thing is that we should not let disappointment make us old. The greatest problem of all is to remain young. Our real enemy is not scandal, nor poverty nor hardship nor even our vices—but Time. It is love that brings Time to a halt.'

Many of the tribal people live in natural surroundings of exceptional loveliness but on the whole they do not make many beautiful things. But I have sought for them in remote villages and little huts where one would least expect them. It has not been easy and the total result of thirty years' seeking may not be very much. But it is something.

Beauty is so rare a thing
So few drink of my fountain.

Unhappily during the later years of the British regime a wave of ugliness passed over the whole of India. In spite of the protests of Tagore and the active opposition of Gandhi, vast quantities of cheap foreign goods poured into the country. The western world, says Herbert Read, 'has evolved a civilization of vast and all-pervasive vulgarity, a civilization without a decent face'. Its business-dominated economy soon gave India 'an architecture of poverty and meanness in the manufacture of everyday things'. It spared no aspect of Indian life. The harmonium corrupted Indian music; western idioms deeply disturbed Indian painting and sculpture; mass-produced textiles nearly killed the Indian handloom industry, and even when this was revived left it with a heritage of debased designs or purely utilitarian aims. The Indian home became a vulgarized, secondrate copy of lodgings in Balham or Tooting Bec. The old beauty was driven underground and the Indian countryside is, as a consequence of the Community Development movement, being defaced with the ugliest and most unsuitable architectural constructions that it has known in its long history. Many official buildings in the villages look like police lines and sometimes even like public lavatories. A development headquarters should not resemble a third-rate mental home, yet in many cases the plans for building our houses are lacking in both art and imagination and there is little attempt at adaptation to the rural scene.

Of all things, beauty must not be forgotten. Beauty, eternally renewed in every generation, undiscouraged by big business or bad taste, is the most vital thing in the world and must triumph in the end. The hill people of India, itself a country which has always been dedicated to ideals of grace and loveliness, still have much beauty in their lives. By desiring to preserve it, I have not been trying to check their progress in the modern world: I have been helping them to inspire that world.

From my Oxford days I had been attached to the idea of Aletheia, the ultimate truth or reality, as it appears in the Johannine writings. Gandhi emphasized this idea for me in his teaching on truth as God. Among the tribes too I wanted the truth as a philanthropologist. The truth about the tribes makes its contribution to our knowledge of mankind, and it is only as the truth about them is known that they will be properly regarded and rightly treated.

In India one of the chief enemies of beauty and even of truth, especially in the tribal areas, is Puritanism and this is so important that I must give a few pages to discussing it.

IV

India is not, repeat not, by temperament, history or tradition, a Puritan country. Puritanism invaded her from the West, to some extent through Protestant missionaries who also, I suspect, influenced Gandhi more than he would have cared to admit. There is today a self-conscious and self-righteous Puritanism in the country which is destructive of many of the aesthetic values of life and, particularly when applied to simple village people, is ruinous to their happiness.

Perhaps the most fundamental of the Puritan's mistakes is a false sense of values, 'A Puritan', said G. K. Chesterton, 'is a person who pours righteous indignation into the wrong things.' He is for ever wanting to do other people good, never happy unless he is showing something up.

Puritanism must be carefully distinguished from asceticism. The Puritan did not seek to annihilate the sensitivity of the senses, or attain the passivity of the will or seclusion from the world. He sought rather, as Crane Brinton has said, 'to select among his worldly desires those which would further his salvation, and to curb and suppress those which did not'. He thought that 'many pleasures to which the human race was addicted—light music, dancing, gambling, fine clothes, drinking and playgoing—were the kind of thing Satan liked' and so they were forbidden. But he did not believe in mortifying the flesh, in the manner of the Catholic monk or the Hindu sadhu. He liked to eat well, sleep well, and have a comfortable house.

One of the things that the Puritans have created throughout India is a self-consciousness about the beauty of the human body and a fear of its warm and breathing loveliness. This has particularly affected the tribal people who in former days had no artificial inhibitions and often went about half-clothed or even not clothed at all and were very beautiful when they did so. Today some state Governments have started regular campaigns to dress them up. One such Government has allotted a large sum of money to clothe the graceful people of Bastar in white cloth. In Rajasthan, the home of colour, a photographer once published photographs of some Bhil girls who were bare to the waist. The local Government's reaction was to issue thousands of white saris to these girls so that their shameful semi-nudity might be hidden. The result is that the girls, formerly so beautiful, with the combination of their own charms and the traditional coloured cloth of Rajasthan, today look like Hindu widows.

Puritanism has given its special attention to the cinema. Official censorship today makes it almost impossible to witness a realistic adult film as it should be seen by grown-up persons. At one time it was forbidden to screen anyone drinking alcohol and you were shown, for example, a party where whisky was served to the guests ; they held their glasses in their hands and raised them to their lips, but when the dreadful moment of consummation between the lip and the glass was about to appear there was a flash and you then saw the glass lowered empty to the table.

A recent attack on the Indian cinema and its effect on children declares that 'kissing, embracing and obscene conversations and songs' have come to dominate the screen and that film-goers cannot help 'seeing a hundred ways of making love'. This is characteristic of many ignorant criticisms of the film industry, for it is just not true, and as for seeing a hundred ways of making love in a cinema, even the author of the *Kama Sutra* could not, by stretching his imagination to the limit, think of more than eighty-four.

Censorship, whether of books, films or pictures, is ineffective and insulting, especially when it is combined with a lack of interest in the education of public taste. The subject of good taste, the development of a literary or moral fastidiousness, is ignored in our Universities and we try to gain by muddled and obscure legislation what could surely be better achieved by a trained public opinion.

Recently there has been a silly campaign about immoral cinema posters. Shortly after this started I went to Calcutta and decided to see some of them for myself. I was rather excited about it and went round the streets searching for something interesting. There was nothing that could possibly have excited even my fairly inflammable mind and, in fact, the cinema posters of India are of a remarkably mild character. But ardent social workers have been tearing down pictures which have any relation to the love between men and women, and this in a country where kissing is forbidden on the screen.

At one time there was even a move to destroy the marvellous sculptures of Khajuraho and Konarak. An important Congressman actually suggested to Gandhi that the erotic figures of Konarak should be removed and their place taken by statues of national leaders.

Prohibition is often attributed to Puritanism, but I am not quite sure about this, although it is the Puritans who have taken the most active part in trying to enforce it. My own objection to Prohibition is simply my lifelong objection to imposing things on people. I entirely agree with Bishop Magee when he said, at a time when there was a move to introduce it in England: 'If I were given the choice I should say that it would be better that England should be free than that England should be sober—for with freedom we must eventually obtain sobriety but, on the other hand, we should lose both freedom and sobriety.' Not long ago the American President said that he did not know any figure in the world who was more committed to individual liberty than Mr Nehru, and on his own account I do not believe that he would ever impose prohibition on India.

I naturally look at this problem from the point of view of the tribal people and while I think that rice-beer is a thing which should not only not be banned but should actually be encouraged, for it is nothing more than a nourishing and palatable soup with a kick in it, there can be little doubt that distilled liquor, which has been positively supported by Governments in order to inflate their revenues, is injurious. If I had my way I would close the licensed liquor shops and would have a special branch of the Community Development Ministry to teach the brewing of beer.

The Puritans had a strong bout of activity shortly after Independence. For example, there was a fuss made about Indian girls even shaking hands, for it was pointed out that *panigrahanam,* the clasping of hands, is a symbol of marriage, and a Calicut writer wrote that 'India's womanhood has kept its standard of purity so high that only a husband, father or brother is allowed to touch a member of the opposite sex. In Indian households, after the girls grow up, even their brothers do not touch them. Indian girls should not link arms with men or shake hands with them'. This author continues that 'the time may not be far off when we find ourselves whirling round and round to the tune of luscious music under dim lights, our arms round the waist of other women'.

National leaders, especially Congress leaders, frequently appeal to the public to be good, though there is some divergence of opinion as to what goodness is. Very often they ask women to give up ornaments, sometimes they inveigh against lipstick and cigarettes. During the debate on Prohibition in the Constituent Assembly some speakers advocated a ban on tobacco as well as on alcohol.

In 1950 a Parliamentary *Who's Who* was published, in which there are some examples of this self-conscious do-goodism. Under 'recreations', one M.P. put 'Mixing among the poor and downtrodden peasants and workers for the uplift of their life through cooperative effort'. Another described his hobby as 'Uplift of the common man'.

I am not specially worried about Puritanism as it affects me, but for the tribes it is a cruel and wasteful creed,

> The adroit castrator
> Of art: the bitter negation
> Of song and dance and the heart's innocent joy.
> You have botched our flesh and left us only the soul's
> Terrible impotence in a warm world.

There are many people, greatly admired by society, who have devoted their entire lives to robbing the tribal folk of what little they have. They turn them into vegetarians and thus take from them an essential item of their diet and give nothing in its place. By introducing Prohibition among them they rob them of a much-needed tonic and deprive their festivals and marriages of their former gaiety and even their funerals of some sort of comfort. By suggesting that their simple natural way of dress is indecent they lay on them a new economic burden. They cast a shadow on the sweet delights of young love. To steal colour, beauty and freedom from poor people is just as bad as to exploit them in more obvious ways.

I believe in compassionate and universal love towards the world, but this does not mean that one should be a jellyfish. To be too charitable to the wrong people can be a betrayal of those who need you. The following Malediction, therefore, is not really inconsistent: its chief fault is that it has not been very effective.

Mr Verrier Elwin's Monday Morning Malediction

> Attend, my Muse, and hear the curse
> Which on the tribesmen's foes I call
> And listen as I now rehearse
> On whom my maledictions fall.
>
> On puritanic theorists
> Looking at Nehru's plans askance,
> Whose minds are clouded by the mists
> Of prejudice and ignorance.

On Uplift workers trying hard
To change, improve and interfere
In tribal custom, and to guard
Against the crimes of beef and beer.

On those who would assimilate
Into the dead Sanatan scheme
Of caste and custom those who late
Lived free and happy as a dream.

On those who're shocked by nakedness,
Who stare and snigger, peep, and try
The human form divine to dress
In millcloth which the poor must buy.

On those who trade in short and shirt,
Who think a singlet is the thing,
However quickly stained with dirt,
Who'd make a coolie of a king.

On moneylender, lawyer's tout,
Corrupt official, landlord ; then
On the slick merchant growing stout
By cheating good and simple men.

On pastors tricking boys to church
By lying threats of hell and fire,
On those who nose about in search
Of happy love and young desire.

On those who take joy from the poor,
Who stifle laughter, mar delight,
Stop dancing, rob the ancient store
Of beauty, zest and colours bright.

On those debasing tribal art
In melody, design or form,
Who sentimental hymns impart
And on harmoniums perform.

On those who think morality
Can be a substitute for brains,
And, proud of their own purity,
Exult in peering into drains.

On every man whose empty heart
Is void of poetry and grace,
And his own dullness would impart—
On one and all my curse I place.

Yet as far as I am concerned, Puritanism has really been rather kind. I was the first person who dared, in my book *The Baiga,* to write freely about the sexual habits of an Indian tribe. In *The Muria and their Ghotul* I was even more outspoken and detailed, and I included in my collections of folksongs and folktales stories which, while of considerable psychological value, could hardly be read aloud in a drawing-room. Yet in all the hundreds of reviews which I have received, some of which have been very critical on other grounds, I do not think that anybody in India or any newspaper or journal has criticized me on this account. I have been attacked by orthodox religious people in England for what I have written about sex and by South African reviewers for what I have written about politics, but Indian critics as well as the Indian Government have been very generous to me, both for what I have written and also for the photographs I have reproduced in my various books, some of which on the stricter Puritan standards would be regarded as quite shocking.

As I wrote in *Motley,* Puritanism is not native to India. It is entirely alien to the minds of her greatest men. Its existence here today is due to a small faction who are dominated by their reaction against what they erroneously suppose to be ' Western ' pleasures, by a subconscious envy of those who are more liberally educated and modern than themselves. It is of the first importance that its prurient and unclean influence should not inflict incurable wounds on the soul of this tolerant, beauty-loving and traditionally happy land. ' A nation ', declared the first Indian Governor-General, ' needs joy as much as food and knowledge.'

V

When I think of the things that have influenced me and moulded my life, I put poetry first. Music, Western orchestral music, especially the works of Mozart and Beethoven or, in another mood, Stravinsky, has spoken to me, but not enough: my way of life has not allowed me to see a great deal of painting and sculpture in original. The advantage of poetry is that it is portable: even on tours where loads have to be kept to a minimum, you can slip a few slim volumes into your baggage. And so the poets have been my teachers: they have taught me to explore the secret places of my own heart; they have opened a window through which I can see my tribes with clearer eyes.

Then, first in time, were certain aspects of the Christian religion. I do not think that very much has remained,

> But through the water pale and thin
> Still shine the unoffending feet.

That part of Christianity which reflects the neo-Platonic philosophy, the mystical aspect, continues to be important and I still think that in the writings of some of the great Christian mystics (provided we turn a blind eye to the exclusive and narrow aspects of their teachings) there is a great deal to be found. I still feel a stirring of the heart when I think of some of the Catholic Modernists; when I recall, for instance, Pierre Teilhard de Chardin, isolated in the lonely steppes of Asia without bread or wine, offering to God 'on the altar of the whole earth the work and sorrow of the world'.

I do not think anyone can understand me, nor can I understand myself, without realizing that for about five years of my life I intended to be a monk. I still love silence above all things. It is very difficult to find silence even in a village, but you can get it in the high mountains, and sometimes here in our house in Shillong at night there may be a few minutes of perfect silence, which is the most refreshing and strengthening thing I know. If I had the courage I would follow Gandhi's example and refuse to speak a word for at least one day a week or do what we used to do in Poona and not speak for several hours every day.

The fundamental vows of the 'religious life' are Chastity, Poverty and Obedience. I was never particularly enthusiastic about Holy Chastity but Poverty did appeal to me and for many years I followed this ideal, even though today circumstances have forced me to abandon it. But at all times in my life I have found greater satisfaction in austerity than in luxury. To get what you want sometimes seems a little vulgar; to go without things is, I am certain, a great strength to the soul. I believe in Obedience, at least in the wider sense of loyalty.

After Christianity came Gandhi. Like everybody else I take from Gandhi's teachings those ideas which appeal to me and ignore the rest. The rejection of Gandhi's philosophy by India, which began even before his death, was symbolized when his body was taken to the pyre on a weapon-carrier. There are a lot of things I have never been able to accept in Gandhism, particularly its Puritan aspect, but there were at the same time many other things of great inspiration. The centrality of his teaching on truth, his doctrine of love and pacifism, and his austerity as distinct from his Puritanism continue to make a strong appeal. And I shall never lose the memory of that wonderful personality, at once warm and luminous, or the affection he gave me even when I least deserved it, so that still today I cannot hear his name without a thrill of pride and happiness.

I never met Tagore, though he influenced me even from my Oxford days. Curiously enough, I was not first attracted to him by his famous *Gitanjali,* but by his translations of the poems of Kabir, my very first introduction to Oriental verse.

There have always been two sides to me—one side, the world-renouncing, was captivated by Gandhi, but the other side of world-affirmation I found in Tagore. His belief in beauty, rhythm and colour, the fact that so many people in India seemed to be afraid of love and that he was not, awoke an enthusiastic response in my heart. 'He who wants to do good knocks at the gate; he who loves finds the gate open.' Everything about Tagore was positive, affirmative. He made life itself a work of art. He was interested in the tribal Santals and inspired by them. Indeed, I have often felt that the tribal areas should be administered and their policies directed by poets and artists.

India was happy in having these two men to guide her destinies at the critical period when she was advancing towards Independence. Gandhi braced and stimulated people and his hard, stern message was essential to rouse his followers and nerve them for the task of non-violent opposition to a great Empire. But on the aesthetic side he was weak. He did not seem to care much for poetry, except religious poetry. He did little to encourage art. The handloom industry, through which he might have created a whole world of beauty, he used to make plain, unsightly garments in which many of his followers are still clothed, for he wanted to put India in prison-garments as a constant reminder of her status. Without Tagore India might have become dreary and colourless. She might have forgotten the loveliness of the world, the essential poetry of human beings and of the things they make. Tagore was a perfect counter-influence and the combination of the two men was needed both for India as a whole and certainly for myself. It is true that there are aspects of Tagore's teaching which I felt were a little woolly—such a definition, for example, of human life as 'the ceaseless adventure to the Endless Further'. But at its best his work remains supreme and is full of wisdom.

My appreciation of Tagore's work was increased by a wonderful performance of a dramatization of his poem, *Samanya Kshati*, by Uday and Amala Shankar. They came to Shillong and Amala visited us and later I visited Uday, and although I had never met them before, I felt that sense of immediate kinship which I am always seeking but do not, I must admit, very often find. Their presentation of Tagore's poem, which itself is a little masterpiece with its understanding of village life, was superb, and young Wasant said to me afterwards, 'Daddy, that is the best thing I have ever seen in my life.'

I have said a good deal about Gandhi's effect on me, especially in the early years, but in the last decade I have come much more under the influence of Mr Nehru. This is partly due to his inspiration simply as a great human being, partly to his policy for the tribes which I am sure is the chief hope for them, if only people in India will pay sufficient attention to it. I have called myself 'a missionary of Mr Nehru's gospel' for the tribes. U. N. Dhebar, rather pessimistically, once said I was its only missionary.

In his foreword to my *Philosophy for NEFA,* Mr Nehru wrote generously, too generously, questioning this. He describes how his views on the tribes had 'developed under the impact of certain circumstances and of Verrier Elwin's own writings. It would be more correct to say that I have learnt from him rather than that I have influenced him in any way.'

But in fact Mr Nehru's influence on me has been paramount: he is so vitalizing a person that every time I meet him my ideas are enriched with new life. In him are combined Gandhi's austere devotion to truth and peace with the world-affirming attitude of Tagore; the hardness and realism of Gandhi with Tagore's warm love of beauty and children. Into our thinking about the tribes he has brought science, humanity and respect; and I liked the man who once remarked to me that 'the whole of the Prime Minister's tribal policy can be summed up in one word—humility'.

I have sometimes been accused of having a prejudice against Hinduism, which is ridiculous. It is true that I have expressed my opinion that certain aspects of Hinduism are not very good for the tribes. Hindu 'reformers' are apt to import worse things into tribal society than they banish from it. Hinduization of the tribes in central India has often meant a belief in caste that is more rigid even than that of the ancient Brahmins, and there are places where widow-remarriage, which formerly had never been questioned, has now been forbidden, and boys and girls are married at an earlier age than formerly so that they may be saved from 'sin'. A whole set of new taboos on food and drink have been imported. Worst of all, as Hinduism spreads in a tribal area the tribes tend to sink down to the bottom of the social scale.

But this is not real Hinduism. It is that parody of it which the Hindu leaders are doing their best to banish. True Hinduism has a power and beauty that no one acquainted with it can regard with anything but the deepest respect. You have to approach it of course, as you would approach poetry, with a willing suspension of disbelief. The Hindus, even highly educated Hindus, have the capacity of accepting the most extraordinary ideas. But this does not matter very much. Above all the fads and irrational notions rises the great edifice of Hindu philosophy, painting, architecture and poetry. Its best men gain an exceptional strength from it and I myself have drawn a great deal of strength from it through them.

There is one trifling complication—that many Hindus make you feel uncomfortable because they are so much 'better' than you are. They make you feel worldly and luxurious—one does not smoke, another drinks only milk, a third has taken a vow never to read novels. Those of us who do all these things and many others sometimes find a Hindu friend just a little difficult to live up to.

In recent years perhaps the chief spiritual influence of my life has been a very simple form of Buddhism. This I met first in Ceylon, then in Thailand. I found its true spirit in little village-homes among the north-eastern mountains and in the Khampti temples in the foothills of NEFA. What little I know of Buddhism has not come to me through the gurus or philosophers but through very simple and ordinary people and in small, sometimes brokendown, shrines and temples

On one side of me I am hardly a good subject for Buddhism. I love life ; I love this good and kindly world ; I love the rich provision of the senses, the enticements of the eye, the ear, the tongue ; I like good food, beautiful things and people, children, amusing friends, tobacco, wine. My emotions are constantly entangled with causes, ideas and individuals.

But, as I have said already, there is another side to me which values a certain mental austerity and detachment. I like the good things of life but I can manage happily without them, and in fact, I generally have to. And above all, I have gradually come to see that unless I have peace inside me, my enthusiasm for life will not get me very far. The weakness that comes from anxiety, from small jealousies, bad temper, flurry and attachment, not only hinders a man's spiritual progress but even destroys his capacity to enjoy the good and beautiful things of this world. Inner strength is essential both for happiness and for good work.

Just at a time when I was feeling this rather acutely and growing impatient with the mean and shabby bonds that held me back, I began to study Buddhism. I do not pretend to understand its philosophy. It would be nice to be reborn as a better man ; deep down inside me is the desire ultimately to attain something we can call Nirvana or, in another discipline, to reach Point Omega. But this is a long way off. For the moment at least let me control my temper, at least let me banish dislike from my heart.

The Buddhist scriptures speak of Five Hindrances which the pilgrim must overcome if he is to climb the mountain of reality and lose himself in the shining vision at the summit. He must put away the hankering after the world. He must banish the corruption of the will to injure, remaining with a heart free from ill-temper and purifying his mind of malevolence. He must be free of sloth and weakness and purify his mind of doubt. It is very important that he should 'put away flurry and worry, and with heart serene within, free himself of irritability and vexation of spirit'. These practical down-to-earth principles may seem elementary enough, yet it is only when we try seriously that we realize how hard it is to fulfil them, and even at the age of sixty I am staggered when I realize what little progress I have made. For to overcome the Five Hindrances demands ceaseless vigilance and untiring effort. It also requires a certain attitude of mind, the realization that the world is only a bridge, that its prizes are but shadows, that by pursuing happiness too eagerly we may destroy our happiness. The perfect vision, which sets the soul free, comes in serenity, from the contentment that is regardless of the world.

The building up of an inner strength, equipping the soul like a well-guarded frontier fort by gentleness, compassion and a love that extends to all the world, makes it possible for a man to tread the path of liberation. This is not achieved only by detachment: it must be very positive. 'As thou would'st guard against suffering and sorrow, so exercise the spirit of helpfulness and tenderness towards mankind.'

The first Hindrance is the hardest to overcome, for the world is attractive and I cannot accept the psychological trick which makes the way easy by regarding everything temporal, mundane or human as unworthy of attention. I would not take passion out of love. Yet it is possible to bring an element of detachment into our attitude to the world and people.

The other Hindrances are more straightforward. A great sense of freedom comes to the heart that purifies itself of dislike, resentment, anger. Weakness and uncertainty are other obvious enemies. Anxiety and vexation of spirit, getting into a flap about things, are my own special Hindrances. I am the victim of various kinds of *angst,* especially when I travel, even when I am to meet people. From the early days when I was so constantly criticized and sometimes ostracized, I have suffered from a 'not-wanted' complex so that I often read into an unintentional coldness something that is not really there at all.

But what is exciting is the discovery that all these things can be overcome. The freedom and the gladness are within our grasp if only we are determined to have them. Dante had a special place of torment reserved for those who deliberately lived in sorrow and I meet many people who, instead of taking the freedom that is potentially theirs, cling to their grievances and hatreds, weaken themselves and lose their chance of happiness. A sense of grievance is the occupational disease of Government servants. But the wise man, as the Buddhists say, will free himself from bondage, bondage even to the gods—bondage to his own ideas, his rights, his privileges.

And when he has won his freedom, when the Five Hindrances have been put away from him, the pilgrim can look on himself as 'freed from debt, rid of disease, out of jail, a free man, and secure. And gladness springs up within him on his realizing that, and joy arises to him thus gladdened, and so rejoicing all his frame becomes at ease, and being thus at ease he is filled with a sense of peace, and in that peace his heart is stayed.'

VI

I am not sure about the meaning of life but I am sure that it has a meaning. Where many people go astray is in thinking that they must interpret this meaning in theological terms and when they find that they cannot believe in a God or a specific religion, they give up too much: they lose their belief in the meaning of life altogether. I do not think this is necessary. I am not greatly concerned whether there is a God or not or whether we can look forward to some kind of life after death. I certainly do not see any point in putting down here my views on these obscure and mysterious subjects. After all, God does not depend on our votes for his existence. He is either a fact or He is not. In the same way some kind of future life is or is not a fact, and my little opinion is not going to alter it and I do not think it is even going to alter me. In the old days when we believed in the now generally discarded doctrine of rewards and punishments in a future life for what we did in this, it was another matter. But most thinking people today, whatever their theology may be, do not really believe that there is some unseen accountant noting down and totting up our merits and demerits against a final settlement.

I have, however, found through contemplation experiences of such power as to suggest that our short human life on this planet is not the final word. In the ecstasy of human love, in the appreciation of beauty, in the recognition of goodness we have brief glimpses of a greater love and a greater reality than anything we can know in our ordinary lives. The mystical experience, to my mind, is the strongest argument for something beyond ourselves.

But I do not think my own salvation or my own theological or philosophical opinions are of great importance. It is interesting to speculate; theology is the queen of sciences. But it is not belief that saves a man.

What then should we aim at during our life on earth? In spite of what I have said, we have to begin with ourselves because, unless we have some measure of self-realization, some achievement of peace and love inside ourselves, we shall not be equipped for the tasks which give the ultimate meaning to our lives. We may find this peace, this love, through religion (the realization of 'this thing'), through poetry or art, through joy or suffering—it does not matter how it comes to us, but we must have it in some measure. We must learn to interpret our experiences in spiritual terms.

And in the context of this, let us turn to our immediate neighbourhood, to what, on the human, down-to-earth plane, is worth having.

The attainment of wealth or high office, even if it is possible, is not an end in itself. I put first, among the good things possible to ordinary people like myself, a happy home. There is no greater fulfilment than the love of wife and children who love you in return. There is no greater discipline or challenge to self-denial than to live in a family which you take seriously.

And then there must be some kind of work that is worth doing. In the Tawang lamasery there is a painting of a water-carrier who performed his duties so faithfully that he is now regarded as a saint. The work may be of any kind provided—to put it in religious terms—it is done as an act of worship. Most fortunate are those who are captured by a cause, such as the well-being of the tribal people, which demands a lifelong devotion, even though it may open the door to anxiety, frustration and deep sorrow in sympathy with others.

In T. S. Eliot's *The Cocktail Party,* Celia is inspired by somewhat similar ideas to mine (except that I had not been crossed in love). She has to face the problems of both the spiritual and the physical forest, and Reilly suggests that compassion may be a clue towards finding the way out. She replies:

> But even if I find my way out of the forest
> I shall be left with the inconsolable memory
> Of the treasure I went into the forest to find
> And never found, and which was not there
> And perhaps is not anywhere? But if not anywhere,
> Why do I feel guilty at not having found it?

I too went to find a treasure. It was, I think, the perfect vision of love, truth and beauty, for even then I was thinking in those terms, though the vision was not to be found in solitary contemplation but in the active impulses of compassionate love, and I searched for it in the diseased, the unhappy, the dispossessed. I did not find the Vision Splendid; perhaps the discovery of the Vision Squalid was ultimately more important. In the end human beings proved to be so needy—and so lovable—that God had to take a back seat. From the very beginning I craved for a reality which was hidden from me by the artificiality, however gracious, of Oxford and by the urgent political excitements, however idealistic, of Sabarmati.

Of course, to go to the physical forest is not necessary to find the treasure that every man seeks. Heaven and hell are within ourselves. A man must make his pilgrimage over the rugged uplands of his own spirit, and the search goes on wherever one may be. I did not find the ultimate treasure in the forest; perhaps it is not there: it may not be anywhere.

And yet I suspect that there is a treasure which every man may find if he searches for it.

That treasure, I believe, is love, the brother and ally of peace, in all its variety and depth. To quote from my Patel lectures again:

Love illuminates knowledge; it gives meaning to beauty; it is the heart of virtue; it is the dearest guest of the home. Love's great artillery is more powerful than the weapons of hatred and, properly directed, can overcome them. Love gives dignity and stature to every man—it chastens the proud and redeems the sad, the guilty and the ashamed, and gives to the poorest a meaning and reason for life. It is, as Traherne said, 'the most delightful and natural employment of the soul of man'. It is, indeed, natural, for man is born, he exists, to co-operate, to live in harmony with his fellows, not to compete or conflict with them. This is what is to be really human, for when man is brought by love to realize his part in the life of the whole world, he no longer is open to the isolating power of loneliness; his personality is expanded to a sense of unity with all things. Love brings him freedom from fear. It brings him peace and fills his soul with a gentle power that will unite conflicting forces.

Love and the duties it imposes is the real lesson of the forest. I did not find spiritual enlightenment, indeed, some people may say that I found spiritual disaster, but I did discover urgent and challenging demands. Among very poor and exploited people there was the need to maintain those imponderable values that give dignity to the life of man; to restore to them their self-respect, the feeling of being loved. There was the necessity of working for peace and reconciliation—there is no greater cause to which a man can dedicate himself. There was the need of reverence, reverence for all life, reverence too for the ideas, the pitiful hopes and aspirations of the children of mankind. Another thing which became very clear in the forest was the importance of 'a steady will for a new social order', and of very practical measures to banish poverty. Above all, I felt that there was no greater expression of love than to work for beauty, freedom and happiness, to preserve it where it existed and restore it where it was lost.

The realization of these things may not be the great treasure of which the saints and mystics speak. But in this life we must do what we can ; we may not reach to the heavens, but there is plenty to do on earth.

Index